EXPLORING FRANCE
by Peter and Helen Titchmarsh

Halt beside the Dordogne near Beynac
Photograph by Peter Titchmarsh

Contents

Page

Introduction 2
Acknowledgements 2
How to Use This Book 3
Information 3
Books on France. 4
Maps of France. 5
Learning the Language 5
Climate 5
Types of Holiday. 6, 7, 8
Journeying to France. 8, 9
En Route...The Roads of France 9, 14, 15
Charts and Planning Map 10, 11, 12, 13
Trains 15
Bus and Coach Services 15
Cycling in France 16
Walking in France. 16
Bird Watching 16
National Parks & Regional Nature Parks 17
Eating and Drinking in France 17, 18
Entertainment 18
Services, etc. 18, 19
Opening Times 19
Shopping in France .19
The Historical Background . . . . .20 – 21
The Regions of France indicating the
    Départements which they comprise 22
The Départements of France indicating the
    Region in which each one is located . . .23

Page

French Architecture 24
Paris . . . . .25 – 38
Alsace and Lorraine-Vosges . . . . .39 – 46
Aquitaine . . . . .47 – 57
Auvergne . . . . .58 – 67
Brittany. . . . . .68 – 77
Burgundy . . . . .78 – 87
Champagne-Ardenne . . . . .88 – 94
Corsica . . . . .95 – 101
Côte-d'Azur . . . . .102 – 110
Franche-Comté . . . . .111 – 117
Île-de-France . . . . .118 – 128
Languedoc-Roussillon . . . . .129 – 139
Limousin. . . . . .140 – 147
Loire Valley — The Centre Region . . .148 – 164
Loire Valley — West . . . . .165 – 174
Midi-Pyrénées .175 – 186
Nord – Pas-de-Calais. . . . . .187 – 193
Normandy . . . . .194 – 207
Picardy . . . . .208 – 216
Poitou-Charentes . . . . .217 – 225
Provence . . . . .226 – 240
Rhône Valley . . . . .241 – 250
Savoy and Dauphiny Alps. . . . . .251 – 259
Index of Places . . . . .260 – 270
Index of Persons . . . . .270 – 271

Introduction

My first glimpse of France was from the deck of a small troopship edging its way into Dieppe on an early March morning in 1946. Our 'draft' was on its way to the Middle East, and we were sent in a war-weary train over a still battered railway line, down a circuitous route to the south. And so to Toulon, and on again by boat away from the shores of France for over two years. However that two day journey across the still mysterious French countryside, with its mile-upon-mile of dense woodlands, quiet fields and deep mountain gorges, left an impression of remote beauty that remains with me still. I came back as soon as I could, by various means....hitch-hiking up from the south, back from North Africa, driving across the Massif Central in a 1934 London taxi, riding a motor cycle down to Marseille en route for Algiers.... on a number of carefree visits.

With student days behind us we soon came back again, first on honeymoon to Sanary, and then a few years later, with our own children in a long suffering motor-caravan, travelling to the quiet corners of Burgundy, the Jura and Provence, as well as to the beaches around

Toulon and St-Raphaël. And now the children go on their own holidays, so the two of us travel by car again, sometimes down the autoroutes to the Mediterranean and sometimes on quieter journeys of exploration to some of the more remote places described in this guide.

We are still deeply embroiled in our love affair with France, and we hope that for several years to come, we shall continue to experience that special sense of excitement as we set out on yet more journeys of discovery and refreshment. *Exploring France* is largely a factual guide, but we have compiled it in the hope that at least a proportion of our readers will be persuaded to follow our unashamedly romantic lead, and set out on their own explorations through this most seductive land.

We hope that you find *Exploring France* useful, as well as tempting. If you have any suggestions for improving its contents, either by addition or amendment, do please write to us.

Still Exploring France... sunny September in the Tarn Gorge Country Photograph by Peter Titchmarsh

Peter and Helen Titchmarsh,
Kineton, Warwick.

Acknowledgements

We would like to thank Mrs. Pauline Hallam and her colleagues at the French Government Tourist Office in London, for all their help and advice; for allowing us to select so many excellent photographs from their files; and for giving us permission to reproduce these in our guide. Unless otherwise stated, the illustrations are reproduced here with the permission of the French Government Tourist Office. A few photographs are our own and several more have been kindly supplied by other organisations individually acknowledged below the illustrations in question. We are much indebted to these organisations for their help and also to a large number of Regional, Départemental and local Tourist Information Offices, and the owners of numerous châteaux, wildlife parks, zoos, etc. throughout France, for the generous supply of descriptive material. Their response to our appeal for assistance, together with that of the French Government Tourist Office typifies the enthusiastic and generous reception that visitors to France are likely to receive during their own visits.

How to Use This Book

We have divided up the main part of this book into twenty-three sections, one covering Paris, and one covering each of the twenty-two regions into which France is divided. After a brief introduction to each region we have described its outstanding features. You will note that there is a number in brackets after each place mentioned (except in the Paris section, where this is replaced by a map reference). This is the département number and this number also appears on the accompanying map of each region, allowing you to cross refer to the map as quickly as possible. We have also listed the Département names and numbers at the head of each Regional Introduction and there is a list of Regions on Page 22 and a master list of Départements in alphabetical order on Page 23. At the end of each Regional section, we have made a brief reference, where appropriate, to the chief wine areas in that region, and their approximate extent is shown on the relevant maps.

We have indicated the distance in kilometres of each place mentioned, either from the nearest main town, or from Paris. If you refer to the Distance Charts on pages 10 & 11, and the Planning Map on pages 12 & 13, it should be reasonably simple to estimate the distance between the place mentioned in the text, and your own home town, using the Channel crossing of your choice. If you wish to convert from kilometres to miles, you will find the necessary Conversion Chart on page 10.

While we have provided as much information as we could in the space available, we are conscious that for the serious traveller this may only be regarded as an introduction to France. For this reason we have included as much guidance as possible on the best sources of further information, advice, maps, and books.

Information
'The Traveller in France'

There is a wealth of information available on France, but without any doubt the first item you should obtain one or more of the magazine-style brochures on various themes which are being published from time to time in English by the French Government Tourist Office in London, under the family title *The Traveller in France*. We are advised at the time of writing that they will have individual titles such as *'The Touring Traveller in France'*, *The Short Break Traveller in France*, *The Camping Traveller in France* and *The Active Traveller in France*, and will be available from them (but not normally all at the same time) at 178, Piccadilly, London W1V 0AL (write sending 80p IN STAMPS — do not send cheques, money-orders, cash or envelopes). They contain a series of colourfully illustrated articles and a wealth of helpful advice, and readers are invited to write for more detailed information on specific subjects. There are also advertisements for certain ferry services, air lines, train services and package holidays. But perhaps the meatiest section is the reference guide supplement which lists a great variety of special holidays and packages together with the addresses of over two hundred organisations offering these various services. There are also pages covering 'Helpful Hints' and 'How to Get There', together with useful maps.

We have devoted considerable space to these publications as we feel that they provide an up to date complement to our own guide, and the combination provides an ideal introduction for anyone contemplating a visit to France.

Beside the Dordogne at Limeuil
Photograph by Peter Titchmarsh

Information Offices

Apart from the ever helpful French Government Tourist Office, at 178, Piccadilly, who will provide a wealth of specialist literature in addition to a copy of *The Traveller in France*, each tourist region has a Regional Tourist Office (any addresses not in the *The Traveller in France*, will be provided by the Piccadilly office). At a more local level, there are over five-thousand Syndicats d'Initiative... local tourist information offices, situated in every town of any significance. This network can not only help with genuine tourist information, but will also assist with hotel reservations, and provide advice on restaurants, entertainment and local transport.

Books on France

There is a bewildering selection of books on France, but here are a few which we think you will find useful:

GENERAL

Michelin Red Guide.
This is published annually and is an invaluable companion and friend on any journey across France (see also Hotels, page 6), with its most reliable merit listing of hotels and restaurants; its town plans locating hotels, information offices, post offices, and major sites of interest; its listing of garages, and its distances between towns. It also cross refers to the position of each town on the relevant Michelin maps, and to the name of the relevant Michelin Green Guide in which it appears.

Michelin Green Guides.
These are a series of nineteen books covering all France, some of which are available in an English edition. These are Paris, Burgundy, Brittany, Châteaux of the Loire, Dordogne, French Riviera, Normandy, and Provence. The whole series cover places of interest and excludes hotels and restaurants, being complementary to the Red Guide. These guides are full of detailed information, with many outline maps, and if you wish to explore a particular area in detail they are most useful.

Michelin Camping Caravanning en France.
In our view this is by far the best annual guide for campers and caravanners. Each site is categorised and is fully described and mapped. There is also a cross reference to the Michelin series of Maps.

The Penguin Travel Guide to France.

The A.A./Hachette Guide to France (in English).

The Blue Guide to France. Published by Benn.

Collins Guide to France.

The Rough Guide to France.

Eating and Drinking in France. (For details see page 17.)

A Wine Tour of France. (For details see page 17.)

Eperon's French Wine Tour. Published by Pan.

Discovering the Vineyards of France. By Worthington. Published by Ward Lock.
The Wine Roads of France. By Millon. Published by Mildmay.

Guide to the Wines and Vineyards of France. By Alexis Lichine. Published by Weidenfeld & Nicholson.
A most entertaining and descriptive volume.

The Châteaux of France. By Hubert Fenwick. Published by Robert Hale.
This is a large and splendid book, covering almost all the significant châteaux. It is excellently illustrated and lacks only a map. However this small shortcoming may be overcome with the help of our own guide.

Traveller's Art Guide to France. By Michael Jacobs and Paul Stirton. Published by Mitchell Beazley.

France the Quiet Way. By John Lilley

Cruising French Waterways. By Hugh McKnight
The two books above form a delightful introduction to the pleasures of travelling on the French Waterways.

Holiday Cruising in France. By Gerard Morgan-Grenville. Published by David & Charles.
A very practical guide, to be read in conjunction with the same author's *Barging into France*, and his *Barging into Southern France*.

Where to Watch Birds in Europe. By John Gooders. Published by Pan.
This attractive paperback has 24 pages on France. These cover eighteen of the best bird watching areas, and is complete with several maps and photographs. Well worth its modest price, even if you never plan to bird watch in Finland, Turkey, etc.

REGIONAL BOOKS (Series)

Collins Companion Guides.
Paris. The South of France. Burgundy. South-West France. The Loire. Île de France. Normandy.

Moorland Publishing.
Île de France. Normandy. Dordogne. Beyond the Bordogne. Provence. Languedoc-Roussillon. Burgundy. Eastern France. Auvergne. The North of France. Brittany. French Pyrénées.

Helm French Regional Guides.
Languedoc-Roussillon, The Loire Valley, Auvergne and the Massif Central, Dordogne and Lot, Provence and the Côte d'Azur.

REGIONAL BOOKS (Individual)

Portrait of the Auvergne. Published by Robert Hale.

Portrait of Normandy. Published by Robert Hale.

The Loire. By Vivian Rowe. Published by Eyre Methuen.

The Loire and its Châteaux. By Eugene Pepin. English edition by Thames & Hudson.

Oyster River. By George Millar. Published by Bodley Head.
A wonderfully evocative description of sailing on the Gulf of Morbihan in Brittany.

Three Rivers of France. By Freda White. Published by Faber & Faber, and re-issued in paperback.
The classic description of the Lot, Dordogne and Tarn valleys.

West of the Rhine and **Ways of Aquitaine.** Both by the above author and publisher.

Brittany and the Bretons. By Keith Spence. Published by Victor Gollancz.

The Somme Then and Now. By John Giles. Published by Bailey Bros. & Swinfen.

Maps of France

There are two good sources of maps covering France...the Institute Géographique National (IGN) and Michelin. In our view the best general road map is the Michelin *Grandes Routes* (1:1,000,000), but this is admirably supplemented by the IGN Map No. 902 entitled *Principales Richesses Historiques et Artistiques*, which shows not only the principal historic monuments, but also all National Parks and Regional Nature Parks. To explore in more detail use the IGN *Série Rouge*, which covers France in 16 sheets at a 1:250,000 scale, and which shows all roads, all historic sites, all forests and all National Parks and Regional Nature Parks. The Michelin 1:200,000 series is in our view clearer than the *Série Rouge*, and takes over 30 sheets to cover the whole country, or in 17 larger 'Regional' sheets at the same scale. Both are cross referenced with the Red Michelin Guide, and we find them an invaluable companion on our own journeys of exploration. If you only wish to consult these maps in your car, they are now incorporated into an atlas covering the whole of France. Published by Hamlyn, it is outstanding value. IGN publish a 1:100,000 and 1:50,000 series, together with special maps covering the Environs of Paris, individual National Parks, and many of the Regional Nature Parks, various mountain massifs, islands and forests and a National Footpath Map (*Sentiers de Grande Randonnée*). Michelin publish a Motorway Atlas, three maps of differing scales centred upon Paris, and a very fine *Paris Plan*, either as a map, or an indexed Atlas.

Michelin maps and guides are widely available, but if you require help either with the supply of these or with the IGN series, write or call, Stanfords International Map Centre, 12 – 14, Long Acre, London WC2 9LP (Tel: 01-836 1321), or McCarta Map and Guide Shop, 122, King's Road, London WC1X 9DS (Tel: 01-278 8276).

Learning the Language

Many French people speak a little English, but it will be much appreciated if you have mastered at least a few words of French. You will also find that it increases the enjoyment and interest of your holiday if you can ask the way, give elementary greetings and other small courtesies. May we suggest a simple phrase book and a small dictionary, and if you are a little more ambitious, a Linguaphone Travel Cassette, or a series of evening classes. However do not let a lack of French deter you from a first visit...it is fun finding out, and if any small problems do arise, there will usually be someone close to hand who will be able to help you.

Climate

It is not easy to generalise, but the north of France has weather very similar to southern England, although further away from the coast the Continental land mass ensures slightly warmer and drier summers, and slightly colder winters. As one travels south, the influence of the Mediterranean becomes more apparent, especially in the Saône-Rhône valley; and the Mediterranean coastlands, especially when sheltered by the Alps, are notable for their mild sunny winters, and hot dry summers. The Atlantic coast, as far south as Nantes, has a climate similar to Cornwall, with mild but rainy weather

Collioure... one of France's sunniest resorts
Photograph by Peter Titchmarsh

coming in from the west. Further south the Atlantic coast becomes warmer, but rain and wind are still hazards that may be encountered, even in the summer months. The heat and dryness of summer is more evident in central and southern France facing the Mediterranean, but even here the Mistral can sometimes blow cruelly down to the sea, with only the very sheltered parts of the Côte d'Azur escaping its excesses. However throughout the summer months, the chances of hot or warm sunshine are excellent in most parts, and we would not like our comments to discourage you in any way. Pack a light raincoat and the odd pullover...you may need neither, but just in case...

With these thoughts in mind, when are the best times of the year to visit the various regions of France? During the winter months there is ski-ing in the Alps, the Pyrenees, the Vosges and the Auvergne, and there is sufficient warmth to tempt visitors to the Côte d'Azur (which once had its main season during these months). Most other areas however are not really suitable for visiting before the late spring, or Easter at the earliest. In many areas, late May, June and early July are the best times, with everything and everyone fresh, and the summer storms and the French holiday crowds still far away. (Bastille Day, July 14th, marks the beginning of the great French holiday exodus.) If school holidays make July or August obligatory, it is still possible to enjoy your visit to France then, but if you can wait until September, this can be a very pleasant month to travel across France, with the sun still warm, and the roads and beaches already much clearer.

Types of Holidays

HOTELS

French hotels are officially inspected, signed, and graded into five categories…1 Star, 2 Star, 3 Star, 4 Star, and 4 Star Luxe. 2 and 3 Star hotels should prove adequate for British visitors and the 1 Star hotels are often quite acceptable. The facilities provided are often simpler than those to be found in Britain, but the prices of hotel rooms in France are exceptionally reasonable and usually offset the price of the meals which may prove to be a little more expensive than their English equivalent.

In our own search for hotels while en route we normally use the Red Michelin Guide, an invaluable annual publication. Before attempting to use it, take an hour or so to study the introductory pages, which, once mastered, will enable you to get so much more out of this splendid publication than a casual glance will allow. When in search of good value we steer by the series of maps charting those small hotels offering 'Good Food at Moderate Prices', and which are marked in the text with a red R. If in luxuriant mood we use the maps marking those establishments which have been awarded at least one star (nothing to do with the official hotel stars referred to above), as the Michelin star really does indicate culinary excellence. However when referring back to the text, the cost of the particular establishment's meals has sometimes sent us scurrying back to the red Rs…one cannot have culinary excellence without paying for it!

At Les Hospitaliers, Poët Laval… one of our favourite hotels
Photograph by Peter Titchmarsh

There are many other guides including the very helpful one published by the Logis et Auberges de France (available free of charges — usually from March onwards — from the French Government Tourist Office, 178 Piccadilly, London W1V 0AL, but send 80p for postage). The standards of the 5000 or so family-run hotels (none in Paris) in this 40-year-old federation are frequently checked and the almost always provide excellent value. The Relais Routiers organisation sprung from the needs of French lorry drivers for inexpensive food and a basic resting place for the night, and their guide is therefore perhaps more appropriate for its advice on meals rather than accommodation.

GÎTES DE FRANCE

These are cottages, farmhouses, village houses, chalets, flats and even a few châteaux, which are all in rural France, and are registered with the Fédération Nationale des Gîtes Ruraux de France, as being up to a suitable standard for letting on a self-catering basis. A wide variety of gîtes are listed in the *French Farm and Village Holiday Guide* and the *Country Welcome Guide*, which are published annually and via the normal book trade, and which contain all the details required for making a booking. There is also an official handbook of the British Section of the Gîtes de France, listing many other gîtes. This may be obtained from Gîtes de France, 178, Piccadilly, London W1V 0AL,

VILLAS

There are many agencies arranging the letting of holiday villas and flats, and many of these will be found on the holiday pages of Sunday papers like the *Sunday Times,* the *Observer*, the *Mail on Sunday*, or the *Sunday Telegraph.*

HOLIDAY VILLAGES

These are to be found in many holiday areas and it is possible to book a package in one of two, with French Travel Service, Georgian House, 69 Boston Manor Rd., Brentford, Middx TW8 9JQ, , or with several operators including Club Méditerranée and Mark Warner. Club Méditerranée run a series of exotic holiday villages in Corsica, the south of France, the Alps, Vittel and Pompadour, and they offer a very special concept in holiday-village life. For further details write to them at 106 – 108 Brompton Road, London SW3.

CAMPING AND CARAVANNING

Taking Your Own Equipment.

The opportunities in France for these twin activities are limitless. If you wish to take your tent or caravan with you, and having been caravanners for years we can greatly recommend it, we would suggest that you first purchase a copy of Michelin's *Camping Caravanning en France*. This is another invaluable companion and enables the reader to plan much of his holiday in advance, should he wish to do so, as it has reasonably detailed maps in addition to an easily understandable list of sites, showing their various features and facilities. Before going to France make sure that you have a Camping Carnet, as many sites insist on retaining this while you are on the site, and will at best insist on holding your passport as an alternative, or at worst, not have you on the site at all. Camping Carnets may be obtained from the AA, the RAC, or one of the camping or caravan clubs. If you plan to camp at peak times in a popular holiday area try to book in advance if possible, either by writing or telephoning. You will also find the French Government Tourist Office's leaflet *Camping and Caravanning in France* most useful.

The Camping or Caravan Package.
There are now many organisations advertising in the Sunday papers and elsewhere, who will provide a package with erected tents and equipment, ferry crossings, and even tents at sites en route, or hotel rooms en route. This can be combined with use of our own car, or with travel by air, coach or rail. Our family had grown up before this concept was introduced, but it appears to us that many of these packages offer very good value for family holidays in France. Details of names and addresses of many recognised companies may be obtained from your local travel agents.

AIR HOLIDAYS.
These are on offer via the normal travel trade and consist of packages involving Air/Self Drive...now better known as Fly-Drive, Air/Hotel, Air/Villa or Flat. For those of more independent mind there is a wide choice of un-packaged air routes to France, and again, the normal travel agent can be of most use. Details of internal routes covering France may be obtained from Air France.

CANAL HOLIDAYS.
There is an extensive and well maintained network of canals and navigable rivers in France, as illustrated on the map on page 7. This network offers a wide variety of holiday opportunities which can be divided into two main groups:

Hotel Boats
This involves cruises of various lengths, with a crew looking after all requirements, and usually includes short excursions to places of interest in the nearby countryside. There is a wide choice of cruises including ones on the Yonne between Fontainebleau and Auxerre; from Paris into the Champagne country, on the Marne, Aisne and Oise; on the canals of Brittany radiating from Nantes; on the canals of Burgundy as far south as Chalon; on the canals of Alsace, Lorraine and Franche-Comté between Dijon and Strasbourg, and on the canals of the south between Bordeaux and Sète. Details of some of these delightful cruises may be obtained from Travel Solutions, 93 Trafalgar Road, Greenwich, London SE10; or from European Canal Cruises, 79 Winchester Road, Romsey SO51 8JB.

'Self-Drive' Boats.
These can be hired from various points and the three most popular cruising areas are the canals of Brittany, the canals of Burgundy and the canals of the south (between Bordeaux and the Rhone delta). There are several operators, but many of the boats* may be booked via Blakes Holidays, Wroxham, Norwich NR12 8DH, or Hoseasons, Sunway House, Lowestoft, Suffolk, NR32 3LT, both of whom provide colourful brochures showing the boats available and giving a good impression of the lovely canalside scenery of France. Anyone contemplating an exploration of the French canals is strongly recommended to buy a copy of John Lilley's *France, the Quiet Way*, or Hugh McKnight's *Cruising French Waterways*. You will also find the French Government Tourist Office's leaflet *Afloat in France* most useful.
* See list of other operators and agents in *The Traveller in France*.

CANOEING.
A fine introduction to this pastime may be obtained on the Ardèche (see page 241, for the Ardèche Gorges). PGL Young Adventure Ltd., Station Road, Ross-on-Wye, Hereford & Worcester HR9 7AH, organises excellent holidays for the young and not so young, which includes a thirty kilometre descent by canoe through the dramatic Ardèche Gorges, and this trip can be combined with a camp at Port Grimaud (see page 236) on the Mediterranean.

CANALS AND NAVIGABLE WATERWAYS OF FRANCE

Canoes on the banks of the Dordogne below Castelnaud   *Photograph by Peter Titchmarsh*

SAILING.

It is now possible to hire sailing cruisers individually, or to become involved in the increasingly popular concept of 'flotilla cruising'. This enables the hirer to feel reasonably independent while at the same time being able to draw upon the experience and local knowledge of the flotilla leader. Hoseasons, Sunway House, Lowestoft, Suffolk, NR32 3LT, will provide details of Flotilla Sailing in the South of France and Corsica, and details of other organisations offering individual charters may be obtained from your local travel agent. The French Government Tourist Office's leaflet *Afloat in France* provides a wealth of useful information for those planning to take their own boat to France.

The Dordogne near Trémolat
Photograph by Peter Titchmarsh

OTHER SPECIAL HOLIDAYS.

France offers an immensely wide variety of holiday experiences…from lying on a hot beach, to learning to cook, from horse riding to courses in pottery. It is impossible to provide details but the names and addresses of organisations offering a variety of specialist holidays will be found in the French Government Tourist Office's invaluable *Active Traveller in France* (write sending 80p IN STAMPS, if possible mentioning, *Exploring France*, to 178, Piccadilly, London W1V 0AL. Do NOT send cheques, money-orders, cash or envelopes). Holidays listed in this publication include Art, Archaeology & History, Carnivals and Music Festivals, Châteaux Tours, Coach Tours, Cookery Courses, Farm Holidays, Gastronomic and/or Wine Tours, and Language Tours.

Journeying to France

PLANNING (See charts and map on pages 10 – 13.)

If you intend to travel to France by air, we would suggest that you put yourself in the hands of a good travel agent and let him advise you on the most suitable flights, whether or not this is to be part of a package including hotel or camping accommodation, the hire of a car or a canal cruiser. However if you wish to travel by car and make your own plans we have included a map showing the principal ferry crossings to France with a chart showing the distance (in kilometres) from the major British cities to all

relevant British ferry ports, and another chart showing the distance from all relevant French ferry ports to the major French cities. With the help of this map and the accompanying charts you should be able to work out the shortest route between your own home area and the area you plan to visit. Naturally road distance is not the only factor to be considered and you will wish to study the various ferry crossing times and costs, and the type of roads likely to be encountered. As an example, someone living in the Midlands will do well to avoid London if at all possible, even if this means using the Southampton crossings rather than those from Dover.

BOOKING THE FERRY

Having decided on which crossing you favour, you should if at all possible book well in advance. This may be done via your travel agent, via the AA or RAC, or with the ferry operators direct. The merits of various crossings, various companies, and the comparative effectiveness of boat against hovercraft, could be discussed at great length, but each has its merits. We happen to be rather poor sailors and tend therefore to favour one of the short crossings… normally Dover – Calais. However some of the longer crossings further westward can save an appreciable amount of motoring… We leave you to work this out, once you have studied our charts and the various ferry operators' brochures.

'En route'… at Sévérac le Château
Photograph by Peter Titchmarsh

PAPERWORK

Make sure that your Passport is in order. Visas are not required for stays of up to three months. Take out adequate Holiday Insurance, but keep in mind that a large percentage of medical costs can be recovered in respect of employed persons, with the help of a document available from British Social Security offices. Ask for Form E111 well before travelling. Ensure that your Driving Licence (and those of any co-drivers) is in order... a UK Driving Licence is acceptable, but the holder must be at least 18 years old. Ensure that you take your Vehicle Registration Document, and if you are not the registered owner, ensure that you have written authority from the owner. Ensure that you have adequate insurance cover for your vehicle by way of an International Motor Insurance Certificate (a Green Card). If you are camping independently take an International Camping Carnet (ask the AA, the RAC, the agent or organisation through which you book your ferry crossing.

LEGAL REQUIREMENTS

You are required by French Law to display a GB plate (we assume that you are a UK resident). It is also necessary to carry a red warning triangle to place on the road as an advance warning if you have a breakdown or an accident. You should also have a complete set of spare bulbs. All these items may be obtained at most garages or accessory shops.

No driving is allowed on a provisional licence, and minimum age to drive in France is 18. Under tens may not travel in the front seats (unless the vehicle has no back seat). Stop signs mean **stop**; do not creep up in first gear, but come to a complete stop.

YOUR VEHICLE

If you are planning a long journey across France we would suggest that you have a detailed service a few weeks before setting out. This is preferable to leaving it until the last minute as service by even the most efficient garage can sometimes disturb the fuel or ignition system during the course of a service. It also avoids the possibility of any delay in the supply of a spare part, the need for which could arise during the service. At the same time book your vehicle in to have the necessary modification to its headlights carried out immediately before you set out. You may be able to do this yourself... it depends on the make and model of your vehicle. It is necessary to ensure that your lights swing over to the right rather than to the left when dipping, and that if possible, they are coloured yellow. Special paint is now available for this purpose.

Picnic in the wooded countryside of the Drôme
Photograph by Peter Titchmarsh

En Route...On the Roads of France

Now you are off. We assume that you have already read our section on books and maps, and that you are equipped with at least a good general road map of France, and that if you plan to stay en route at unbooked hotels or camp sites, you have a relevant guide or guides. We mention this right at the outset, because we wish to stress to you the merits of taking your time on your journeys through France. You and your passengers will almost certainly be itching to put plenty of kilometres between you and the channel port... we have seen this revealed on the faces of neighbouring drivers on the ferry car decks, as the ramps come down and they start their engines just that little earlier than necessary. BUT PLEASE... resist this urge... do not try to cover too much ground, especially on your first day. So, drive quietly off the boat, KEEP TO THE RIGHT, and ask one of your passengers to read this section on French driving regulations.

Maximum speed limits, unless otherwise indicated are as follows. For **dry** roads — 130 kmph (82 mph) on toll motorways; 110 kmph (69 mph) on dual carriageways and non-toll motorways; 90 kmph (56 mph) on other roads, and 60 kmph (37 mph) in towns. However, on **wet** roads these maxima are reduced to 100 kmph (69 mph) on toll motorways; 100 kmph (62 mph) on dual carriageways and non-toll motorways, and 80 kmph (50 mhp) on other roads. There is also a **minimum** speeds limit of 80 kmhp (50 mph) for the outside lane of motorways during daylight, on level ground and with good visibility.

Most road signs are indicated pictorially, but verbal signs may sometimes be encountered. Here are a few popular specimens:
TRAVAUX — Road Works. FIN DE CHANTIER — End of Road Works. CHAUSSÉE DÉFORMÉE — Uneven Road Surface. NIDS DE POULES — potholes ROUTE BARRÉE — Road Closed. DÉVIATION — Diversion. FIN DE RÉSTRICTION DE VITESSE — End of Special Speed Limit. FIN D'INTERDICTION DE STATIONNER — End of No Parking. SERREZ À DROITE —Keep well into Right. VERGLAS — Danger from Black Ice. RAPPEL — A reminder (— still in built-up area, or speed restriction still applies)

How Far Is It? *(See map on pages 12 and 13.)*

All distances in kilometres.

	Plymouth	Weymouth	Southampton	Portsmouth	Newhaven	Folkestone	Dover*	London
Aberdeen	967	888	853	886	890	896	900	792
Birmingham	328	246	206	240	272	290	293	177
Bristol	189	111	121	154	233	290	301	187
Cardiff	257	179	185	219	298	359	362	248
Carlisle	626	547	515	549	578	590	594	479
Edinburgh	775	697	661	695	698	705	708	600
Exeter	67	95	169	203	283	386	389	274
Glasgow	777	698	668	702	729	742	745	631
Holyhead	524	446	432	467	507	528	531	417
Hull	547	460	394	383	367	386	389	273
Inverness	1,029	951	916	949	952	959	962	854
Ipswich	455	328	240	230	206	198	201	115
Leeds	502	420	360	394	404	410	413	306
London	340	212	124	114	93	112	116	—
Manchester	446	365	331	365	393	407	410	296
Newcastle	645	565	500	534	540	543	547	439
Northampton	352	236	171	204	202	217	220	104
Norwich	513	386	304	293	285	260	264	179
Oxford	289	172	104	138	169	204	208	92
Sheffield	452	367	309	343	352	365	368	255
Stoke-on-Trent	388	309	273	307	335	349	352	237
Stranraer	788	710	679	713	740	753	756	642
Swansea	322	434	249	283	362	423	426	309
York	532	446	380	414	414	422	425	317
	Plymouth	Weymouth	Southampton	Portsmouth	Newhaven	Folkestone	Dover*	London

* Distances also approximately the same to Ramsgate.

Conversion Chart . . . kilometres to miles

All distances in this book are indicated in kilometres, but if you wish to convert into miles the conversion chart below should be of some help.

Kilometres	Miles	Kilometres	Miles	Kilometres	Miles	Kilometres	Miles
1	.62	20	12.4	39	24	300	186
2	1.2	21	13	40	25	400	249
3	1.9	22	13	41	25	500	311
4	2.5	23	14	42	26	600	373
5	3.1	24	15	43	27	700	435
6	3.7	25	15	44	27	800	497
7	4.4	26	16	45	28	900	559
8	5	27	17	46	29	1,000	621
9	5.6	28	17	47	29	1,100	684
10	6.2	29	18	48	30	1,200	746
11	6.8	30	18	49	30	1,300	808
12	7.5	31	19	50	31	1,400	870
13	8	32	20	60	37	1,500	932
14	8.7	33	20	70	43	1,600	994
15	9.3	34	21	80	50	1,700	1,056
16	10	35	21	90	56	1,800	1,118
17	10.6	36	22	100	62	1,900	1,181
18	11.2	37	23	200	124	2,000	1,242
19	11.8	38	24				

If you have a calculator: Convert kilometres to miles by multiplying by .6214.
Convert miles to kilometres by multiplying by 1.6093.

	Roscoff	St-Malo	Cherbourg	Le-Havre	Dieppe	Boulogne	Calais	Paris
Agen	809	652	785	761	802	927	961	643
Aix-en-Provence	1,172	987	1,078	981	923	1,000	1,034	752
Aix-les-Bains	981	796	887	790	732	809	843	566
Amiens	541	401	357	179	112	125	156	150
Angers	339	195	284	311	336	470	504	284
Arras	608	468	419	264	139	116	114	178
Aurillac	800	643	709	681	692	794	843	545
Avignon	1,101	916	1,003	912	854	931	965	686
Bayonne	842	685	819	796	837	962	996	739
Belfort	929	785	772	656	598	644	642	432
Besançon	856	712	729	613	555	601	599	400
Béziers	1,086	929	1,033	857	926	1,010	1,044	823
Biarritz	851	694	830	805	846	971	1,005	747
Bordeaux	667	510	643	619	660	785	819	560
Bourges	593	408	488	403	372	474	523	227
Brest	62	221	403	482	558	683	717	592
Caen	305	165	121	108	166	306	340	240
Cannes	1,315	1,130	1,191	1,081	1,023	1,110	1,134	910
Carcassonne	1,008	851	945	917	928	1,030	1,079	905
Chalon-sur-Saône	805	661	679	563	505	582	616	338
Châlons-sur-Marne	722	531	501	367	301	328	326	185
Charleville-Mézières	734	594	559	404	300	277	275	224
Chaumont	757	613	592	476	502	463	465	253
Clermont-Ferrand	800	591	663	586	555	639	673	390
Dijon	773	629	655	539	481	543	540	312
Gap	1,086	901	993	883	825	901	936	667
Geneva	968	783	860	744	686	748	745	546
Grenoble	983	798	890	780	722	798	833	568
Lille	660	520	472	289	197	116	108	219
Limoges	628	471	537	509	520	622	671	379
Lyon	877	692	783	686	628	705	739	462
Le Mans	337	193	269	222	256	381	415	200
Marseille	1,192	1,007	1,097	1,006	948	1,025	1,059	777
Metz	871	691	650	501	435	439	437	330
Monaco	1,366	1,181	1,302	1,132	1,074	1,151	1,185	957
Montluçon	710	471	565	514	465	567	616	320
Moulins	691	506	586	501	470	572	621	290
Nancy	838	694	652	518	452	479	477	310
Nantes	332	175	308	387	430	555	589	370
Nice	1,348	1,163	1,284	1,114	1,056	1,133	1,167	933
Orléans	475	331	389	292	261	363	412	120
Paris	560	370	360	204	200	243	295	—
Pau	858	701	834	810	851	976	1,010	750
Périgueux	689	547	611	602	624	723	772	528
Perpignan	1,123	966	1,057	1,039	1,014	1,098	1,132	910
Poitiers	510	353	417	408	430	555	589	335
Le Puy	928	719	791	714	683	767	801	513
Reims	653	513	478	323	257	284	287	150
Rennes	213	69	208	278	360	485	519	347
La Rochelle	478	321	454	494	568	693	727	476
Rouen	433	293	244	86	58	183	217	139
Strasbourg	974	834	803	669	603	630	595	488
Toulon	1,256	1,071	1,163	1,072	1,009	1,086	1,120	838
Toulouse	917	760	854	826	837	939	988	684
Tours	445	263	357	306	328	453	487	233
Troyes	662	518	497	381	323	391	388	157
Valence	977	792	883	786	728	805	839	561
	Roscoff	St-Malo	Cherbourg	Le-Havre	Dieppe	Boulogne	Calais	Paris

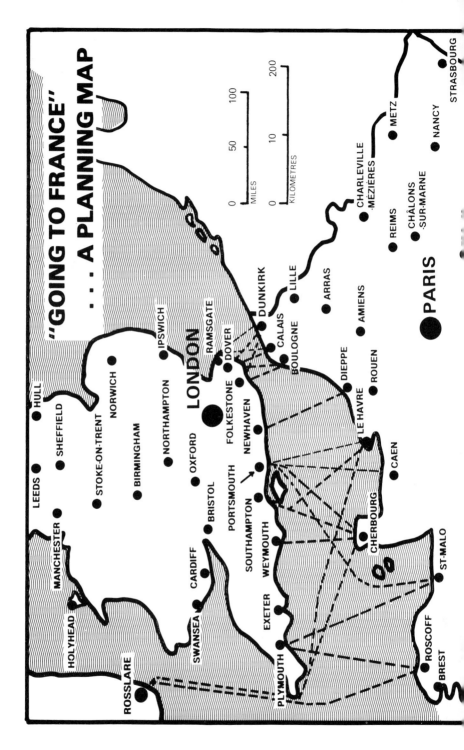

"GOING TO FRANCE"
. . . A PLANNING MAP

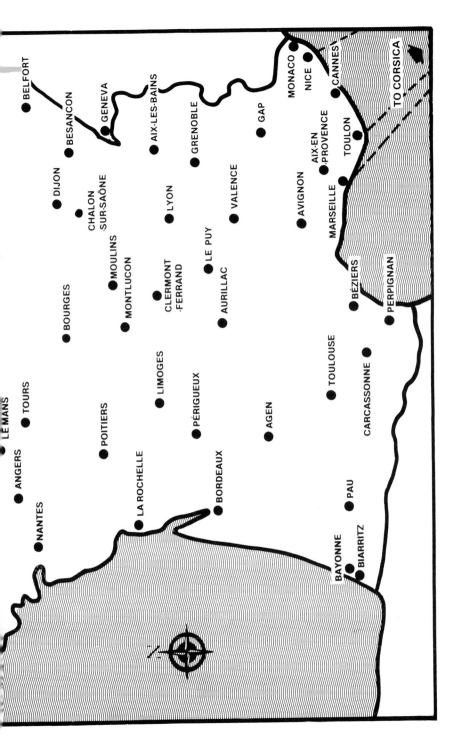

13

HOLIDAY ROUTES.

At peak holiday times, alternative 'holiday routes' are signed by green arrows for long distances and by yellow arrows for up to sixty kilometres. The *Bison Futé* ('The Clever Indian') is a cartoon character promoting these routes and there are a series of *Bison Futé* or *Itinéraires Bis* (as they are now more usually called) Information Centres on the road and at service stations, where free maps and advice are available (especially during July and August).

OVERTAKING

Observe the no-overtaking sign (a red car alongside a black one). This is the most common traffic infringement by British drivers in France. Do not cross a solid white or yellow line unless there is a broken line on your side of the solid one. Do not overtake a stationary tram when passengers are leaving or entering. Restrict your speed to 30 kph (18 mph) when overtaking funerals, marching troops or processions. Keep your offside indicator flashing when overtaking and use your nearside indicator when about to pull back in to the right.

PARKING

Common sense in the observation of international NO PARKING signs will serve in most instances, but remember that parking is not allowed near intersections, bends, hill summits, in front of police stations, on roads on the outskirts of towns, hospitals, post offices and private entrances. If parking outside built-up areas, pull right off the road. Street parking is sometimes allowed on alternative sides of the street, and this is governed either by splitting into even and uneven dates (Jours Pairs, or Jours Impairs), or by splitting into the first and second half of the month (1 – 15, or 16 – 30). Most towns have Blue Zones (Zones Bleus) where street parking is allowed for short periods, and for which discs may be obtained from tourist information offices, garages, police stations, and tobacco kiosks. Ignore these restrictions at your peril... there are substantial fines, and especially in Paris there is considerable chance of finding that your car has been towed away.

SEAT BELTS

The wearing of seat belts by driver and front seat passenger, and by children in the back, is compulsory outside towns.

PEDESTRIANS

Watch carefully at all times and remember that pedestrians have a right of way once they have started to cross an uncontrolled crossing indicated by studs or white stripes.

HORNS

Do not use horns in towns and only during daylight in the country. Use flashing headlights at all intersections at night.

Autumn at the Pont-du-Gard
Photograph by Peter Titchmarsh

BREAKDOWNS

Wise motorists will have taken out some form of insurance against mechanical breakdowns, but the first thing to do is to phone the police from the nearest telephone using the word *panne* for breakdown, as opposed to *accident* for accident, and giving the registration number of your car in French if at all possible. Usually the police will summon the assistance of *Touring Secours France*. We have broken down a few times and have usually found everyone most helpful.

DRIVING ON THE RIGHT

You will find this much easier than you feared, but keep ever vigilant, as it is possible to have a moment's confusion after a day or two, especially when turning from one road into another, or drawing out from a garage, camp site or hotel. Small children will normally be delighted to provide a 'KEEP TO THE RIGHT, DADDY' service, although one has known this to be overdone on a hot afternoon in the middle of a long cross country journey.

ROADS

French roads are on the whole very good, and they are divided into the following categories:

Motorways (Autoroutes). These are prefixed by the letter A and are almost all subject to tolls. In most cases drivers are handed a card when joining an autoroute, and the toll is collected when the card is surrendered (either when leaving the autoroute, or when leaving a particular section). In some cases tolls may be paid by throwing coins in automatic collecting boxes, but this only applies to certain short lengths, usually in the vicinity of large towns and cities. The autoroutes are well maintained and signed and are provided with excellent services...filling stations, restaurants, snack bars, lavatories, information points and picnic areas. The tolls are expensive but they tend to keep the volume of traffic lower than it would be otherwise, and we feel that they offer excellent value to holiday motorists who only have a limited time at their disposal. There is no doubt that anyone journeying across France using nothing but the autoroutes misses the whole flavour of France, and we would suggest that an intelligent blending of autoroutes with the smaller roads running in approximately the same direction, is the best compromise for most visitors.

The Main Roads (Routes Nationales). These are prefixed by the letter N. Many of them are excellent, but they are often over-used by traffic which includes large trucks and trailers avoiding the payment of autoroute tolls, and they are also often subject to very pronounced cambering, and varying surfaces caused in many cases by the uneven pavé base beneath the asphalt. However not all Routes Nationales are subject to these drawbacks and they are generally much wider than British main roads, and are very often lined with splendid trees, providing welcome shade from the hot sun on a summer day.

The Secondary Roads (Routes Départementales). These are prefixed by the letter D. We think that the ideal journey across France may be planned using a combination of Autoroutes and D roads, and if time was no object we should use D roads almost without exception. They are in most instances well surfaced, remarkably under-used, and take visitors through the very heart of the tranquil French countryside, with considerable distances even between the smallest of towns. In addition to this guide your invaluable companions on journeys of this nature would be the Michelin Red Guide (see Books, page 4, and Hotels, page 6) and the relevant Michelin Yellow 1:200,000 maps (see Maps, page 5), which indicate the most usable of the D roads for cross-country motoring by colouring them in yellow. Those left white should generally be left for exploration from your final holiday destination and not used for long distance motoring.

The Minor Roads (Chemins Vicinaux). These are prefixed by the letter V and are also reasonably well surfaced, but they are not numbered on the normal tourist maps and should only be used for local exploration.

Trains

France has a fine railway network, with fast and efficient services across the country, ranging down from the *TGV* (Train à Grande Vitesse) (the fastest train in the world, running on a special high-speed line from Paris to Lyon, and to many other destinations including the Alps, Marseille and the Côte d'Azur), to the *Rapide*, the *Express*, the *Direct* and the *Omnibus*, a local service stopping at every station. If you wish to avoid the long road journey to your destination you can use the *Motorail Service*, carries cars and passengers overnight from Boulogne, Calais, Dieppe and Paris to all the main holiday areas. Alternatively French Railways offer a Self-Drive Hire Service from nearly 200 towns served by their rail network. They also offer a wide selection of packages combining rail from any British station, ferry crossing and French rail journey, with a variety of hotels, holiday villages, apartments, car tours making use of the Motorail Service and hotels, camping, and cycling. There is also an inclusive Air France Rail Service which links various UK airports with many French cities, via Paris. Colourful illustrated leaflets describing all these services may be obtained from French Railways, 179, Piccadilly, London W1V 0BA, or in many cases from your local travel agent. Under 26's qualify for up to 50% reduction on rail travel with a "Carré Jeune" or "Carte Jeune" railcard depending on date of travel. These are available on personal application to French Railways in Piccadilly, or in French railway stations. French Railways also offer a form of 'Railrover' ticket entitled 'France Vacances', giving unlimited travel throughout France on any 4 days during a period of 15 days or on any 9 or 16 days during a period of one month, in 1st or 2nd class. Various valuable travel concessions are also offered to France Vacances ticket holders.

Bus and Coach Services

Although there is no separate long distance coach service within France, the French Railways run a *Europabus* service which is largely a complementary extension of their own rail network, with many tours starting from centres served by trains. They do however also run coach services between several of the large cities, including two routes between Paris and Nice, and one between London and Paris, operated jointly with Britain's National Bus Company. Further details of these services are available from French Railways, 179, Piccadilly, London W1V 0BA. There are regular coach services running from London to a large number of French destinations. For details contact your travel agent, your local National Express Office, or Euroways, 52 Grosvenor Gardens, Victoria, London SW1 0AU.

Cycling in France

Some of the cross-Channel ferry operators offer free transport for bicycles (scan the brochures with care) and the quieter roads of France offer many tempting opportunities for cyclists, especially when combined with the use of the smaller hotels and restaurants with bedrooms, listed in the Logis de France guide (just the right size for the saddle-bag) or with the many camp-sites listed in the Michelin camping guide. It is also possible to hire bicycles from over 200 railway stations throughout France. Books on cycling in France include *Cycle Touring in France* (published by Oxford Illustrated Press) and *Susi Madron's Cycling in France* (published by George Philip). For further helpful details, write to the Touring Department, Cyclists Touring Club, Cotterell House, 69 Meadow. Godalming, Surrey GU7 3HS.

Walking in France

Several travel organisations provide walking holidays in France. Their programmes cover such diverse areas as Brittany, the Cévennes, Provence and the Alps. However if you wish to organise your own walking holiday you can obtain interesting information from the Comité National des Sentiers de Grande Randonnée, the organisation responsible for the splendid network of long distance footpaths across the length and breadth of France. The IGN (see Maps, page 5) publish a map of France showing all these long distance footpaths and the Comité publish a series of *Topoguides* covering many of the paths individually (these are in French and their maps are very basic). Robertson McCarta publish a series of walking guides based on the French Topoguides, including *Normandy and the Seine, Walks in Provence, Walking through Brittany, Walking the Pyrénées* and *Walks in Auvergne*. Other excellent books on walking in France include *Walking in France* and *Classic Walks in France* (both published by Oxford Illustrated Press), *Walking through France* (published by Collins), and *Walking through Northern France* (published by Moorland).

In our view you would be advised to purchase the IGN 1:50,000 (1¼" to the mile) maps of the area you wish to cover. All these maps and guides are available from McCarta Map & Guide Shop, 122, King's Cross Road, London WC2, or Stanford's International Map Centre, 12 – 14, Long Acre, London WC2 9LP.

Walking in the wooded foothills of the Pyrenees near Luchon   *Photograph by Peter Titchmarsh*

Vulture-watching near Le Rozier (See page 135)
Photograph by Peter Titchmarsh

If you aim to walk in high mountain country, please make sure that you have adequate experience and equipment, and walk in the company of anyone with mountain experience. However walking in France can be undertaken by anyone with virtually no experience providing they keep to the plains, the valleys and the low hills. We think that the Vosges or the Jura in summer, or the quieter parts of Provence in spring or autumn, would all be ideal… but ponder over the maps and dream your dreams during the coming winter… the possibilities are limitless.

Bird Watching

We make reference in our book list to *Where to Watch Birds in Europe*, by John Gooders, and we would strongly recommend you to purchase this most useful paper-back before setting out for France. Most holiday locations are within striking distance of at least one of the eighteen areas to which Mr. Gooders refers (which range from the Somme estuary to the Vanoise National Park, and from the Golfe du Morbihan to the Camargue). We are not expert bird watchers, but we find this book to be quite mouth-watering in its descriptions of the quiet marshlands and lagoons, so beloved by birds and watchers alike.

Here is a list of official 'Ornithological Reserves' open to the public: In *Brittany*…Cap Sizun, nr. Goulien (29), Cap Fréhel, nr. Plevenon (22), Sept-Îles, nr. Perros Guirec (22), Belle Île-en-mer, nr. Pointe de Nar Hor Morbihan (56). In *Provence*…The Reserve de Camargue (13). In the *Gironde*…Banc d'Arguin, nr. Arcachon (33), Teich, nr. Arcachon (33). In *Picardy*…Marquenterre (80). In *Vendée*…Île d'Olonne, nr. Sables d'Olonne (85), St-Denis du Payré, in the Marais Poitevin (85).

National Parks and Regional Nature Parks

There are five **National Parks**: The Cévennes, The Écrins, The Port Cros, The Pyrénées Occidentales, and the Vanoise. These are large, virtually uninhabited areas, and in this respect differ from the **Regional Nature Parks**, in that the latter are in inhabited country areas, 'where rural economic development is pursued hand in hand with policies to preserve and enhance natural assets...' (to quote from an official statement).

There are no fewer than twenty **Regional Nature Parks**: Armorique, Brière, Brotonne, Camargue, Corsica, Forêt d'Orient, Landes de Gascogne, Haut Languedoc, Lorraine, Luberon, Marais Poitevin, Montagne de Reims, Morvan, Normandie-Maine, Pilat, Queyras, St-Amand-Raismes, Val de Sèvres et Vendée, Vercors, Volcans d'Auvergne, and Vosges du Nord.

The difference between the two types of Park, apart from that mentioned above, appears to be largely an administrative one, and need not concern the normal visitor. The areas concerned are for various reasons specially protected against exploitation and over-development, and without exception are a pleasure to visit. Within some of them, the Camargue for instance, certain areas are partially restricted as *Nature Reserves* and access is limited.

NATIONAL PARKS, REGIONAL NATURE PARKS AND ORNITHOLOGICAL RESERVES

- ⬤ NATIONAL PARKS
- ◯ REGIONAL NATURE PARKS
- ● Ornithological Reserves

Eating and Drinking in France

However far along the 'self-catering' road you intend to travel, please ensure that you devote a considerable proportion of your funds to the pleasures of eating in French restaurants. Almost all display their priced menus outside and it is well worthwhile making a survey of the various set meals offered.

In the Regional Nature Park of Brière (See page 167)

THE PRINCIPAL WINE GROWING AREAS OF FRANCE

Calvados
Champagne
Loire Valley
Alsace
Vouvray
Chablis
Muscadet
Sancerre
Saumur
Pouilly
Nuits
Burgundy
Beaune
Chalonnaise
Côtes
Mâconnais
du Jura
Beaujolais
Cognac
Savoy
Bordeaux
Medoc
St-Émilion
Graves
Bergerac
Sauternes
Côtes du
Rhone
Armagnac
Languedoc
Côtes de
Provence
Roussillon

Your meal may prove a little more expensive than you had hoped, especially if you are several in family, but meals out in France can still be one of the outstanding experiences of your holiday. We have, from time to time, had disappointing meals in France, but happily the standards of most of the small family-run restaurants are still well maintained, even in these days of plastic everything. The Red Michelin Guide will prove useful in locating good food at moderate prices or something rather special (see Hotels, page 6), especially if you are planning ahead on a journey. However, if you are walking around a town, personal observation of the restaurants and their menus, is at least as important when making your choice, and the process is a most pleasurable experience in itself.

Cafés are for drinking and although some serve sandwiches, we think that restaurants offer far better eating value. Soft drinks and ice-creams tend to be expensive in cafés and when holidaying with a young family visits to cafés should usually be regarded as a special treat only.

We do not claim to be food and wine experts, but we find that advance reading on both subjects greatly enhances the pleasures of a holiday in France. There are many books on these subjects but we would like to make special mention of Glynn Christian's *Edible France* (published by Ebury Press) and *A Wine Tour of France* by Frederick S. Wildman (published by Cassell & Co.). Both authors have great enthusiasm and a wide knowledge, and both write with considerable humour…read Frederick Wildman on his introduction to the pleasures of Château Yquem (at the tender age of six), and the disastrous consequences. Should you wish to place yourselves completely in the hands of experts there are tours for gourmets and wine lovers, details of which may be obtained from your travel agent.

Entertainment

Cinemas and theatres are not to be recommended to those who do not speak French fluently, and we think that the best holiday entertainment in France is to sit at a pavement café or restaurant table and watch the world go by. If you are staying near a château or other historic building with 'Son-et-Lumière', those 'sound and light' shows are well worth attending. Discos, 'dancings' and night-clubs can all be fun, but we can only suggest you follow your own particular inclination. We would probably rather spend our money on a reasonable and well prolonged meal, followed by a short stroll round the town or village in which we are staying, but perhaps this is rather a middle-aged view.

Services, etc.

POLICE

The French Police Force is divided into two arms…the nationally organised *Gendarmerie Nationale* and the locally organised *Agents de Police*. Traffic Police can impose hefty spot fines on tourists as well as on native Frenchmen, for drink infringements, speeding, non-wearing of safety-belts, and other traffic offences. If you put yourself at risk, have ready cash available…it will save considerable trouble. However, we feel sure that you will find no difficulty in keeping within the law.

POSTAL SERVICES

Post Offices are normally open on weekdays from 8 a.m. until 7 p.m., and on Saturdays from 8 a.m. until 12 noon. However stamps may also be purchased from tobacconists who are signed with a red cigar, and from various small shops selling post-cards, but if you buy at the latter, make sure that you have also purchased their post-cards…you will be most unpopular otherwise. Post boxes are painted yellow and are marked *Boite Aux Lettres*. Poste Restante letters should be marked as such, and also marked *Poste Centrale*, with the name of the town and the Département. When you go to collect a Poste Restante letter, make sure that you have your passport with you.

TELEPHONE

The French telephone service is now much improved. You may dial any UK number from a call box or other phone. First dial 19, wait until a continuous tone occurs, then dial 44 followed by the UK STD number, minus the first '0'. e.g. A London number becomes 19-44-1-499-6911 instead of 01-499 6911 if dialled from within Britain. To telephone from the UK to France, dial (010) (33), then either (1) plus the eight-figure number for Paris, or simply the eight-figure for the provinces.

BANKS

Banks are normally open on Monday – Friday, except in a town that has a regular Saturday market, when they are open from Tuesday – Saturday. Opening hours are usually 9 – 12, 2 – 4. Take your passport with you when cashing Traveller's Cheques. If you are travelling only to France, take French France Traveller's Cheques, as you are then protected against fluctuations in the rate of exchange, and encashment is much simpler. Ask your bank for the latest advice regarding Eurocheques and Cheque Cards. For regular travellers, credit cards such as Access, Barclaycard, American Express and Diner's Club are useful. The Michelin Red Guide indicates which hotels and restaurants accept which credit cards.

PUBLIC HOLIDAYS

(Keep this list in mind...it may save you trouble.)

New Years Day	1st January	Bastille Day	14th July
Easter Monday	–	Assumption	15th August
Labour Day	1st May	All Saints Day	1st November
VE Day	8th May	Armistice Day	11th November
Ascension Day	6th Thursday after Easter	Christmas Day	25th December
Whit Monday	2nd Monday after Ascension		

N.B.: – If any of the above fall on a Sunday, the following day may be treated as a holiday. If any falls on a Tuesday or a Friday, the day between this and the weekend is also a holiday... What a splendid arrangement!

PUBLIC LAVATORIES

These may be rather sparse in some towns, but do not be afraid to ask to use the toilettes of bars, restaurants and cafés, even if you have not purchased a drink or a meal. You should however leave a small tip in the saucer usually provided. Gents will be entitled *Messieurs* or *Hommes,* and Ladies, *Dames* or *Femmes.*

ELECTRICTIY

Generally 220 volt AC is now available, but most sockets are two pin. Adaptors for these sockets are available at most electrical shops in Britain. If in doubt about the possible use of any appliance on a two pin adaptor, query with your local electrical shop before departure.

TIPPING AND SERVICE CHARGES

All restaurant prices are now 'service compris', but most people still leave small change as a token of appreciation. In hotels tipping is not necessary. Taxi drivers expect 15% and theatre and cinema usherettes expect about 2 francs (at the time of writing). Attendants in public lavatories also expect a small tip.

OPENING TIMES FOR PLACES MENTIONED IN THIS GUIDE

We have not included details of opening times in this guide as they might become misleading with changing conditions. However details will be found in leaflets available from the local Syndicats d'Initiative, which are usually most helpful. To generalise, many places will be closed all day on Tuesdays, but will usually open for the rest of the week from about 9.30 – 12, and 2.30 – 5.

Shopping in France

We love window shopping along the smart streets of Paris and the large provincial and holiday towns, and we also enjoy walking around the large department stores where prices are very similar to those in Britain. However the great pleasure of shopping in France is in its food markets, food shops, and to a lesser extent, its super-markets and hyper-markets. The latter can be useful if your French is non-existent, but if you have even a few words it is much more fun to shop in the markets and in the small food shops. We thoroughly enjoy our continental breakfast (petit déjeuner), with hot or still warm croissants, and delicious coffee; and our dinners out in restaurant or hotel, but our lunch (déjeuner) is almost invariably a picnic, and it is shopping for this meal that provides us with almost as much pleasure as its consumption a few hours later... well, almost! Fresh crusty bread, pâté of infinite variety, a little sliced ham, some local cheese, a bottle of wine or mineral water, fresh tomatoes, peaches, a melon, or grapes, and perhaps a puff pastry from the pâtisserie. If you are forced to 'eat in', in flat, gîte, villa or camp-site, shopping for your evening meal becomes a fraction less frivolous, but it can still be fun, especially if you enjoy fish and salads. However, to repeat ourselves, do try to eat out in the evenings as often as possible... the French will be quite used to seeing young children out to dinner, and most restaurants start serving at about seven.

Normal Opening Hours: Food Shops 7 a.m. – 6.30/7.30 p.m.
Others Shops 9 a.m. – 6.30/7.30 p.m.
Many shops close all day on Monday.
Many small food shops, especially bakers, open on Sunday mornings.
Most hypermarkets remain open until 9 or 10 p.m., although many of them
do not open on a Monday morning.

France . . . The Historical Background

Evidence of prehistoric France remains in the form of cave paintings, largely in the Dordogne, and in chambered tombs (dolmens) and standing stones (menhirs), the most dramatic of which are to be found in Brittany. The Iron Age Gallic (or Celtic) tribes, having driven out the earlier inhabitants by the 6th century BC, established themselves, as in Britain, in large hill forts, many of whose earthworks have survived.

Gaul was conquered by the Romans under Julius Caesar between 58 and 49 BC, and for several hundred years the whole area was exposed in varying degrees to the effects of Roman civilization, the south-eastern part being inevitably affected more intensively. The remains of this Gallo-Roman civilization are a most interesting feature of tourist France, with an especial emphasis on the towns and cities of Roman Provence. However there is much else to be seen, and reference is made within our guide to several other sites throughout France.

The declining power and influence of Rome left a political and military vacuum in Gaul and it was to be many centuries before a uniform and centralised control could be once again imposed. First the Visigoths established themselves between the Loire and the Pyrénées in the 5th century, but they were overcome by the tribes that were to give modern France its name. . . .the Franks. The greatest King of the Frankish Merovingian dynasty, Clovis, became a Christian in 496, and the Merovingians ruled over a considerable area until they in their turn were replaced by the stronger Carolingians, who up to that time had been their palace mayors.

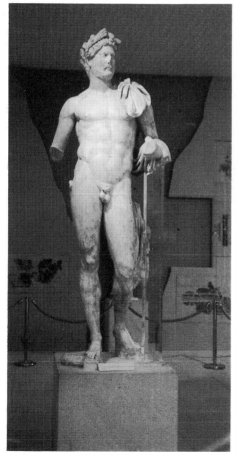

Charles Martel, the first of the Carolingians, turned the tide against the Saracens who had spread across the Pyrénées into much of southern France, at the famous Battle of Poitiers in 732. The third Carolingian, Charles Martel's grandson, the great Charlemagne, established control over a great Empire stretching from the Baltic to the Ebro, and also east and south to Calabria, and he had himself crowned 'Holy Roman Emperor' at Aachen on Christmas Day AD 800. However his Empire was split into three parts after his sons and grandsons fell out over their inheritance, and the western third had declined in size to a small area around Paris, the 'Île de France', by the time that Hughes Capet became the first true King of France in the year 987.

Despite the menace of the Vikings, or Norsemen, established in Normandy, the presence of the Bretons to the west, the Burgundians to the east and the various other feudal dukedoms, principalities and kingdoms to the south... despite all this, it was from the time of Hughes Capet's coronation in 987, that the Île de France was to gradually expand into the modern state of France. It was the persistent goal of the French monarchy to give France her 'natural' frontiers upon the Rhine, the Alps and the Pyrénées, and like their more successful English counterparts, to establish strong central authority throughout this enlarged realm.

The story of this struggle is too involved to follow here in detail, but it was only in the 15th century that the English, established here for many centuries for dynastic reasons, were finally driven out of their lands in the south and west (1453). Burgundy reverted to the French crown a few years later (1477), and in 1480 Provence also became part of France. In 1499 Brittany was finally incorporated, on the marriage of Anne of Brittany to Louis XII. And so, by the end of the 15th century a substantial part of modern France had been united under the monarchy.

In the museum at Vaison-la-Romaine
Photograph by Peter Titchmarsh

In the century that followed, this building process was rudely interrupted by the devastating 'Wars of Religion', between the Roman Catholics and the Protestant Huguenots, which lasted from 1562 until 1598. The savagery of this struggle was highlighted by the infamous 'St-Bartholomew's Eve Massacre' of 24th August 1572.

The 17th century saw the establishment of much central authority by the great Cardinals, Richelieu and Mazarin, and on the death of the latter in 1661, the establishment of the greatest autocrat King of all French history... the 'Sun King' himself, Louis XIV, who ruled until his death in 1715, having been aided by such capable servants as Colbert and Turenne and the great military engineer, Vauban.

However French defeats at the hands of Marlborough during the War of the Spanish Succession, and the sporadic warfare that went on between France and Britain over their North American colonies, led to widespread poverty throughout France. Louis XV, under the influence of his mistresses, Madame de Pompadour and Madame du Barry, did not appear to have realised the importance of these colonies, and despite reforms both in the armed services and in the civil service, he left France a much weaker and much poorer nation than he had inherited, when he died in 1774.

Chenonceaux

Photograph by Peter Titchmarsh

Louis XVI soon found himself facing the twin evils of acclerating inflation and rising unemployment, but despite this, it would be wrong to see the opening stages of the Revolution as being a popular movement in response to these pressures. It sprung largely from the upper-middle classes and the minor aristocracy, who saw unrestrained monarchy as an obstacle to much needed reform, as propounded by the political philosphers of the 'Age of Reason'. The tragic deterioration of order and the savageries of the years following 1789 are too well known to repeat, but the longing for strong central control and a return to law and order, was eventually satisfied by the emergence of Napoleon Bonaparte, who was declared First Consul, and then Emperor in 1804.

The 19th century saw the destruction of Napoleon's Empire and the re-establishment of the Bourbons for a short period (1815 – 1830). Then the 1830 Revolution led to the establishment of a constitutional monarch, Louis-Philippe, who ruled for eighteen years. Then a Second Republic (1848 – 1852), followed by a Second Empire ruled over by Bonaparte's nephew, Louis-Napoleon (1852 – 1870). With the defeat of the French by the Prussians, at Sedan in 1870, the Second Empire collapsed, and after the tragic events of the Paris Commune, it was not until 1875 that the Third Republic was created. This lasted until 1940, and was replaced in 1946 by the Fourth Republic, and in 1958 by the Fifth Republic, the creation of the great Charles de Gaulle, following the near fatal dissensions over the struggles for independence in Algeria.

The Fifth Republic remains today, and despite the political upheavals over the past two hundred years, France now finds herself strong, prosperous, and less divided than her neighbour across the Channel. She is a vital nation which looks forward more often than she looks back, and the visitor will be excited by the many manifestations of this vitality... an ever growing network of superb autoroutes, new rail routes, great hydro-electric undertakings and irrigation schemes, modernised, wide canal systems, urban motorways like the Paris 'Boulevard Péripherique', and many highly automated modern factories... all this is in splendid contrast to the tranquillity of its great stretches of under-populated countryside, a priceless asset that is becoming increasingly valued by the French themselves, in addition to their visitors from abroad.

THE REGIONS OF FRANCE
indicating the Départements which they comprise

(75) PARIS (Pages 25 – 38)

ALSACE AND LORRAINE-VOSGES (Pages 39 – 46)
54 Meurthe-et-Moselle
55 Meuse
57 Moselle
67 Bas Rhin
68 Haut Rhin
88 Vosges

AQUITAINE (Pages 47 – 57)
24 Dordogne
33 Gironde
40 Landes
47 Lot-et-Garonne
64 Pyrénées-Atlantiques

AUVERGNE (Pages 58 – 67)
03 Allier
15 Cantal
43 Haute-Loire
63 Puy-de-Dôme

BRITTANY (Pages 68 – 77)
22 Côtes-du-Nord
29 Finistère
35 Ille-et-Vilaine
56 Morbihan

BURGUNDY (Pages 78 – 87)
21 Côte-d'Or
58 Nièvre
71 Saône-et-Loire
89 Yonne

CHAMPAGNE-ARDENNE (Pages 88 – 94)
08 Ardennes
10 Aube
51 Marne
52 Haute Marne

CORSICA (Pages 95 – 101)
20 Corsica

CÔTE-D'AZUR (Pages 102 – 110)
06 Alpes-Maritimes

FRANCHE-COMTÉ (Pages 111 – 117)
25 Doubs
39 Jura
70 Haute-Saône
90 Territoire-de-Belfort

ÎLE-DE-FRANCE (Pages 118 – 128)
77 Seine-et-Marne
78 Yvelines
91 Essonne
92 Hauts-de-Seine
93 Seine-St-Denis
94 Val-de-Marne
95 Val-d'Oise

LANGUEDOC-ROUSSILLON (Pages 129 – 139)
11 Aude
30 Gard
34 Hérault
48 Lozère
66 Pyrénées Orientales

LIMOUSIN (Pages 140 – 147)
19 Corrèze
23 Creuse
87 Haute-Vienne

LOIRE VALLEY . . . THE CENTRE REGION
(Pages 148 – 164)
18 Cher
28 Eure-et-Loir
36 Indre
37 Indre-et-Loire
41 Loir-et-Cher
45 Loiret

LOIRE VALLEY WEST (Pages 165 – 174)
44 Loire-Atlantique
49 Maine-et-Loire
53 Mayenne
72 Sarthe
85 Vendée

MIDI-PYRÉNÉES (Pages 175 – 186)
09 Ariège
12 Aveyron
31 Haute-Garonne
32 Gers
46 Lot
65 Hautes-Pyrénées
81 Tarn
82 Tarn-et-Garonne

NORD-PAS-DE-CALAIS (Pages 187 – 193)
59 Nord
62 Pas-de-Calais

NORMANDY (Pages 194 – 207)
14 Calvados
27 Eure
50 Manche
61 Orne
76 Seine-Martime

PICARDY (Pages 208 – 216)
02 Aisne
60 Oise
80 Somme

POITOU-CHARENTES (Pages 217 – 225)
16 Charente
17 Charente-Maritime
79 Deux-Sèvres
86 Vienne

PROVENCE (Pages 226 – 240)
04 Alpes-de-Haut-Provence
05 Hautes-Alpes
13 Bouches-du-Rhône
83 Var
84 Vaucluse

RHÔNE VALLEY (Pages 241 – 250)
01 Ain
07 Ardèche
26 Drôme
42 Loire
69 Rhône

SAVOY AND DAUPHINY ALPS (Pages 251 – 259)
38 Isère
73 Savoie
74 Haute-Savoie

THE DÉPARTEMENTS OF FRANCE
indicating the Region in which each one is located

		(Pages)				(Pages)
01	Ain	Rhône Valley	(241 – 250)	49	Maine-et-Loire	Loire Valley West	(165 – 174)
02	Aisne	Picardy	(208 – 216)	50	Manche	Normandy	(194 – 207)
03	Allier	Auvergne	(58 – 67)	51	Marne	Champagne-Ardenne	(88 – 94)
04	Alpes-de-Haut-Provence	Provence	(226 – 240)	52	Haute-Marne	Champagne-Ardenne	(88 – 94)
05	Hautes Alpes	Provence	(226 – 240)	53	Mayenne	Loire Valley West	(165 – 174)
06	Alpes-Maritimes	Côte-d'Azur	(102 – 110)	54	Meurthe-et-Moselle	Alsace and Lorraine-Vosges	(39 – 46)
07	Ardèche	Rhône Valley	(241 – 250)	55	Meuse	Alsace and Lorrane-Vosges	(39 – 46)
08	Ardennes	Champagne-Ardenne	(88 – 94)	56	Morbihan	Brittany	(68 – 77)
09	Ariège	Midi-Pyrénées	(175 – 186)	57	Moselle	Alsace and Lorraine-Vosges	(39 – 46)
10	Aube	Champagne-Ardenne	(88 – 94)	58	Nièvre	Burgundy	(78 – 87)
11	Aude	Languedoc-Roussillon	(129 – 139)	59	Nord	Nord – Pas-de-Calais	(187 – 193)
12	Aveyron	Midi-Pyrénées	(175 – 186)	60	Oise	Picardy	(208 – 216)
13	Bouches-du-Rhône	Provence	(226 – 240)	61	Orne	Normandy	(194 – 207)
14	Calvados	Normandy	(194 – 207)	62	Pas-de-Calais	Nord-Pas-de-Calais	(187 – 193)
15	Cantal	Auvergne	(58 – 67)	63	Puy-de-Dôme	Auvergne	(58 – 67)
16	Charente	Poitou-Charentes	(217 – 225)	64	Pyrénées-Atlantiques	Aquitaine	(47 – 57)
17	Charente-Maritime	Poitou-Charentes	(217 – 225)	65	Hautes-Pyrénées	Midi-Pyrénées	(175 – 186)
18	Cher	Loire Valley Centre	(148 – 164)	66	Pyrénées-Orientales	Languedoc-Roussillon	(129 – 139)
19	Corrèze	Limousin	(140 – 147)	67	Bas-Rhin	Alsace and Lorraine-Vosges	(39 – 46)
20	Corsica	Corsica	(95 – 101)	68	Haut-Rhin	Alsace and Lorraine-Vosges	(39 – 46)
21	Côte-d'Or	Burgundy	(78 – 87)	69	Rhône	Rhône Valley	(241 – 250)
22	Côtes-du-Nord	Brittany	(68 – 77)	70	Haute-Saône	Franche-Comté	(111 – 117)
23	Creuse	Limousin	(140 – 147)	71	Saône-et-Loire	Burgundy	(78 – 87)
24	Dordogne	Aquitaine	(47 – 57)	72	Sarthe	Loire Valley West	(165 – 174)
25	Doubs	Franche-Comté	(111 – 117)	73	Savoie	Savoy & Dauphiny Alps	(251 – 259)
26	Drôme	Rhône Valley	(241 – 250)	74	Haute-Savoie	Savoy & Dauphiny Alps	(251 – 259)
27	Eure	Normandy	(194 – 207)	75	Paris	Paris	(25 – 38)
28	Eure-et-Loir	Loire Valley Centre	(148 – 164)	76	Seine-Maritime	Normandy	(194 – 207)
29	Finistère	Brittany	(68 – 77)	77	Seine-et-Marne	Île-de-France	(118 – 128)
30	Gard	Languedoc-Roussillon	(129 – 139)	78	Yvelines	Île-de-France	(118 – 128)
31	Haute-Garonne	Midi-Pyrénées	(175 – 186)	79	Deux-Sèvres	Poitou-Charentes	(217 – 225)
32	Gers	Midi-Pyrénées	(175 – 186)	80	Somme	Picardy	(208 – 216)
33	Gironde	Aquitaine	(47 – 57)	81	Tarn	Midi-Pyrénées	(175 – 186)
34	Hérault	Languedoc-Roussillon	(129 – 139)	82	Tarn-et-Garonne	Midi-Pyrénées	(175 – 186)
35	Île-et-Vilaine	Brittany	(68 – 77)	83	Var	Provence	(226 – 240)
36	Indre	Loire Valley Centre	(148 – 164)	84	Vaucluse	Provence	(226 – 240)
37	Indre-et-Loire	Loire Valley Centre	(148 – 164)	85	Vendee	Loire Valley West	(165 – 174)
38	Isère	Savoy & Dauphiny Alps	(251 – 259)	86	Vienne	Poitou-Charentes	(217 – 225)
39	Jura	Franche-Comté	(111 – 117)	87	Haute-Vienne	Limousin	(140 – 147)
40	Landes	Aquitaine	(47 – 57)	88	Vosges	Alsace and Lorraine-Vosges	(39 – 46)
41	Loir-et-Cher	Loire Valley Centre	(148 – 164)	89	Yonne	Burgundy	(78 – 87)
42	Loire	Rhône Valley	(241 – 250)	90	Territoire de Belfort	Franche-Comté	(111 – 117)
43	Haute-Loire	Auvergne	(58 – 67)	91	Essonne	Île-de-France	(118 – 128)
44	Loire-Atlantique	Loire Valley West	(165 – 174)	92	Hauts-de-Seine	Île-de-France	(118 – 128)
45	Loiret	Loire Valley Centre	(148 – 164)	93	Seine-St-Denis	Île-de-France	(118 – 128)
46	Lot	Midi-Pyrénées	(175 – 186)	94	Val-de-Marne	Île-de-France	(118 – 128)
47	Lot-et-Garonne	Aquitaine	(47 – 57)	95	Val-d'Oise	Île-de-France	(118 – 128)
48	Lozère	Languedoc-Roussillon	(129 – 139)				

Please Note: Départemental numbers are incorporated into vehicle registration and you can tell at a glance which Département any vehicle comes from (refer to the last two numbers). Postal Codes also incorporate Départemental numbers (refer to the first two numbers).

French Architecture — A Brief Summary

Please note: All dates shown represent an over-simplification, and are only an indication of the times when the gradual changes in architectural styles were developing.

EARLIEST PREHISTORIC TIMES
Chambered tombs (dolmens), standing stones (menhirs), and cave paintings.

GALLO-ROMAN (50 BC – AD 450)
Cities, towns, villas, arenas, temples, triumphal arches, aqueducts.

MEROVINGIAN (450 – 730)
Little remains of this period apart from a few crypts and baptisteries. They all derived their styles from Rome, and the buildings above them (now vanished) must have been built on the 'basilica' plan.

CAROLINGIAN (730 – 1000)
Little remains of the earlier parts of this period, although the church of Germigny-des-Prés (see page 156) in the Loire Valley, is an interesting example. However the Romanesque style was now beginning to evolve.

ROMANESQUE (1000 – 1200)
This represents a development of styles evolving from the use of the Roman arch, but with a much more complex inter-relationship than is found in Roman buildings. Romanesque architecture flowered to the full in France, and many of its great cathedrals and abbeys have survived as superlative examples of the style.

Reims Cathedral

GOTHIC (1150 – 1500)
The development of the pointed arch and the great steps forward in vaulting and load bearing that it made possible introduced a new lightness in design. This style appears to have come to fruition in the Île de France and the resulting early buildings, many of which survive today, are a wonder to visit… Sens, St-Denis, Laon, Chartres. The style quickly spread throughout France, and the rest of civilized Europe and there is of course a wealth of Gothic architecture in city, town and village throughout France.

FLAMBOYANT GOTHIC (1400 – 1550)
This was an elorate evolution of the normal Gothic style, which was named thus because of the flamelike tracery of its windows. The pointed arch tended to become depresed and the vaulting more decorative.

THE RENAISSANCE (1500 – 1600)
This great art movement had its origins in Italy, when artists of all kinds had started to look back to classical times for their inspiration. Nobles coming back from the wars in Italy brought these ideas back with them, and at the same time the unification of France and the imposition of central power made the medieval fortress no longer necessary. Some of the great Loire châteaux were actually built by Italian craftsmen, and almost all of those built at this time were pleasure palaces rather than fortified castles. At the same time, formal gardens were laid out, also in the Italian manner.

THE CLASSICAL PERIOD (1600 – 1800)
This is the great period of elegance, not only in the châteaux and town houses themselves, but also in their interior decoration and furnishings, and in their splendid gardens. Men like Le Nôtre, the great garden designer, the architects Mansart and Hardouin Mansart, the interior decorator Le Brun, all come to mind. This was the age of the great palaces including Louis XIV's Versailles, the greatest of them all, and of elegant town houses and city churches.

THE NINETEENTH CENTURY
Not a great number of individual buildings come to mind, but the great town planner Baron Haussmann's ruthless re-design of Paris in the 1850s is now much appreciated. Sacré Coeur and the Eiffel Tower are enduring monuments of doubtful taste, but they too are now much loved by all…Parisians and visitors alike.

THE TWENTIETH CENTURY
There are several brilliant new buildings worthy of note, including Le Corbusier's chapel at Ronchamp (page 116), some of the buildings of La Défense (page 122) and possibly the controversial Beaubourg Centre (page 29), but we prefer the clean sweeping lines of some of the great new hydro-electric dams in the Alps and the Massif Central. But all France awaits you…find your own favourites from every period.....

Paris

Goethe once described Paris as a 'universal city where each step upon a bridge or square recalls a great past', and to all who come here, it appears to have many added charms... there is a warm vitality to be found in its people, and a certain luminescence in its skies. Its cafés and restaurants are a delight, especially in summertime when the pavements are invaded. Its old narrow streets and its quiet quays beside the Seine provide an attractive contrast to the noise and bustle of the great boulevards, and the lush parks and colourful public gardens are a perfect foil for the massive public buildings.

In the Tuilleries Gardens   *Photograph by Peter Titchmarsh*

Through it all flows the lovely river Seine, dividing the city into the 'Right Bank'... the northern two thirds traditionally devoted to fashion, finance and Montmartre; and the 'Left Bank'... the southern third, devoted to young people, artists and the Latin quarter. However this is a misleading generalisation and should not be relied upon too closely.

We have tried to describe briefly some of the outstanding features of this great city, and we would suggest that you use this guide in connection with a good street plan, and limit yourselves to a few items each day. Make use of the excellent Metro (underground railway) and bus services, and if your street plan does not include details of these services, ask at the Paris Tourist Office, 127, Champs Elysées for copies of the vital Metro and bus route maps. Do not begrudge the effort of getting here, as this office is most helpful, and the Champs Elysées is an excellent point of departure in any case.

If you are staying any length of time in Paris, a copy of the splendid Michelin Green Guide (English Edition) will provide a great deal of useful and interesting information to supplement this guide. Now you are fully equipped for your exploration of this fascinating city. So Good Hunting... but remember... don't try to take in too much on your first day, or even on your first week. Paris will always be ready to welcome you on your return... and return you will.

Paris... a stormy afternoon on the Seine   *Photograph by Peter Titchmarsh*

Paris... Hints for the Visitor

Public Transport. While we have in the past toured Paris both by car and by motor-caravan, we would suggest that it is now infinitely preferable to use public transport. The Metro service is excellent and with a free map easily obtainable it is very simple to follow, each line being numbered, and identified by the name of its terminal stations. Connections between different lines are clearly signed CORRESPONDANCE on the platforms of the stations served by more than one line. The bus service is not as easy to follow but it obviously provides a fine way of seeing more of the city. Maps of the bus service are also available free at tourist offices.

Combined tourist tickets (entitled **Paris Visite**) for unlimited travel within certain zones, for periods of three or five days on Metro, Bus and Regional Express Network (fast trains across Paris) are obtainable from thirty of the main Metro stations, main railway stations, Paris airports and the tourist offices at 53, Quai des Grands Augustins, or Place de la Madeleine, Marché aux Fleurs. Alternatively it is possible to buy books of ten tickets covering both the Metro and the bus services.

Taxis. As in London, these may be hailed in the street, or picked up from a rank. These will be marked 'Tête de Station'.

Car. If you do come to Paris by car, or you are passing through and wish to stop, we would suggest that you purchase **in advance** the Michelin 'Plan de Paris', which is No 10 in their series. This marks every building of interest, indicates all one-way streets and also shows the location of all large car parks. The line of the old outer 19th century walls of Paris with its 'gateways'... the Porte de Bagnolet, etc, etc... is now followed by the motorway-style Boulevard Périphérique, with three lanes in each direction; and with

the help of the Michelin map motorists could use this to locate an exit from the Périphérique which is close to both a car park and a Metro Station... thus hopefully avoiding a drive to the centre of the city. However, those still wishing to drive further in (and you have been warned), may wish to use the George Pompidou Expressway which runs along the right (or north) bank of the Seine right across the centre of Paris.

Books. We have mentioned further reading about Paris in our Book Section on Pages 3 & 4, and should you wish to make any purchases of books in English, either on Paris, or on France in general, may we suggest W. H. Smith at 248, rue de Rivoli, and Brentanos, at 37, avenue de l'Opéra.

Shopping Hours. Almost all large stores and shops open from 9.30 – 6.30 from Monday to Saturday. Some smaller ones may close down during the lunch hour and many food shops close completely on Mondays.

Museums and other Public Buildings. Enquire at tourist office for up to date information on opening times, but beware... many places are closed on Tuesdays (although the Orsay Museum closes on Mondays). Don't overlook the **Carte Musée** — a pass providing 50% discount on the entry charges to about 60 national and municipal museums and monuments in the Paris area. It is valid for one, two or five days and costs 50F, 100F or 150F accordingly. It can be obtained from any of the participating museums and monuments, and from main Metro stations.

The Beaubourg Centre, Paris... a controversial example of 20th century architecture   *Photograph by Peter Titchmarsh*

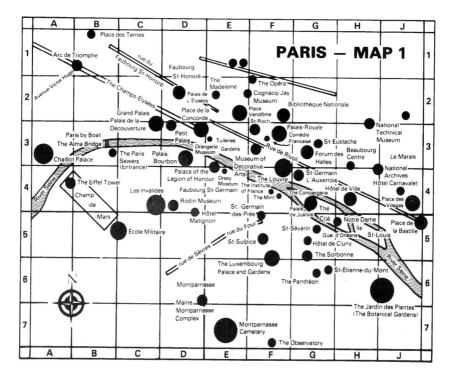

PARIS — MAP 1

Place des Ternes
Arc de Triomphe
Avenue Victor Hugo
rue du Faubourg St-Honoré
The Champs-Elysées
Faubourg St-Honoré
The Madeleine
The Opéra
Cognacq-Jay Museum
Bibliothèque Nationale
Palais de L'Elysées
Place Vendôme
St-Roch
Grand Palais
Palais de la Découverte
Place de la Concorde
Palais-Royale
Comédie-Française
St-Eustache
National Technical Museum
Paris by Boat
The Alma Bridge
Petit Palais
Orangerie Museum
Tuileries Gardens
Rue de Rivoli
Forum des Halles
Beaubourg Centre
Le Marais
Chaillot Palace
The Paris Sewers (Entrance)
Palais Bourbon
Museum of Decorative Arts
St-Germain L'Auxerrois
National Archives
The Eiffel Tower
Palace of the Legion of Honour
Orsay Museum
The Louvre
The Conciergerie
Hôtel de Ville
Hôtel Carnavalet
Champ -de -Mars
Les Invalides
Faubourg St-Germain
The Institute of France
The Mint
Place des Vosges
Rodin Museum
Hôtel Matignon
St.-Germain -des-Prés
Palais de Justice
The Cité
Notre Dame
Place de la Bastille
École Militaire
rue du Four
St-Sulpice
St.-Séverin
Quai d'Orléans
St-Louis
rue de Sèvres
St-Sulpice
Hôtel de Cluny
The Sorbonne
The Luxembourg Palace and Gardens
The Panthéon
St-Étienne-du-Mont
River Seine
Montparnasse
Maine- Montparnasse Complex
Montparnasse Cemetery
The Jardin des Plantes (The Botanical Gardens)
The Observatory

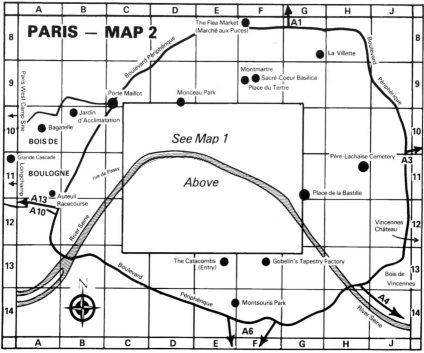

PARIS — MAP 2

The Flea Market (Marché aux Puces)
A1
Boulevard Périphérique
La Villette
Boulevard
Paris West Camp Site
Porte Maillot
Monceau Park
Montmartre
Sacré-Coeur Basilica
Place du Tertre
Périphérique
Jardin d'Acclimatation
See Map 1
Bagatelle
BOIS DE
Above
Père-Lachaise Cemetery
A3
Grande Cascade
BOULOGNE
Longchamp
rue de Passy
Place de la Bastille
A13
Auteuil Racecourse
A10
River Seine
Vincennes Château
The Catacombs (Entry)
Gobelin's Tapestry Factory
Bois de Vincennes
Boulevard
A4
Périphérique
Montsouris Park
River Seine
A6

Advice and help. For further information call in at one of these addresses:
Accueil de France, 127, Avenue des Champs-Élysées,
Accueil de la Ville de Paris, Hôtel de Ville, 29, Rue de Rivoli.
Thomas Cook, 2, Place de la Madeleine.
American Express, 11 Rue Scribe.

Camping in Paris. We have stayed many times at the excellent Paris West Camp Site, on the banks of the Seine, on the west side of the Bois de Boulogne. However, be warned... it will be necessary to arrive very early and to have an International Camping Carnet (See Camping, Page 6). Even then you may not be lucky enough to enjoy this splendid facility... especially if the holiday season is in full swing.

Paris by boat, with the Chamber of Deputies in the background.

Exploring the Paris Sewers

The Arc de Triomphe

Sculptural detail, the Arc de Triomphe

PARIS BY BOAT (B-3)

A visit to Paris without a boat trip on the Seine would be very sad. There are frequent departures from various points along both banks, but if in doubt contact one of the following: Bateaux Mouches, Pont de l'Alma (B-3), Tel: 42-25-96-10... Vedettes Paris Tour Eiffel, Tel: 45-51-33-08... It is also possible to explore the city's canals, and details are available from 'Paris Canal' (Tel: 48-74-75-30).

SHOPPING IN PARIS

It is impossible to offer detailed guidance, but if you wish to start by just window shopping, may we suggest the following... the rue du Faubourg St-Honoré, the rue de la Paix (E-2), the Place Vendôme (E-2), the Avenue Victor Hugo (A-2,ETC), the rue de Passy (C-11), the rue de Sèvres (E-5,D-6), and the rue du Four (E-5, F-5). When you have soaked up some of the atmosphere, try a few of the large stores... Les Galeries Lafayette, 40, boulevard Haussmann (E-1), Au printemps, 64, boulevard Haussmann (E-1), or Aux trois quartiers, 17, rue de la Madeleine (E-2).

THE PARIS SEWERS (B-3)

It is possible to explore part of the Paris sewer system, starting from the Place de la République, at the junction of the Quai d'Orsay, with the Pont de l'Alma. Open Monday, Wednesday and the last Saturday of each month. Closed on days before or after holidays, and (understandably) after heavy rain.

THE ALMA BRIDGE (B-3)

The old bridge was replaced by a new steel one in 1972, but the famous stone Zouave (one of a series of carvings of soldiers) has been retained. For many years he has served as a high-water mark for Parisians, and in the famous floods of 1910 the river rose up to his chin.

ARC DE TRIOMPHE (B-1)

This great archway was commissioned by Napoleon in 1806 to stand in the star shaped square (The Place de l'Etoile) upon which only five avenues then converged. The Arch was finally completed in 1836, and in 1854 the famous Baron Haussmann redesigned the square, adding a further seven avenues. Now beneath the Arch, there is buried an Unknown Soldier, to represent those who died in the 14–18 War, and Etoile has been renamed the Place Charles-de-Gaulle. It is possible to climb to the Arch Platform between April and September (closed Tuesdays) and there are fine views down the twelve great avenues, out over the city. To reach the Arch use the subway from the end of the Champs-Élysées.

PLACE DE LA BASTILLE (G-11)

The royal fortress and prison was stormed on July 14th 1789, and the remaining prisoners (a mere seven) were set free... thus marking the beginning of the Revolution. All signs of the notorious building were soon swept away, but its plan is marked out on the paving stones of the Place. The great square is dominated by the July Column, which commemorates, not 14th July 1789, but the death of so many Parisians in the cause of liberty in July 1830 and 1848.

THE BEAUBOURG ART AND CULTURAL CENTRE (H-3)

This is a brilliantly designed modern building on the Plateau Beaubourg, and known officially as the Centre National d'Art Georges Pompidou. Its intention is to 'bring together and stimulate this century's art forms and expressions of culture'. We are quoting here from an official leaflet, but it should be stressed that although the aims may sound lofty, the whole project is a most exciting one, and there is something here for everyone (including the outstanding National Museum of Modern Art). Do not miss a visit to this 'cultural power house'... there's a fine view from its top floor, and from the transparent escalators, which cling to its strange exterior surfaces.

Escalating visitors at the Beaubourg Centre Photograph by Peter Titchmarsh.

THE BIBLIOTHÈQUE NATIONALE (F-2)

This, the great National Library of France originated in the royal collections made in the Middle Ages, and grew in size from the time when the Copyright Act of 1537 dictated that a copy of every publication be deposited in the collection. There is limited access by means of a conducted tour, which is however well worth taking.

Riding in the Bois de Boulogne
Boating in the Bois de Boulogne

BOIS DE BOULOGNE (A-11, ETC)

This is the great park of Paris, with no fewer than 2224 acres of grass and woodlands, with two racecourses (Longchamp and Auteuil), over a dozen lakes, sports fields and even a 'Grande Cascade'. There are beautiful gardens at Bagatelle, but those visitors with children should head for the Jardin d'Acclimatation, a delightful amusement park for the young, which can be approached from the Porte Maillot by a miniature railway train.

THE HÔTEL CARNAVALET (J-4)

Handsome 16th century Renaissance town house, which was the last home of the famous Marquise de Sévigné, and which now houses a most interesting museum devoted to the last four hundred years of Parisian history. This is one of the great town houses for which the Marais quarter is noted (See Page 38).

Bagatelle, in the Bois de Boulogne

THE CATACOMBS (E-13)

These are quarry caves beneath the city, which were turned into ossuaries (storage for bones, skulls, etc.) in the late 18th century. Entry in the Place Denfert-Rochereau, open some Saturdays. Take a torch. Not for the squeamish. We have not been down!

CENTRE POMPIDOU (See Beaubourg Centre, above)

CHAILLOT PALACE (A-3)

The present building was erected as part of the Exhibition of 1937, and now houses a theatre, and four

Continued *In the Catacombs*   *In the Catacombs*

Paris

The Chaillot Palace

museums: the Maritime Museum, the Museum of French Monuments (a very fine introduction for those about to explore the buildings of France), the Museum of Man, devoted to Prehistory, Anthropology and Ethnography; and a Cinema Museum. There are fine views from its gardens, across the Seine to the Eiffel Tower and the gardens of the Champ-de-Mars, with the École Militaire beyond.

THE CHAMPS-ÉLYSÉES (C-2 ETC)

This most famous of all the great Paris thoroughfares owes its origins to Le Nôtre, who extended the Tuileries vista with an avenue of trees, which was renamed the Champs-Élysées (The Elysian Fields) in 1709. It was further extended in the 18th century, to the Chaillot Mound (where the Arc de Triomphe now stands in the Place Charles-de-Gaulle), and beyond to the Neuilly Bridge (although this is the Avenue de la Grande Armée). Today the avenue is full of cinemas, the offices and showrooms of motor manufacturers and airline and tourist offices, but it still retains much of its past atmosphere.

CHAMP-DE-MARS ((B-4, ETC))

A long series of formal gardens running between the Eiffel Tower and the École Militaire, laid out on what was a great parade ground attached to the École (Hence Champ-de Mars). Many great exhibitions were held here in the 19th century, and the Eiffel Tower is in fact a 'left-over' from the Great Exhibition of 1889.

The Champs-Élysées

THE CITÉ (G4, H-5)

This small island in the Seine is the very heart of Paris, the medieval core from which the great city has grown. The Quays along the banks of the Seine, and around much of the Île de la Cité, and the neighbouring Île St-Louis (See Page 32), are one of the great attractions for the visitor to Paris, with gorgeous views, of buildings and bridges, and of the River Seine itself. In many places bookstalls line the Quays, where books, maps and prints may be purchased, where browsing is delightful, but bargains no longer easy to find. But of course, all that come to the Cité, will be looking for Notre Dame Cathedral (See Page 35), and when you have completed your visit there, walk westwards to look at the Palais de Justice (See Page 35), the Sainte-Chapelle (See Page 37), and the Conciergerie (See Page 31).

Bookstalls near Notre Dame
Photograph by P. Titchmarsh

The Champ-de Mars, from the Eiffel Tower

THE HÔTEL DE CLUNY (G-5)

This largely 15th century building was the town house of the Abbots of Cluny in Burgundy (See Page 82), and happens to be situated above the excavated ruins of an extensive series of Roman baths. These now form part of the exhibits of the charming Cluny Museum, which is otherwise devoted to the Arts and Crafts of the Middle Ages. Do not miss this.

THE COGNACQ-JAY MUSEUM (E-2)

25, boulevard des Capucines

An exquisite collection of painting and furniture emanating from the late 17th and the 18th century, including works by Fragonard, Watteau, Greuze, Canaletto and Gainsborough.

THE COMÉDIE-FRANÇAISE (F-3)

The famous home of the French classical theatre is situated on the Place du Théâtre Français, at the southern end of the Avenue de l'Opéra.

The Cluny Museum

Roman Baths beneath the Cluny Museum

THE CONCIERGERIE (G-4)

This formed part of the medieval Royal Palace on the Île de la Cité, and is adjacent to the Palais de Justice (See Page 35). It incorporates three fine Gothic Halls, built in the 14th century, but it is best known for its use as a prison for those awaiting death by the guillotine, including Marie-Antoinette, Charlotte Corday, Madame du Barry, Danton and Robespierre... not a particularly happy place.

PLACE DE LA CONCORDE (D-3)

This was laid out in the mid 18th century in honour of Louis XV, but it was here on 21st January 1793 that a guillotine was set up for the execution of Louis XVI. Moved to a new location in the Place, the 'nation's razor' ended no fewer than 1343 lives in the next two years, including those of Marie-Antoinette, Charlotte Corday, Danton and Robespierre. The Place was really completed in 1790 with the opening of the Concorde Bridge, and the erection of an obelisk, and the addition of two fountains and eight statues representing the principal towns of France. Overlooking the Place are the famous Hôtel Crillon, the American Embassy and the Hôtel de la Marine, housing the Headquarters of the Navy and the Ministry of the Environment.

The Conciergerie

The Place de la Concorde

MUSEUM OF DECORATIVE ARTS (F-3)

Situated on the Rue de Rivoli between the Louvre and the Tuileries Garden, this is a fine museum devoted to the decorative arts in general; something akin to London's Victoria and Albert Museum, with a splendid series of displays.

The Place de la Concorde

LA DEFENSE (See Page 122)

THE EIFFEL TOWER (A-4)

When completed in 1889 this great metal tower was the world's highest structure (at 984 ft). It has since been overtaken by several skyscrapers and television towers, although it has itself been heightened to 1051 ft by the addition of a television mast. Stand beneath its feet to appreciate the vast latticework of metal girders. It is possible to climb to the top on foot, but most visitors will use the lifts to climb to the first, second, or third stage. The views out over Paris and the surrounding countryside are breathtaking, and are perhaps at their best when the sun is low, towards the end of the day.

FAUBOURG ST-GERMAIN (D-4, E-4)

This is perhaps the most aristocratic quarter of Paris, with many handsome town houses of the 18th century still to be seen. Here are many of the great government buildings including the Palais-Bourbon, the seat of the National Assembly, several Ministry buildings, foreign Embassies, the Hôtel Matignon, which is the Paris residence of the Prime Minister, and the Palace of the Legion of Honour.

FAUBOURG ST-HONORÉ (D-1, D-2)

The Rue du Faubourg St-Honoré runs parallel with the Champs Élysées, and apart from the honour of having the Palais de L'Élysée (the Presidential Palace) upon it, it has a wonderful variety of elegant 18th and 19th century buildings. Here will be found the British Embassy, and a wonderful selection of the great names of French haute couture and perfumery.

The Eiffel Tower

Paris

The Quai aux Fleurs (The Flower Market)

Les Invalides.   Photograph by Peter Titchmarsh.

Napoleon's Tomb, in Les Invalides

THE FLEA MARKET (Marché aux Puces) (F-8)

This amazing assortment of market stalls is situated to the north and north-west of the Porte Clignancourt, in several blocks. Another guide book's reference to a "motley throng" is no understatement... but the Flea Market is still worth visiting. Items on sale range from antiques, old clothes, old books and records, to almost anything imaginable!

FLOWER MARKETS OF PARIS

These will be found in the Place Louis Lépine, on the Île de la Cité (F-3), on the east side of the Madeleine church (E-2), and on the Place des Ternes, north of the Arc de Triomphe (B-1).

GOBELIN'S TAPESTRY FACTORY (F-13)

Established by Jean Gobelin in about 1440, Gobelin tapestry has for centuries been under royal and later, state control. It is now established in a modern building, but traditional methods are still employed, and to watch craftsmanship with such an outstanding tradition is well worthwhile.

LES HALLES AND THE FORUM DES HALLES (G-3)

This quarter takes its name from the vast complex of buildings erected in the 19th century on the site of Paris' medieval markets, and now removed to a site at Rungis, near Orly Airport. The old site now is occupied by the Forum des Halles, a brilliant new shopping complex with over two hundred shops and boutiques, and several restaurants. See also the interesting Museum of Holography, and the Parc Océanique Cousteau, which explores the magical world of the ocean bed. (Open daily except Mondays).

HÔTEL DE VILLE (H-4)

Vast 19th century building housing the city government of Paris, and situated to the immediate north of the Seine, overlooking one of the bridges across to the Île de la Cité (See Page 30).

THE ÎLE ST-LOUIS (H-5)

This is the smaller of the two islands in the Seine that comprise the Cité, the other being the Île de la Cité (See Page 30). It has many pleasing 17th century houses, and is a comparatively quiet area in which to stroll. Do not miss the exquisite views of Notre Dame from the Quai d'Orléans, near the Pont St-Louis, which links the two islands.

THE INSTITUTE OF FRANCE (F-4)

This dignified 18th century building is the home of the Académie Francaise, admission to which is limited to forty outstanding contributors to French life... who are henceforth known as the 'immortals'.

LES INVALIDES (C-4, ETC)

This institution was founded in 1670 by Louis XIV for wounded and infirm soldiers (Chelsea Hospital is London's equivalent), and Les Invalides is at outstanding example of 17th century architecture. It incorporates the Church of St-Louis, in which are buried many of the great soldiers of France, and the massive Dome Church, designed by the master architect Hardouin-Mansart, and in which the magnificent tomb of Napoleon is situated, along with the tombs of several of France's notables. While here do not miss a visit to the very interesting Army Museum... one of the world's great military museums.

THE JARDIN DES PLANTES (The Botanical Gardens)
(J-6, ETC)

This great botanical garden contains no fewer than 10,000 plant specimens. There is a maze, galleries of Mineralogy and Palaeontology, as well as a Zoo, with Vivarium and Aquarium, and also a Natural History Museum.

THE LOUVRE (Museum and Art Gallery) (F-3, ETC)

This, the world's largest Royal Palace, was built over the centuries on the site of a fortress erected by Philippe Augustus in about 1200. It was Catherine de Medici, widow of Henri II, who built the Tuileries to its immediate west, in the mid 16th century, and although much of this was burnt down in 1871, its far corner pavilions were rebuilt, and gardens were laid out on its site. The Grande Gallery was first opened as a museum in 1793, but it was Napoleon Bonaparte, and Napoleon III who really established the Louvre as it is today... one of the world's greatest art collections.

The new entrance is through an architecturally exciting glass pyramid built in front of the Pavillon de l'Horloge, and most of the collections are the subject of major re-organisation. Their very size is daunting, with collections of Oriental and Egyptian antiquities, European paintings and sculpture; ivories, jewellery and tapestries. Do not try to take in everything on your first visit, but concentrate for instance on the French and Italian paintings.

The Pyramide du Louvre

THE LUXEMBOURG PALACE AND GARDENS (F-5)

Splendid 17th century Palace built by Marie de Medici, the widow of Henry IV, and now housing the Senate, the Upper House of the French Parliament. Much of the interior may be visited on Sundays or on holidays, and the very extensive gardens are a true delight.

THE MADELEINE (E-2)

The great Church of St. Mary Magdalene was built in the style as a Greek temple, largely as a result of Napoleon's wish to have a temple erected to the glory of his army, although it was not consecrated until 1842. It is a most impressive building, and from its steps there are fine views down the Rue Royale to the Place de la Concorde. Don't miss the luxury shops in the Rue Royale.

MAINE-MONTPARNASSE COMPLEX (D-7, ETC)

A vast, modern, commercial, shopping and leisure complex built around the Gare Montparnasse, with department stores, luxury shops, offices, sports centre and swimming pool. The Maine-Montparnasse Tower is one of the tallest office buildings in Europe, and there are dramatic views from its 'observatory', which may be visited from morning to late evening.

The Louvre   Photograph by Peter Titchmarsh

LE MARAIS (See Place des Vosges and the Marais, Page 38) (J-4 ETC).

THE MINT (HÔTEL DES MONNAIES) (F-4)

Fine 18th century building which may be visited, although most of the actual production work has been moved to Pessac in the Gironde.

MONCEAU PARK (D-9)

Behind the beautiful 19th century gates along the Boulevard de Courcelles, lie the remains of a splendid 18th century garden, complete with pagodas and artificial ruins, both so fashionable at the time it was laid out.

The Luxembourg Gardens

Paris

The Mint by night (See Page 33)

St-Pierre de Montmartre

'The Law'

Montmartre

Notre Dame

MONTMARTRE (F-9)

Here on the 'Martyrs' Mound' was the great abbey of Montmartre, the only survivor of which is the abbey church of St-Pierre, an interesting 11th – 18th century building between the Sacré-Coeur Basilica (See Page 37) and the Place du Tertre. The whole area to the south and west of the hill is also within Montmartre, and is noted for its narrow little streets, steep steps and terraces. Here will be found colourful night-life, and many memories of the Bohemian artist life of the 19th and early 20th century; while to the west is the cemetery of Montmartre, last resting place of many of the great 'Bohemians'.

MONTPARNASSE (D-6, ETC)

This quarter was at the height of its fame at the turn of the century when it was the great centre of Bohemian café life. However by the time the '39 – 45' War started it had lost much of its flavour, and plans were already afoot for a great new commercial and shopping complex. (See Maine-Montparnasse Complex, Page 33).

MONTPARNASSE CEMETERY (E-7)

Here will be found the tombs of such well known figures as de Maupassant, César Franck, Beaudelaire, Saint-Saëns and André Citroën.

MONTSOURIS PARK (F-14, ETC)

Pleasant park laid out by Baron Haussmann, complete with lake and waterfalls, and dominated by a reproduction of the Bey of Tunis' Palace, made for the Exhibition of 1867.

THE NATIONAL ARCHIVES (H-4, ETC)

These are housed in the Soubise Palace and the nearby Hôtel de Rohan. In the former there is the Historical Museum of France, where unique plays referring to many periods of French history are presented 'in their historical context' (to quote one official guide). The Cardinal's Apartments in the Hôtel de Rohan are used for temporary exhibitions, but otherwise admission to the archives in either building is only obtained by written application.

THE NATIONAL TECHNICAL MUSEUM (H-2, H-3)

Within the Conservatoire National des Arts et Métiers

A fascinating series of technical and scientific displays including the famous pendulum used by Foucault to demonstrate the rotation of the earth.

NOTRE DAME CATHEDRAL (H-5)

A magnificent 12th, 13th and 14th century Gothic building, on the site of several earlier churches, and which is of course the religious focal point of all France. The west front is in our opinion its finest external feature, while the lovely 13th century Cloister Portal and the stained glass windows are particularly memorable. Do not miss the tiring, but richly rewarding climb to the north and south towers… the views of Paris from here are somehow more intimate than those from the Eiffel Tower, and are moreover greatly enriched by the gargoyles and flying buttresses so often in the fore-ground.

THE OBSERVATORY (F-7)

Built in the 17th century on exact north-south, and east-west axes, it formed, until replaced by Greenwich, the basis for international longitudinal calculations... the Paris Meridian. It is the home of the International Time Bureau, and its cellars house equipment accurate to less than a millionth of a second.

THE OPÉRA (F-2)

This impressive building was opened in 1875. Its extravagant facade looks out over the Place de l'Opéra, and gives more than a hint of the opulence to be found inside if one is lucky enough to be able to attend a performance.

AVENUE DE L'OPÉRA (F-2, F-3)

Running south-eastward from the Opéra to the Rue de Rivoli, this is a fine shopping street, originally laid out by Baron Haussmann between 1854 and 1878. Banks and large commercial houses favour this thoroughfare.

THE ORANGERIE MUSEUM (E-3)

This is situated in one of the two pavilions at the end of the Tuileries, close to the Place de la Concorde and the Quai des Tuileries. It houses a fine collection of paintings, mainly from the 1920s.

THE ORSAY MUSEUM (E-4)

Housed in the massive *fin de siècle* former Gare d'Orsay, this museum's outstanding collection covers the period between about 1848 and the 1914 – 18 War. It includes the magnificent collection of impressionist paintings that once hung in the Jeu de Paume.

PALAIS DE LA DÉCOUVERTURE (C-3)

This is situated on the Avenue Franklin-Roosevelt to the south of the Rond Point des Champs-Élysées, and is a most interesting museum devoted to modern science, with a first class planetarium in its midst.

PALAIS DE JUSTICE (G-4)

These are the principal Law Courts of France, and are built on the site of an early Royal Palace, from which justice was dispensed. Most of the buildings may be visited, but visitors with a limited time at their disposal will be advised to go directly to the lovely 13th century Gothic Sainte-Chapelle (See Page 37), which is situated in one of its courtyards. Do not miss a visit to the Conciergerie (See Page 31) which adjoins the Palais de Justice.

THE PALAIS-ROYALE (F-3)

This was originally built by Cardinal Richelieu, although it became a Royal Palace after his death in 1642. It had a chequered history following the Revolution, but now houses the Council of State and other Government offices, and is not open to the public.

THE PETIT PALAIS (D-3) AND THE GRAND PALAIS (C-3)

These lie to the south of the Champs-Élysées, to the immediate west of the Place de la Concorde, and were part of the 1900 World Exhibition. The Grand Palais is now a cultural centre, with exhibitions of the work of various modern French artists. The Petit Palais contains the Museum of Fine Arts of the City of Paris... a series of collections including many works by 19th century French painters.

View from Notre Dame (See Page 34)

In the Orsay Museum   Photograph by Peter Titchmarsh

The Opéra

Palais de Justice

The Pantheon .   *The Pantheon .*

THE PANTHEON (G-6)

This magnificent building was originated by Louis XV, as the result of a vow made by him in 1744 during a serious illness. Ironically it was not finally completed until 1789 (the year that the Bastille fell), and two years later it became the National Pantheon, a lay temple in honour of many of the great men of the Revolution, and subsequently of France in general. Here are buried the ashes of Mirabeau, Voltaire, Rousseau, Victor Hugo, Emile Zola, and nearer to our times, one of the great heroes of the Resistance, Jean Moulin.

THE PÈRE-LACHAISE CEMETERY (H-11, ETC)

This great cemetery standing on Mont Louis covers almost 100 acres and contains a bewildering and often beautiful collection of tombs, the majority in classical styles. It was here that the Communards made their last stand, on 28th May 1871, the survivors being rounded up and shot in the north-east corner, and finally buried in a communal grave where they fell. However most visitors will wish to know the names of those of the famous that are buried here... they include Oscar Wilde, Marshal Ney, Sarah Bernhardt, Edith Piaf, Chopin, Baron Haussmann, and many many others (For a list of 30 notable tombs with their locations, see the Michelin Green Guide to Paris).

The Rue de Rivoli.

POMPIDOU CENTRE (H-3)

(See Beaubourg Centre. Page 29)

RUE DE RIVOLI (E-3, F-3)

Famous thoroughfare running south eastwards from the Place de la Concorde, alongside the Tuileries Garden, and the Louvre. The arcaded buildings on the other side of the road contain a mixture of luxury shops and others largely devoted to the sale of souvenirs.

At the Père-Lachaise Cemetery   *The Balzac Room, the Rodin Museum*

RODIN MUSEUM (D-4)

A splendid collection of the great sculptor's works housed in the Hôtel Biron, an 18th century building in a pleasant park. Do not miss this.

ST-ROCH CHURCH (F-3)

A richly endowed 17th and 18th century church, with a fine series of monuments within. This is situated on the west side of the Rue des Pyramides, and to the north of the Rue St-Honoré.

ST-ÉTIENNE-DU-MONT CHURCH (G-6)

Impressive Gothic and Renaissance building situated to the immediate north-west of the Pantheon. This church was the burial place of both Pascal and Racine, and it has a magnificent rood screen, the only surviving specimen in the whole of Paris.

ST-EUSTACHE CHURCH (G-3)

Fine 16th and 17th century church on the northern edge of the former Halles area (See Page 32). This is essentially a Gothic building, but its interior is enriched with many Renaissance details. Note especially the splendid Flamboyant style vaulting to both nave and chancel.

The Rodin Museum

ST-GERMAIN-L'AUXERROIS CHURCH (G-4)

A Gothic and Renaissance building, once richly decorated by the Kings and Queens that lived in the neighbouring Louvre, and who used St-Germain as their parish church. Although desecrated during the Revolution it was well restored in the 19th century and houses the remains of many poets and artists. It was the bells of this church that signalled the start of the infamous St-Bartholomew's Day massacre of the Huguenots, on the night of 24th August 1572.

ST-GERMAIN-DES-PRÉS CHURCH (F-5)

Delightful 11th and 12th century monastery church, with many fine tombs within its Romanesque interior. This stands on the northern side of the St-Germain-des-Prés — Luxembourg quarter, with its fascinating little streets, old shops, and its small restaurants and cellars.

St-Germain-des-Prés

ST-SÉVERIN CHURCH (G-5)

The present church dates from the beginning of the 13th century, but its outstanding feature is the lovely Flamboyant style double ambulatory, built some two hundred years later.

ST-SULPICE CHURCH (F-5)

Handsome 16th and 17th century church with a fine 18th century facade by the Florentine architect, Servandoni. The splendidly proportioned interior is dominated by a series of mural paintings by the famous Delacroix.

THE SAINTE-CHAPELLE (G-4)

A delightfully graceful little Gothic building situated in a courtyard of the Palais de Justice (See Page 35). It was built in the 13th century to house one of the great medieval relics... 'The Crown of Thorns' (now in the Treasury of Notre Dame). It is an outstandingly beautiful two storeyed building, with splendid pillars and buttresses giving sufficient strength to allow the remaining 'walls' to be made of windows in which there is some of the finest medieval stained glass in France.

Sainte-Chapelle   *Sainte-Chapelle*

SACRÉ-COEUR BASILICA (F-9)

Although this great white building was begun in 1873, it was only completed in 1910. It is one of the great features of the Paris skyline, with dramatic views from its dome, both over the buildings of Paris, and downwards into its interior. Combine a visit here with a look at the medieval abbey church of St-Pierre and the attractive Place du Tertre, which is the very heart of Montmartre (See Page 34). *It is possible to ascend to Sacré-Coeur by funicular railway from the Marché St-Pierre.*

The Sorbonne

THE SORBONNE (G-5)

Founded in 1253 by the Confessor of St-Louis it became, after many transformations, the main centre of higher education in France. Cardinal Richelieu's tomb stands in the chancel of its church. The Sorbonne is situated in the Montagne Ste-Geneviève Quarter, an area devoted largely to learning and the student life... the 'Latin Quarter'. To sample its lively flavour, start your exploration from the Place Maubert, the traditional meeting place for students and hangers-on for many years.

PLACE DU TERTRE (B-1)

This is the very heart of Montmartre (See Page 34), and is situated a short distance to the west of the Sacré-Coeur Basilica (See above). There are several open-air cafés here, and many artists who will paint or draw your

The Sorbonne   *Sacré-Coeur*

Paris

In the Tuileries Gardens Photograph by Peter Titchmarsh

The Quai des Tuileries   *The Place Vendôme*

The Place des Vosges

Le Géode... at La Villette

portrait. It is a great tourist haunt, especially at night, and the art shops seem to keep open almost as long as the lively cafés and cabarets.

THE TUILERIES GARDENS (E-3)

These splendid gardens are situated between the remaining pavilions of the Tuileries and the Place de la Concorde, and were laid out by the great garden designer, Le Nôtre, in the 17th century. Walk along the Bord de l'Eau Terrace for fine views out over the gardens, and over the Seine. The two pavilions at the 'Concorde' end of the gardens are the Orangerie, which houses a museum devoted largely to the art of the 1920s (See Page 35) and the Jeu de Paume, which is now used only for temporary exhibitions.

PLACE VENDÔME (E-2)

Elegant late 17th century square, originally intended as a worthy setting for a statue of Louis XIV. However this was destroyed during the Revolution and eventually replaced by the famous Austerlitz column, which incorporates a bronze spiral made from the melted remains of the twelve hundred cannons captured at that battle. This was topped by a statue of Napoleon, a replica of which was placed here by the Third Republic, after a series of changes following the various political unheavals of the mid 19th century. The Place Vendôme is noted for its luxury shops, and is a fitting introduction to the equally elegant Faubourg St-Honoré, and the Rue de la Paix, both of which are close by.

PLACE DES VOSGES (J-4)
AND THE MARAIS (H-3, J-4, ETC)

This, the oldest square in Paris, lies on the south eastern edge of the Marais, once a marsh, and then in the 16th, 17th and 18th centuries, the most fashionable part of Paris. The Marais then fell on hard times and it is only since the 1960s that it is again acquiring some of its former elegance. Once known as the Place Royale, the Place des Vosges has the lovely Queen's Pavilion on its north side, and the smaller King's Pavilion on its south side. To the west of the Place lie many handsome town houses, or Hôtels, the best known of which is the Hôtel Carnavalet (See Page 29). Do not miss a visit to the Picasso Museum in the Hôtel Salé.

LA VILLETTE (G-8)

An exciting 55-acre park which is a showpiece of French technology. It includes the re-furbished Grande Halle, which is used for exhibitions and conferences; the Géode, a great sphere with mirrored exterior and an interior which houses a giant semi-circular cinema; the City of Science and Industry; and (opening in about 1990) the City of Music.

BOIS DE VINCENNES (J-13, ETC)

This large park just beyond the ancient confines of Paris, contains the Château of Vincennes (See below), a racecourse, an outstanding 'Floral Garden', a large lake with rowing boats, an African and Oceanic Museum, a Transport Museum, and one of the great zoos of France.

VINCENNES CHÂTEAU   *(To East of J12)*

Spendid Royal Palace, fortress and prison... the nearest building in Paris to London's 'Tower'. It was built largely in the 13th century by Philippe VI of Valois, and it has the highest and probably the best preserved keep in Europe. See the château itself, the Sainte-Chapelle and the Historical Museum..... all providing a fascinating insight into the history of France.

Alsace and Lorraine-Vosges

Comprises the following Départements:
Meurthe-et-Moselle (54) Bas Rhin (67)
Meuse (55) Haut Rhin (68)
Moselle (57) Vosges (88)

Bounded by the Rhine on its eastern flank, this is the great north-east frontier region of France, with the plateau of Lorraine divided from the Alsatian plain by the beautifully wooded mountain country of the Vosges.

In the Alsace plain are the three cities of Alsace... Strasbourg, Colmar and Mulhouse... while to their west on the low hills beneath the Vosges, are the lovely little villages and fortified towns of the Alsace wine country... most of them strung out along the ninety mile long Wine Road (Route du Vin). Running parallel with this road, well to the west, is the Crest Road (Route des Crêtes) which provides an ideal introduction to the varied pleasures of the Vosges.

Behind the Vosges lies the great plateau country of Lorraine, through which the lovely Meurthe, Moselle and Meuse rivers flow. Here will be found the beautiful cities of Nancy and Metz, the little village of Domrémy-la-Pucelle where Joan of Arc was born, and vast areas of forest, all set in gently rolling countryside so typical of France.

ABRESCHVILLER (57) *71k W Strasbourg*
Modest village in lovely forest country on the western slopes of the Vosges, with a multitude of paths and tracks to be explored. There is a fascinating little Forest Railway 6ks in length, with steam and diesel trains giving rides to visitors.

Forest Railway, Abreschviller. Photograph by Forest Railway

ALSACE WINE ROAD (67)(68)
This runs for nearly 140 kilometres across the wine clad hills of Alsace from Thann (to the west of Mulhouse) northwards to Nordheim near Strasbourg, taking the visitor through a wonderful series of old towns and villages, some of which are included in this guide. For full details ask for the English language leaflet entitled 'The Wine Road of Alsace' from the Centre d'Information du Vin d'Alsace, 68004, Colmar, France.

ALTKIRCH (68) *18k SSW Mulhouse*
Picturesque little town on a hill above the river Ill, with fine views out over the surrounding countryside from the gardens around the church.

AMMERSCHWIHR (68) *7k NW Colmar*
Minute wine producing town on the eastern slopes of the Vosges. Following virtual destruction in the 39 – 45 war, it has been attractively rebuilt incorporating its tall 13th century gateway and fortifications. It lies on the famous Alsace Wine Road (See above).

Ammerschwihr village

ARGONNE FOREST (51, 55) *W of Verdun*
(See Page 89, in Champagne-Ardenne Region.)

BAR-LE-DUC (55) *57k SSW Verdun*
Lying in well wooded country, this is a largely industrialised town, and the capital of the Meuse Département. However much of the old town survives above the south bank of the River Ornain, with its famous 12th century clock tower, its castle gate and the church of St-Étienne with its gruesome skeleton statue*. See also the attractive and interesting Town Museum.
The work of Ligier Richier of nearby St-Mihiel (See Page 44).

Vosges foresters *Storks of Alsace*

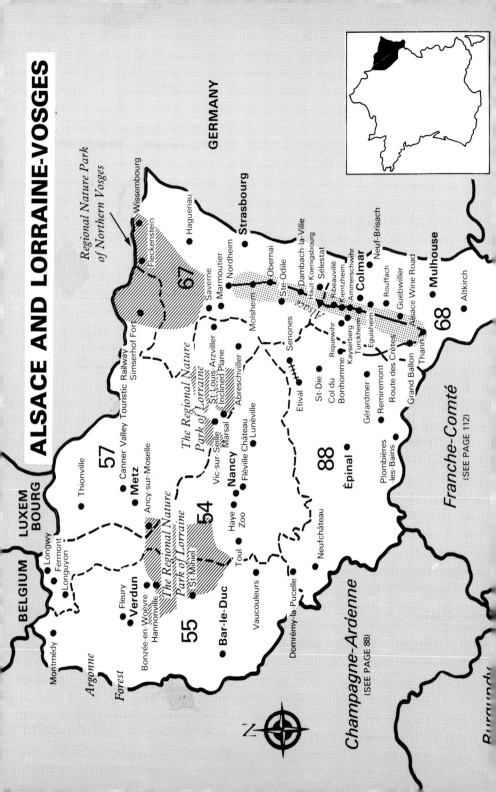

ALSACE AND LORRAINE-VOSGES

CANNER VALLEY TOURISTIC RAILWAY (57) *14k NE Metz*

An attractive 8-mile standard gauge steam railway running northwards to Kedange-sur-Canner.

COLMAR (68) *444k E Paris, 69k SSW Strasbourg*

Its medieval walls have been replaced by wide boulevards, but within their confines lies a picturesque old town, with narrow streets, beautiful half-timbered houses and little waterways crossed by charming old bridges. See especially... the restored Tanner's Quarter, the splendid Unterlinden Museum, the cathedral of St-Martin, and the statues and fountains by local sculptor, Bartholdi, who is best known for his Statue of Liberty in New York harbour.

Colmar *Colmar*

ROUTE DES CRÊTES, OR THE CREST ROAD (68)

Built for strategic reasons in 1914, this magnificent route runs from Thann (to the west of Mulhouse) to the Col du Bonhomme, and links some of the highest mountains of the Vosges including the Grand Ballon, from which there are splendid views. (For details see the Michelin yellow map No. 87.)

DAMBACH-LA-VILLE (67) *38k SW Strasbourg*

Attractive flower-bedecked village astride the hilly Alsace Wine Road. See the fortifications with three ancient gateways, and the chapel of St-Sébastien which has a rich Baroque altar.

Dambach-la-Ville *Domrémy-la-Pucelle*

DOMRÉMY-LA-PUCELLE (88) *57k SW Nancy*

Joan of Arc was born in this small village on the Meuse, in 1412, and the house in which she was born still stands. There is a museum next door, and to the south of the village, a modern Basilica marking the spot where Joan heard voices prompting her to fight for France.

EGUISHEIM (68) *7k SSW Colmar*

Picturesque village in Alsatian vineyard country, with a castle and many old houses. There is also a pleasant art gallery.

ÉPINAL (88) *370k E Paris, 70k W Colmar*

Capital of the Vosges, Épinal is situated on the River Moselle and surrounded on almost every side by attractive forest country. See especially the Basilica of St-Maurice, the 'Castle Park' with its ruined castle and fine views of the river; and the museum which specialises in medieval sculpture.

Joan of Arc's birthplace, Domrémy

FLÉVILLE CHÂTEAU (54) *9k SSE Nancy*

Elegant Renaissance château incorporating the keep of a 12th century castle, and which has a pleasantly decorated and furnished interior.

GÉRARDMER (88) *52k W Colmar*

Pretty town on the shores of a lake of the same name, in a wooded hollow in the Haut Vosges. A well known winter and summer resort, this makes an excellent base for exploring the Vosges mountains and forests.

GUEBWILLER (68) *25k SSW Colmar*

Busy town at the southern end of the Alsatian vineyard country, with a splendid Rhenish-Romanesque church, a handsome town hall and a museum in a 14th century former Dominican church. The town lies a short distance to the east of the Ballon de Guebwiller (or Grand Ballon), the highest mountain in the Vosges.

Guebwiller

Alsace and Lorraine-Vosges

Haguenau   Haut Koenigsbourg

Kayserberg

Kayserberg Castle   Lunéville

Marmoutier

HAGUENAU (67)   *30k N Strasbourg*
Small town to the south of the great forest of Haguenau, through which there are many lovely forest tracks and pathways. In the town, see the lovely 14th century church of St-Nicholas, the town museum and several woodworking shops.

HAUT-KOENIGSBOURG (67)   *13k W Sélestat*
Near this small village on the western slopes of the Vosges will be found the splendidly titled 'Mountain of the Apes'… a zoo with a difference!

HAYE ZOO (54)   *5k W Nancy to N of N4*
Small zoo specialising in European animals, in the forest of Haye, to the east of Velaine-en-Haye.

KAYSERBERG (68)   *10k NW Colmar*
Small town in wine growing country, renowned as the birthplace of Dr. Albert Schweitzer. See the medieval castle, the fortified bridge, the lovely Romanesque west front to the church, and the many old half-timbered houses.

KIENTZHEIM (68)   *3k E Kayserberg, 10k NW Colmar*
Attractive old village dominated by a great castle in the grounds of which there is an Eagle Park and Stork Centre, which should not be missed. Storks will also be found at Hunawihr about 6ks to the north.

LONGUYON (54)   *48k NNE Verdun*
Small town in wooded country near the Belgian border. 5ks to the NE are the great Maginot Line* fortifications of Fermont which are open to visitors.
See Simserhof Fort, (Page 45).

LONGWY (54)   *65k NW Metz*
Busy industrial town close to the borders with Belgium and Luxembourg, Longwy has a 'higher town' with fortifications by Vauban.

THE LORRAINE REGIONAL NATURE PARK
(54)(55)(57)
460,000 acres in the Départements of Meuse, Moselle, and Meurthe-et-Moselle, in two blocks on either side of the Metz-Nancy axis. Here are great areas of forest country, with several lakes. Visit the House of Salt at Marsal (Moselle) and the House of Rural Art and Traditions at Hannonville (Meuse). Information Centres at Ancy-sur-Moselle, Vic-sur-Seille, St. Mihiel, Marsal and Bonzée-en-Woëvre.

LUNÉVILLE (54)   *35k ESE Nancy*
Retains some of the elegance of the 18th century, when the Dukes of Lorraine had their home here. Their castle is now an interesting museum and its grounds have made a fine park for the town. See also the 18th century church and several woodworking shops. There is extensive forest country on three sides of the town, through which there are several attractive minor roads.

MARMOUTIER (67)   *32k ENE Strasbourg,*
5k S Saverne
Small village in wooded forest country, with an interesting Romanesque abbey church and many pleasant woodland walks.

METZ (57)   *330k ENE Paris, 160k NW Strasbourg*
Capital of the Moselle Département, this thriving modern city has retained its picturesque old town, with narrow streets and many quaint old houses. See especially the fine Gothic cathedral, with its outstanding stained glass, its marble Merovingian throne, and Romanesque crypt. Rabelais was the town physician of Metz in the mid 16th century.

MOLSHEIM (67)   *25k WSW Strasbourg*
Old town on the Wine Road, at the foot of the Vosges. See La Metzig ('Large Slaughter House'), the famous Bugatti Car Museum, and the park with storks. There is an interesting church 3ks north... St-Pierre at Avolsheim.

Metz Cathedral

MONTMÉDY (55)   *50k N Verdun*
Village in hilly wooded country close to the Belgian border, with impressive 16th and 17th century fortifications.

MULHOUSE (68) *170k ESE Paris, 115k S Strasbourg*
Busy industrial city situated between the Vosges and the Black Forest, with a fine Renaissance town hall (1552), a church with some interesting stained glass (St- Étienne), and an outstanding zoo in a 50 acre park. There are various museums here including the National Railway Museum, the fabulous National Automobile Museum, and others devoted to such diverse subjects as Fire Engines, Wallpaper, and Textiles.

Metz   *Mulhouse*

NANCY (54)   *310k E Paris, 145k W Strasbourg*
Capital of the Meurthe et Moselle Département, and once the Ducal capital of the dethroned King of Poland, Stanislaus Leszczynski (Lorraine having been given to him as a consolation). It is to this monarch that we are indebted for one of Europe's loveliest groups of buildings... Stanislaus Square... together with several other squares in the rectangular 'new' town. See also the triumphal arch, north of the square, the beautiful little Chapelle de Bonsecours (1738) containing the tombs of Duke Stanislaus and his Duchess, and the Museum of Fine Arts.

NEUF-BRISACH (68)   *15k ESE Colmar*
Small town only five kilometres from the Rhine and the border with Germany. See the interesting Vauban Museum, in part of the Citadel built by this master of fortification. See also the huge locks and hydro electric works at nearby Voelgrun, where the Grand Canal d'Alsace joins the Rhine, and take a trip on the 16 km long 'touristic railway' running north from here beside the Rhine to Marckolsheim. This can be combined with a boat trip.

The Place Stanislaus, Nancy

NEUFCHÂTEAU (88)   *60k SW Nancy*
An ancient hill-town on the upper reaches of the Meuse, with forest country never far away. The Town Hall has a splendid staircase and there are a number of interesting old houses.

OBERNAI (67)   *30k SW Strasbourg*
Picturesque town on the Wine Road, with an attractive market square, medieval walls, and a 16th century Town Hall... all accompanied by a wealth of lovely old houses, shops and inns. Do not miss the famous six-bucket well, nor the interesting Horse and Carriage Museum at the Domaine de la Léonardsau, three kilometres to the east of the town.

Cathedral treasure, Nancy

In the Museum at Nancy

Remiremont

Old houses at Riquewihr

Ribeauvillé

PLOMBIÈRES-LES-BAINS (88)   *33k S Épinal*
A modest spa town in Vosges forest country. There are fine views from La Feuillée Nouvelle five kilometres to the south.

REMIREMONT (88)   *27k SSE Epinal*
Pleasant old town on the banks of the Moselle, with arcaded shops on either side of its 'Grande Rue'. There are many fine old houses and an interesting 11th century crypt beneath the church.

RIBEAUVILLÉ (68)   *15k NNW Colmar*
Pretty wine producing village (on the Wine Road), at the feet of no fewer than three castles. See the 15th century church and the notorious Tower of the Butchers (Tour des Bouchers).

RIQUEWIHR (68)   *13k NW Colmar*
Minute 'town' (only 1400 inhabitants) in the foothills of the Vosges which can justly claim that it has lost little of its medieval character. The ancient walls enclose many rich middle class houses and the elegant Château now houses an interesting Postal Museum. Inevitably this town is on the Wine Road.

ROUFFACH (68)   *15k S Colmar*
Attractive little Alsatian town with many old gabled houses, and a quiet square overlooked by an interesting 13th century Gothic church. See also the Sorcerer's Tower.

ST-DIE (88)   *50k ENE Épinal*
Although burnt down in 1944 by the retreating Germans, this town amongst the wooded hills of the Vosges is now an attractive holiday centre, with miles of forest tracks and pathways to be explored. Do not miss the fine 15th and 16th century cathedral cloisters.

ST-LOUIS-ARZVILLER INCLINED PLANE (57)
16k E Sarrebourg, 13k W Saverne
This amazing engineering structure on the Marne-Rhine Canal replaced a flight of seventeen locks, and by means of cables, counterweights and great moving tanks of water, enables fully laden barges to be lifted from one level of canal to another in a few minutes, a task which took the best part of a day through the old locks. Take the D98 south from Lutzelbourg to view this fascinating device in action.

ST-MIHIEL (55)   *33k NE Bar-le-Duc*
Small town on the western edge of the great Regional Nature Park of Lorraine, with its great forests and several lakes. There is a lovely statue of the Virgin in the church of St-Mihiel, and a tomb in the church of St-Étienne, both by the local sculptor Ligier Richier, who was a pupil of Michelangelo.

STE-ODILE (67)   *42k SW Strasbourg, 12k SW Obernai*
The great plateau on which the restored convent of Ste-Odile stands is surrounded by a wall formed by great blocks of sandstone dovetailed together. There are splendid views from here, out over the foothills of the Vosges to the Rhine valley.

'Fête des Vins', at Riquewihr

SAVERNE (67)   39k WNW Strasbourg

Pleasant town below the wooded eastern slopes of the Vosges, with a fine 18th century château of red sandstone. There are colourful botanic gardens below the Col de Saverne, just to the west of the town.

SÉLESTAT (67)   22k N Colmar

A bustling industrial and commercial town which still retains many of its old narrow streets. See especially the splendid Romanesque church of St-Foy, the 13th century Gothic church of St-George and the town walls high up above the River Ill.

Château at Saverne

SENONES (88)   47k SE Lunéville

Agreeable little town in wooded Vosges country with a Romanesque church and a fascinating little steam railway leading 9ks down the valley of the Rabodeau to Etival.

SIMSERHOF FORT (57)   4k W Bitche,
                                   30k E Sarreguemines

This is one of the great underground fortresses of the ill-fated Maginot line, the formidable defence line built between Sedan and the southern end of the Franco-German border in the 1930's. Simserhof provided for a garrison of up to 1,200 men and could maintain itself for three months without external support. It has over ten kilometres of tunnels, and is a fascinating example of military engineering. We believe that visits by groups can sometimes be arranged by writing in advance to: M. l'Officier chargé des relations publiques, Bureau Emploi à l'État-Major de Metz, 57998 Metz-Armée, France.

Tower of the Sorcerers, Sélestat

Palais des Rohan, Strasbourg

STRASBOURG (67)   488k E Paris, 595k SE Calais

Capital of the Bas Rhin Département and a major European city, Strasbourg has over a quarter of a million inhabitants. It stands on the Rhine, at a point where that river is joined by the Ill, and the Rhine-Marne and Rhine-Rhône canals. It is also the seat of the European Parliament and the European Court of Human Rights. The fascinating old town (which can if necessary be explored on a mini-train) is entirely surrounded by water, while to its south-east, stands the fine 13th century red sandstone cathedral, with its splendid west front, its 'pillar of angels' and its famous astronomical clock. See the handsome classical Palais des Rohan, built by Robert de Cotte, the architect of Les Invalides dome, and which now houses the Musée des Beaux Arts; also take a launch tour around France's fifth largest port, and visit at least some of Strasbourg's variety of interesting museums.

Astronomical clock, Strasbourg Cathedral

In Strasbourg Cathedral

THANN (68)   88k SW Épinal

Small town on the River Thur with its old quarter dominated by the dramatic ruins of Engelsbourg Castle. The church of St-Théobald is a splendid Gothic building with a fine 16th century tower. There is a small museum in the Corn Market.

THIONVILLE (57)   30k N Metz

Large, heavy industrial town on the Moselle with the remains of a 13th century castle which includes the 'Tour aux Puces' or Flea Tower. There is also an arcaded market place and a partly medieval Hôtel-de-Ville.

Boat trip at Strasbourg

45

TOUL (54)   *23k W Nancy*

Pleasant town on the upper Moselle, the old part of which is contained within fortifications erected by the great military engineer Sébastien Vauban. See especially the old cathedral of St-Étienne, and the church of St-Gengoult, both of which have lovely cloisters.

TURCKHEIM (68)   *7k W Colmar*

Attractive little wine village below the eastern slopes of the Vosges. Despite damage in the 39–45 war, three of its ancient gates remain, and during the tourist season the village night watchman makes his rounds.

Toul Cathedral   *Turckheim*

VAUCOULEURS (55)   *45k WSW Nancy*

Small village in the rolling wooded countryside of the Meuse valley, with the ruins of a medieval castle, the commander of which was finally persuaded in 1428 by the young Joan of Arc to send her to the king, after she had waited here for so long. There is a gateway close by, through which Joan is believed to have set out with her troop to the royal court... the Porte de France.

VERDUN (55)   *78k W Metz*

Since Roman times, Verdun has been a place of strategic importance, and during the 14–18 War the area to its immediate north and east was the scene of terrible carnage. Those who like to see battlefields should leave by the N18, and then turn north on the N403 about 5k east of the town. (There is an interesting War Museum at Fleury, 5k along N403). Better in our view to look at the fine Romanesque cathedral, the Porte Chaussée, with its great twin 14th century towers, and the dignified 17th century Town Hall.

NORTHERN VOSGES REGIONAL NATURE PARK
(57)(67)

300,000 acres in the Départements of Moselle and Bas Rhin, within a triangle formed by Volmunster, Saverne and Wissembourg, with one side running along the German border. More than half the park is covered by forest and the area is rich in fauna and flora. Opportunities for rambling, water sports and especially canoeing.

WISSEMBOURG (67)   *65k NNE Strasbourg*

Picturesque small town on the border with Germany, with old ramparts, an interesting Romanesque and Gothic church, many attractive old houses and two museums. The magnificent castle of Fleckenstein is situated about 20k to the west.

Vineyards above Turckheim

Porte Chaussée, Verdun   *Wissembourg*

THE WINES OF ALSACE

Most of the significant vineyards of Alsace are situated on the lower slopes of the Vosges mountains, at the point where they merge into the plain some distance from the Rhine. This strip runs about a hundred kilometres from north to south, and is seldom more than five kilometres wide. The vineyards here produce a wide variety of predominantly light, white wines. The series of charming little wine towns are linked by the fascinating 'Alsace Wine Road' (See Page 39).

Vendanges in Alsace

Aquitaine

Comprises the following Départements:
Dordogne (24) Lot-et-Garonne (47)
Gironde (33) Pyrénées-Atlantiques (64)
Landes (40)

This is a region of fascinating contrasts. In the far west it is bound by the great Atlantic beaches stretching over 250 kilometres, from the mouth of the Gironde to the rocky shores where the Pyrénées meet the sea at the Spanish frontier. Behind the beaches lie the great dunes, lagoons and pine forests of the Landes, while beyond the Landes are the great winelands of Bordeaux. Beyond these lie the splendid western fringes of the Massif Central, penetrated by such rivers as the Isle, the Dordogne and the Garonne. In this entrancing countryside will be found a wealth of prehistoric remains, and medieval castles and fortified towns, reminding us of England's long involvement with Aquitaine in the middle ages. In the far south Aquitaine embraces the French part of the Basque country, with its unique traditions and folk-lore; and the western end of the great Pyrennean range, with its wealth of fine forests and wildlife, its snow capped peaks and wonderfully varied mountain flowers. In short, whatever you search for in a holiday, is almost certainly to be found in this astonishingly varied region.

ABBADIA CHÂTEAU (64)　　　*2k NE Hendaye*
A 19th century neo-medieval château from which there are fine views southwards to the Pyrénées. It is furnished in the rich style of the Second Empire and is well worth visiting.

AGEN (47)　　　*142k SE Bordeaux*
The centre of one of France's most important fruit growing areas, Agen is noted for its delicious prunes. It is a busy commercial town, but there are old arcaded streets, some of which run along the banks of the Garonne. The Museum contains the famous Venus du Mas, an exquisite Greek marble statue; and several paintings by Goya. Attractive old bridges over the Garonne, include a fine aqueduct carrying the Canal Latéral.

Arcachon

AIRE-SUR-ADOUR (40)　　*33k SE Mont-de-Marsan*
Small town astride the Adour, with a 12th century cathedral built on the Benedictine plan, and a church with a 5th century sarcophagus in its Romanesque crypt.

ARCACHON (33)　　　*62k W Bordeaux*
Bustling summer resort with a splendid sandy beach over ten kilometres long, and a yacht harbour with 1800 moorings, on the sheltered lagoon of the Bassin d'Arcachon. Facilities include an Aquarium, a skating rink and a swimming pool. At nearby Pyla there are sand dunes almost 400 feet high, the highest in Europe.

ASSON ZOO PARK (64)　　　*24k SSE Pau*
An extensive collection of animals and birds in a magnificent setting beneath the Pyrénées, together with a museum of items from Madagascar, and a fine collection of cacti. Combine with a visit to the Bétharram Grottoes (See Page 49).

Climbing the Pyla Sand Dunes

BAYONNE (64)　　　*175k SW Bordeaux*
Seaport town where the river Nive joins the Adour, only about five kilometres from the sea. This was a busy Aquitaine trading centre, and was in English hands between 1152 and 1451. Its Citadel, built by Vauban in the 1670's still stands. See also the largely Gothic cathedral, the Musée Bonnat, with its outstanding art collection, the attractive promenades encircling the town (replacing the old walls), and the Musée Basque, which is devoted to the Basque culture (Bayonne being the spiritual capital of the French Basques).

In the Pyla Dunes

In the Musée Basque, Bayonne

AQUITAINE

Poitou-Charentes
(SEE PAGE 218)

Limousin
(SEE PAGE 140)

Jumilhac-le-Grand

Puyguilhem

Brantôme
Bourdeilles
Merlande Priory

Hautefort

Périgueux

The

Pauillac

Blaye

Médoc

33

Pomerol

Le Bouilh
Libourne
St-Emilion

Bordeaux

Route du Médoc

Graves
St-Émilion
Entre
-deux-Mers
Sauternes

Langoiran Zoo
Labrède
Arcachon
Le Teich
Ornithological Park
Roquetaillade
Villandraut
Bazas

Regional
Nature Park
of the Landes
de Gascogne

Luxey

Marquèze
Sabres

40

Mont-de-Marsan

Ravignan

Dax
Hossegor

Aire-sur-Adour

Biarritz
Guéthary
Bayonne
St-Jean-de-Luz and Ciboure
Abbadia
Hendaye
Cambo-les-Bains

64

Orthez

Pau

St-Jean Pied-de-Port

Oloron-Sainte-Marie
Asson Zoo Park
Bétharram Grottoes

Pyrénées National Park

SPAIN

24

Montignac
Thonac
Les Eyzies-de-Tayac
Le Bugue
Limeuil
Trémolat
Montaigne
Bergerac
Monbazillac
Lanquais
Beaumont
Cadouin
Duras
Villéréal
Monflanquin
Fontirou Caves

St-Amand-de
Lascaux Cave
La Roque-Gageac
Sarlat
Beynac
Montfort
Fénelon
Domme
Monpazier
Biron
Castelnau
Les Milande
Bonaguil

47

Villeneuve-sur-Lot

Agen

Nérac

Midi-Pyrénées
(SEE PAGE 175)

N

La Réole

MILES
0   10   20   30   40   50

KILOMETRES
0   20   40   60   80

BAZAS (33)   *58k SE Bordeaux*

Small town on a bluff above the Beuve valley, with a Gothic cathedral much restored in the 15th century, but retaining splendid 13th century Romanesque west portals. These look out over a wide, arcaded square, and there are pleasant views out over the Beuve from a nearby terrace.

BEAUMONT (24)   *66k S Périgueux, 29k ESE Bergerac*

Built in 1272, this modest village was one of the earliest of the English bastides (See Villeneuve, Pages 56 – 57). The church still has four defensive towers, and the market square retains two sides of its delightful arcading.

BERGERAC (24)   *92k E Bordeaux, 47k SW Périgueux*

Bergerac Church   *In Bétharram Grottoes*

Pleasant town on the river Dordogne, in a wine and tobacco growing area (Dordogne is France's leading tobacco Département). See the interesting Tobacco Museum in the Hôtel de Ville, and explore the old streets centred upon the covered market-place. Cyrano de Bergerac, the gentleman with the large nose, was a 17th century soldier and writer, later to be immortalised by the playwright Edmond Rostand.

BÉTHARRAM GROTTOES (64)   *16k W Lourdes, 28k SE Pau*

Dramatic limestone caves in the slopes of the Pyrenees which may be visited with the aid of a boat, a miniature train and a cable car. Do not miss this.

BEYNAC CHÂTEAU (24)   *64k SE Périgueux, 12k SW Sarlat*

This is a fine medieval castle perched on the edge of a sheer cliff above the Dordogne. It has been excellently restored in recent years, and is well worth visiting. Park by the river and walk up the steep streets of little Beynac town. Also take a boat trip on the lovely Dordogne.

BIARRITZ (64)   *183k SW Bordeaux*

Internationally famous holiday resort, still retaining a flavour of the late 19th and early 20th century, when most of the crowned heads of Europe visited here. Rocky coves, five magnificent beaches, casinos, horse racing, bull fights, and Basque folklore festivals, including the unique Basque game of pelota.

BIRON CHÂTEAU (24)   *8k SSW Monpazier*

Beynac
Photograph by
Peter Titchmarsh

Romantically situated above the Dropt valley, this château dates from the 12th to the 17th century, and is now being restored following centuries of ill fortune. The two storeyed chapel (lower for the villagers, upper for the castle folk) contains two lovely 16th century tombs, but two other, finer specimens, are in the Metropolitan Museum in New York.

BLAYE (33)   *51k N Bordeaux*

The town itself is of little interest but the great citadel build by Louis XIV's fortification expert, Vauban, to control the entrance to the Gironde is well worth visiting. This was complemented by further forts, one on the island of Paté in mid stream and one on the opposite shore, Fort Médoc. There are hydrofoil services across to Lamarque and Pauillac... a rather more rapid means of transport than that used by the pilgrims crossing here on one of the great routes to St-James of Compostella.

Biron Château

Aquitaine

Palais-de-la-Bourse, Bordeaux Quay

The River Dronne at Brantôme.
Photograph by Peter Titchmarsh.

Brantôme Abbey. *Photograph by Peter Titchmarsh.*

BONAGUIL CHÂTEAU (47)   *64k NE Agen*
A massive late 15th century fortress, which although never put to the test, has always been regarded as completely impregnable. This was erected when most nobles were building elegant Renaissance pleasure palaces, but it certainly provided its builder, Bérenger de Roquefeuil, a means with which to ignore the opinions and good will of his neighbours.

BORDEAUX (33)   *560k SW Paris*
Capital of Aquitaine and one of the most important towns of France... both as an industrial town and seaport, and as a tourist centre. In the hands of the English between 1154 and 1453, it grew prosperous as a wine shipping port, and today it is the port of one of the world's great wine areas. Too extensive to describe here adequately, but see especially... the busy quays along the River Garonne, with their wine merchants' warehouses, the Cathedral, the church of St-Michel, the Maritime Museum, the Customs Museum, the Beaux Arts Museum, the Decorative Arts Museum, the splendid facade of the Grande Théâtre, and the Grosse Cloche, one of two surviving 13th century gate towers.

LE BOUILH CHÂTEAU (33)   *17k N Bordeaux*
Vast late 18th century neo-Classic mansion, which was never completed, due to its owner the Marquis de la Tour du Pin being guillotined during the Revolution. It is pleasantly situated amongst vineyards.

BOURDEILLES CHÂTEAU (24)   *10k SW Brantôme*
Splendid medieval castle, with a Renaissance front, on a rocky spur overlooking the river Dronne. It has an interesting interior, including a 16th century 'gilded salon'. This castle was the family home of Brantôme (See Brantôme, below).

BRANTÔME (24)   *27k N Périgueux*
Charming town built on an island in the river Dronne, with vines and weeping willows adorning the gardens of old houses, and with a Renaissance balustrade bordering both banks (All beautifully floodlit). Parts of the abbey may be visited, and there is a small museum housing the curious works of a local artist who worked under the influence of a medium. Pierre de Bourdeille, better known as Brantôme (1540 – 1614), brought fame to the abbey, as he did most of his writing while he was 'abbot' here.

LE BUGUE (24)   *41k SSE Périgueux*
Small town on the Vézère a short distance above its confluence with the Dordogne. There is an attractive zoo garden here with about 200 animals on display. Le Bugue is only 11k W of Les Eyzies, the great cave centre of the Vézère valley, and just to the west of the village is the great cavern of Bara-Bahau, while the Proumeyssac chasm lies about 3k to the south.

CADOUIN (24)   *36k E Bergerac*
Small village in wooded countryside to the south of the Dordogne valley, with a Cistercian abbey church and cloisters which are worth visiting. This was a great centre of pilgrimage for centuries as the abbey held a piece of cloth in which the head of Christ was believed to have been wrapped. It was only in 1933 that this was subjected to scientific examination, when it was found to have been woven in Egypt in the 10th century. Pilgrimages ceased forthwith and Cadouin has now returned to tranquillity after eight centuries of renown.

CAMBO-LES-BAINS (64)   *20k SSE Bayonne*
Small spa town in the foothills of the Pyrénées, astride the little river Nive. There is an attractive road south-east from here, up the Nive valley to St-Jean-Pied-de-Port (See Page 56). The author of 'Cyrano de Bergerac', Edmond Rostand, lived at Cambo and his house is now a Rostand Museum.

CASTELNAUD CHÂTEAU (24)   *11k SW Sarlat*
There are fine views up the Dordogne Valley to Beynac from this ruined castle, which is dramatically sited above a sheer rock face. The riverside just beyond the bridge offers fine picnic possibilities.

Nive valley near Cambo (Roland's Pass)

DAX (40)   *142k S Bordeaux*
Small town on the banks of the river Adour, noted for the curative properties of its hot water springs. These were used as early as Roman times, and parts of the Gallo-Roman town wall have survived (in the park). The 17th century cathedral incorporates a fine doorway from the Gothic cathedral built by the English. Dax was one of the last English-occupied towns to fall to the French (1451).

DOMME (24)   *75k SE Périgueux, 12k S Sarlat*
Delightful bastide town overlooking the Dordogne with narrow streets within its old fortifications and three surviving gateways. There are fine views northwards out over the Dordogne river, and the covered market hall in the square stands over the entrance to an interesting series of caves which may be visited.

DURAS CHÂTEAU (47)   *76k ESE Bordeaux, 22k S Ste-Foy-la-Grande*
Splendidly sited castle dating from the 12th century, but much altered in the 16th and 17th centuries into a classical château. This is now being lovingly restored and together with Duras village with its arcaded market square, is well worth visiting.

LES EYZIES-DE-TAYAC (24)   *45k SE Périgueux*
Sites of prehistoric importance are to be found in many parts of the Dordogne, but most of the outstanding ones are in the vicinity of the Vézère valley, and to understand their significance, go first to the National Museum of Prehistory in the castle overlooking Les Eyzies. Here you will be inspired to visit various sites, but concentrate first on the Grand Roc Cave, and the Laugerie Deposits, both to the NW of the village. See also the reserve in the Gorge d'Enfer where living animals similar to those portrayed in the caves are in semi-capitivity, and the Museum of Speleology (caving) in the fort at Tayac. Other caves in the area worth visiting include La Mouthe, de Rouffignac, des Combarelles, and de Font-de-Gaume. To explore the area properly use Michelin Map 75.

Castlenaud Château... perched high above the Dordogne   Photograph by Peter Titchmarsh

FÉNELON CHÂTEAU (24)   *15k ESE Sarlat*
Massive 15th and 16th century castle with outer walls and towers, and some 17th century 'domestic' modifications within its courtyard. There are fine views out over the Dordogne valley, and an interesting interior which includes mementoes of Bishop Fénelon, the prolific writer and philosopher who spent his childhood here.

In the Museum at Les Eyzies Château

Hautefort Château   The Lagoon at Hossegor

Labrède Château

Resin tapper in the Landes   Landes shepherd in traditional costume

The Sabres-Marquèze Railway (In the Landes).
Landes Regional Nature Park Photograph

FONTIROU CAVES (47)   *18k NNE Agen, to W of N21*
Interesting limestone caves with the bones of prehistoric animals found here on display.

GUÉTHARY (64)   *9k SW Biarritz*
Attractive Basque village and sea-side holiday resort. Sandy beach, with rocks and rock pools. Ideal for families with young children.

HAUTEFORT CHÂTEAU (24)   *45k E Périgueux*
Fine 17th century château on the site of a medieval castle, on a rocky outcrop overlooking the Auvézère valley. It was badly damaged by fire in 1968, but has been well restored. See also the charming village below, with its many medieval features.

HENDAYE (64)   *14k W St-Jean-de-Luz*
Busy seaside resort and frontier town, with a wide variety of hotels and fine golden sands. The small port looks across the estuary of the Bidassoa to the Spanish town of Fuenterrabia.

HOSSEGOR (40)   *20k N Bayonne*
Cheerful holiday resort situated on a salt water lagoon, with pine woods and great dunes close by, and the sea not far away. Splendid beach, although sometimes dangerous. Open-air cinema, surfing, riding and pelota (the unique Basque game). Also an interesting Motor Museum.

JUMILHAC-LE-GRAND (24)   *56k NE Périgueux*
    19k NE Thiviers
Romantic medieval castle with Renaissance alterations and 17th century additions, on a rocky site above the picturesque Isle gorge. With its pepperpot turrets and steep roofs this is a fairytale castle par excellence. See the 'room of the spinner' where Louise de Hautefort was apparently incarcerated by her jealous husband, and from where she is supposed to have sent messages to her lover written in her own blood, and let down on thread from her spinning wheel. See Jumilhac, and you will believe anything.

LABRÈDE CHÂTEAU (33)   *17k SE Bordeaux*
Small medieval château with Renaissance front, on two islands in a small lake... all within a park in the English style, inspired by one of the owner's frequent visits to England. This was the noted essayist Montesquieu. He died in 1756, but his descendants still live at Labrède.

THE LANDES DE GASCOGNE REGIONAL NATURE PARK (33, 40)
This encompasses a vast area stretching south-eastwards from the Arcachon basin to the village of Sabres in the heart of the great Landes forest country. There are ecological museums at Luxey (80k SE Arcachon), and at Marquèze which can be reached from Sabres by a fascinating little scenic railway. Visit both these and you will learn much about life and work in the attractive Landes area which extends behind the Atlantic coast almost as far down as Bayonne. Use Michelin Map 78.

LANGOIRAN ZOO (33)   *25k SE Bordeaux*
This collection of reptiles and birds of prey is situated just to the north of Langoiran village which is itself situated on the north bank of the Garonne.

LANQUAIS CHÂTEAU (24)   *18k E Bergerac*
The original fortress here was largely destroyed by the English during the Hundred Years War, but there are some medieval parts remaining, to which is attached a handsome Renaissance building, with an interesting interior. See especially the toile-de-Jouy hangings in the dining hall.

Lanquais Château   *Lanquais Château*

LASCAUX CAVE (24)   *49k SE Périgueux*
                                       2k SW Montignac
This was discovered by schoolboys in 1940, and contains many hundreds of outstandingly impressive prehistoric animal paintings. Sadly it was closed to the public some years ago, due to deterioration of the paintings, but at Montignac, just to its north, it is possible to visit a remarkably exact replica, 'Lascaux 2'. For further details of other caves in the area, visit the museum at Les Eyzies (see page 51).

Lascaux cave art

LIBOURNE (33)   *30k E Bordeaux*
It is at this point that the Dordogne becomes navigable to ocean going vessels, and wine is still exported from here. This trade was established when the town was built by an Englishman, Roger de Leyburn... a village in the far off Yorkshire Dales), and Libourne is in fact one of the largest of the bastide towns (See Villeneuve, Pages 56 – 57). Attractive arcaded town square, but the Tour du Grand Port is the only other relic of the bastide plan.

MERLANDE PRIORY (24)   *9k NW Périgueux*
A largely 12th century priory church in a quiet forest valley only a few kilometres from Périgueux, but remote for all that. There is a clear spring just behind the church and a round tower not far from a moat, part of the old priory buildings.

LES MILANDES CHÂTEAU (24)   *15k SW Sarlat*
Late 15th century castle pleasantly sited above the south bank of the Dordogne, and created into a lovely children's home by the American cabaret star of the 20's and 30's, Josephine Baker. It is open to the public.

MONBAZILLAC CHÂTEAU (24)   *5k S Bergerac*
Elegant 16th century château at the heart of the famous vineyard of Monbazillac, the best known of the Bergerac vineyards, and producing a high quality sweet white wine. Well restored exterior, and fine views from terrace.

MONFLANQUIN (47)   *17k NNE Villeneuve-sur-Lot*
This small village looking out over the Lède valley was a French bastide, and it retains its arcades on all four sides of the square. The fortified church dominates the village and there are enchanting views out over the surrounding countryside.

Libourne Château   *Monbazillac Château*

MONPAZIER (24)   *45k SE Bergerac*
This has often been described as a typical 'bastide' town (See Villeneuve Pages 56 – 7). It was founded by Edward I in 1284, at almost the same time as he was having Winchelsea, near Rye laid out by a certain Itier Bochard, a builder of bastides from this part of the country.

MONTAIGNE CHÂTEAU (24)   *53k E Bordeaux*
                                       18k E St-Émilion
Only the tower and delightful gardens are open, but *Continued*

The Square, Monpazier

Mont de Marsan

Mont de Marsan

Montfort Château

Nérac

13th century bridge at Orthez

Palm trees at Pau

Bernadotte's House at Pau

this tower is the surviving part of the home of the great 16th century essayist, Michel de Montaigne, and his bedroom on the first floor above the chapel may be visited. There are fine views northwards out over the Landais forest from the other side of the château.

MONT-DE-MARSAN (40) 127k S Bordeaux
This medium sized town is the capital of the Landes Département, and is perhaps best known to visitors for its light-hearted form of bull fighting. A wealth of good hotels and restaurants here, also an interesting museum.

MONTFORT CHÂTEAU (24) 6k SE Sarlat
Splendidly sited, high above the river Dordogne, this castle dating from the 16th century, is actually the fifth on the site, the first having been destroyed by the elder Simon de Monfort in 1214. (Not open.)

NÉRAC (47) 30k WSW Agen
Delightful little market town, with lovely tree-shaded walks beside its river. Only a wing of the once fine château survives, and this houses a local history museum. Petit Nérac, across the river from the modern town, is a charming huddle of old streets with many overhanging houses. Nérac is believed by some to be the setting of Shakespeare's 'Love's Labours Lost', as this was briefly one of the sites for the court of Navarre.

OLORON-SAINTE-MARIE (64) 32k SW Pau
The old part of this small town stands on a hill overlooking the union of two small rivers. There are two churches of interest... St-Croix, with a dome over its crossing, and St-Marie with a fine Romanesque west doorway.

ORTHEZ (64) 37k SE Dax
Small town in the valley of the Gave-du-Pau a few kilometres north west of the great natural gas field of Lacq. The Tour Moncade is all that remains of its once great castle. This was the capital of Béarn (See also Pau below) from 1194 to 1464, and the famous chronicler Jean Froissart describes a visit he made here to the court of the legendary Gaston Phoebus.

PAU (64) 190k S Bordeaux, 750k SW Paris
This large town was the capital of the province of Béarn, which in the middle ages was almost an independent kingdom... especially under Gaston Phoebus, who was largely responsible for its splendid castle. It was here that Henri of Navarre, later to become Henri IV, was born. Considerably restored in the 19th century, this is well worth visiting. Do not of course miss the splendid view of the Pyrénées (if the weather is clear) from the nearby Boulevard des Pyrénées. See also the Beaux Arts Museum, and the small museum with mementoes of Count Bernadotte, Napoleon's marshal, who became King of Sweden. Pau is an excellent centre from which to explore the western Pyrénées.

PAUILLAC (33) 51k NNW Bordeaux
Small town on the western shore of the broad Gironde estuary. Visit if possible the splendid Musée du Vin (Wine Museum), which is attached to the Château Mouton-Rothschild (2k NW). In the neighbourhood of Pauillac will be found three of the world's great vineyards... Lafite, Latour and Mouton-Rothschild.

PÉRIGUEUX (24)   *528k SW Paris, 120k NE Bordeaux*
Once the capital of Périgord, a region stretching between Limousin and the east of Aquitaine, Périgueux is now the capital of the Département of Dordogne. It is dominated by the great white dome, towers and pinnacles of the largely 19th century exterior of St-Front cathedral... a precursor of Sacré-Coeur in Paris. There are of course splendid views from its roofs. Also see the fascinating old streets between the cathedral and the Allées de Tourny, the Périgord Museum, the prehistoric section of which will remind you that we are in an area which is world famous for its prehistoric sites (notably its caves). See also the Tour de Vesone, which is the remains of a circular Roman temple, and the Romanesque church of St-Étienne. Do not leave Périgueux without sampling the truffles and pâtés-de-foie, for which it is so renowned.

Périgueux Cathedral

PUYGUILHEM CHÂTEAU (24)   *13k NE Brantôme*
A handsome 16th century Renaissance château with towers reminding us that medieval times were a very recent memory in the hill country in which it was built.

PYRÉNÉES NATIONAL PARK (64 & 65)
(See Page 183).

RAVIGNAN CHÂTEAU (40)   *20k E Mont-de-Marsan*
3k SE Villeneuve-de-Marsan
An 11th century castle which has been absorbed within a Louis XIII château, with parts added in very recent years. This is situated in the heart of the Armagnac country, and there is a distillery here which can be visited. The château itself is pleasantly furnished, and there is an interesting collection of 18th century court uniform on display.

Périgueux Cathedral   *In the Dordogne Gorge*

LA RÉOLE (33)   *68k ESE Bordeaux*
Pleasant small town on slopes above the Garonne, with a ruined castle, a largely 13th century church (with modern tower) and a fascinating 12th – 14th century market hall.

LA ROQUE-GAGEAC (24)   *9k S Sarlat*
Charming small village on the banks of the Dordogne, beneath steep cliffs, largely bare of vegetation. Park your car and wander along the riverside road.

In the foothills of the Pyrénées

ROQUETAILLADE CHÂTEAU (33)
52k SSE Bordeaux, 11k NNW Bazas
Large 14th century castle in a pleasant park, with central keep and six round towers, all restored in the grand manner by the great 19th century architect Viollet-le-Duc. The interior is full of 19th century neo-medieval flavour and well worth visiting.

ST-AMAND-DE-COLY (24)   *21k N Sarlat*
Small village in a quiet valley setting, with an exceptionally interesting fortified church. This abbey church was built by monks in the 12th century. Although the abbey and the cloisters have disappeared the church and much of the ramparts have survived. The high bare interior with its defensive features conveys the spirit of medieval times when the worship of God was carried out against a background of violence and disorder.

Lakeside Picnic in the Landes
Photograph by Peter Titchmarsh

Aquitaine

St-Émilion

Folk-dancing at St-Jean Pied-de-Port

Sarlat

Sarlat

Sarlat

The Dordogne near Trémolat
Photograph by Peter Titchmarsh

ST-ÉMILION (33)   *38k E Bordeaux*

Wonderfully situated hill-top town looking out across the Dordogne valley. There are medieval town walls almost entirely intact, and within them a wonderfully unspoilt medieval town. See especially the rock cut subterranean church, to which is attached the hermitage cell of St-Émilion. This town gives its name to one of France's most well known wine areas (See Page 57).

ST-JEAN-DE-LUZ AND CIBOURE (64)
15k SW Biarritz

Set in a wide bay at the foothills of the Pyrénées, with splendid sands and an old tunny fishing port to lend a salty flavour to this already lively resort. Basque folklore festivals in summer. Louis XIV was married in the 16th century church.

ST-JEAN PIED-DE-PORT (64)   *54k SE Bayonne*

This attractive little town lies below the famous pass (hence its name) of Roncesvalles, the scene of Roland's heroic defence in 778 against the invading Moslems, pressing over the Pyrénées from Spain. There is a pleasant bridge across the river Nive, which is overhung with a series of quaint old houses. The old citadel overlooks all.

SARLAT (24)   *67k SE Périgueux*

Attractive little town which makes a good base for exploring southern Périgord, including the most interesting stretch of the Dordogne valley. In the 19th century a new road was driven right through the old town, but apart from this intrusion, there are many lovely streets, lined with a wonderful variety of old buildings. See the Bishop's Palace, now a theatre, the cathedral, and the house of la Boëtie, (1530 – 1563) the poet and translator, whose early death inspired Montaigne to write his well known essay on friendship. Also visit the interesting aquarium in the rue du Commandant Maratuel.

LE TEICH ORNITHOLOGICAL PARK (33)
11k E Arcachon

This is an extensive bird reserve in the saltings and marshes between the little port of Le Teich and the shoreline of the Arcachon basin. Parts of this (near Le Teich itself) are open to the public and a wide variety of sea birds and waterfowl may be observed. This is situated on one of the great migratory routes and while about 75 species build their nests, over 240 species have been observed in total.

THONAC (24)   *50k SE Périgueux*

Visit the Prehistoric Art Centre at Le Thot nearby. There are slides, films and pictures, and also a park in which will be found the animals most frequently represented in the cave paintings in the area.

TREMOLAT (24)   *34k E Bergerac*

With its rugged castle-like church and its charming hotel (the Vieux Logis — one of our favourites) this attractive village lies close to a great bend in the Dordogne, known as the Cingle de Trémolat (the Trémolat Meander). The cingle, which encloses a vast patchwork of fields, is overlooked by high wooded cliffs, and there is a viewpoint providing a dramatic panorama, just to the north of the village. 7 kms to the east is the little village of Limeuil, with its steep streets dropping down to grassy banks which overlook the confluence of the Dordogne and the Vézère.

VILLANDRAUT (33)   *58k SE Bordeaux*

Small village on the edge of the Landes forest and dominated by the great four square ruined castle, built by Pope Clement V, who was born at Villandraut in 1264, and who is perhaps best remembered for moving the papal court to Avignon.

VILLENEUVE-SUR-LOT (47) *29k N Agen*

Busy little market town with an accent on fruit and vegetables, this was one of the strongest bastides* in the area. See especially the town gateways, the old bridge, built by the English, and the church of St-Catherine (20th century with medieval stained glass).

Bastides were fortified towns of the 13th and 14th centuries, built by both the French and the English, all on a chequered plan, and centred upon a square surrounded by covered arcades or cornièrs. Most bastides had a fortified church, and all had a town wall with towers and gateways.

VILLÉREAL (47) *37k SE Bergerac*

This small village is a good example of a French bastide town (See Villeneuve above), many of which, like this one, were built by Alphonse de Poitiers, the brother of St. Louis, in an attempt to halt the advance of the English. See the narrow streets, with many overhanging houses, the fortified church, and the covered market.

Bridge over the Dordogne near Trémolat
Photograph by Peter Titchmarsh

GREAT WINE AREAS OF BORDEAUX

THE MÉDOC. This is the area lying to the west of the Gironde estuary, taking up a large proportion of the tongue of land extending northwards from Bordeaux between the Gironde and the Atlantic coast. Here are produced the great red wines of Bordeaux. The names of the 'Grand Crus' in this area are many, but they include at their head, Château-Lafite-Rothschild, Château-Margaux, Château-Latour, and Château-Mouton-Rothschild. Drive north from Bordeaux to follow the well signposted 'Route-du-Médoc', which turns right off the D-1, about 7ks north of the city, following the D2E.

SAUTERNES. A small area on the west bank of the Garonne, about 35 kilometres south-east of Bordeaux, comprising the towns of Sauternes, Barsac, Bommes, Fargues and Preignac. From here come some of the world's finest sweet wines including the superlative Château-d'Yquem.

GRAVES. This area stretches south-eastwards from Bordeaux, about fifty kilometres and in fact envelopes the Sauternes area, being also situated to the west of the Garonne. Here are produced red wines and medium dry and sweet white wines, all of very considerable quality. Haut-Brion is one of the most distinguished red wines from this area, the château having once been owned by Napoleon's Foreign Minister, Talleyrand.

The Dordogne at Limeuil *Photograph by Peter Titchmarsh*

ST-ÉMILION AND POMEROL. A small area lying to the north of the river Dordogne about forty kilometres to the east of Bordeaux, and centred upon the delightful town of St-Émilion. This area was already popular during the English occupation of Aquitaine and today it provides many excellent red wines including those of Ausone, Cheval Blanc and Beauséjour. The Pomerol area lies to the immediate north west of the St-Émilion area, with Libourne, on the Dordogne, at its foot, and the best of its fine red wines rival those of the Médoc.

ENTRE-DEUX-MERS. This area extends south-east-wards from Bordeaux between the Dordogne and the Garonne, and should by rights be described as being between 'two rivers' rather than 'two seas'. Both red and white wine is produced here, but it is the light dry wines of the area that carry its name, and these are especially drinkable with sea-food.

In the blacksmith's forge at Limeuil
Photograph by Peter Titchmarsh

Sunny afternoon at Limeuil
Photograph by Peter Titchmarsh

Aquitaine

Auvergne

Comprises the following Départements:
Allier (03)   Haute-Loire (43)
Cantal (15)   Puy-de-Dôme (63)

This is the very heart of the Massif Central... a country of splendid mountains, many of which are volcanic in origin, lush green valleys and blue, tree bordered lakes. To the north of the area lies the less dramatic plateau country of the Bourbonnais (the homeland of the Bourbon family), but everywhere will be found quiet unspoilt countryside enriched by little medieval towns and villages, fascinating Romanesque churches and nearly five hundred ancient castles. Amongst the old summer pastures of the Auvergne there are many small pilgrimage towns, in addition to the great centre of pilgrimage at Le Pûy-en-Velay, and for those searching for modernity there are the great hydro-electric dams on the Sioule, Dordogne, Cère and Truyère rivers with their attendant lakes. But above all, this region should be visited by those in search of tranquillity... by exploring quiet roads, walking in the hills and forests, or simply sitting in the sun in some quiet town square.

The Moulin Richard-le-Bas, Ambert

Alleuse Château

Hill country near Besse-en-Chandesse

ALLEUZE CHÂTEAU (15)   *10k S St-Flour*
The dramatic ruins of a great 13th century castle on a hill above one of the inlets created by the Grandval Barrage, about eight kilometres to the south.

AMBERT (63)   *78k ESE Clermont-Ferrand*
Small town which was the centre of a thriving paper-making industry in the 15th, 16th and 17th centuries. Four kilometres east of the town there is an interesting paper mill still in operation... the Moulin Richard-le-Bas. Here you may watch paper being made by traditional methods, and visit the small museum. About five kilometres to the south-east of Ambert, will be found the pleasant Le Bouy Zoo Park. In Ambert itself, see the late Gothic church of St-Jean, and the monument to Emmanuel Chabrier, born here in 1842.

ANJONY CHÂTEAU (15)   *22 N Aurillac*
Fine 15th century castle situated on a spur above a deep wooded valley, with central keep and round corner towers. There are 16th century wall paintings in the chapel, and Flemish and Aubusson tapestries in the castle itself.

AURILLAC (15)   *157k SW Clermont-Ferrand*
This medium sized town grew up around the great abbey, built here by Saint Géraud, and from which originated the first French Pope... Gerbert, or Sylvester II. Both town and abbey were largely destroyed by the Huguenots in 1569, and few medieval buildings remain. However do not overlook the Maison Consulair, a 16th century merchant's house, now occupied by a savings bank; the beautifully restored abbey church of St-Géraud, the Rames Museum, nor the attractive view of the river Jordanne from the Pont Rouge.

BESSE-EN-CHANDESSE (63)
51k SSW Clermont-Ferrand
Charming medieval village with an old gateway and steep streets lined with houses built of black volcanic rock. The Romanesque church houses the famous 'Black Virgin' of Vassivières, except when she is taken up to the mountain chapel of that name in July and September, in solemn pilgrimage. The winter-sports resort of Super-Besse, situated about seven kilometres west, at the foot of the Monts Dore, has a cableway up to the summit of Puy Ferrand (1846m).

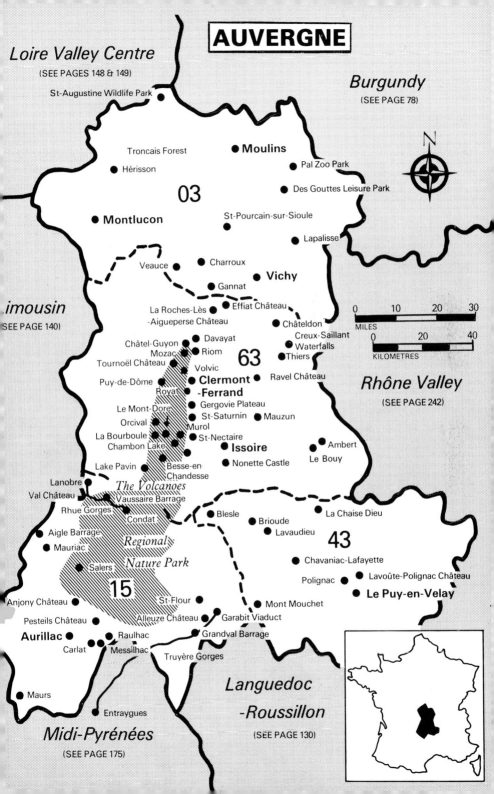

Riding near La Bourboule

La Bourboule

Plage on Lake Chambon

BLESLE (43) *36k S Issoire*

This little town situated at the junction of three deep valleys grew up around a wealthy nunnery. See the interesting Romanesque abbey church, the remains of the medieval town walls, the old streets with overhanging houses, many of which are half-timbered. The nearby d'Alagnon gorges should not be missed.

LA BOURBOULE (63) *52k SW Clermont-Ferrand*

Health resort and summer holiday town to the west of the Monts Dore, with a wide variety of hotels, and many facilities for sportsmen. There is a cableway up from the town to the Plateau de Charlannes, and about eight kilometres to the north-east, the 'chimney' of an extinct volcano, known as 'La Banne d'Ordanche' from which there are splendid views.

BRIOUDE (43) *70k SSE Clermont-Ferrand*

Bustling little market town in flat country just to the west of the river Allier, which is noted hereabouts for its salmon. The Romanesque church of St-Julien is a fine building, the largest of its period in the Auvergne, and well worth visiting.

CARLAT (15) *17k ESE Aurillac*

Here once stood one of the most important castles of the Cantal region, on a great rocky platform, from which there are still fine views out over the mountains for those who are prepared to climb up to this windswept point.

LA CHAISE DIEU (43) *57k SE Issoire*

Little village standing over 1000 metres above sea level, with fine views out over the southern Auvergne... hence the name... 'The Seat of God'. Here are the remains of a great Benedictine abbey, rebuilt by a former monk who had become Pope Clement VI, and which was later sacked by the same Huguenots who destroyed Aurillac. In the abbey are buried the remains of the last Anglo-Saxon queen of England, Edith, the wife of King Harold. See especially, the grim 'Danse Macabre' wall painting, the choir stalls, the 'Tour Clementine', and the splendid cloister.

CHAMBON LAKE (63) *37k SSE Clermont-Ferrand*

Like Lake Pavin, this lies in the crater of an extinct volcano, and is most attractively sited amidst wooded volcanic hills. There is a plage at its eastern end, and several hotels nearby. Visit the interesting 13th century château of Murol about 3k E.

CHARROUX (03) *25k W Vichy*

Pleasant medieval village with the remains of its fortifications, and many picturesque old streets, amongst which will be found a belfry (the symbol of a 'free-town') and an interesting 11th and 12th century church.

CHÂTELDON (63) *21k SSE Vichy*

Minute town surrounded by vine covered hills, with a tree shaded stream running between its half-timbered houses. There is a 14th century clock-tower and a church containing handsome baroque statues. Drive fourteen kilometres south and east to explore the valley of the Credogne including the lovely waterfalls of Creux-Saillant. Use Michelin Map 73.

Chaise Dieu

Chaise Dieu

Lake Chambon

CHÂTEL-GUYON (63)
6k NW Riom,
21k NNW Clermont-Ferrand

Pleasant little spa town with a wide choice of hotels. The centre of the town is dominated by a Calvary on a small hill, from which there are fine views out over the Monts Dômes and the Monts du Forez.

CHAVANIAC-LAFAYETTE (43)
40k WNW Le Puy

This large château in pleasant gardens was the birthplace of the famous Marquis de Lafayette, one of the heroes of the American War of Independence, and it is now maintained by an American foundation as a Lafayette Museum.

Mementoes of Lafayette at Chavaniac-Lafayette

CLERMONT-FERRAND (63)
390k S Paris

'Capital' of the Auvergne, and capital of the Département of Puy-de-Dôme, Clermont Ferrand is an important commercial and industrial city (owing much of this importance to the Michelin brothers who established their tyre factory here in 1886). The centre of the town is situated on the top of a long extinct volcano, and the 13th century Cathedral is built of a black volcanic rock. See also the Romanesque Basilica of Notre-Dame-du-Port, the various attractive fountains, the old streets, the beautiful Jardin Lecoq and the Bargouin and Ranquet Museums. The great scientific and religious philosopher, Pascal, was born here in 1623.

Châtel-Guyon

Notre-Dame-du-Port, Clermont-Ferrand

DAVAYAT (63)
7k N Riom

Small village with a charming Louis XIII manor house. This has some pleasantly furnished rooms and delightful gardens with ornamental stonework.

EFFIAT CHÂTEAU (63)
17k SW Vichy

Dignified 17th century château with its mansard roofs looking out over charming formal gardens, complete with canals and statues. The interior is furnished in a style contemporary with the building, and has a delightful 'lived-in' atmosphere.

GANNAT (03)
19k W Vichy

A modest town with two churches worth visiting, and a museum in its 15th century castle containing a fine collection of treasures, together with a complete harness room, a Bourbonnais kitchen and a cobbler's shop.

Davayat Manor House

Davayat Manor House

GARABIT VIADUCT (15)
12k SE St-Flour

Dramatic single spanned viaduct built by the great civil engineer Eiffel in 1883, some six years earlier than his stupendous tower in Paris. This viaduct spans the Truyère river near the head of the vast lake created by the Grandval Barrage (See Page 62).

GERGOVIE PLATEAU (63)
12k S Clermont Ferrand

This high plateau overlooking the road south from Clermont Ferrand to Issoire, was the site of a victory over Caesar's troops by the Gallic Arvernes, whose capital it was. They were lead by Vercingétorix, who was later forced to surrender to the Romans at Alise-Ste-Reine (See Page 78). Remains of camp visible. Monument. Fine views eastwards. Restaurant.

Garabit Viaduct

Auvergne

DES GOUTTES LEISURE PARK (03)   *30k SE Moulins*
2k N Thionne

An extensive 'pleasure park' with many ponds for fishing and boating. Children's recreation areas, pony rides, animal reserves. Trout and crayfish streams.

GRANDVAL BARRAGE (15)   *18k S St-Flour*

Large dam across the Truyère with an equally large hydro-electric generating station. The lake behind it stretches north and east as far as the Garabit viaduct, another interesting feature of the Truyère gorges.

HÉRISSON (03)   *27k N Montluçon*

The priory church of Châteloy, with its fine murals, overlooks the lovely Aumance valley in which stands the little town of Hérisson. Lovely old houses and the impressive ruins of a medieval castle.

ISSOIRE (63)   *35k S Clermont-Ferrand*

Small town on the river Couze, with splendidly carved capitals in the fine Romanesque church of St-Austremoine. This was one of the few buildings to survive the sacking of the town by the Duc d'Alençon in the Wars of Religion. Comfortable little hotels.

JONAS CAVES (63)   *22k W Issoire*

Interesting caves in hill country to the south east of Mont-Dore. The bones of prehistoric animals have been found here, and occupation by man extended from prehistoric times to the middle ages, when a chapel was installed. Son-et-lumière in July and August.

LANOBRE (15)   *75k SW Clermont-Ferrand,*
7k NE Bort-les-Orgues

The 12th century Romanesque church has finely sculptured capitals, and not far from the village is the Château-de-Val. This was built in 1450 on a hillside overlooking the Dordogne, but due to the creation of a lake for hydro-electric purposes, it is now even more attractively sited, with water on three sides. It has an interesting interior and there is a beach and boat harbour close by. Boat trips on the lake.

LAPALISSE (03)   *20k NE Vichy*

Small town below a large 12th century castle, which was converted into a handsome Renaissance château by its owner on his return from the wars in Italy in the 15th century. The rich interiors are well worth visiting.

LAVAUDIEU (43)   *10k SE Brioude*

Here in a quiet valley is a late 11th century Benedictine abbey church with splendid wall paintings and attractive cloisters, together with the ruins of the abbey itself.

LAVOÛTE-POLIGNAC CHÂTEAU (43)   *12k N Le Puy*

Small medieval castle romantically sited above a bend in the Loire as it passes through a steep sided gorge. The interior includes an interesting collection of Polignac family portraits.

Hérisson

Romanesque capitals at Issoire

Lapalisse Château

Auvergne

MAURIAC (15)
114k SW Clermont-Ferrand
Small market town and holiday centre on the edge of the upper Dordogne region. The Romanesque church has a splendid west doorway and a high interior in which there is a statue of Our Lady of Miracles... a 13th century carving in black wood. Twelve kilometres to the north west is the Barrage de l'Aigle, a hydro-electric dam across the Dordogne.

MAURS (15)
45k SW Aurillac
Picturesque village delightfully situated amongst chestnut woodlands on a hillside above the river Rance. The 14th century church contains a richly ornamented reliquary in the form of a bust of St-Cézaire... an outstanding 13th century art treasure.

Barrage de L'Aigle, near Mauriac *Le Mont-Dore*

MAUZUN (63)
30k ESE Clermont-Ferrand
Dark stone castle ruins on a bramble covered hilltop from which there are fine views out over the surrounding hills. Of its original nineteen towers eleven are still standing, and it is easy to imagine how strong Mauzun must have been in its heyday.

LE MONT-DORE (63)
47k SW Clermont-Ferrand
Busy little spa town taking its name from the mountains in which it lies and popular as a summer holiday resort and winter sports centre. There is a wide selection of hotels, restaurants, ski lifts and cableways, and with the help of one of the cableways the peak of Puy de Sancy (5ks S) may be ascended. There are many other lakes, waterfalls and villages to be visited in the surrounding area. (Use Michelin Map 73).

MONTLUÇON (03)
320k S Paris,
90k NW Clermont-Ferrand
Large industrial town on the river Cher, with a pleasant old quarter above the south bank. The 12th century church of St-Pierre has a pleasant interior, but it is not of outstanding interest.

MONT MOUCHET (43)
30k E St-Flour
This was the site of the Resistance H.Q. for the whole Massif Central region, and there was a considerable battle here in June 1944 when the German army attempted to eliminate Resistance forces concentrating in the area prior to 'D' Day. There is a monument and a museum recording sad times and brave deeds.

Monument on Mont Mouchet

MOULINS (03)
290k S Paris
Capital of the Allier Département, this town on the Allier river was the capital of the Duchy of Bourbon from 1368 until 1527. See the narrow cobbled streets, the Gothic cathedral with its lovely choir, its fine stained glass windows and its well known 15th century triptych by the Maître de Moulins. See also the lovely mausoleum of Duke Henri II in the Lycée Banville, and the folklore museum in the remains of the Ducal Palace.

MOZAC (63)
To the immediate west of Riom
Only part of the abbey church of Mozac survives and its interior is not very attractive. However do not miss the splendid Romanesque carvings within... nor the lovely 12th century enamelled casket in its treasury.

Moulins   *Moulins*

Auvergne

Murol   Murol

MUROL (63)   37k SW Clermont-Ferrand
Small village with several modest hotels, on a hillside beneath the dramatic ruins of a 12th century castle... all in pleasant pine covered countryside with Lake Chambon close by. An ideal base for those wishing to explore on foot.

NONETTE CASTLE (63)   10k S Issoire
The ruins of a great castle on a hill within a bend of the river Allier. This was one of the most important fortresses of the Auvergne, but it was dismantled on the orders of that great imposer of central power, Cardinal Richelieu. The hills of the Monts Dore make an impressive backdrop to the Allier valley when viewed from here.

Orcival   Polignac from the Castle

ORCIVAL (63)   27k SW Clermont-Ferrand
Minute village and pilgrimage centre (four small hotels), with a fine 12th century Romanesque church housing a contemporary carving of a black Virgin and Child. See also the prisoners' iron collars and chains hanging from the arches and the capitals with carved leaf-work.

PAL ZOO PARK (03)   30k ESE Moulins
4k N St. Pourcain-sur-Besbre
Large zoo park with a fine collection of animals in open country surrounded by woodlands and lakes. There are are also a wide variety of attractions, especially for children, as well as picnic area, buvettes, souvenir shop and cafeteria.

LAKE PAVIN (63)   40k SSW Clermont-Ferrand
Situated in the crater of an extinct volcano, this lake with its thickly wooded shores, is one of the loveliest in the whole Auvergne region.

Puy-de-Dôme Country near Orcival

PESTEILS CHÂTEAU (15)   10k NE Aurillac
Ancient fortress overlooking the Cère valley, almost completely rebuilt in the 18th and 19th centuries. There are feudal dungeons, with interesting frescoes and splendidly decorated rooms in the main building.

POLIGNAC CASTLE (43)   5k NW Le Puy
The impressive ruins of a 15th century castle complete with a great square keep and low walls, all dominating the village below the flat topped hill on which it stands.

PUY-DE-DÔME (63)   10k E Clermont-Ferrand
1464 metres high mountain top, once crowned by a Roman temple to Mercury, and now unfortunately the site of a television mast and an observatory. There is a toll road, and then a short walk up from the car park to the summit, from which there are splendid views south west down the 'Chaîne des Volcans'... the famous range of extinct volcanoes.

LE PUY-EN-VELAY (43)   513k S Paris
128k SE Clermont-Ferrand
'Le Puy' means 'the peak', and this busy town lies in a flat plain punctuated by dramatically sharp volcanic peaks. The fine Romanesque cathedral, which should be visited, was a great place of pilgrimage in the middle ages, being astride one of the routes to St-James of Compostella in north western Spain. One of the volcanic peaks (which rises above the cathedral) is

Route to the summit of   The summit of the Puy-
the Puy-de-Dôme   de-Dôme

Continued

topped by a statue of the Virgin, while to the north another is topped by an 11th century chapel. See also the Crozatier Museum, which specialises in lace (for which Le Puy is famed); and the 14th century church of St-Laurent.

RAULHAC (15)   20k E Aurillac
Small village with several attractive old farm houses, and fine views. Not far to the south is the château of Messilhac, beautifully sited above the Cère valley. This medieval fortress has fine Renaissance decoration.

RAVEL CHÂTEAU (63)   28k E Clermont-Ferrand
Medieval castle converted in the 17th and 18th centuries into an elegant château, with delicious views across to the Monts Dômes from its terrace, which was established by Le Nôtre. The quietly dignified interior with its echoes of former glory is well worth visiting.

RHUE GORGES (15)   W from Condat, which is 80k
SSW of Clermont-Ferrand
These are followed by a road stretching westwards for about thirty kilometres, from Condat to Bort-les-Orgues, passing the great hydro-electric barrage of Vaussaire, and close to the attractive Cornilloux Waterfall. The steep sides of the gorges are beautifully wooded and they are wonderfully cool on a hot summer day. Use Michelin Map No. 76.

St-Michel Chapel, Le Puy

RIOM (63)   15k N Clermont-Ferrand
This little town was once the capital of the Auvergne, until it was overtaken by Clermont Ferrand. Wander along its pleasant old streets and look at the 14th century St-Chapelle, with its fine stained glass windows (within the Palais-de-Justice), the tapestries in the Palais itself, the lovely 14th century carving of the Virgin in Marthuret church, the various attractive fountains, and the Museum of the Auvergne.

LA ROCHE-LÈS-AIGUEPERSE CHÂTEAU (63)
19k NNE Riom
Late medieval castle with fine views of the 'Chaîne des Volcans' from its battlements. The interior contains much of interest including a collection of ancient arms and some Aubusson tapestries.

Ravel Château

ROYAT (63)   5k SW Clermont-Ferrand
Elegant 'thermal resort' now almost a suburb of Clermont-Ferrand, with the wide choice of hotels and restaurants making it an excellent centre for exploring the Auvergne. In the 'old village' there is an 11th century fortified church, above a 10th century crypt.

ST-AUGUSTINE WILDLIFE PARK (03)
44k NW Moulins, 6k NW le Veurdre
A sixty acre wildlife reserve in the park of a Louis XV château, complete with a drive-in lion enclosure. It is possible to take a boat across one of the four lakes.

Bedroom in Ravel Château

Auvergne

St-Flour

Procession at St-Flour

St-Nectaire

ST-FLOUR (15) *68k S Issoire*

This small town is the commercial centre of the 'Haute Auvergne' area, and is situated on a dramatic rocky spur above the meeting of two rivers. Walk around the old streets, see the fine view northwards from the Terrasse des Roches, and the Gothic cathedral which contains a splendid 15th century sculpture of Christ, and an earlier one of the Virgin and Child... both well worth seeing.

ST-NECTAIRE (63) *22k W Issoire*

Outstanding Romanesque church splendidly sited above a little village. The beautifully sculptured capitals are full of interest and the treasures of the church include a Romanesque Virgin in gilded copper.

ST-POURCAIN-SUR-SIOULE (03) *31k S Moulins*

Small town noted for its excellent trout fishing and also for its delectable local wine (which may be sampled at the co-operative's 'Cave'). There is a fine Romanesque and Gothic abbey church here, with a wealth of interesting features.

ST-SATURNIN (63) *15k S Clermont-Ferrand*

Charming fortified market town (small enough to be a village), complete with outstanding Romanesque church, medieval dovecote, 15th century fountains and attractive views down the Monne valley.

SALERS (15) *19k SE Mauriac*

Small village nearly a thousand metres above sea level, on the basalt plateau overlooking the Maronne valley. There are many fine houses in the upper part of the town, and there are splendid views from the Promenade de Barrouze. The interior of the church contains several items of interest, including a 15th century 'Entombment of Christ' of painted stone.

THIERS (63) *42k E Clermont-Ferrand*

Pleasant old town rising above the banks of the river Durolle. Here will be found several half-timbered houses, which are a rarity in this area. Thiers has been a cutlery town since the middle ages, and there is a Cutlery Museum. There are two Romanesque churches... St-Genès, which is being restored, and St-Pierre Moûtier, an early specimen dating from the 10th century.

TOURNOËL CHÂTEAU (63) *8k WSW Riom,*
22k NNW Clermont-Ferrand

A largely 14th century castle dramatically sited on a rocky peak in the eastern foothills of the Monts Dômes, with spendid views eastwards over the Allier valley to the Monts du Forez (There is an 'Orientation Table' near the entrance). Although this is a ruin, much of the internal structure remains and one can climb to the top of the great round keep. Do not miss this.

TRONÇAIS FOREST (03) *35k NNE Montluçon*

A splendidly wooded area with several lakes, picnic places, two camping sites and a variety of pleasant forest walks. (Use Michelin Map 69)

Mountain road to Salers   *Thiers*

Thiers

TRUYÈRE GORGES (15)   *From 12k SE St-Flour*
These stretch south-eastwards from near St-Flour to Entraygues,* a total distance of about 140 kilometres (much of which is in the Midi-Pyrénées region), and although it is not possible to follow their exact course by road all the way, there are many places where road and gorge coincide, and many others where the gorges can be reached by paths from the road. See separate entries covering the Garabit Viaduct, the château of Alleuze, and the barrages of Grandval, Sarrans and Couesque. Use Michelin Map 76, and if possible the Michelin Green Guide to the Auvergne (in French only).
*(See Page 179).

Auvergne folk-dancers

VAL CHÂTEAU (15)   (See LANOBRE, Page 62)

VEAUCE (03)   *35k W Vichy*
Small village on the south-eastern fringes of the lovely Colettes forest, with a 12th century church and a 13th and 14th century castle on a rocky site overlooking the little river Veauce.

VICHY (03)   *350k S Paris*
A spa town on the Allier river, famous for its curative waters since Roman times. Its extensive range of hotels make it an excellent centre for exploration of the surrounding countryside. See especially the tree shaded Parc des Sources. Theatres, cinemas, casino, tennis, golf, sailing and swimming.

THE VOLCANOES REGIONAL NATURE PARK
(63 & 15)
This thickly wooded mountain area covers the former volcanic zone in the centre of France and extends from the Monts Dômes (west of Clermont-Ferrand) to the Monts du Cantal (west of St-Flour). The little village of Volvic (20k NNW of Clermont Ferrand) lies at the foot of a great outpouring of lava from the extinct volcano of la Nugière, and there is an interesting underground quarry from which this lava stone was extracted... the Maison de la Pierre, which may be visited. This is splendid country to explore on foot, and long distance footpath GR-4 crosses it from St-Flour in the south, to the vicinity of Volvic. It is not so easy to drive along its spine, but many roads pass across it from west to east. Use Michelin Maps 73 and 76. For further information write to: Syndicat Mixte du Parc des Volcans, Centre d'Information, 28 rue St-Esprit, 63000 CLERMONT-FERRAND.

Val Château

Crater lake in the Volcanoes Regional Nature Park

Sporting facilities at Vichy

Auvergne

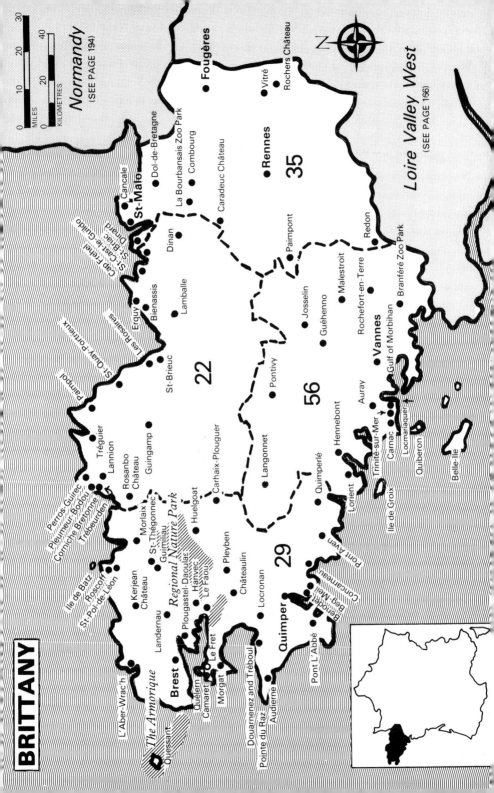

Brittany

Comprises the following Départements:
Côtes-du-Nord (22) Ille-et-Vilaine (35)
Finistère (29) Morbihan (56)

Here is a strange land, always remote from the heartland of France. In the 6th and 7th centuries it was colonised by Celts from Cornwall and Wales, with their Christian monks very much to the fore; and despite subjugation by Charlemagne in 799, and repeated incursions by the Normans in the centuries that followed, it was only in 1491 that Brittany was finally united with France. However to this day the Celtic traditions still survive, with the Breton language closer to Welsh than French, and with the deeply moving religious festivals known as Pardons, celebrating the local saints, many of whom had set out as missionary monks from Wales. Here is the great 'promontory of Europe', with over six hundred miles of coastline... a splendid succession of wild, rocky headlands, long sandy beaches, lively holiday resorts, quiet tree-backed coves, and little sheltered harbours.
Inland will be found wooded hills and moorland, quiet valleys and a charming patchwork of small stone-walled fields. Prehistoric remains, old castles and manor houses, unique parish closes and walled medieval towns... all combine with the lovely coastline to create a unique holiday experience.

L'ABER-WRAC'H (29) *28k N Brest*

A well sheltered sailing harbour, still used by lobster men, L'Aber-Wrac'h is an attractive little holiday resort, with lovely views out over its broad estuary. The lighthouse on the nearby Island of the Virgin is the highest in the world.

L'Aber-Wrac'h *The Pointe du Raz, near Audierne*

ARGOAT, THE... INLAND BRITTANY

This is the countryside of little stone-walled fields, wooded hills, open moorlands, quiet villages and hidden valleys... this is inland Brittany, an area often passed through speedily on the way to the coast. Here will be found great castles, attractive manor houses, and a wealth of little chapels... it is a magical countryside far removed from the busy coastal resorts, and is well worth exploring.

ARMORIQUE REGIONAL NATURE PARK (29)

This is a large area situated around Brest and the island of Ouessant, with a wide variety of flora and fauna under its protection. Full details are available from the Maison du Parc, Menez Meur, Hanvec, 29224 Daoulas. The Maison du Parc also includes an information centre, which is open to the public... it is at Hanvec, approximately 30 ks ESE of Brest.

On the Island of Ouessant, in the Armorique Regional Nature Park

AUDIERNE (29) *35k W Quimper*

Busy little fishing and pleasure port with its main square close to colourful quays. It is beautifully sited on the estuary of the Goyen beneath a wooded hillside. There are boat trips across to the Île-de-Sein from here. The famous headland, the Pointe du Raz, lies 15 kilometres to the west and should not be missed.

AURAY (56) *18k W Vannes*

Situated at the head of a long creek running into the Gulf of Morbihan, Auray has an interesting little quay and old streets in the St-Goustan quarter. Visit the Carthusian Monastery (5k NE), and take a boat trip to the Gulf of Morbihan.

BEG-MEIL (29) *21k SE Quimper*

Delightful little holiday resort at the mouth of a wide bay, with two beaches, both bordered by luxuriant woodlands, nurtured by its particularly mild climate.

Audierne

Le Palais, Belle-Île   Benodet

Ramparts at Brest

Quiet moorings at   Memorial at the Pointe
Camaret   de Pen Hir, near Camaret

Cancale

Brittany

BELLE-ÎLE (56)   *1 hour S Quiberon*
This is the largest of the Breton islands and is easily reached from Quiberon (1 hour crossing). There is a lively little port... Le Palais, great sea cliffs, little sandy beaches and quiet inlets. There are coach and boat excursions around the island, but it is also good walking country.

BENODET (29)   *16k S Quimper*
Attractive seaside resort at the mouth of the Odet estuary, with a little port, popular with sailing men, and three sandy beaches facing south. Do not miss a trip up river to Quimper.

BIENASSIS CHÂTEAU (22)   *15k NNE Lamballe*
17th century château, the ground floor of which may be visited. There is a double moat and delightful 'French' gardens.

LA BOURBANSAIS ZOO PARK (35)   *15k SE Dinan*
Here you can combine your visit to an excellent zoo with a visit to the delightful Renaissance château in the grounds of which the zoo is situated. See also the stud farm and the pack of fifty hounds.

BRANFÉRÉ ZOO PARK (56)
31k ESE Vannes, near le Guerno
Lively zoo with over 2000 animals and birds at liberty in a large park with trees and ponds. Do not miss a visit here.

BREST (29)   *592k W Paris, 245k W Rennes*
Very badly damaged during the second world war, Brest has been rebuilt in fine style, befitting its position as one of France's principal naval ports. There are fine views over the beautiful roadstead, especially from the Cour Dajot, on the old ramparts. The naval dockyard and arsenal are probably only open to French citizens, but foreign visitors should not miss a trip across the roadstead to Quélern or Le Fret, or out to the island of Ushant (Ouessant).

CAMARET (29)   *66k S Brest*
This colourful little fishing port is France's most important lobster centre. The Pointe de Pen Hir to the south-west is a magnificent viewpoint. There are several well sheltered beaches nearby.

CANCALE (35)   *14k E St-Malo*
Small fishing port and seaside resort, noted for its oysters and its fine views out over the bay of Mont-St-Michel. Boat Club, sailing school, skin diving school and also water-ski training.

CAP FREHEL (22)   *38k W Dinard*
High red and black cliffs tower over the sea, and there are fine views, especially from the lighthouse (Open when official duties permit). On a headland 4 kilometres to the south east is Fort la Latte, a medieval castle, restored in the 17th century, and worth visiting.

CARADEUC CHÂTEAU (35)   *21k SSE Dinan,*
1k W Bécherel
Handsome 17th century château in an extensive park.

CARHAIX-PLOUGUER (29)   *47k SE Morlaix*

Bustling little market town and a route centre of the Finistère peninsula since Roman times. This is largely unspoilt by tourist development and is consequently full of character.

CARNAC (56)   *31k W Vannes*

Lively holiday resort with splendid long beach, protected by the Quiberon peninsula. Carnac is perhaps better known as the centre of Brittany's outstandingly interesting prehistoric past. In the town there is a Museum of Prehistory and a prehistoric burial mound (or tumulus) which can be explored... but it is to the immediate north east that the great megalithic stone 'alignments' stand... see especially the Lines of Ménec... over a kilometre in length and thirty metres wide.

Prehistoric 'Alignment' near Carnac

CHÂTEAULIN (29)   *28k N Quimper*

Pleasant small town in wooded country on a bend of the river Aulne, the banks of which are lined by quays, and which is noted for its salmon. Come here at spawning time and you will see salmon leaping the weirs in their brave fight to reach their spawning grounds upstream.

COMBOURG (35)   *24k E Dinan*

This little town is dominated by the great château in which the poet and writer Châteaubriand spent two years of his early life, and there is a small Châteaubriand Museum within. The château is romantically sited overlooking a broad lake.

The Lines of Ménec, near Carnac

CONCARNEAU (29)   *23k SE Quimper*

This busy fishing port is one of the world's great centres for tunny, and the harbours are well worth visiting. See also the interesting Fishing Museum and the attractive streets of the old walled town, which is built on an island, only linked to the mainland by two small bridges. There are lovely beaches just outside the town.

DINAN (22)   *370k W Paris, 51k NW Rennes*

An old town built on a cliff at the head of the Rance estuary, with a small harbour below. It has an old castle, town walls and old streets centred upon the twin squares of the Cordeliers and the Apport. See also the partly Romanesque church of St-Sauveur and, below the walls, the lovely terraced gardens overlooking the Rance.

DINARD (35)   *373k W Paris, 72k NW Rennes*

Elegant and still fashionable seaside resort in a splendid setting at the mouth of the Rance estuary opposite St-Malo. There are several sandy beaches, one facing the estuary, and the others, the sea. There is a Marine Museum and aquarium. Take the ferry across to St-Malo, an excursion by water to Cap Frehel, or to the tidal powerhouse on the Rance estuary.

Combourg Château   *On Concarneau Quay*

DOL-DE-BRETAGNE (35)   *24k SE St-Malo*

Small town with an early Gothic cathedral, built largely with funds provided by King John of England in reparation for his having burnt down the original Romanesque building. Do not miss the fascinating carved arm rests on the eighty 14th century choir stalls. There are fine views of the granite mound of Mont Dol, 3 kilometres to the north, from the Promenade des Douvres just behind the cathedral.

Dinan Château

Brittany

Douarnenez   Tréboul

Douarnenez Bay

Low tide at Erquy

Medieval strength at
Fougères

Guimiliau Calvary

DOUARNENEZ AND TRÉBOUL (29)

22k NW Quimper

Douarnenez is a busy fishing port, noted for its sardines and crayfish, and it has two sailing schools and a genuine nautical flavour to its quays and narrow streets. This is complemented by the lively, more conventional holiday resort of Tréboul, to which it is connected by a bridge across the Pouldavid estuary.

ERQUY (22)

40k W Dinard

Small fishing port and seaside resort in an attractive bay, with fine beaches overlooked by pine topped cliffs.

LE FAOU (29)

30k SW Brest

Minute town at the head of the Faou estuary, with many pleasant old houses overhanging its streets.

FOUGÈRES (35)

300k W Paris, 47k NE Rennes

This is largely an industrial town, but is worth visiting for its great castle, which once controlled much of the frontier between Brittany and France. Visitors may walk right round the massive wall, which has no less than eleven towers. See also the Flamboyant Gothic church of St-Sulpice.

GUÉHENNO (56)

20k NNE Vannes

Minute village with a remarkable 16th century calvary to its immediate south. Do not miss this.

GUIMILIAU (29)

18k SW Morlaix

This small village is famed for the beauty and interest of its parish close (See Page 74). The 16th century Calvary includes over two hundred figures, and the church porch has wonderfully detailed sculpture-work. See also the interior of the church with its 17th century pulpit and font cover.

GUINGAMP (22)

31k WNW St-Brieuc

Charming old town on the river Trieux, with some of its medieval walls surviving and many narrow streets within them. Parts of the 15th century castle are also still standing and there is a fine Gothic and Renaissance basilica, which is the site of one of the great Pardons of Brittany (on the 1st Saturday in July).

HENNEBONT (56)

10k NE Lorient

Charming little fortified town at the head of the Blavet estuary. The gateway and ramparts suffered considerable damage during the 39 – 45 war, but they are still of interest. The 16th century church of Notre-Dame-de-Voeu has a Flamboyant Gothic tower topped by a tall spire, which looks out over the wide town square. It is possible to visit the impressive local stud farm.

HUELGOAT (29)

29k S Morlaix

Small quiet town in a countryside of boulders, rocks and woodlands, a spendid area to explore on foot, and much in contrast to some of the crowded coastal resorts. Use Michelin Map 58, and if possible the Michelin Green Guide, which provides detailed suggestions for a variety of walks around Huelgoat.

JOSSELIN (56)

72k W Rennes

This small town is romantically sited on the banks of the canalised river Oust. The great medieval castle of the Rohan family stands above the river, its high curtain walls
Continued

concealing a gentler more domesticated range of buildings within. Behind the castle is the little town with its Flamboyant Gothic church and its attractive 17th century fountain.

KERJEAN CHÂTEAU (29) *28k W Morlaix*
Handsome early Renaissance building protected by a moat and ramparts. Part of the interior now houses a folk museum. Son et Lumière.

LAMBALLE (22) *55k WSW St-Malo*
Small town dominated by its handsome, partly fortified collegiate church, from the terrace of which there are fine views out over the surrounding countryside. There is an interesting stud farm here.

Reflections at Josselin

LANDERNAU (29) *11k ENE Brest*
Interesting old market town at the head of the Elorn estuary, with quays along the river banks overlooked by a pleasant bridge. The small 16th century church is dedicated to St-Thomas of Canterbury.

LANGONNET (56) *26k N Quimperlé*
There is an interesting zoo park at Le Harlay containing animals from five continents.

LANNION (22) *63k WNW St-Brieuc*
Busy market town with many attractive old streets and an interesting Romanesque and Gothic church founded by the Knights Templar on a hill to its immediate north.

LOCMARIAQUER (56) *31k SW Vannes*
Little fishing village and holiday resort situated near the end of a long peninsula between the sea and the Gulf of Morbihan. It is best known for the prehistoric chamber tombs (or dolmens) of Mané Lud, and the Merchant's Table; and the largest standing stone in France, The Great Menhir, which is broken into five pieces weighing about 350 tons each.

Kerjean Château

Lannion

LOCRONAN (29) *17k NW Quimper*
Charming little town situated on a steep hillside, with a pleasant square surrounded by handsome granite houses, many dating back to the Renaissance. These signs of past prosperity are due to the importance of Locronan as a centre for the making of sailcloth for the navy. See the 15th century Penité chapel near the church and the museum depicting Breton life and work.

Wood carver at Lannion

LORIENT (56) *146k SW Rennes*
This great naval, commercial and fishing port was virtually destroyed during the 39 – 45 war, but has since been rebuilt with panache (See especially the Dame-de-la-Victoire church, the Town Hall and the Place Alsace-Lorraine). Foreigners are probably not allowed to visit the famous submarine base, but you should not miss the Keroman fishing port, nor an excursion by boat to Belle-Île or the Île de Groix.

MALESTROIT (56) *35k ENE Vannes*
Little medieval town on the banks of the canalised river Oust, along which there are pleasant walks. The church of St-Gilles is of the 12th and 16th centuries, and its south doorway is of particular interest. There are several Gothic and Renaissance houses close to the church, several of which have carvings upon their
Continued

Fishing boats at Lorient

Brittany

Old house at Morlaix

Drying the fishing nets

Net makers in traditional costume

The Calvary at Guimiliau

Details from the Calvary
at Guimiliau

Perros-Guirec

façades (Do not miss the one depicting a man in his nightshirt beating his wife).

MORBIHAN, GULF OF (56)   *S of Vannes*

This fascinating inland sea, swept by high swirling tides, is best explored by boat, and excursions can be taken from Vannes, Locmariaquer or Auray. There are many oyster beds and fishing is still a flourishing local industry. To capture the true flavour of the area, read the delightful 'Oyster River' by George Millar (Pub. Bodley Head).

MORGAT (29)   *58k NW Quimper*

Charming seaside resort on the northern shore of the Bay of Douarnenez, with a long sandy beach and a small harbour still used by tunny fishermen. Walk southwards to the lighthouse which may be visited, or take a boat trip beyond this point to the sea cave of 'l'Autel'.

MORLAIX (29)   *532k W Paris, 59k NE Brest*

This town is attractively sited in a deep valley at the head of the Dossen estuary and is dominated by its great viaduct. Much of the town is inevitably built on slopes, and this gives great character to many of its old streets and alleyways, which should be explored on foot.

PAIMPOL (22)   *46k NNW St-Brieuc*

Fishing town and holiday resort with its pleasant harbour at the head of a deep-set sandy bay. Oysters are cultivated on a large scale here and there are fine views from the Tour de Kerroc'h, three kilometres to the north-east. Drive three kilometres south-east to visit the extensive ruins of the 13th century abbey of Beauport, in a beautiful setting not far from the shore.

PAIMPONT (35)   *40k SW Rennes*

Small village set beside a pool in enchanting woodland country, with pine and fir perhaps more plentiful than the older beech and ash. Also visit the village of Les Forges, the châteaux of Comper and Trécesson, and the valleys of Serein and La Chèze.

PARDONS

These are a form of pilgrimage unique to Brittany, and every town, village and hamlet has one at some time during the year... although most are held in the summer, and are well worth attending. Details, including dates, in Brittany leaflet available from FGT offices.

PARISH CLOSES AND CALVARIES

Together these form a typical monumental group to be found all over Brittany. The close is built round the cemetery, often entered through a triumphal arch, and comprises the church, the calvary, and the ossuary or bone-house. The calvaries of Brittany were built and elaborated over several centuries, and are full of fascinating sculptural detail.

PERROS-GUIREC (22)   *11k N Lannion*

Lively holiday resort with a number of beaches separated by rocky headlands. There is a wide variety of hotels and restaurants, making this an ideal place from which to explore western Brittany. The twenty eight kilometre long 'Corniche Bretonne' runs along the coast

Continued

from here, and around to Trébeurden, and provides a splendid series of sea views over granite rocks and small sandy bays. Use Michelin Map 59, and the Michelin Green Guide for details.

Young Bretons at Pont-Aven *An older Breton at Pont L'Abbé*

PLEUMEUR-BODOU SPACE COMMUNICATION STATION (22) *9k NW Lannion*
This is the French equivalent of Britain's Goonhilly Downs 'Earth Station'. It provides multi-channel radio links to various parts of the world via earth satellites, and it was one of the points from which communications were first made via Telstar in 1962. The great dish aerials are most impressive, and at the time of writing it is still possible to visit the station during the summer months.

PLEYBEN (29) *10k ENE Châteaulin*
Small town with an outstandingly interesting parish close complete with 18th century triumphal arch, charnel house, and the largest calvary in Brittany. The church itself is also worth visiting.

PLOUGASTEL-DAOULAS (29) *8k E Brest*
In this village at the entrance to the unspoilt peninsula of Plougastel, with its strawberry fields, narrow roads and heavily indented coastline, will be found one of Brittany's outstanding calvaries (See Page 74).

Pontivy Fortress

PONT AVEN (29) *37k NW Lorient*
Attractive little town, in a deep wooded valley, at the point where the river Aven opens out into an estuary. This was the seat of the Pont Aven 'school' of painters... the best known of whom was Gauguin.

PONT L'ABBÉ (29) *19k SSW Quimper*
A small market town of considerable character with the dammed-up waters of the Pont-L'Abbé river providing attractive sheets of water to the immediate north of the château, which houses a local folklore museum.

Quiberon

PONTIVY (56) *64k SSW St-Brieuc*
Small town on the river Blavet, at the point where it is joined by the Nantes-Brest Canal. The medieval part of the town is grouped around its ancient fortress which has been recently restored, and there are narrow streets lined with half timbered houses. The 'new town' was built on a grid plan on the orders of Napoleon for strategic reasons and for a short time was known as Napoléonville.

QUIBERON (56) *46k SW Vannes*
Pleasant family holiday resort at the end of the long Quiberon Peninsula. Busy sardine port, long sandy beaches, boat trips to the Gulf of Morbihan, and Belle Île.

Quimper Cathedral *Old houses near Quimper Cathedral*

QUIMPER (29) *207k W Rennes*
Pleasant old cathedral town situated in a small valley, at the tidal limit of the river Odet. The ancient capital of the medieval kingdom and then duchy of La Cornouaille, Quimper is now the capital of Finistère Département. See the fine Gothic cathedral (the spires are 19th century additions), the old houses on the Place Terre-au-Duc, the Museum of Fine Arts, the Breton Museum, and visit one of the working potteries, carrying on Quimper's long ceramic traditions. Take a boat trip down the Odet to Benodet.

Brittany

Breton pipers at Quimperlé

The Palais St-Georges, Rennes

The Thabor Gardens, Rennes

At Roscoff

QUIMPERLÉ (29)   *20k NW Lorient*
Attractively sited at the junction of two rivers, Quimperlé is a charming little town with two interesting churches and several old houses.

REDON (35)   *57k E Vannes*
Small market town on the Vilaine, crossed here by the Nantes-Brest Canal. The 12th century tower of the church of St-Sauveur is particularly impressive and in the 13th century choir below there is a beautiful high altar, a gift from Cardinal Richelieu.

RENNES (35)   *347k W Paris*
Important industrial town and both the administrative and cultural capital of Brittany, Rennes was largely destroyed by fire in 1720, and most of its buildings post date this disastrous event. However part of 'old Rennes' survives and its quaint narrow streets should be explored. Another building to survive was the splendid 17th century Courts of Justice, built by de Brosse, the architect of the Luxembourg Palace in Paris. Do not miss this, nor the lovely Thabor Gardens, the early 19th century cathedral, the Museums of Fine Art Archaeology, and of Breton Art, and the 15th century Porte Mordelaise, Rennes' only surviving town gate.

ROCHEFORT-EN-TERRE (56)   *34k E Vannes,*
                                       78k SW Rennes
Pleasant old village (or small town) built on a high promontory between two valleys, with a covered market, a street of 16th and 17th century houses, an interesting church, and a ruined castle.

ROCHERS CHÂTEAU (35)   *6k SE Vitré*
14th century château remodelled in the 17th century, with extensive gardens, laid out by the famous Le Nôtre. It is best known as one of the homes of Madame de Sévigné, whose letters describe her life here so vividly.

ROSCOFF (29)   *560k W Paris, 63k NE Brest*
This small fishing port and seaside resort is now also a ferry town, with daily crossings to and from Plymouth for cars and passengers. Once the lair of privateers, and more recently the home town of many of those famous bicycle-borne onion sellers, Roscoff remains a town of great character, with many old houses, a 16th century church and a splendid aquarium. Excursion to the nearby Île de Batz with its many sandy beaches.

ROSANBO CHÂTEAU (22)   *15k SW Lannion*
Interesting château dating from the 14th century, with additions and alteration in the 17th and 19th centuries. It is well furnished with Breton and Florentine Renaissance furniture and the formal gardens were laid out by Le Nôtre. There are pleasant views out over the valley of the little river Bo from one of its terraces.

ST-BRIAC (35)   *10k W St-Malo*
Charming little seaside resort at the mouth of a small estuary, here crossed by a long bridge. There are good sands and an attractive little harbour.

ST-BRIEUC (22)   *58k W Dinan*
Pleasant market town and capital of the Côtes-du-Nord with the long white beach of Les Rosaires about eight kilometres to the north. The canalised river Gouët
continued

connects it with the little port of Légué. See the cathedral, the Town Hall with its small museum. and the many old houses close by.

ST-MALO (35)   *370k W Paris*
A most attractive seaport, with its old walled town guarding the entrance to the Rance estuary, opposite Dinard. The town wall was ruined in 1944, when the Germans refused to surrender to the Americans, but it has been rebuilt with loving care. Do not miss a walk around the walls (about 1 hour). Also visit the islet of Grand-Bé, where the poet Châteaubriand is buried, the castle, the former cathedral, and the port itself. Take the ferry across to Dinard, an excursion by boat to Cap Frehel, or to the tidal powerhouse on the Rance estuary.

Yachts at St-Malo

ST-POL-DE-LÉON (29)   *23k NW Morlaix*
Small town in prosperous market garden country, with an interesting former cathedral, and an outstandingly beautiful tower and spire to its Kreisker Chapel... a largely 15th century building.

ST-QUAY-PORTRIEUX (22)   *22k NNW St-Brieuc*
St-Quay is a lively holiday resort with fine sandy beaches and Portrieux is a busy little harbour town, dealing both with fish, and the shipping of early vegetables to England.

ST-THÉGONNEC (29)   *13k SW Morlaix*
Here is a small village with a splendid parish close (See Page 74), including 17th century calvary, and an interesting church.

In St-Thégonnec Church

TRÉGUIER (22)   *61k NW St-Brieuc*
Small town on a hillside overlooking the Jaudy estuary, with a Gothic cathedral and cloisters... one of Brittany's most harmonious architectural groups. The writer Ernest Renan was born here, and his birthplace is open to visitors.

TRINITÉ-SUR-MER (56)   *30k WSW Vannes*
Pleasant holiday village on the shore of the Crac'h estuary, with a long sandy beach and a sheltered fishing and pleasure harbour. There are some excellent restaurants here, making it an ideal port of call for hungry yachtsmen.

St-Thégonnec Calvary   *Trinité-sur-Mer Harbour*

VANNES (56)   *106k SW Rennes*
Busy agricultural and tourist centre, Vannes has retained a fine stretch of its old walls, at the foot of which lie lovely gardens, which are floodlit during the season. See the interesting cathedral, the Place Henri IV, with its old gabled houses, and narrow streets and alleys nearby, and the outstanding Archaeological Museum in the Château Gaillard. Vannes lies immediately inland of the fascinating Gulf of Morbihan, and several boat excursions may be taken from here.

VITRÉ (35)   *35k E Rennes*
The medieval walled town is set on a spur overlooking the valley of the Vilaine, with a fine castle at its head. See especially the castle itself with its three museums, the 15th century church, and the 15th century St-Nicholas Hospital, below the castle to the north of the river.

Ramparts at Vannes   *Vitré*

Burgundy

Comprises the following Départements:
Côte-d'Or (21)   Saône-et-Loire (71)
Nièvre (58)   Yonne (89)

This wonderful region is rich in artistic treasures… in its cities, towns and villages, its prehistoric and Roman sites, and its châteaux and abbeys. It has great areas of gently rolling countryside, and extensive wooded hills, notably in the Morvan. It has some of the world's most famous vineyards, splendid rivers like the Sâone and the Yonne, and several entrancing canals. Its hospitable people have brought the art of eating and drinking to near perfection, and in their shops, restaurants and hotels, will be found a most civilized appreciation of these good things of life. Burgundy, astride the great Autoroute A6, is easy to reach from the channel ports, and once over the great watershed on the hills to the north of Beaune, one feels that the warmth and colour of the Mediterranean world is already within reach. Resist the feeling and linger in Burgundy… you will be amply rewarded.

ALISE-SAINTE-REINE (21)   *15k SE Montbard*

This village is dominated by Mont Auxois, on which stands Millet's immense statue of Vercingetorix, the Celtic chieftain defeated and then besieged by Julius Caesar in 52 BC. See the Gallo-Roman remains, both in the field and in the museum… also the Carolingian and Romanesque church, restored in 1965.

ANCY-LE-FRANC (89)   *53k E Auxerre*

Splendid 16th century Renaissance castle, with lovely courtyard and a series of magnificently decorated and furnished apartments.

ARCY-SUR-CURE CAVES (89)   *33k SSE Auxerre*

A fine series of caves just to the south of Arcy village, with a small lake of emerald green water inside near the entrance, and many well illuminated stalactites.

Ancy-le-Franc

ARNAY-LE-DUC (21)   *57k WSW Dijon*

Minute town in the Arroux valley, with a 15th-18th century church and a massive 15th century tower… all that remains of a great medieval castle largely destroyed during the Wars of Religion.

AUTUN (71)   *290k SE Paris*

Interesting old town with wooded country to the south and the great *Morvan* forests not far to the north. The Roman town of Augustodonum was of great importance, and there are the remains of two gateways, a large amphitheatre, and an impressive temple. The splendours of the cathedral are due to its having housed relics of St-Lazare (Lazarus)… outstanding medieval carvings. See also the Lapidary Museum and the Rolin Museum.

Temple of Janus, Autun   *Distant view of Autun*

AUXERRE (89)   *167k SE Paris*

Lovely medieval city on the River Yonne, best viewed from the right bank. See especially St-Etienne cathedral, with its Romanesque crypt and beautiful stained glass; St-Germain abbey church which has a 9th century crypt with Carolingian murals; several other churches and charming 15th and 16th century houses in the old boatmen's quarter. Many cherry orchards in the surrounding countryside.

AUXONNE (21)   *32k SE Dijon*

A pleasant town on the banks of the Saône (camping, swimming, boating), with fortifications partly built by Vauban. Napoleon served here as a young 2nd lieutenant, and there is an interesting Bonaparte Museum in the château.

The Place St-Nicholas, Auxerre

Quiet street in Avallon
Photograph by
Peter Titchmarsh

Courtyard of the
Hostellerie de la Poste,
Avallon
Photograph by
Peter Titchmarsh

The Hospice, Beaune

In the Hospice Kitchen,
Beaune

The Hôtel-Dieu, Beaune.
Photograph by Peter Titchmarsh

Berzé-le-Château

Brancion

AVALLON (89)   224k SE Paris
Delightful old fortified town with ramparts overlooking the deep Cousin valley toward the wooded hills of the *Morvan*. See St-Lazare church, with its fine Romanesque doorways, the attractive clock tower, once a town gate, and the interesting museum.

AZÉ CAVE (71)   20k NNW Mâcon
This is on the north side of the village of Azé, and has a stream running through it. A small museum in the village displays prehistoric and Gallo-Roman items discovered here.

BEAUMONT-SUR-VINGEANNE CHÂTEAU (21)
                                              34k NE Dijon
Charming little 18th century château, built by Claude Jolyot, a royal chaplain, with a series of elegantly furnished and decorated rooms, and standing in a small, delightfully landscaped park.

BEAUNE (21)   315k SE Paris
This lovely old city is situated in the heart of the Burgundy vineyards, and the fascinating Hôtel-Dieu, a Gothic building founded in 1443 for the shelter of poor and sick people, remains richly endowed with the wealth that several of the most famous vineyards produce. In the Hôtel-Dieu, see the furniture, the kitchens, the copperware, the pharmacy... still all intact. Also visit the wine cellars, some of which are in casemates of the old ramparts; the Wine Museum, Notre Dame collegiate church, and the fine collection of tapestries in the adjoining hall. The Hospice de la Charité also benefits from the sale of the local wines, and should be visited, as also the Fine Arts Museum and the Museum of Burgundy Crafts in the same building as the Hôtel de Ville.

BERZÉ-LE-CHÂTEAU (71) *16k NW Mâcon 8 k S Cluny*
This pleasant medieval château is situated on a slope amongst the vineyards of the Mâconnais and there are fine views from its terraces which may be visited during the holiday period.

BLANOT CAVES (71)   28k NNW Mâcon
These are a series of caves in the slopes of Mont Romain just to the north of the village of Blanot and are worth visiting.

BOURBON-LANCY (71)   72k SE Nevers
Small spa town with views out over the Loire valley from its hilly site. See especially the museum in the old church of St-Nazaire, the 15th century clock tower and fortified gateway, and the 'wooden house' of about the same date.

BRANCION (71)   15k WSW Tournus
Attractive little hill village dominated by an interesting medieval castle which may be visited. There is a communal bakehouse which was used up to the 1930's, and several houses dating back to the 15th century. The late 12th century church contains some fine 14th century wall paintings.

BUSSY-RABUTIN CHÂTEAU (21)   *16k SE Montbard*
Fine 17th century mansion, with elegant garden front, and beautiful interior decoration, with many portraits of Bussy-Rabutin's contemporaries.

CHABLIS (89)   *20k E Auxerre*
The attractive little town is the centre of the wine growing district that produces that rather special white wine... Chablis. The Chablis vineyards are the most northerly in France apart from those of Champagne. See the church of St-Martin, on one of whose doors are nailed votive offerings of horse-shoes, one of which may have come from Joan of Arc's horse.

Bussy Rabutin Château

CHALON-SUR-SAÔNE (71)   *338k SE Paris*
Busy industrial and commercial town, with a river port on the Saône. Canal du Centre links the Saône/Rhone system to the Loire. Unexceptional cathedral. Denon Museum (Denon was a great engraver and museums expert). Fine views from 15th century Doyenné Tower.

CHARITÉ-SUR-LOIRE (58)   *24k NNW Nevers*
This once busy river port is still a prosperous market town with a long tree-lined quay beside the east bank of the river. The abbey church of Notre-Dame, built by the Benedictines, was once the largest church in France after Cluny, although the western end of the nave was burnt down in 1599 and never replaced. However it remains a magnificent building, with its original Romanesque choir, and fine octagonal tower over its domed crossing.

The 'Salle des Grands Hommes', Bussy Rabutin

CHAROLLES (71)   *55k WNW Mâcon*
Small market town in the rolling, partly wooded countryside noted for the breeding of the famous Charolais cattle, many of which are now to be seen in the fields of England. There is a genuine flavour of rural France in its busy little streets.

CHÂTEAU-CHINON (58)   *37k WNW Autun*
Small town on the eastern edge of the Morvan (See Page 84), of which it is the 'capital'. There is a calvary and an 'Orientation Table' on the steep hill above it, and this is well worth climbing for its fine views out over the wooded hills of the Morvan.

Romanesque sculpture, Charité-sur-Loire

CHÂTEAUNEUF-EN-AUXOIS (21)   *50k SW Dijon*
Medieval castle dramatically sited on a hillside with views westwards to the Morvan hills. There is a drawbridge and five great towers, with some rooms shown to visitors. Attractive little village around it, with late medieval and early Renaissance houses.

CHATILLON-SUR-SEINE (21)
83k E Auxerre, 33k NE Montbard
Attractive little town, much damaged by an air raid in 1940, but well restored. Old streets, lime tree shaded promenade, and above all, the Archaeological Museum, which houses the fabulous 'Treasure of Vix', 6th century Graeco-Italian grave-goods from an Iron Age burial at Vix a few kilometres away... do not miss this.

Charité-sur-Loire

The Refectory, Cîteaux Abbey

Clamecy Church

Old house at Clamecy

Doorway at Clos Vougeot. Photograph by Peter Titchmarsh

Cluny Abbey

Vineyard near Cluny

Cormatin Château

CHAUMONT CHÂTEAU (71)
15k NE Charolles, 50k WNW Mâcon
A largely 19th century château with a 16th century east front. However it is the splendid 17th century stable building that is open to the public. At one time this housed 99 horses (it being the royal prerogative to stable 100 or more), and there is still accommodation for 18 horses together with a fine display of horse-drawn vehicles.

CÎTEAUX (21)
23k S Dijon
Little remains of the great abbey founded here in 1098, and from which grew the great Cistercian Order, the fame of which was largely created by St. Bernard who came here in 1114. However the Cistercians have returned and there are Gregorian chants to be heard in the chapel each Sunday morning at 10.45.

CLAMECY (58)
43k S Auxerre
Small town on the river Yonne. It was from here that logs from the Morvan forests were made up into great rafts for floating down to Paris, but regrettably this timber now goes by road. There is an interesting museum in the old town on its hill, with some good pictures and also some illustrations of the timber 'floatage' referred to above. Do not overlook the 13 – 15th century church of St-Martin.

CLOS VOUGEOT (21)
16k S Dijon
This well known Renaissance château amongst its vineyards was originally a 'clos' of nearby *Cîteaux Abbey*, and the great winepresses may still be seen in the 13th century cellars. Here no less than 15 banquets are held each year by the owners, the Chevaliers du Tastevin.

CLUNY (71)
24k NW Mâcon
This small town gave its name to the Cluniac order of monks, for it was in 910 that the great abbey was founded. The abbey church, built between 1088 and 1130, was the largest in Christendom until St. Peter's, Rome was built, but it was almost entirely demolished in the early 19th century. See the remains of the south transept, stone fragments in the abbey flour mill, and the Ochier Museum in the Abbot's House.

COMMARIN CHÂTEAU (21)
40k W Dijon
17th century moated château with fine facade. Do not miss splendid 16th century reredos in nearby church.

CORMATIN CHÂTEAU (71)
25k W Tournus
Charming Renaissance château in attractive countryside to the north of Cluny. There were once three wings making a 'U' shaped building around a central courtyard, but one of these has been demolished. There are some splendid 17th and 18th century interiors to be seen here.

COSNE-SUR-LOIRE (58)
52k NNW Nevers
Bright, bustling town on the Loire, which is joined here by the river Nohain. There is a Romanesque priory church and another church with an impressive square tower.

DECIZE (58)   *34k SE Nevers*

All the old part of this small town is situated on an island in the Loire, with steep streets and a church with a 7th century Merovingian crypt.

DIGOIN (71)   *92k SE Nevers*

Small pottery town on the Loire, here crossed by a fine aqueduct carrying a branch of the Canal du Centre over the river. There is good eating here in at least two establishments.

Fountain in Dijon

DIJON (21)   *312k SE Paris*

One of France's most interesting and historic towns, Dijon was from 1364 to 1477 the capital of the Dukes of Burgundy whose domain extended as far north as Flanders. It was one of the great centres of European civilization in the 15th century and ample evidence of this remains. See especially the Ducal Palace and Palace of States, the Fine Arts Museum, which is housed in these buildings, the cathedral, Notre-Dame church, St-Michel church, the Palais de Justice, and the monastery of Chartreuse de Champmol.

EPOISSES CHÂTEAU (21)   *25k E Avallon*

Fine Burgundian château-fort turned manor house, with an interesting interior including several tapestries. Madame de Sévigné often stayed here. Do not miss the vast dovecote, with its wooden ladder on a central pivot post, giving access to 3000 pigeon holes.

Tombs in the Ducal Palace, Dijon

FLAVIGNY-SUR-OZERAIN (21)   *19k SE Montbard*

A medieval village with ramparts. There is a Carolingian crypt to the abbey church incorporating Gallo-Roman pillars, probably from Alise-Sainte-Reine, and an interesting interior to the church of St-Genest. Flavigny and the surrounding countryside was praised by Chateaubriand, and painted by Augustus John and William Rothenstein.

FLEURIGNY CHÂTEAU (89)   *14k NNE Sens*

Delightful Renaissance château complete with conical capped towers, and surrounded by a moat complete with swans. There is a window in the chapel by the local craftsman Jean Cousin (1490 – 1560), who is best known for his work at Sens cathedral (See Page 86). Cousin was also responsible for the splendid mantlepiece in the guard room. Do not miss the forge and the dovecote, with its revolving ladder.

Old kitchen in the Ducal Palace, Dijon   *Distant view of Flavigny*

FONTENAY (21)   *5k NE Montbard*

Delightfully sited in a narrow wooded valley, Fontenay is the oldest Cistercian abbey in France, and the second foundation of St. Bernard who came here in 1118. Turned into a paper mill at the Revolution, it has been restored since 1906, and gives a very good impression of the Cistercian way of life. Fine forest country between here and Chatillon.

JOIGNY (89)   *147k SE Paris*

An unspoilt medieval town on the banks of the Yonne, with many sloping, narrow streets which are best explored on foot. Visit the churches of St-Thibault, St-André, and St-Jean, and walk across the 18th century bridge for a delightful view of the riverside with its quays and tree shaded towpath.

Cloisters at Fontenay Abbey

Memories of Lamartine at Mâcon

Les Settons in the Morvan (See Page 86)

The northern edge of the Morvan Forest from the ramparts of Avallon   Photograph by Peter Titchmarsh

Nevers

Craftsman at Nevers

The Porte de Croux, Nevers

MÂCON (71)   395k SE Paris

Busy commercial town on the banks of the Saône, which links it to the Mediterranean. Only the twin towers of the old cathedral survived the Revolution. The great poet and liberal Lamartine was born here, and there is a small museum largely devoted to him.

MONTBARD (21)   73k ESE Auxerre

Busy small town on the river Brenne and on the Canal du Bourgogne. Georges Buffon, the great naturalist, was born here in 1707, and on his retirement from the Royal Gardens in Paris, he returned to Montbard and created a fine park for himself around the ancient castle of the Dukes of Burgundy. This park is still well worth visiting and includes the little pavilion in which Buffon spent so many hours.

MONTCULOT CHÂTEAU (21)   24k WSW Dijon

Elegant 18th century manor house above the Ouche valley. This was inherited from his uncle by Lamartine and its quiet setting in the hills provided the poet with much inspiration during the first thirty years of the 19th century. This gentle, atmospheric place is not open very frequently.

MONTRÉAL (89)   13k NE Avallon

A medieval town splendidly sited on a spur overlooking the Serein valley, with ramparts and gateways enclosing a delightful mixture of 15th, 16th and 17th century houses. The church has a most interesting interior including carved pews and an exquisite 15th century reredos.

MORVAN REGIONAL NATURE PARK (21)(58)(71)
Approx. 250k SE Paris

175,000 hectares of heavily wooded upland country between Autun in the south west and Vézelay in the north east. Beech and oak predominate. There is sailing on Lac des Settons, Lac de St. Agnan, and Lac du Crescent. Never over 3,000 feet, it is ideal walking country.

Information: La Maison du Parc Naturel du
                      Morvan,
                      Saint-Brisson,
                      58230 Montsauche.

NEVERS (58)   240k S Paris

Busy town at the union of the Loire, the Nièvre and the Allier. See especially the cathedral, a mixture of styles from the 10th to the 16th century, the fine Romanesque church of St-Etienne, and the great Porte de Croux, a 14th century gate tower. The film 'Hiroshima mon Amour' featured many of Nevers' old streets, and these are well worth exploring.

NOYERS-SUR-SEREIN (89)   40k E Auxerre

Remarkably well preserved medieval town, with no fewer than 16 towers along its walls. Narrow streets and attractive little squares.

PANNESIÈRE-CHAUMARD BARRAGE (58)
13k N Château-Chinon

This is a great dam across the upper waters of the river Yonne, on the eastern edge of the wooded Morvan country (See above.) There are attractive minor roads around much of the large lake, which is best reached from Château-Chinon (Use Michelin Maps 65 and 69).

Burgundy   84

PARAY-LE-MONIAL (71)   70k W Mâcon

This is probably the second most popular place of pilgrimage in France... devoted to worship of the Sacred Heart. The priory church is a replica of Cluny abbey church, and is a fine Romanesque building.

PONTIGNY ABBEY (89)   20k NE Auxerre

This massive abbey was founded by the Cistercians in 1114, being only the second foundation by Cîteaux. In 1164 it provided shelter for Thomas-à-Becket after his quarrel with Henry II, and he stayed here for no less than six years. Stephen Langton also stayed here after his quarrel with King John, between 1208 and 1213. Do not miss a visit to this fine Romanesque church.

Paray-le-Monial   *Paray-le-Monial*

RATILLY CHÂTEAU (89)   60k SW Auxerre,
          28k NE Cosne-sur-Loire

Stout 13th century moated castle of red stone with four pepper-pot towers. The owners run pottery courses here throughout the summer, but it is also open to the public during the holiday season.

LA ROCHEPOT CHÂTEAU (21)   15k SW Beaune

15th century fortress based on the remains of an earlier castle and much restored at the end of the 19th century. However its high pitched roofs and pepperpot towers make a fine picture of late medieval Burgundy.

ROMANECHE ZOO PARK (71)
          15k SSW Mâcon, on N6

A good collection of animals and birds easily reached from the autoroute, via the Belleville or Mâcon South exits. There is a picnic area, play area, a little train, souvenir shop and bars.

Râtilly Château

ST-FARGEAU CHÂTEAU (89)   45k WSW Auxerre

Medieval castle transformed in the 17th century into a Renaissance château and further altered in the 18th century. There is a five sided courtyard and a grass covered moat, beyond which is a fine lake. It has retained its twin medieval towers and mellow brickwork.

ST-FLORENTIN (89)   45k SE Sens

Modest little town above the river Armance, with attractive streets leading up to its 14th – 17th century church, which contains some outstandingly beautiful stained glass. There are delicious views out over the valley from the tree shaded Priory Walk.

La Rochepot

ST-POINT CHÂTEAU (71)   25k W Mâcon

Partly medieval château restored by the poet, Lamartine. Visit his bedroom, study and salon. He and his English wife are buried in a chapel in the village nearby.

SAULIEU (21)   40k SE Avallon

Small town on the N6, with a reputation for gastronomic delights, and a 12th century collegiate church with a splendid series of carved capitals on the nave pillars. Museum displays work by sculptor Francois Pompon (born here 1855).

SAVIGNY-LES-BEAUNE (21)   5k N Beaune

Pleasant village with 14th century château housing an interesting Motor-Cycle Museum.

Lamartine's bedroom, at St-Point

Semur-en-Auxois   *Solutré Rock*

Tanlay Château

Tonnerre

SEINE, SOURCE OF THE (21)   *35k NW Dijon*
The Seine rises in a small valley planted with fir trees two kilometres west of the N71, Châtillon-Dijon road, and its source is enlivened by a statue of a nymph personifying the 'spirit of the Seine'. Archaeological excavations have revealed this to have been a site of religious significance since Bronze Age times.

SEMUR-EN-AUXOIS (21)   *40k E Avallon*
Delightful little town on a bend in the River Armaçon, with ramparts shaded by chestnut trees, and dominated by four circular 14th century towers. See also the lovely 13th century church and many charming old houses.

SEMUR-EN-BRIONNAIS (71)   *28k S Paray-le-Monial*
Charming village overlooking quiet countryside, with a 10th century castle and a handsome Romanesque church with an octagonal tower and a fine west portal.

SENS (89)   *120k SE Paris*
Roman provincial capital and a former bishopric, Sens remains a town of considerable interest. The splendid Gothic cathedral contains outstanding stained glass and has one of Europe's richest Treasuries. See also the Synodal Palace, and the Municipal Museum.

LES SETTONS (58)   *60k S Avallon*
This beautiful lake covers 360 hectares and is the most popular of several in the Morvan Regional Nature Park. Hire of sailing dinghies and canoes. Camping at Chevigny, and le Cernay.

SOLUTRÉ (71)   *8k W Mâcon*
A well known prehistoric site, which is situated below the escarpment of the great Solutré Rock. This stands 400 metres high, overlooking the famous Pouilly-Fuissé vineyards. Archaeological finds from here may be seen in the museum at Mâcon.

SULLY CHÂTEAU (71)   *15k ENE Autun*
Elegant Renaissance château surrounded by a wide moat and set in a large park. It is only possible to view the outside but it is a pleasure to look at the handsome front, with its square towers and five arched bridge over the moat.

TALMAY CHÂTEAU (21)   *37k E Dijon*
A largely 18th century building with a massive 13th century keep the only surviving feature of a medieval castle demolished in 1760. The interior of the keep is delightfully furnished and there are fine views from the top, especially south-eastwards to the Jura mountains.

TANLAY CHÂTEAU (89)   *9k E Tonnerre*
Splendid Renaissance château, surrounded by a moat, with woodlands close by. Magnificent interior decoration. This is Burgundy's finest château, and one of the loveliest in France.

TONNERRE (89)   *35k E Auxerre*
Small town on the Canal de Bourgogne. See the 'Old Hospital', founded by Margaret of Burgundy in 1293; the church of St-Pierre: and above the town, the Fosse Dionne, an attractive spring which supplied water from Roman times.

TOURNUS (71)   *27k S Chalon-sur-Saône*

Delightful town, with old stone quays on the banks of the Saône. Noted for its many pleasant eating places and its smart kitchen ware. However do not miss the splendid Romanesque abbey, with its fine west front and very impressive interior. 18th century pharmacy in the Hôtel-Dieu, and two other museums, one devoted to painter J. B. Greuze, born here 1725.

VÉZELAY (89)   *15k W Avallon*

Wonderfully preserved medieval hill-top town, with ramparts, town gates, and fine views from the castle terrace. However the crowning glory of Vézelay is its splendid church of Sainte-Madeleine… one of the great masterpieces of Romanesque art. Vézelay was a most important place of pilgrimage in the Middle Ages… St-Bernard preached the 2nd Crusade in 1146, and Philip Auguste and Richard the Lion Heart met here for the 3rd Crusade in 1190. The writer Romain Rolland spent his last years here.

VILLENEUVE-SUR-YONNE (89)   *13k S Sens*

Delightful little town with much of its medieval walls intact, including two fine gateways and a 12th century keep, the Tour Louis-le-Gros. See also the 18th century house, the Maison des Sept-Têtes and the Romanesque and Gothic church of Notre-Dame, with its handsome Renaissance facade, and interesting interior.

In Tournus Abbey   *Tournus Abbey*

GREAT WINE AREAS OF BURGUNDY (See Map)

CHABLIS. Situated between Tonnerre and Auxerre and centred upon the village of Chablis. Here is produced a crisp, dry wine, which is especially well suited for drinking with shell fish generally, and oysters in particular.

CÔTE-DE-NUITS. The south-eastward facing slopes of a narrow ridge running between Dijon and Nuits-St-Georges. These produce smooth, full red wines, including Chambertin, Clos-de-Vougeot, Musigny and Vosne-Romanée.

CÔTE-DE-BEAUNE. The south-eastward facing slopes of the ridge of hills extending south-west between Ladoix and Chagny, producing delicate red wines and some of the best white wines in the world. Aloxe-Corton, Pommard, Volnay, Meursault and Montrachet are some of the great names of the Côte-de-Beaune.

CÔTE-CHALONNAIS. This extends southwards along the low line of hills beyond the Côte-de-Beaune, from Chagny to Montagny. Agreeable red wines and dry white wines not up to the best of the wines from the côtes to the north, being lighter in quality, but also not quite as expensive.

MÂCONNAIS. In the low rolling hills to the immediate west of the Saône, from just north of Tournus to Pouilly-Fuissé, just south of Mâcon. The white wines from this area are better known than its reds, and the most renowned of the whites is Pouilly-Fuissé, a marvellous dry, fruity wine.

The Nave, Vézelay

Countryside near Vézelay

Burgundy

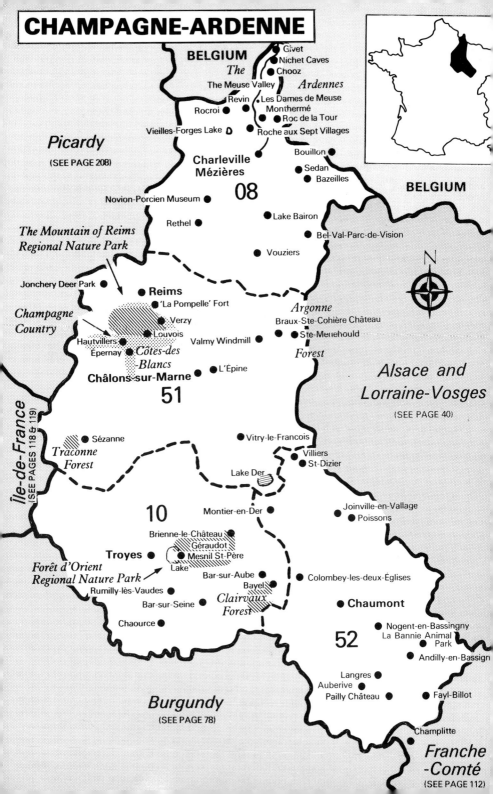

CHAMPAGNE-ARDENNE

BELGIUM

The

Givet
Nichet Caves
Chooz

The Meuse Valley

Ardennes

Revin · Les Dames de Meuse
Rocroi · Monthermé
Roc de la Tour

Vieilles-Forges Lake · Roche aux Sept Villages

Picardy
(SEE PAGE 208)

Bouillon

Charleville Mézières

Sedan
Bazeilles

08

BELGIUM

Novion-Porcien Museum

Lake Bairon

The Mountain of Reims Regional Nature Park

Rethel · Bel-Val-Parc-de-Vision

Vouziers

Joinchery Deer Park · **Reims**

Argonne

'La Pompelle' Fort

Braux-Ste-Cohière Château

Champagne Country

Verzy · Ste-Menehould

Louvois

Valmy Windmill

Forest

Hautvillers
Epernay · *Côtes-des-Blancs*

Châlons-sur-Marne

L'Épine

Alsace and Lorraine-Vosges
(SEE PAGE 40)

51

Île-de-France
(SEE PAGES 118 & 119)

Sézanne

Vitry-le-Francois

Villiers
St-Dizier

Traconne Forest

Lake Der

Joinville-en-Vallage
Poissons

10

Montier-en-Der

Brienne-le-Château
Géraudot

Troyes

Mesnil St-Père
Lake

Colombey-les-deux-Églises

Forêt d'Orient Regional Nature Park

Bar-sur-Aube
Bayel

Chaumont

Rumilly-lès-Vaudes
Bar-sur-Seine · *Clairvaux Forest*

52

Nogent-en-Bassingny
La Bannie Animal Park

Chaource · Andilly-en-Bassign

Langres
Auberive
Pailly Château · Fayl-Billot

Burgundy
(SEE PAGE 78)

Champlitte

Franche-Comté
(SEE PAGE 112)

N

Champagne-Ardenne

Comprises the following Départements:
Ardennes (08) Marne (51)
Aube (10) Haute Marne (52)

Interest in this region inevitably centres upon Reims and Épernay where the massive underground galleries (or caves) of all the great Champagne houses are to be found. However there are many other towns and cities worth visiting, including Châlons-sur-Marne, Troyes, Chaumont, Langres and Charleville-Mézières. There are also the great forests of the Ardennes and the Argonne, the lakes of Der-Chantecoq and Forêt d'Orient, and the wooded valleys of the Meuse and the Marne.

There is a Wildlife Park and two Regional Nature Parks, a Motor Museum and at least two Military Museums, and those who value the history of France will wish to visit the last resting place of Charles de Gaulle. In addition to the 'champagne' wine growing area centred upon Reims and Épernay, there is mile upon mile of gentle pastoral countryside punctuated by smiling villages and small towns, lakes, ponds and great woodlands. In short this is an ideal area for a family exploring holiday, with sufficient diversity to please everyone, and to provide a warm introduction to the real flavour of France and the French.

ANDILLY-EN-BASSIGNY (52) *18k NE Langres*
There are interesting Gallo-Roman remains just to the north of this small village in the hills of the Bassigny.

ARGONNE FOREST (51, 55) *40k E Châlons-s-Marne*
Richly wooded hill country lying on a north-south axis along the 'border' between the Champagne and the Verdun regions (See Alsace and Lorraine-Vosges section). This area, with its many ponds and caves, was a favourite of both Victor Hugo and Alexandre Dumas. Ste-Menehould, just off the A4 Autoroute, is an ideal starting point for explorations of the Argonne Forest, by car, or on foot.

Camp site at Bar-sur-Aube

AUBERIVE (52) *23k SE Langres*
Not far to the west of this village is the Auberive Boar Park. This is in fact three small reserves, one for fallow deer, one for roe deer and a third for wild boar.

BAIRON LAKE (08) *30k SSW Sedan*
Attractive lake, with swimming and sailing facilities, just to the north of the D947 Vouziers-Sedan road at le Chesne.

LA BANNIE ANIMAL PARK (52) *43k NW Langres*
A 250-acre park near Bourbonne-les-Bains, sheltering wild boar, fallow deer, and wild sheep.

BAR-SUR-AUBE (10) *53k E Troyes*
Attractive small market town, a few kilometres north of the Forest of Clairvaux.* There are two ancient churches, that of St-Pierre having an unusual wooden gallery around the outside.
St-Bernard's famous monastery is now a detention centre, and is not of interest.

BAR-SUR-SEINE (10) *33k SE Troyes*
This minute town has a Gothic and Renaissance church with an interesting interior. There are also the ruins of a medieval castle and several pleasant 16th, 17th and 18th century houses.

BAYEL (10) *60k E Troyes, beyond Bar-s-Aube*
Small village on the northern edge of the Forest of Clairvaux, with fine sculptures of the Virgin and Child in its church, and an interesting glass works (We are not sure if this can be visited and would suggest that you enquire locally).

BAZEILLES (08) *4k SE Sedan*
Small village with a charming Regency château, which has fine wrought-iron gates (grounds open to visitors).

Bazeilles Château

Continued

Châlons-sur-Marne Church

Mézières

Here also is the 'Maison des Dernières Cartouches' (the House of the Last Cartridges) the last position to be held in the village by heroic French troops in the Battle of Sedan (1870). This house may be visited.

BEL-VAL PARC DE VISION (08) *30k S Sedan*
Extensive wildlife Park, 30k east of Vouziers, just to the north of the D947. Here in splendidly wooded country will be found wild boar, deer, wild sheep, elk and bison. Motorists may take a 7 kilometre road through the most picturesque area.

BRAUX-STE-COHIÈRE CHÂTEAU (51)
6k W Ste-Menehould, 23k ENE Châlons-sur-Marne
Small 16th and 17th century château in mellow brick, with a regional museum in its octagonal dovecote and varying displays in the buildings around its courtyard.

BRIENNE-LE-CHÂTEAU (10) *40k ENE Troyes*
This village is renowned as the site of the Military College where Napoleon studied from 1779 to 1784, and there is an interesting Napoleonic Museum here. The handsome château dates from the 18th century, and is situated in a fine park. See also the interesting old timber-framed market hall.

The Place Ducale, Charleville

CHÂLONS-SUR-MARNE (51) *185k E Paris*
Large busy town and third only to Reims and Épernay as a champagne centre. It has a fine cathedral with an outstanding series of 16th century windows, and two interesting Romanesque churches... Notre-Dame-en-Vaux and St-Alpin. There are several elegant 18th century buildings and a pleasant series of tree shaded walks following the former lines of the ancient walls.

CHAMPAGNE ROAD, THE (51)
This is in fact comprised of three routes... The Blue, The Red and The Green... and together they cover most of the champagne growing areas lying between Reims and Épernay, and in the case of the Green Route, to the south of Épernay. Apply to Office de Tourisme, 3, boulevard de la Paix, 51100 Reims, for a copy of the excellent leaflet in English.

Friendly encounter on the Champagne Road
Photograph by Peter Titchmarsh

CHARLEVILLE-MÉZIÈRES (08) *224k NE Paris*
Until 1966 this was in fact two towns... Mézières was a medieval walled town situated on the south bank of the Meuse, while Charleville was established on the north bank in 1606, and is an interesting example of 17th century town planning. See especially the basilica of Notre Dame in Mézières, where Charles IX married Elizabeth of Austria in 1570; the elegant Ducal Square, which is the centre-piece of Charleville, the house where the poet Rimbaud was born in 1854 (14, rue Thiers), and the Museum of the Ardenne in the Vieux-Moulin.

CHAUMONT (52) *95k E Troyes*
Busy town built on a promontory between the rivers Suize and Marne which meet here. See especially the church of St-John the Baptist and the great railway viaduct crossing the Suize to the west of the town.

COLOMBEY-LES-DEUX-ÉGLISES (52)
27k WNW Chaumont
Here, on the northern edge of extensive forest country between the Aube and Marne rivers, you will come across the great pink granite cross of Lorraine, erected as a memorial to that great Frenchman, General Charles de Gaulle, who maintained a modest family home here. Also see the General's grave in the simple village churchyard.

Chaumont Viaduct

Champagne-Ardenne

DER LAKE (51)   *50k SE Châlons-s-Marne, beyond Vitry-le-François*
This splendid stretch of water is claimed to be the largest artificial lake in Europe. There are several access points, and good facilities for sailing, swimming and water-skiing.

ÉPERNAY (51)   *27k S Reims*
Attractive town in the Marne valley, and 'capital' of the Champagne producing area, with the great cellars of Möet et Chandon and Mercier both situated here. Visit the cellars, and also the Museums, both of Champagne and of Prehistory.

Épernay

L'EPINE (51)   *7k E Châlongs-s-Marne*
Small village with a fine late medieval pilgrimage church (built to house a miraculous statue of the Virgin found by shepherds in a thorn bush). Almost opposite the church will be found the Aux Armes de Champagne, a hotel which has provided us with several memorable meals.

FAYL-BILLOT (52)   *24k ESE Langres*
Small village in hilly country which is noted for its basketware. A National School of Basketware has been established here, and craftsmen can be seen at their fascinating work. See also Champlitte where there is an interesting Folklore Museum... only 20ks S, but in Franche-Comté (See Page 113).

Champagne Country near Épernay
Photograph by Peter Titchmarsh

FORÊT D'ORIENT REGIONAL NATURE PARK (10)   *20k E Troyes*
An extensive forest area, with a great lake lying mostly to its south and east. There are public sailing facilities at Mesnil St-Père, and sandy bathing beaches, both at Mesnil St-Père and at Géraudot. The quieter parts of the lake are excellent for bird watching.

GIVET (08)   *55k N Charleville-Mézières*
This is in effect two little towns separated by the lovely river Meuse, and is situated close to the Belgian border. The Nichet caves (3k SE) may be visited with a guide in summer. The Nuclear Power Station at Chooz (6k S) may, we believe, be visited on request.

HAUTVILLERS (51)   *3k N Épernay*
Attractive village in the Marne valley, just south of the wooded 'Mountain of Reims' Nature Park. It was in the abbey here that Dom Perignon perfected the formula for producing 'champagne', in the latter half of the 17th century and he is buried in the parish churchyard here.

Hautvillers... the abbey where Dom Perignon 'discovered' champagne

JOINVILLE-EN-VALLAGE (52)   *30k SE St-Dizier*
Small town on a hill above the Marne, with the remains of an old castle, and an elegant 16th century château. In the valley there are attractive rows of old houses beside the water, giving, in the words of a local guide, 'aquatic perspectives which remind one of Bruges or Amsterdam'.

JONCHERY DEER PARK (51)   *17k W Reims on N31*
The 'Parc aux Daims' has pleasant woodlands, with deer, sheep, ducks and swans, and is complete with antique shop and bar.

Sailing boats on Fôret d'Orient Lake

The Meuse at Givet

91

Renaissance houses at Langres

The Meuse, between Revin and Fumay (North of Monthermé)

The Meuse at Monthermé

Montier-en-Der Church

LANGRES (52)   *285k SE Paris*

Fascinating fortified town on a high plateau with splendid views out over the Marne valley. Four kilometres of ancient walls surround a town of old cobbled streets, and there are six gateways and seven fine medieval towers. See especially the Cathedral of St-Mammes and the two museums. The author and philosopher Diderot was born at Langres in 1713.

THE MEUSE VALLEY
(NORTH OF CHARLEVILLE-MÉZIÈRES) (08)

The road northwards from Charleville-Mézières to Revin, and onwards to Givet on the Belgian border, follows the course of the lovely Meuse, through the richly wooded country of the Ardennes. There are many dramatic rocky sites, notably Les Dames de Meuse, north of Monthermé, and several old forts and châteaux, but it is the river itself and the glorious forest country that provides most pleasure here.

MONTHERMÉ (08)   *17k N Charleville-Mézières*

This is not an outstanding village, but it is beautifully situated on a bend in the Meuse not far from its confluence with the Semoy. Ask locally for directions to the Roche aux Sept Villages, the Roc de la Tour, and Les Dames de Meuse (Ref. Michelin Map No 53... an invaluable companion for your exploration of this lovely Ardennes countryside).

MONTIER-EN-DER (52)   *24k SSW St. Dizier*

A village eight kilometres south of the Der Lake, with an abbey church dating back to the 10th century, and a National Horse Breeding Centre.

THE MOUNTAIN OF REIMS REGIONAL NATURE PARK (51)

This is an attractive forest area lying to the south of Reims. Perhaps the single most interesting feature is the 'Faux de Verzy' a large group of unique trees, with umbrella shaped tops, believed to be developed from a mutation in the structure of the common beech. Verzy is 15k SE of Reims. Children will enjoy a visit to the Pony Club at Louvois, 17k SSE of Reims.

NOGENT-EN-BASSIGNY (52)   *24k SE Chaumont*

Situated on a hillside overlooking a wide valley, in pleasantly wooded country, this village is noted for the manufacture of surgical instruments and 'artistic cutlery' (It is possible to visit some of the workshops concerned). There is an interesting prehistoric chambered tomb near the village... the dolmen, 'De la Pierre Alot'.

NOVION-PORCIEN MUSEUM OF THREE WARS (08)   *50k NE Reims, beyond Rethel*

Here will be found a most interesting War Museum, with an accent on the Battle of the Ardennes... the last great battle of World War II.

PAILLY CHÂTEAU (52)   *10k SE Langres*

A largely Renaissance château incorporating the remains of an earlier feudal castle. A fine example of the Renaissance period, this building is unfortunately (at the time of writing) not open.

POISSONS (52)   *7k ESE Joinville*
Delightful little village in a quiet wooded valley, with a mill on its trout stream, an interesting parish church, and a hairpin bending road up through 'Little Switzerland' just to the north (This is used for hill climbs during the latter half of August).

'LA POMPELLE' FORT (51)   *9k SE Reims (On N 44)*
This is an interesting museum devoted to the 1914 – 1918 War housed in an old fort, the contents of which include a unique collection of German helmets... no fewer than five hundred of them.

REIMS (51)   *150k ENE Paris*
Important and historic city, whose origins date back to pre-Roman (Celtic) times. There was a Roman

The Roman 'Gate of Mars', Reims

provincial capital here, and the 3rd century 'Gate of Mars' is an impressive reminder of this period. The great 13th century Gothic cathedral is on the site of an earlier building where Clovis, the first Christian king of France was baptized in 496, and most of the kings of France were crowned here. See especially the western façade, with its splendid rose windows and lovely statuary. While in Reims be sure to visit at least one or two of the cellars belonging to the great Champagne houses, such as Mumm, Piper-Heidsieck, or Tattinger (Details from the Syndicat d'Initiative). See also the Art Gallery in the Abbey of St-Denis which is especially memorable for its tapestries and pictures; the Palais du Tau which houses the treasures of the cathedral and a Coronation Museum; the Abbey of St-Remi; and the interesting 'Le Vergeur' Museum. The room where General Eisenhower received the German surrender in 1945 is also worth visiting.

Cathedral and Bishop's Palace, Reims

ROCROI (08)   *30k NW Charleville-Mézières*
This 16th century village is a perfect example of a star-shaped fortification with streets radiating from its central square.

RUMILLY-LÈS-VAUDES (10)   *22k SE Troyes*
Small village on the northern edge of extensive woodlands, looking out over the broad Seine valley. See the fine 16th century church, and the old manor house with its exterior timber gallery and four round towers (This is now the 'town hall'). Drive south-west through lovely forest country to Chaource.

ST-DIZIER (52)   *85k NE Troyes*
Industrial town, with a 'New Town' begun only in 1952 close by. See the church of St-Martin, and at Villiers-en-Lieu (4k NW) the splendid Motor Museum in a modern purpose-built setting.

13th century sculpture, Reims Cathedral

West front, Reims Cathedral

SEDAN (08)   *20k SE Charleville-Mézières*
Ancient citadel town on the Meuse, lying at the foot of the beautifully wooded Ardennes, and now considerably industrialised. It claims to have the largest fortified castle in Europe and this is open to visitors.

SEMOY, VALLEY OF
This river joins the Meuse at Monthermé, north of Charleville-Mézières, in the heart of the deeply wooded Ardennes. There is an attractive minor road following up the valley into Belgium, and on to Bouillon, from here one can drive south over the border back to Sedan in France.

Old manor house at Rumilly

Fortifications at Sedan

Champagne-Ardenne

Troyes

Troyes Cathedral

Old street in Troyes

Valmy Windmill

Grapes for Moët-et-
Chandon

In the Cellars of Möet et
Chandon, Épernay

SÉZANNE (51) *57k SW Châlons-sur-Marne*
Pleasant little market town to the north east of the lovely Traconne Forest. It has a Flamboyant Gothic church with a fine Renaissance tower and an interesting interior. There is a wide promenade following the line of the old ramparts, from which there are attractive views over the nearby vineyards.

TROYES (10) *157k ESE Paris*
Ancient city on the Seine, with Gallic and Roman origins, Troyes became prosperous during the Middle Ages owing to the number of great fairs held there. This prosperity lasted well into the Renaissance period and Troyes is rich in both medieval and Renaissance art. Its cathedral, its many churches and its Renaissance houses are especially rich in sculpture and stained glass. See especially the cathedral, the basilica of St-Urbain, the churches of Ste-Madeleine and St-Pantaléon, the Museum of Fine Arts, the Museum of Modern Art, the houses of Marisy, Ursins, Mauroy and Vaulisant; and the old narrow streets with their oversailing timber-framed houses.

VALMY WINDMILL (51) *30k ENE Châlons-s-Marne*
This famous landmark celebrates the first victory of the Revolutionary forces in 1792, and the reconstructed windmill overlooks the Autoroute de l'Est from its slight rise to the north.

VIEILLES-FORGES LAKE (08)
15k NW Charleville-Mézières
Beautiful lake in wooded country on the edge of the Ardennes Forest, with facilities for swimming and sailing.

VOUZIERS (08) *56k ENE Reims*
Small market town on the river Aisne, with a 16th century church which has a fine Renaissance triple portal.

'CHAMPAGNE COUNTRY'
The finest vineyards of Champagne are situated within twenty five kilometres of Épernay and although the splendid city of Reims is also greatly involved in the production of this delectable sparkling wine, Épernay is the true Champagne 'capital'. Dark skinned grapes are used largely in the Montagne de Reims area and in the Marne valley, while white grapes are used in the area to the south and west of Épernay, hence its name... the Côtes-des-Blancs.

Vendage in Champagne *Photograph by Peter Titchmarsh*

Visit to the Champagne Country
Photograph by Peter Titchmarsh

Corsica

This outstandingly lovely island cries out to be explored. Here are a thousand kilometres of coastline with hundreds of long smooth beaches, and thousands of small sandy coves and rocky inlets, while inland there are the mountains. These rise to over 2500 metres in a few places and their peaks are snow covered from November to May. In the high valleys will be found delightful forests of chestnut, beech and pine, while the lower slopes are covered in places by terraced cultivation, and everywhere else by the unique maquis, a complex tangled mass of vegetation including juniper, holm oak, arbutus, bay, thyme, rosemary and lavender. Corsica's most famous son, Napoleon, claimed that he would recognise his island blindfolded, by its scent alone, and there is no doubt that it justly deserves its title, 'The Scented Isle'.

Apart from a brief interval in the 18th century, when Pasquale Paoli fought for its independence, Corsica has always been under external domination... by Greece, Rome, the Vatican, Pisa, Aragon and Genoa... until it became part of France in 1796. Genoa ruled it from 1453 until 1729 and the Genoese citadels in its main towns and the watch towers along its coast are ample evidence of their occupation. However there are also interesting prehistoric, Graeco-Roman and Pisan remains to be observed; and of course the birthplace of Napoleon in Ajaccio.

An ideal holiday in Corsica might combine relaxation upon its shores with a gentle exploration of at least a small part of its wooded mountain interior. Take your car on one of the ferries from southern France, hire a car on the island, or use the bus services and the attractive railway, which has a truly scenic quality. Above all, do not attempt to explore it all too quickly, for we are certain that you will wish to return.

AJACCIO (20)   83k SW Corte

Founded by the Genoese in the 15th century, Ajaccio is now the capital of the island, and is only just a few hundred less in population than Bastia. Like Bastia it has its spacious squares and wide streets, in contrast to the picturesque buildings in the old town around its fishing port. Napoleon was born here on 15th August 1769, and his birthplace, the Casa Bonaparte is well worth visiting. See also the Musée Napoléonien and the Musée and Palais Fesch, with its splendid collection of Italian paintings (Cardinal Fesch was Napoleon's uncle). There is a wide selection of hotels and restaurants in Ajaccio, and a series of splendid beaches along the road to La Parata Point (twelve kilometres to the point). Off this point lie the Îles Sanguinaires, which can be reached by a popular boat trip from Ajaccio.

Ajaccio

ALERIA (20)   72k S Bastia

Village near the mouth of the Tavignano river, with the extensive remains of a Graeco-Roman town nearby. There is an interesting museum with an outstanding collection of Greek pottery.

ALGAJOLA (20)   15k ENE Calvi

Small holiday resort village with fine beaches and an old citadel. There are at least two hotels and a good camp site. The interior of the church is worth visiting.

ASCO (20)   64k SW Bastia

Small village situated half way up a long gorge of the same name, eighteen kilometres from the main N193, Bastia-Corte road at Ponte Leccia. There is a small hotel here. About twelve kilometres further on, the road comes to an end at Haut Asco, where there is another small hotel. This is good skiing country, and in summer there is the lovely forest of Carozzica to be explored.

A Gentleman of Corsica

The Îles Sanguinaires (See Ajaccio)

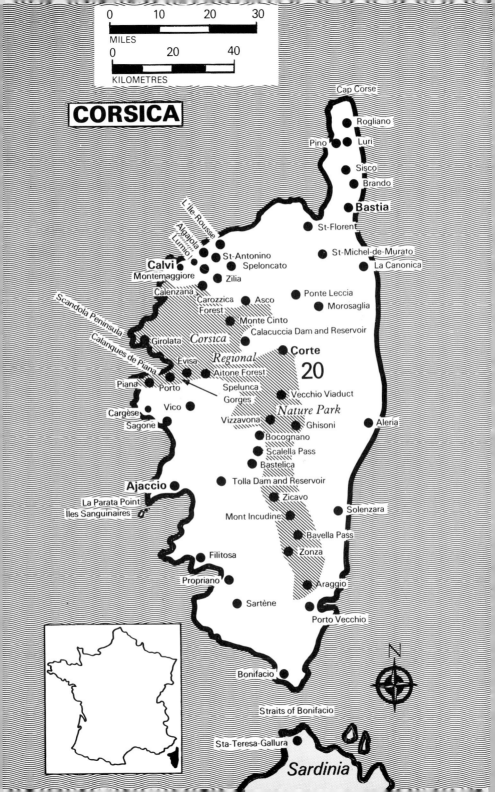

BASTELICA (20)
41k ENE Ajaccio
Bright little mountain resort and ski centre near the head of the Prunelli valley (See Tolla Dam, Page 101). There is adventurous motoring north from here, over the Scalella Pass... not to be undertaken lightly.

BASTIA (20)
70k NE Corte
This was the Genoese capital of Corsica, and with a population of over 50,000, it is the largest and busiest city on the island. The new port and new town are both centred upon the busy Place St-Nicholas, while the attractive old port and old town are situated to its south. The old fishing port is approached by narrow streets overlooked by tall houses, and the fine Palace of the Genoese Governors at its southern end is now an interesting Ethnographical Museum. There are no fewer than four richly decorated Baroque churches which are well worth visiting. The beaches in the Bastia area are not outstanding, but it is a lively city with many pleasant hotels and restaurants. Cafés around the Place St-Nicholas are good value especially at the time of the 'evening parade' (*the passeggiata*), when all the young men and girls are out for their stroll.

BAVELLA PASS (20)
46k NE Sartène
Dramatically bleak pass on the long narrow mountain road between Zonza and Solenzara. There are fine views, and a restaurant which is open from June to September.

Bastia

BOCOGNANO (20)
40k NE Ajaccio
Charming village in the upper Gravone valley, astride the main Ajaccio-Corte road. Here one is surrounded by chestnut woods, but after a short distance, the road climbs up towards the Vizzavona Pass into high mountain country, which is much favoured by skiers. There is at least one hotel in Bocognano.

BONIFACIO (20)
140k SE Ajaccio
Small town situated on a limestone rock above the sea on the very southern tip of the island, looking across the Straits of Bonifacio to Sardinia, only eight miles away (There is a vehicle ferry to Sta-Teresa-Gallura). Here is a walled town with narrow streets, old churches and a citadel where the young Napoleon served in 1792. This is connected to its little harbour in a deep inlet, by one small road and a stepped path, believed to have been cut out of the rock in a single night during a siege in 1420 by King Alphonso of Aragon. If the weather is calm, there are several interesting boat trips from here.

Bonifacio, on its cliffs

CALACUCCIA DAM AND RESERVOIR (20)
27k W Corte
This great dam across the Golo river, in the mountains to the west of Corte, is one of several built since 1955 by the Somivac Company for the irrigation of the eastern plains of Corsica. The village from which the dam takes its name lies on the road south westwards to Evisa and Porto, through the forests of Valdo Niello and Aitone. There is at least one hotel in Calacuccia, and there is good trout fishing in the reservoir between March and the end of June.

Bonifacio waterfront

Corsica

Above the Calanques de Piana

Calvi

Corte

Corte

Evisa

CALANQUES DE PIANA (20)   *9k WSW Porto*

Literally the Creeks of Piana, these are a succession of natural sculptures in red granite visible from about two kilometres of road between Porto and Piana. For superlative effect, see these at sunset or dawn.

CALVI (20)   *93k W Bastia, 5½ hours by sea from Nice*

The Genoese citadel of this relatively small town dominates a great sweeping bay, with splendid sands, and a high mountain backdrop. Here are many hotels, restaurants, cafés and bars with dancing, and a luxurious yacht harbour. Calvi is always lively from March to October and the massive camping sites on the bay attract many younger holidaymakers. Nelson lost his eye during the bombardment of Calvi in 1793.

CANONICA, LA (20)   *20k S Bastia*

Interesting Romanesque basilica situated close to the site of the Roman town of Mariana... this all lies a short distance beyond the airport of Poretta.

CAP CORSE (20)   *40k N Bastia*

A complete tour of this splendid peninsula, northwards from Bastia covers 123k, and is well worth doing. There is a succession of small, unsophisticated fishing ports; with inland villages in richly wooded valleys up from the coast. Near the head of the peninsula is Rogliano with its medieval castle and ruined monastery. Between Luri and Pino, is the Tower of Seneca where legend has it that Seneca spent his years in exile; and at Brando and Sisco there are Romanesque chapels worth visiting.

CARGÈSE (20)   *51k NW Ajaccio*

Small village founded in 1676 by Greeks fleeing from Turkish tyranny, and still retaining a Greek Catholic church, and a certain Greek flavour. There are pleasant beaches and several hotels.

CORSICA REGIONAL NATURE PARK (20)

This covers a vast area of the Corsican mountains together with 80 kilometres of coastline, northwards from Porto. This also includes a Nature Reserve covering the whole Scandola peninsula beyond Girolata. Traversing the Park from north-west to south-east, there is a long distance footpath between Calvi and Porto Vecchio (GR20).

CORTE (20)   *70k SW Bastia, 83k NE Ajaccio*

This town is situated in the approximate centre of the island at the junction of two rivers, the Tavignano and the Restonica, on a mountain spur, capped by a 15th century Genoese citadel. This was the seat of the short lived Corsican republic in the 18th century, and the house where Napoleon's mother and father lived may still be seen. Explore up the little road along the Restonica gorge, about twenty kilometres, or walk up the Tavignano gorge.

EVISA (20)   *72k N Ajaccio, 23k E Porto*

Small summer resort in hilly country reached via the dramatic Spelunca gorges from Porto. To its immediate east lie the great pine forests of Aitone. A walk to the north east leads to the Aitone waterfalls, near which is a splendid viewpoint.

FILITOSA
20k NW Propriano

Here in the Taravo valley some five kilometres from the sea, will be found extensive Megalithic (Stone Age) remains... standing stones with primitive carvings on their surfaces. This is regarded as one of the most impressive Megalithic sites in the Mediterranean area.

GHISONI (20)
42k S Corte

Small terraced village on a steep hillside overlooking a deep ravine. This is an excellent base for trout fishermen from June onwards. Lovely wooded country.

L'ÎLE-ROUSSE (20)
24k NE Calvi

This was founded by Pascale Paoli, the great Corsican patriot, in the 18th century, to compete with ports still under Genoese domination. It is a relatively small town, but one of the oldest holiday resorts on the island, with several excellent hotels and restaurants. This is a colourful holiday town with a lively night life, and it is also a good base for exploring that part of north west Corsica known as the Balagne, the coastline of which stretches between here and Calvi.

LUMIO (20)
10k ENE Calvi

Attractive little village with views out over the Gulf of Calvi towards Calvi. There are beautifully sandy beaches and a yacht marina at St-Ambroggio 2ks north. There are fine views from the hill village of St-Antonino about 10ks east of Lumio.

MONTE CINTO (20)
30k SE Calvi

At 2707 metres above sea level, this is Corsica's highest mountain. This and the many other high peaks are snow capped from November to May. There are of course ample opportunities for climbing, but this should only be tackled by experts.

MONTEMAGGIORE (20)
15k ESE Calvi

Delightful hill village with splendid views out from its small square, itself overlooked by a charming Baroque church. Combine with a visit to the neighbouring villages of Calenzana and Zilia using the little N844. Calenzana is THE Corsican wine centre.

MOROSAGLIA (20)
38k NE Corte

This hill village was the birthplace of the Corsican patriot Pascale Paoli (1725), and his birthplace is now a museum. Drive 4ks east for fine views from the Col de Prato.

PORTO (20)
83k N Ajaccio, 86k W Corte

Small town with several hotels situated on the beautiful gulf of Porto, at a point where the Spelunca gorge reaches the sea. Here is an old watch tower, deep waters and lovely pink granite cliffs. Explore eastwards up the gorge to Evisa, and south westwards to the Callanches de Piana (The creeks of Piana). The eighty kilometre drive northwards to Calvi (mainly within sight of the coast) is an exhausting, but rewarding experience.

PORTO VECCHIO (20)
27k NNE Bonifacio

This old fortified town stands at the head of a deep inlet whose shores are clad with pines and cork-oaks. There are many safe bathing beaches for children, a harbour, and splendid opportunities for sailing and water skiing. There is a wide choice of hotels and

continued

Standing stones at Filitosa

Hotel at Ghisoni

L'Île Rousse

Watch tower and beach, at Porto

Corsica

Propriano

restaurants here. The ruined castle of Araggio lies about eight kilometres to the north, and there are fine views from here.

PROPRIANO (20)   *73k SSE Ajaccio*
Pleasant holiday resort town in the deep Gulf of Valinco, with an old port, sandy beaches and a good selection of hotels and restaurants.

RAILWAYS OF CORSICA (20)
There are 230 kilometres of railway in Corsica, with a line reaching south westwards to Ajaccio from Bastia via Corte, with a 'branch' from the mountain junction of Ponte Leccia, north and west to Île-Rousse and Calvi. Almost all of these lines pass through splendid scenery, and are well worth travelling on for this reason alone. The great Vecchio Viaduct (about 20k S of Corte) was built by Eiffel, and was one of his most remarkable engineering feats. It is best seen from the road, north of Vivario.

ST-FLORENT (20)   *23k W Bastia*
Attractive little fishing port, with its old houses surrounding the ancient Genoese citadel. This is a pleasantly quiet resort with several hotels. The Romanesque cathedral of Nebbio, a town demolished by the Moors, stands to the east of the village (Ask for key at the Hôtel de L'Europe).

ST-MICHEL-DE-MURATO (20)   *17k S St-Florent*
About three kilometres south of the Col de San Stefano, there is a small village called Murato, near which is a remarkable example of 12th century Romanesque architecture of the Pisan school… the little chapel of St-Michel or San Michele. Do not miss this.

Chapel at Murato

SAGONE (20)   *38k N Ajaccio*
Small village on the Gulf of Sagone with at least two hotels and a particularly attractive beach. There is a pleasant hill road inland from here (13ks) to the village of Vico where there is a Franciscan monastery.

SARTÈNE (20)   *86k SSE Ajaccio*
Dark little granite town with a medieval flavour. It is noted for its dramatic Good Friday procession, the Catenaccio, when a hooded figure representing Christ carries a great cross through the streets. Not many years ago the parts of Christ and Simon where enacted by criminals, and the watching crowds used to spit on and even beat these unfortunate men. There is an adventurous minor road south and east of Bonifacio (54k).

SOLENZARA (20)   *103k S Bastia*
Small holiday resort on the east coast, with at least two hotels, and a restaurant, together with holiday camp sites. There are pleasant beaches in the area.

SPELONCATO (20)   *32k E Calvi*
A most attractive hill village, with fine views out over the surrounding countryside from its craggy site. There is a small hotel here.

SPELUNCA GORGES   *Approx. 15k E Porto*
A series of deep gorges in the mountains between Porto and Evisa cut by the turbulent waters of the Porto

Sartène

continued

river. The RF9 road wends up these gorges, a total distance of twenty four kilometres between the two places.

TOLLA DAM AND RESERVOIR (20) *30k ENE Ajaccio*
A large dam across the Prunelli river in high mountain country to the east of Ajaccio. This has been stocked with trout, the best period for fishing being between March and the end of June.

VIZZAVONA (20)   *31k SSW Corte*
Attractive mountain resort on the northern side of the splendid Vizzavona Pass, with chestnut, beech and pine much in evidence. There are at least two hotels, and a wonderful selection of walks (The GR20 crosses the main road near here... See Corsica Regional Nature Park, Page 98). Do not stray too far into the mountains without adequate experience and equipment.

ZICAVO (20)   *63k E Ajaccio*
Small village with lovely chestnut woods and fine views south eastwards to the great Mont Incudine (2136 metres). Zicavo is not reached without effort, as a study of the Michelin 1:200,000 (Yellow) map of Corsica will reveal... there being many kilometres of narrow mountain road to be traversed, either east from Ajaccio, or south from Corte.

ZONZA (20)   *37k NE Sartène*
Attractive mountain village where four roads meet. Here are at least two small hotels. The mountain scenery is superb, and there are extensive forests of chestnut and pine.

Above the Spelunca Gorge

Zonza

Corsica

Côte-d'Azur

Only containing one Département, the Alpes-Maritimes, ,his is the smallest of France's 'Regions'. It is here that the Alps meet the sea, and the result is a superbly scenic coastline, wonderfully sheltered from the cold northerly winds. During the last 150 years this coast has given birth to a series of luxurious resorts, both large and small, but there are still some quiet corners to be explored even within sight of the sea. Away from the coast there are many fascinating little hill towns and villages, and expeditions can be made by car, bus (or even by train in some cases) to the gorges and valleys to which we shall refer. There are also at least three zoos, a host of lively museums and art collections, together with ruined castles and a ruined monastery. The coast itself is often crowded in high summer and we suggest May, June or early July (before 14th), or even September or early October as the best times for visiting.

ANTIBES AND JUAN-LES-PINS (06)
11k ENE Cannes

These two towns straddle the base of Cap d'Antibes mid-way between Nice and Cannes. Antibes was first established in the 5th century BC by Greek traders, who in their turn were followed by the Romans. It continued to be important during the Middle Ages, and in the 17th century the great fortification builder Vauban created Fort Carré, which still stands, to the immediate north of the port. Napoleon was a prisoner here for a time, following the fall of Robespierre. Although some of the walls were demolished in the 19th century, enough of the old Antibes remains, to ensure that it is one of the more fascinating old towns of the Côte d'Azur, with its narrow streets and houses built into the ramparts... all in delightful contrast to the luxurious resort of Juan-les-Pins, with its splendid beaches, hotels, bars, casinos and night clubs. This latter half of the joint town was the creation of American millionaire, Frank Jay Gould, as recently as 1925.

The Cathedral and the Grimaldi Castle, Antibes

While in Antibes do not miss the Picasso Museum in the Grimaldi Castle, nor the lovely Jardin Thuret, on the road south towards Cap d'Antibes. At Eden-Roc, near the Cap, there is an interesting Naval and Napoleonic Museum housed in an old coastal defence tower.

AURON (06)
100k NNW Nice

Popular ski resort situated well above the valley of the River Tinée, at 1608 metres. There is a cable car service to Las Donnas, a mountain to the south that is open between mid November and mid October, and there are certain hotels open in high summer as well as the ski season. The 12th century chapel has an interesting interior.

Auron

BEAULIEU-SUR-MER (06)
10k NE Nice

A small but most elegant resort, which has retained its Edwardian flavour. There are two lush yachting harbours, a palm sheltered promenade in the direction of St-Jean-Cap-Ferrat, and the faithful reproduction of a Greek villa (Kerylos), which should not be missed. Beaulieu's exceptionally sheltered position makes it one of the warmest spots on the Côte d'Azur in winter, and has earned it the title of 'Little Africa'. If funds allow, visit the splendid 'Réserve'... a hotel with an international reputation, and one which typifies the elegance of Beaulieu.

BIOT (06)
18k NE Cannes

Attractive village five kilometres inland from the busy coast, with an arcaded 'place' complete with 15th
continued

Beaulieu

The Musée Léger, Biot

La Brigue Church   Haut-de-Cagnes

century church. There is a interesting museum devoted to the works of the artist Ferdinand Léger, who died in 1955. The village is noted for the production of grapes for the table, and for its potteries.

LA BRIGUE (06)   80k NE Nice
A remote place in the mountains to the south east of Tende, with the ruins of a castle and a small Romanesque church. Four kilometres beyond Brigue is the chapel of Notre-Dame-des-Fontaines, a medieval chapel with well preserved Renaissance frescoes (Ask for key at La Brigue Presbytery).

CAGNES-SUR-MER (06)   13k WSW Nice
The part which interests us is the delightful hill village of Haut-de-Cagnes, with its steep narrow streets, leading up to the medieval castle of the Grimaldis, which houses an interesting museum, and from which there are fine views. See also the house where Renoir spent the last twelve years of his life, and the chapel of Notre-Dame-de-la-Protection, with its lovely 16th century frescoes.

Renoir Museum, Haut-de-Cagnes

CANNES (06)   910k SE Paris
Beautifully sited on a lovely bay backed by high mountains and partially sheltered by the Lérins islands, Cannes is perhaps France's most luxurious and elegant holiday resort. Until Lord Brougham was forced to stay here in 1834, by a frontier closed for health reasons, Cannes was little more than a fishing village with a single coaching inn. However he was so enchanted with the climate and the setting that he built himself a villa, which he made his winter home, until his death in 1868. His example was quickly followed by other members of the aristocracy, and royalty including Edward VII, when Prince of Wales; and by the turn of the century Cannes was Europe's most famous winter resort.

Fashions change, and Cannes, like the rest of the Côte d'Azur is now more favoured in summer than in winter, but its mild winters still tempt many members of the older generation to return here when the rest of Europe shivers.

Fashionable Cannes centres upon the colourful Quai Saint-Pierre, on the west side of the harbour, and the long luxurious Boulevard de la Croisette, stretching eastwards from the harbour to the Pointe de la Croisette. Overlooking the harbour is the Tour du Mont Chevalier, from which there are fine views; and there are even wider views out over the Lerins islands and the bay, from the Observatory, which can be reached by a little funicular railway starting from the Boulevard Montfleury.

Cannes   Cannes

CIANS GORGES (06)   75k NNW Nice
Use Michelin Map No. 81 or 195 to explore these deep gorges cut by the River Cians on their way to join the Var. From the village of Beuil they run southwards for twenty five kilometres till they reach the Var, dropping no less than 1600 metres in the process.

DALUIS GORGES (06)   100k NW Nice
Use Michelin Map No. 81 or 195 to explore these remote gorges cut out of red shale by the River Var. The most dramatic views are to be had from Daluis northwards to Guillaumes.

Fishing boats at Cannes

ÈZE (06)   *12k NE Nice*

A highly attractive hill village nearly five hundred metres above the sea which is not far away. The 'streets' here are passages, paths and stairways, and there is a fascinating selection of shops selling pictures, ceramics, jewellery, fabrics and gifts... much of a higher standard than one has come to expect. There are lovely views out over the sea to Cap Ferrat, and near the top of the village a tropical garden built around the ruins of Èze's château.

Èze

GRASSE (06)   *17k NNW Cannes*

Charming old hill town and world renowned centre for the manufacture of perfume. Several of the smaller perfume works may be visited, and the Museum of Provençal Art and History contains several works and many souvenirs of the painter Fragonard, who was born here in 1732. See also the 12th century cathedral and watch tower and the chapel of the Hôpital du Petit Paris, which contains three paintings by Rubens. There are fine views from the terraced promenade of the Cours Honoré-Cresp.

ISOLA 2000 (06)   *95k N Nice*

Modern purpose-built winter sports centre, with at least one hotel open in high summer. Isola is situated at 2000 metres above sea level and is close to the Italian border, crossed here by the small Col de la Lombarde at 2350 metres.

LÉRINS, ÎLES DE (06)

These two islands... the Île Sainte-Marguerite, and the Île Saint-Honorat... lie a short distance off Cannes, with which they are connected by a boat service taking about 15 minutes. Sainte-Marguerite is the nearest, the largest, and also the more hospitable of the two islands. However both are well worth visiting, for they are covered by pine woods which are intersected by many paths. There is an old fortress on Sainte-Marguerite, which once held the mysterious 'Man in the Iron Mask' (whose identity has never been established). The old fortified monastery on Saint Honorat was built in the 11th century as protection against Saracen pirates, but the first monastery was established here by Saint-Honorat himself at the end of the 4th century, and for centuries the Abbots of Lérins were a powerful influence in the Christian world, apart from being the owners of what has become Cannes. The fortified monastery can be visited, but there is a 19th century 'new' monastery still carrying on the tradition of monastic life and work on the island.

Quiet afternoon at Èze.   *Èze*
Photograph by Peter Titchmarsh

Grasse

LOUP GORGES (06)   *40k W Nice*

Use Michelin Map No. 84 or 195 to explore this great cleft in the limestone plateau, cut by the River Loup. Some of the best views may be had from the village of Gourdon, where there is an interesting castle which may be visited. There are dramatic waterfalls further up the gorge, at Saut du Loup, and near Courmes.

LUCÉRAM (06)   *28k NNE Nice*

Little village sited on the steep slopes of a mountainside, with small stepped streets. The late 15th century church contains several interesting items including five lovely 15th century retables.

St-Honorat, Îles-de-Lerins   *In old Grasse*

Côte-d'Azur

Menton

Monte-Carlo, from
Loews Hotel. Photo
by Peter Titchmarsh

La Condamine, from the Palace Square, Monaco.
Photograph by Peter Titchmarsh

The Palace, Monaco

A street in old Nice

Nice Carnival

MARINELAND ZOO PARK *Off N7 17k NE Cannes*

A fascinating 'marine zoo', with performing dolphins, and no fewer than nine pools containing marine mammals from all over the world.

MENTON (06) *28k ENE Nice*

This is one of the great holiday resorts of the Côte d'Azur, with three miles of promenade, stretching almost from the Italian frontier to Cap Martin. Behind and above the port and the Plage des Sablettes, are the steep, narrow and often arched streets of the old town, climbing up to the church of St-Michel and the chapel of the Pénitents-Blancs, which face on to the Place de l'Église where the annual chamber music festival is held each year in August. Modern Menton has something to offer every style of holidaymaker, while retaining at least some of the flavour of gentler days. See especially the Cocteau Museum in the Bastion of the port, which contains some of his tapestries, drawings and gouaches, and the Registry Office in the Hôtel de Ville, with its frescoes also by Cocteau.

MONACO — MONTE CARLO (06) *957k SE Paris*

A Principality of only eight square miles, consisting of the old town of Monaco, the 'new' town of Monte Carlo, La Condamine, the harbour and commercial area between them, and the industrial area of Fontvieille to the west, which has been expanded in recent times, by reclamation from the sea. In Monaco, see the 'Palace of the Prince', of the Grimaldis, the family that has ruled Monaco since 1308; the Oceanographic Museum, the Exotic Garden, the Grotto of the Observatory and the Zoo. In Monte Carlo, see the Museum of Fine Arts, and of course the fabulous Casino.

Be prepared to spend time in this fascinating Principality... in the splendid courtyard of the Palace, with its colourfully dressed guards and fine views out over the harbour. Wander round the harbour itself, with its magnificent array of motor cruisers and yachts; window-shop in the wide streets near the Casino, where many Paris firms are represented, and even 'invest' a franc or so at the Casino before you leave.

LA NAPOULE (06) *8k SW Cannes*

Lively resort with several excellent hotels and restaurants, and three sandy beaches. The Château of Napoule was restored by the sculptor Henry Clews and his wife, and there is an interesting collection of sculpture and a lovely garden, from which there are fine views out over the Bay of Cannes.

NICE (06) *933k SE Paris*

This large bustling city has a population of almost 350,000 inhabitants, (compared to Cannes's 75,000), and there are only five other larger cities in the whole of France. It has a splendid setting below the mountains, and is built upon a gently curving bay. Unlike Cannes, it has been a place of significance since earliest times, and even as a holiday resort it can give Cannes almost a hundred years. The famous Promenade des Anglais was built in the 1820's, at the expense of an English clergyman, to provide work for the unemployed, by which time Nice was already well known to the English traveller. However it was the coming of the railway later in the century that provided the great holiday impetus.

Nice passed back and forth between France and Italy during the 17th and 18th centuries, and there is a *continued*

Côte-d'Azur

considerable Italian flavour amongst the narrow streets and alleys of its old town, which lies below the castle to the west of the port. It is possible to take a lift up to an observation platform in the castle, from which there are fine views. See also the world famous flower market which is held every weekday, the fascinating Masséna Museum, with its furniture, paintings and ceramics, and... if you come in February... perhaps the greatest of European carnivals.. the Carnival of Flowers. At Cimiez, just to the north, there is a ruined Roman amphitheatre and a museum devoted to Matisse, who had a studio here.

NICE TO DIGNE RAILWAY (06-04)
There is a highly attractive railway route between Nice and Digne. The little trains 'of the Five Valleys' take about three and a half hours, during which time they travel through delightful mountain country. Departures from the Gare du Sud, 33 av. Malausséna, 06000 NICE. Details of the service available from this address.

NOTRE-DAME-DE-BRUSC (06)   *6k E Grasse*
A remarkable 11th century church in the countryside to the east of Grasse and to the south of Châteauneuf-de-Grasse. This is built on the site of an early Christian church dating from the 5th century, which is in association with the remains of a Roman camp. Here indeed is evidence of the continuity of Christian worship over the many centuries when its light was all but extinguished in the lands further to the north.

PEILLE (06)   *24k NW Menton*   Nice
Fascinating little medieval town overlooking the Faquin ravine, with occasional glimpses of the distant sea from some of its little cobbled and vaulted alley-ways. See especially the Place du Mont-Agel with old houses looking out over its Gothic fountain, and the 12th and 13th century church, the contents of which include a fine 16th century retable.

PEIRA-CAVA (06)   *40k N Nice*
An attractive winter-sports and summer holiday resort, with a lovely road north up through the Turini Forest. Use Michelin Map No. 84 or 195.

PUGET-THÉNIERS (06)   *65k NW Nice*
Charming old village at the confluence of the Var and the Roudoule rivers, with the ruins of a medieval castle and, in the church, some attractive groups of 17th century carved wooden figures.

Peille

ROQUEBRUNE-CAP-MARTIN (06)
7k NE Monte-Carlo
Attractive resort occupying the area between Monte-Carlo and Menton. The cape is overlooked by the hill village of Roquebrune, with its steep streets and stairways, many of which are arched over. The castle was built in the 10th century, by Conrad, Count of Ventimiglia, as a defence against the Saracens, and is considerably earlier than most castles on this coast. Do not miss a visit here, and if you have time, walk along the western side of the cape from whence there are breath-taking views out over the bay to Monte Carlo, and the heights around La Turbie. The cape itself is

continued *Roquebrune*

Côte-d'Azur

Cap Ferrat

The Ephrussi de Rothschild Foundation, Cap Ferrat

Sheltered beach on Cap Ferrat

St-Martin-Vésubie

St-Paul-de-Vence. Photographs by Peter Titchmarsh

studded with luxury villas and was once a favourite of Winston Churchill's, as well as that of the famous Dutch art forger, Hans van Meegeren.

ST-CÉZAIRE CAVES (06)   *15k W Grasse*

These fine limestone caves are situated to the immediate north of the D613 road and contain a wide variety of stalactites and stalagmites, their reddish hue being due to the presence of iron oxides in the surrounding rocks.

ST-JEAN-CAP-FERRAT (06)   *12k E Nice*

The name Cap Ferrat has for many years been synonymous with luxury, and here will be found the splendid villas and lovely gardens of the very rich. St-Jean is the only real village on the cape, and this has a large marina containing some of the world's most fabulous yachts and motor cruisers. On the road in from Beaulieu is the Ephrussi de Rothschild Foundation, an Italianate villa built by Baroness Ephrussi to house her outstanding collection of art treasures. Do not miss a visit here, for there are also extensive gardens, with fine views across the deep bay to Villefranche. A short distance southwards, there is an interesting Zoo Park, and at the end of the cape, there is a lighthouse which may be visited. If you have time, walk along the delightful Promenade Maurice Rouvier, which follows the coast northwards from beyond St-Jean village almost to Beaulieu, or walk eastwards from the village around the Pointe de St-Hospice.

ST-MARTIN-VÉSUBIE (06)   *65k N Nice*

There is a pleasant drive up from Nice, first along the main N202, and then north east up the Gorges de la Vésubie, and along the upper Vésubie valley... to this attractively sited mountain village, which has at least three hotels. Eleven kilometres beyond the village of Le Boréon is the entrance to the Mercantour Game Reserve (Good walking, but no guns, no dogs). The Italian border is only a few kilometres to the north.

ST-PAUL-DE-VENCE (06)   *20k W Nice*

A most attractive and understandably much visited hill village, with steep narrow streets and pathways, many paved with pink tiles. If funds permit, visit the famous restaurant and hotel, the Colombe d'Or, with its amazing collection of modern paintings (St-Paul has for many years been an 'artist's colony', and many of the paintings were gifts from grateful guests, or were even handed over in lieu of payment). The church contains several interesting items, and one should not be deterred by its outward appearance. See also the ramparts from which there are fine views out over the mountains; and the Maeght Foundation... an outstanding collection of modern art housed in a fascinating building designed by José-Luis Sert, a pupil of Le Corbusier.

SAORGE (06)   *47k N Menton*

Small village on a terrace site above the Roya river, which has cut a series of deep gorges, through which the N204 heads northwards on its way to Tende and the frontier with Italy.

SOSPEL (06)   *45k NNE Nice*

Situated in high mountain country on the Nice-Turin road between the two passes... the Col de Braus and the Col de Brouis. It has attractive old houses lining the banks of the little Bévéra river, and an 11th century toll bridge across it. The paved Place St-Michel is partly bordered by arcaded houses, but is dominated by the large 17th century former cathedral.

TENDE (06)   *85k NE Nice*

Small town astride the road between Nice and Turin. This is some ten kilometres short of the Col de Tende, a once difficult pass, now replaced by a road tunnel. The town is not exceptional, but its setting amongst the mountains is superb.

Sospel   *Sospel*

TOURETTE-SUR-LOUP (06) *6k W Vence, 28k W Nice*

Fascinating old village huddled together on a small rocky plateau, with its outer houses forming defensive ramparts. The 15th century church contains several interesting works of art, and the village is alive with many artists and craftsmen who have settled here.

LA TURBIE (06)   *8k E Monte Carlo*

Pleasant village standing about five hundred metres above sea level, on the edge of the still busy Grande Corniche (The Autoroute runs a kilometre or so further north). Here stands the famous Trophy of the Alps, erected by the Romans in 6BC to commemorate their final conquest of the Ligurian tribesmen, who had proved such a hindrance to communications between northern Italy and Provence. Originally standing at 45 metres, it was plundered over the centuries, until being restored with generous help by an American, Mr. Edward Tuck, to a height of 35 metres. There are splendid views out over Monaco from the area surrounding this unique example of a Roman 'trophy' monument.

Tourette-sur-Loup

TURINI FOREST (06)   *40k NE Nice*

Attractive pine and spruce forest in high mountain country north of the village of Peira-Cava, a well known winter sports centre and summer holiday retreat (at least three hotels).

VALBERG (06)   *85k NNW Nice*

Pleasant ski resort which also caters for visitors in high summer. There are fine views from the Croix de Valberg (1829 metres), a peak to the immediate south of the village. In the village itself there is an interesting church... the Chapel of Our Lady of the Snows. Use Michelin Map No. 81 or 195 to explore this area, linking with the gorges of Daluis and Cians.

The Trophy of the Alps, La Turbie

VALLAURIS (06)   *6k NE Cannes*

Lying a short distance inland from Golfe Juan, Vallauris is a village with an international reputation... thanks to Picasso who came here soon after the 2nd World War and discovered the joys of ceramic as an art medium. It had always had a few potteries, but once Picasso's involvement became known, many more potters followed, and today its streets are lined with

continued

Valberg

Côte-d'Azur

Chapel of the Rosary, Vence

Summer morning at Villefranche.
Photograph by Peter Titchmarsh

Sunday market, Villefranche.
Photograph by Peter Titchmarsh

The Welcome Hotel, Villefranche.
Photograph by Peter Titchmarsh

potteries and pottery shops... some offering items of great beauty and many offering items in quite another category. See also the 'Modern Art Museum', a medieval chapel incorporating decorations by Picasso with the themes of War and Peace.

VENCE (06)   *23k W Nice*

Attractive old cathedral town on a rocky ridge between two valleys. There are many old streets to be explored and the Place du Peyra with its fountain is very pleasant. There are fascinating misericords in the cathedral choir stalls (ask for key at the Syndicat in the Place Clemenceau). The Chapel of the Rosary, off the D2210, on the NE outskirts of the town, was designed and decorated by Matisse and is well worth visiting... especially for its brilliant coloured glass. (Only open Tuesdays and Thursdays).

VILLEFRANCHE-SUR-MER (06)   *6k E Cannes*

Delightful old fishing port, with steep streets and alleys dropping down to its little harbour. There is a charming hotel, The Welcome (where we have spent many happy holidays), and several good restaurants along its quay, and beyond its great citadel, another harbour, filled with lush pleasure cruisers and sailing yachts. The old fishermen's chapel of St-Pierre was decorated by Jean Cocteau in 1947, and is well worth visiting.

VILLENEUVE-LOUBET (06)   *23k NE Cannes*

Small village about two kilometres inland from a busy plage with a Museum of Culinary Art in the house where the famous chef Auguste Escoffier was born. This is to be recommended to all with an interest in good cuisine.

Luxury craft at Villefranche.
Photograph by Peter Titchmarsh

Franche-Comté

Comprises the following Départements
Doubs (25)   Haute Saône (70)
Jura (39)   Territoire-de-Belfort (90)

This region of France can be divided into two parts... the gently rolling plain through which the upper Saône flows, and the gradually rising mountain country of the Jura, which extends over the border into Switzerland. In the far north-east is the Belfort Gap, beyond which the Vosges run northwards into the Alsace-Vosges-Lorraine Region.

The Saône valley country has a certain charm, but the remainder of the region, the Jura mountains, are a sheer delight. Green meadows, great forests, fragrant and cool in summer, deep valleys, rushing streams and thunderous waterfalls, dark gorges and colourful caves, great lakes and vast rolling uplands. Everywhere one looks, nature displays its bounty, and mercifully man has done little to spoil his inheritance here. Small towns and villages, friendly resourceful people, and equally friendly hotels, camp sites and restaurants, make this an ideal holiday area. Ski-ing in winter, and in summer, fishing, walking, riding, sailing and swimming... all these, and more, are well catered for in the Jura... and if it all sounds a little too hearty, remember the local Arbois reference to its wines... 'the more one drinks, the straighter one walks'... What a splendid thought!

AMANCE (70)   *22k NNW Vesoul*
Little medieval market town in wooded country to the west of the Sâone with several 15th and 17th century houses.

ARBOIS (39)   *35k SE Dole*
Pleasant little town at the foot of a steep sided valley, with several pleasant viewpoints nearby. This is a wine growing centre, and some cellars may be visited. See also the house where Pasteur spent most of his boyhood, the 12th and 13th century church, the towers and other remains of the ramparts, and several arcaded 17th century houses.

Arbois

ARC-ET-SENANS (25)   *38k E Dole*
Here, between the River Loue and the forest of Chaux, are situated the fascinating remains of the 18th century Royal Salt Works of Chaux. This is the only completed section of the grandiose 'model town' project of Claude Ledoux, General Inspector of Salt Marshes, in the 1770's. Although now occupied by the 'International Centre for Studies on the Future', the recently restored buildings are open to the public.

BAUME-LES-MESSIEURS (39)
     15k NE Lons-le-Saunier
Small village in a deep valley overlooked by the rocky edge of an eroded plateau, with fine views from the cirque at the head of the valley (The Cirque de Baume). It was from the abbey established here by the Irish monk, St-Colomban in the 6th century that twelve monks set out to found the world famous abbey of Cluny in Burgundy in 910 (See Page 82). See the abbey remains and the interesting Departmental Museum of Arts and Traditions, including its animated presentation of a blacksmith's workshop.

Arbois   *Baume-les-Messieurs*

BELFORT (90)   *432k ESE Paris*
This ancient fortress town is 'capital' of its own Territory of Belfort' and stands guard over the twenty mile gap between the Jura and the Vosges, known as the Trouée de Belfort (the Belfort Gap), or the Porte de Bourgogne (the Burgundy Gate). The old town lies to the immediate east of the River Savoureuse, and here will be found the delightful little square, the Place d'Armes. To the immediate east of the old town is the

continued   *The Royal Salt Works, Arc-et-Senans*

Franche Comté

great citadel built by Vauban in the 17th century, with its impressive gateway, the Porte de Brisach, its 19th century ramparts, complete with a gigantic lion carved by the sculptor Bartholdi, who is best remembered for his great Statue of Liberty in New York harbour. See also the museum, with works by Durer and Courbet among others.

The Porte-de-Brisach, Belfort

In the church of St-Christophe, Belfort

BESANÇON (25)   *400k ESE Paris*

This attractive city is the capital of the Franche-Comté, and since earliest times its strategic importance has been enhanced by its dramatic rocky setting in a loop of the lovely River Doubs. This was further enhanced by the building of a great citadel across the narrowest part of the loop in the late 17th century by the master fortification builder Sébastien Vauban. Almost all of interest is within this loop of the Doubs... pleasant 17th and 18th century streets and squares; the Grenvelle Palace, a fine 16th century building with a colonnaded courtyard, which houses an interesting museum; the houses where Victor Hugo and the Lumière brothers were born (the latter being the inventors of the cinematograph); the 12th century cathedral; the remains of a Roman triumphal arch; the famous astronomical clock housed in a room next to the cathedral; and the citadel itself, which is reached by a path up from the cathedral, and which houses a Zoo, a Natural History Museum, a Museum of the French Resistance and a Museum of the Crafts and Traditions of the Franche-Comté. There is insufficient space to do justice to Besançon here, but mention must be made of its clock making and its man-made fibre industries (Rayon was invented and first manufactured here). Clocks and watches have been made here since the 17th century, and there is a National School of Clock and Watchmaking in the city.

The Préfecture, Besançon

CHALAIN LAKE (39)   *About 25k E Lons-le-Saunier*

This is one of a series of attractive lakes in this part of the Jura (See Michelin Map No. 70), and we have included it here, as it has a lively plage and a large camp site on its eastern shore.

CHAMPAGNOLE (39)   *34k ENE Lons-le-Saunier*

Busy town at the southern end of the Route des Sapins (The Pine Tree Route) (See Page 117). Also explore the valley of the upper Ain including the Billaude waterfall, eight kilometres south.

Besançon

Gateway at Besançon

CHAMPLITTE (70)   *20k NNW Gray*

Picturesque old fortified town on the banks of the Salon river, with wine-growers' houses, and a château of the 16th and 18th century, with an interesting Departmental Museum of History and Folklore. The church with its 15th century bell tower, contains a fine collection of sculptures from the abbeys of Theuley and Champlitte.

CHÂTEAU-CHALON (39)   *15k NNE Lons-le-Saunier*

Old village on a rocky hilltop, with vineyards below. A castle was built here to protect a Benedictine abbey founded in the 8th century. There are splendid views from the ruined castle, and there is an old gate in the ramparts. The vineyards of Château-Chalon are some of the best known in the Jura.

Château-Chalon

Franche Comté

Dole Church

Hérisson Waterfalls. Photograph by Peter Titchmarsh

Joux Château

CHÂTEAU-DU-PIN (39)　　　*5k N Lons-le-Saunier*

With its massive keep and 15th century tower, this château, built in the 13th century on the top of a steep hill, is one of the loveliest in the Franche-Comté.

CLÉRON (25)　　　*25k S Besançon*

This well restored 14th century château is beautifully sited above the Loue river, and is especially noted for its fine chimneypieces.

CONSOLATION CIRQUE (25)　*15k NNW Villers-le-Lac*

This great amphitheatre is the birthplace of the Dessoubre river, and one of the outstanding natural features of the Franche-Comté. There are fine views from the nearby Roche-du-Prêtre.

DOLE (39)　　　*360k SE Paris*

At one time the capital city of the Franche-Comté, Dole is delightfully situated on the banks of the River Doubs, a large town of over 30,000 inhabitants. Although considerably industrialised, there are quiet corners in the old part of the town, with many attractive 17th century houses, especially in the vicinity of the fine 16th century church of Notre Dame. See also the splendid wrought-iron work in the Court of Justice (which was once a convent), the two museums, and the house where Louis Pasteur was born in 1822, which combines material relating to his life, with a museum showing the working of a tannery (the Rue Pasteur, used to be the street of the Tanners).

FAUCOGNEY (70)　　　*15k E Luxeuil-les-Bains*

Small town below the southern fringes of the Vosges, overlooked by a great sandstone rock on which stands a 13th and 14th century chapel. There is a fascinating area of miniature lakes to the south and east which is well worth exploring.

GRAY (70)　　　*46k NW Besançon*

Modest market town attractively sited on the banks of the Saône, with many 16th and 17th century houses, a handsome Hôtel de Ville, and a museum in the château containing many works by the mythological painter, Pierre Prudhon (1758 – 1823).

HÉRISSON WATERFALLS (39) *35k E Lons-le-Saunier*

An impressive series of falls, below and to the west of the Pic de l'Aigle. These should on no account be missed.

JOUX CHÂTEAU (25)　　　*4k SSE Pontarlier*

Dramatic fortress dominating the steep sided defile in the Jura created by the River Doubs, known as La Cluse. For many years it was a state prison, but it now houses an interesting Military Museum.*

*Organised visits

SOURCE OF THE RIVER LISON ((25))

15k E Salins-les-Bains

This river emerges from the Sarrazine Cave, in attractive hill country near the village of Nans-sous-Sainte-Anne. Well worth visiting.

LONS-LE-SAUNIER (39)　*406k SE Paris, 52k S Dole*

Principal town of the Jura Département, Lons-le-Saunier is pleasantly sited in the western foothills of the Jura mountains. See especially the arcaded rue du

continued

Commerce, the home of Rouget-de-Lisle, the composer of the 'Marseillaise', the 11th century crypt of St-Désiré church, the museum in the Town Hall, and the interior of the Cordeliers Church, which was completely restored in the 18th century. Local industries include cheese, clocks, optical instruments and chocolate.

SOURCE OF THE RIVER LOUE (25)
20k NNW Pontarlier
Here in the gorges of Nouailles, the River Loue emerges from a great hole in the ground, and the pretty village of Mouthier Haute-Pierre, with its old Cluniac priory, is only a short distance downstream.

18th century elegance at Luxeuil-les-Bains

LURE (70)
30k ENE Vesoul
Small town in the Ognon valley, with forest country on almost every side, and a fascinating area of woodlands and lakes to the north. There is a pleasant 18th century church.

LUXEUIL-LES-BAINS (70)
366k ESE Paris,
52k WNW Belfort
A 'thermal resort' in pleasantly wooded country, with many 18th century buildings bearing witness to its popularity with those taking the waters, for at least two hundred years. See especially the 15th century 'Maison Carée', the former town hall, now a museum; the church of St-Pierre; the houses of Cardinal Jouffroy and the Abbot François; and the 13th century abbey belfry.

Lake Saint-Point, near Malbuisson

MALBUISSON (25)
15k SSW Pontarlier
Lively holiday resort situated above the shores of the long Lake Saint-Point, with a bathing beach, sailing and boating. Pine woods are much in evidence.

MARNAY (70)
24k SE Gray
Small village attractively sited on the banks of the River Ognon, with a 14th century church and an old fortified castle.

MÉTABIEF (25)
20k S Pontarlier
Popular winter sports and summer resort combining the five localities of Jougne, Les Hôpitaux-Neufs, Métabief, Les-Longevilles and Rochejean. There is a cable-cabin-way up the pine clad slopes of the Mont-d'Or, and excellent hotel and camping facilities.

Montbéliard

MONCLEY (25)
16k NW Besançon
Here is a fine 18th century château, built by the architect Claude-Joseph-Alexandre-Bertrand on a slight mound on a bend in the River Ognon. There is a splendid Neo-Classic portico, and a fascinating fully equipped Neo-Gothic kitchen.

MONTBÉLIARD (25)
22k S Belfort
Busy industrial centre, with the 'old town' of Montbéliard dominated by its hill top castle... re-built in the 18th century, but retaining 15th and 16th century towers, and containing museums of painting and natural history. The Autoroute A36 runs just to the south-east of the town, and the Peugeot car factory is also close by, at Sochaux. Do not miss a visit to the fascinating Peugeot Museum.

At the Peugeot Museum, Sochaux, near Montbéliard

Franche Comté

Morez-du-Jura

The River Loue at Ornans

Le Corbusier's chapel at Ronchamp

MOREZ-DU-JURA (39)   *58k ESE Lons-le-Saunier*
  Small industrial town in the deep wooded valley of the Bienne, with a fascinating assortment of viaducts, which can best be viewed from the Roche-au-Dade, above the D69, just to the west of the town. Morez is noted for its many saw mills, enamelled-plate and clock making factories; and there is a National Centre for Optical Research here. Explore south-westwards along the little D126, which follows down the gorges of the Bienne towards St-Claude.

ORNANS (25)   *25k SSE Besançon*
  Delightful village with old houses lining both banks of the River Loue, some actually overhanging the water (These are floodlit during the holiday season). The mathematician Pierre Vernier (remember the Vernier scale) and the painter Gustave Courbet, were both born in Ornans, and the house and tomb of Courbet may both be seen. See also the Courbet Museum, the 12th and 15th century church and the castle from which there are splendid views out over the whole valley.

OSSELLE CAVES (25)   *20k SW Besançon*
  A fascinating series of chambers and galleries almost two kilometres in length, with fine stalagmites and stalactites. Turn south, off N73 at St-Vit.

POLIGNY (39)   *28k NNE Lons-le-Saunier*
  Pleasant little town at the entrance to the blind valley, the Culée de Vaux, and overlooked by rocky heights. There is a wealth of old buildings including the Hôtel de Ville, in which there is a small museum; two churches, a 15th century convent, 17th century cloisters and an interesting pharmacy in the Hôtel-Dieu. There is attractively wooded hill country to the immediate east, with good walking possibilities. Use Michelin Map No. 70.

PONTARLIER (25)   *455k SE Paris*
  An old town on the Doubs river at the entrance to one of the loveliest valleys cut through the Jura, the Cluse de Joux. See the church of St-Benigne, with its lovely Renaissance porch and the triumphal arch in honour of Louis XV. Situated only a few kilometres from the Swiss border, Pontarlier was for many years known as the 'Key to France', and it makes an excellent base from which to explore this part of the Jura.

RAY-SUR-SAÔNE (70)   *28k NE Gray*
  Handsome 14th and 18th century château overlooking the Saône. The present structure is largely the work of the architect Bertrand, who was also responsible for Moncley about thirty kilometres to the south (See Page 115).

RONCHAMP (70)   *20k WNW Belfort*
  Small village in the lovely Rahin valley, renowned throughout the world for the marvellous chapel on the hill above it, Notre-Dame-du-Haut. This was built in 1955 by the architect Le Corbusier, who brought all his immensely imaginative skills to bear upon the project. Do not on any account miss a visit to this uniquely moving building.

LES ROUSSES (39)   *66k ESE Lons-le-Saunier*
  Winter sports and summer holiday resort in the Jura, close to the Swiss border, with a wide variety of hotels
continued

and restaurants. There is a small lake about three kilometres to the north-east.

ST-CLAUDE (39)
60k SE Lons-le-Saunier

Busy industrial town and holiday centre, dramatically sited at the confluence of the Bienne and Tacon rivers. See especially the fascinating Pipe Museum (St-Claude is renowned for its pipe making), and the Gothic cathedral, with its lovely 15th century choir stalls. Situated in the high Jura, St-Claude is an excellent centre for exploring the numerous waterfalls, caves, and gorges to be found in this area (Use Michelin Map No. 70).

Instruction at Les Rousses

ST-HIPPOLYTE (25)
30k S Montbéliard

Attractive little town in a wooded valley site at the confluence of the Doubs and Dessoubre rivers. There are many 17th century houses with oversailing upper storeys and an interesting 14th century church. This is in some of the loveliest Jura country and the fishing is excellent here.

SALINS-LES-BAINS (39)
42k SSW Besançon

Small health resort sited along the banks of the little river Furieuse, with the remains of its town walls and towers, an elegant little 18th century town-hall, and two interesting churches. There are guided tours of its underground salt workings, and in contrast, tours of the Fort of St-André, from which there are fine views out over the town.

ROUTE DES SAPINS (The Pine Trees Route) (25 – 39)

This is a delightful fifty kilometre scenic route largely through the outstandingly beautiful pine forest of La Joux, from Levier (which is 22k E of Salins-les-Bains) to Champagnole (which is 34k E of Lons-le-Saunier). On the route will be found an arboretum, with pine trees from all over the world; picnic areas and playgrounds; and many giant pine trees.

Early days at Les Rousses   *St-Claude*

VESOUL (70)
50k NNE Besançon

Busy 'capital' of the Haute Saône, with considerable light industry. There are many old houses of the 16th, 17th and 18th century and a pleasant 18th century church (St-Georges). The town is dominated by the dramatic hill-top of La Motte, from which there are outstanding views to the Jura and the Vosges, and which can be reached on foot in about half an hour.

Distant view of St-Claude

VILLERS-LE-LAC (25)
70k ESE Besançon

Popular little holiday resort town close to the Swiss border, and located on the River Doubs, which here widens out to form a lake. Take the river trip down the Doubs to the Saut-du-Doubs, where the river suddenly plunges down a hundred feet; and also the road journey to the Chatelot Barrage (about ten kilometres to the north-east).

VOUGLANS BARRAGE AND LAKE (39)
About 30k SE Lons-le-Saunier

This great dam across the river Ain was completed in 1969, and a lake two thirds the size of Lake Annecy has been created in the lovely Jura mountains. See the dam itself, the daring bridge of La Pyle, and take some of the many forest walks, fish, swim or sail.

Saut-du-Doubs, near Villers-le-Lac

Franche Comté

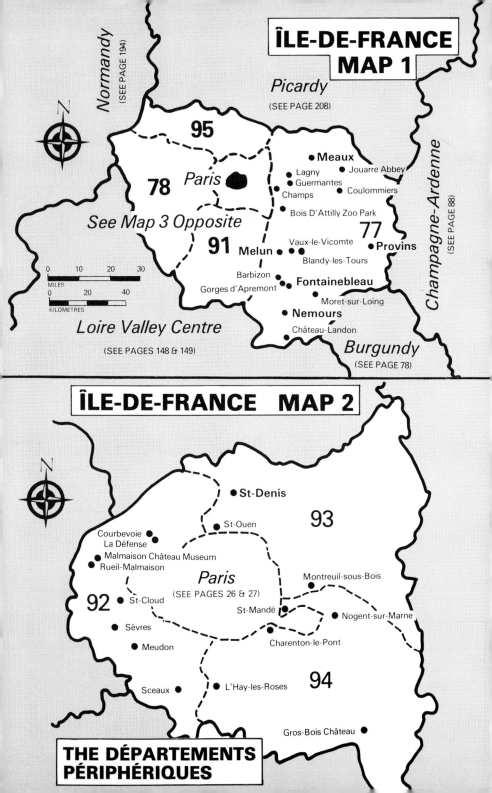

ÎLE-DE-FRANCE MAP 1

Normandy (SEE PAGE 194)

Picardy (SEE PAGE 208)

Champagne-Ardenne (SEE PAGE 88)

95

Paris

78

See Map 3 Opposite

91

MILES
0 10 20 30

KILOMETRES
0 20 40

• **Meaux**

Lagny • Jouarre Abbey

• Guermantes • Coulommiers

Champs

• Bois D'Attilly Zoo Park

77

Vaux-le-Vicomte

• **Provins**

Melun

Blandy-les-Tours

Barbizon

• **Fontainebleau**

Gorges d'Apremont

Moret-sur-Loing

• **Nemours**

Château-Landon

Loire Valley Centre

(SEE PAGES 148 & 149)

Burgundy

(SEE PAGE 78)

ÎLE-DE-FRANCE MAP 2

• **St-Denis**

• St-Ouen

93

Courbevoie
La Défense

• Malmaison Château Museum
Rueil-Malmaison

Paris

(SEE PAGES 26 & 27)

Montreuil-sous-Bois

92

• St-Cloud

St-Mandé •

• Nogent-sur-Marne

• Sèvres

Charenton-le-Pont

• Meudon

• Sceaux

• L'Hay-les-Roses

94

Gros-Bois Château •

THE DÉPARTEMENTS PÉRIPHÉRIQUES

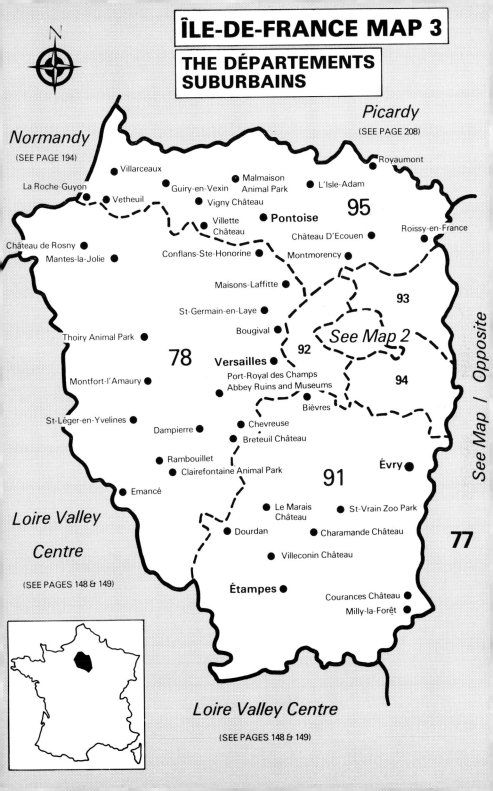

ÎLE-DE-FRANCE MAP 3

THE DÉPARTEMENTS SUBURBAINS

Picardy
(SEE PAGE 208)

Normandy
(SEE PAGE 194)

Royaumont

Villarceaux

Malmaison Animal Park

L'Isle-Adam

La Roche-Guyon

Guiry-en-Vexin

Vetheuil

Vigny Château

95

Villette Château

Pontoise

Roissy-en-France

Château D'Ecouen

Château de Rosny

Conflans-Ste-Honorine

Montmorency

Mantes-la-Jolie

Maisons-Laffitte

93

St-Germain-en-Laye

Bougival

See Map 2

Thoiry Animal Park

78

92

Versailles

Montfort-l'Amaury

Port-Royal des Champs Abbey Ruins and Museums

94

Bièvres

St-Léger-en-Yvelines

Chevreuse

Dampierre

Breteuil Château

Rambouillet

Évry

Clairefontaine Animal Park

91

Emancé

Le Marais Château

St-Vrain Zoo Park

77

Loire Valley

Dourdan

Charamande Château

Centre

Villeconin Château

(SEE PAGES 148 & 149)

Étampes

Courances Château

Milly-la-Forêt

See Map 1 / Opposite

Loire Valley Centre

(SEE PAGES 148 & 149)

Île-de-France

Comprises the following Départements
Seine-et-Marne (77) Seine-St-Denis (93)
Yvelines (78)   Val-de-Marne (94)
Essonne (91)   Val-d'Oise (95)
Hauts-de-Seine (92)

With Paris at its centre, this region was the base from which the French kings gradually extended their suzerainty over the whole country that was to become modern France. With its great forests, many of which were once royal hunting preserves, its great châteaux, its ancient abbeys and its old towns and villages of grey stone and mellow brick, the Île de France is still a true microcosm of France as a whole.

This is also true of the busy inner departments (The Départements Périphériques) which come up to the line of the city walls, in most instances followed by the busy motorway-style Boulevarde Périphérique. Here will be found dramatic modern housing developments, great swaths of motorways, brilliant new factories and public buildings... but never far away, there are small self-contained towns, châteaux, parks and forests.

Beyond the Départements Périphériques lie the Départements Suburbains, with which we have included Seine et Marne (77). The pulse of the great city is still sometimes evident, but here, with splendid forest country never far away, will be found many of the great châteaux of France... Versailles, Fontainebleau, Rambouillet, Vaux-le-Victomte, St-Germain-en-Laye, Maisons-Lafitte and Ecouen. There are also lovely old towns like Montfort, L'Isle-Adam, Moret, Provins and Nemours, the great abbey ruins of Royaumont and Port-Royal, and for the young in heart... river banks and forest glades to be explored, and wildlife parks to be visited. All this is never further than 80 kilometres from the heart of Paris, and much is considerably nearer... so, please, don't spend all your time in that most tempting of all capital cities.

Breteuil Château, with the Marquis and Marquise de Breteuil. Photograph by Almasy

BARBIZON (77)   60k SSE Paris, 8k NW Fontainebleau
A delightful village on the northern edge of the Forest of Fontainebleau, with a fine selection of hotels and restaurants. This was a great favourite of Robert Louis Stevenson's, and the painter Millet had his studio here (Open all the year). Theodore Rousseau also lived here and his house is open at weekends in winter, and daily in summer. Walk south and east from here, into the forest, to visit the Gorges d'Apremont (See Fontainebleau, Page 122).

BIÈVRES (91)   15k SW Paris, To SE of N306
The town hall houses an interesting 'French Museum of Photography'.

BLANDY-LES-TOURS (77)   60k SE Paris, 10k ENE Melun
Minute village with the ruins of an important 14th century castle.

BOIS D'ATTILLY ZOO PARK (77)   25k ESE Paris
(This is near the village of Ozoir-la-Ferrière, which is on the RN4, but access is probably best from the autoroute A4 if travelling from Paris. Leave at Val-Maubuée Interchange, and drive south on N371).

Interesting zoo park with a large collection of mammals and birds, many of which are in large semi-free enclosures.

BOUGIVAL (78)   18k W Paris
This is a charming village on the Seine, much loved and painted by Monet, Renoir and their artist friends. It has at least two outstanding restaurants, and a visit here in summertime is well worthwhile.

BRETEUIL CHÂTEAU (78)   35k SW Paris, 17k ENE Rambouillet
Situated in the valley of Chevreuse, the central part of this impressive château was built in the early 17th *continued*

continued

century. It has been added to over the past three centuries, and the exterior is in the style of Louis XIII. See the splendidly furnished and decorated interiors, and the great park with its picnic areas, lakes and woodlands. Restaurant, tea shop, exhibitions.

CHAMPS-SUR-MARNE (77)   *20k E Paris*
Elegant 18th century château standing high above the Marne on the edge of the Paris suburbs. It was let to Madame de Pompadour, who spent much time and money on improvements and decoration. The formal gardens are the creation of Le Nôtre's nephew, Claude Desgots.

Champs Château

CHARAMANDE CHÂTEAU (91)   *40k S Paris, to E of N20*
Fine château in brick and stone, built by François Mansart in the reign of Louis XIV, with a park laid out by Le Nôtre.

CHARENTON-LE-PONT (94)   *10k SE Paris*
This highly built up area just beyond the Porte de Picpus has a most unusual museum (5, bis, rue Victor Hugo)... The French Museum of Bread. There are tours on Tuesdays & Thursdays.

CHÂTEAU-LANDON (77)   *100k SSE Paris, 22k S Nemours*
Medieval village surrounded by ramparts. A church with 11th century wall paintings has been discovered under the ruined abbey of St-Séverin.

The Salon Chinois, Champs

Madame de Pompadour's Boudoir, Champs

CHEVREUSE (78)   *32k SW Paris*
Old market town with the ruins of a château, and attractive walks in the Vaux de Cernay, about 6ks SW.

CLAIREFONTAINE ANIMAL PARK (DES YVE-LINES) (78)   *55k SW Paris, 8k SE Rambouillet*
Here at the south-eastern end of the Forest of Rambouillet, there is a reserve area where the public are able to spot various species of deer found wild in the forests of the Île de France. Patience and quietness will be required, but a visit here is well worthwhile.

CONFLANS-STE-HONORINE (78)   *30k NW Paris*
This busy town on the banks of the Seine is the great centre for its river navigation, and in the Château du Prieuré, in the town park, will be found a most interesting River Craft Museum, with layouts, photographs and a diorama.

Courances Château

Courances Château

COULOMMIERS (77)   *61k E Paris*
Prosperous market town in the lovely Morin valley, with a museum in its attractive Parc des Capucins.

COURANCES CHÂTEAU (91)   *57k S Paris, 5k N Milly-la-Forêt*
Elegant château, designed by Gilles Le Breton, the architect of Fontainebleau, with outstandingly beautiful gardens and park.

COURBEVOIE (92)   *11k NW Paris*
This busy area of north-west Paris includes 'La Défense', a modern development including several high

continued *The Gardens, Courances Château*

At La Défense

L'Arche... at La Défense

Ecouen Château

Fontainebleau Palace

The Bedroom of the Empress, Fontainebleau

towers, a great exhibition hall and a national industry centre (See Below). The Roybet-Fould Museum has 16th and 17th century tapestries, a fine collection of toys and dolls and some works by Carpeaux, the famous sculptor who died in Courbevoie.

DAMPIERRE (78) *35k SW Paris, 15k NE Rambouillet*
Small village at the gates of a fine 17th century château built by architect J. H. Mansart, and surrounded by a great park laid out by Le Nôtre.

LA DÉFENSE (92) *11k NW Paris*
A brilliant 'new city' situated to the west of the Seine, beyond the Pont de Neuilly. All roads are beneath the city, and there are large open spaces, and many dramatically tall buildings. Many international companies are basing their French operations here, and it is planned that the city will have work for over 100,000 people when completed.

DOURDAN (91) *55k SW Paris*
Small town with quiet forest country to its south and west (the Forest of Dourdan). It has an elegant church, re-built in the 16th century, and the ruins of a castle, built by King Philippe Auguste in the 13th century.

ECOUEN CHÂTEAU (95) *30k N Paris*
Highly elegant Renaissance château, built in the mid-16th century, and now housing a Renaissance Museum based on collections from the Cluny Museum in Paris. See also the stained glass in the nearby church.

EMANCÉ (78) *68k WSW Paris*
At the Château de Sauvage will be found a pleasant Ornithological Park, with a great variety of birds at liberty.

ÉTAMPES (91) *50k SSW Paris*
Pleasant old town with no fewer than four churches (Do not miss the Romanesque Notre-Dame-du-Fort), and a massive 12th century tower... the Guinette, where King Philippe Auguste held his queen, Ingeborg, a prisoner for no less than 12 years.

FONTAINEBLEAU (77) *65k SE Paris*
Small town bounded on the south and east by the magnificent royal palace of the same name, and both in the heart of the great forest of Fontainebleau. The palace dates largely from the 16th and 17th centuries, and was the favourite of Napoleon. The somewhat severe exterior conceals a richly decorated and furnished interior, and the surrounding gardens are delightful. There are a multitude of paths through the forest, but special mention must be made of the Gorges de Franchard (5ks east) and the Gorges d'Apremont (6ks north-east). Here, as in several other areas, the sandstone rock on which the forest stands, lends contrasting colour to the infinite variety of the woodland greens.

FORESTS OF THE ÎLE-DE-FRANCE REGION
This region is particularly rich in forests, and due to their proximity to Paris, they are well served by car parks and other visitor facilities. Space does not allow descriptions, but to visit these forests use Michelin Map No. 97, a special sheet covering all the Île de France

continued

Region. Outstanding forests are:— Armainvilliers, Fontainebleau, Jouy-le-Châtel, Sénart, Sourdin, Fausse-Repose, Marly, Rambouillet, Saint-Germain-en-Laye, Versailles, Verrières, Dourdan, La Malmaison, Meudon, Clichy-sous-Bois, Coubron, Montfermeil, Carnelle, Isle-Adam and Montmorency. For details see the excellent Paris/Île de France brochure, published in English by the Comité Régional de Tourism d'Île-de-France.

GROS-BOIS CHÂTEAU (94) 20k SE Paris, S of Boissy
This impressive château was originally built in the 15th century, but its great days were during the First Empire, when it was owned by Marshal Berthier, the Major-General of the Grande Armée. The Empress Josephine was a frequent guest at the lavish receptions here, and much of the magnificence of this era has been preserved in the château's decoration, furniture and pictures.

In Fontainebleau Forest

GUERMANTES CHÂTEAU (77) 30k E Paris, 3k S Lagny-sur-Marne
Early 17th century château, with a splendid twenty eight metre long, 18th century gallery which was dubbed by contemporaries, 'La Belle Inutile'. This has no fewer than 18 windows opening on to the park, which was designed by Le Nôtre.

GUIRY-EN-VEXIN (95) 55k NW Paris, 8k SE Magny-en-Vexin
Village complete with pleasant 17th century château by Mansart, a small archaeological museum and an interesting 15th and 16th century church.

Gros-Bois Château

L'HAY-LES-ROSES (94) 10k S Paris
Pleasant park on a hillside overlooking the Bièvre valley, and enclosing an extensive rose garden, with more than 3,500 varieties. There is also a Rose Museum.

L'ISLE-ADAM (95) 40k N Paris
Attractive town between the great forest which bears its name and the lovely river Oise, which has one of the largest 'river beaches' in France at this point. See also the old bridge, the church of St-Martin and the Cassan Chinese Pavilion.

Maisons-Laffitte

JOUARRE ABBEY CHURCH (77) 70k E Paris, 3k S La Ferté-sous-Jouarre, 20k E Meaux
Here is a Merovingian crypt containing an astonishing series of Merovingian tombs... the last resting place of several 7th century Christian notables, including Agilbert, Bishop of Paris, who had previously been Bishop of Dorchester. Do not miss a visit here.

LAGNY-SUR-MARNE (77) 33k E Paris
Busy industrial city on the Marne, with a fine 13th century church, and a 14th century gateway, the only real items of interest.

MAISONS-LAFFITTE (78) 20k NW Paris
This was the architect François Mansart's masterpiece... his achievement marking the ultimate flowering of the French Renaissance style. Do not miss this.

The Boudoir, Maisons-Laffitte

The Summer Dining Room, Maisons-Laffitte

123

Malmaison

Napoleon's Bedroom, Malmaison

Mantes Cathedral   *In Meaux Cathedral*

The Seine, near Mantes

MALMAISON CHÂTEAU MUSEUM (92)

15k W Paris

This pleasant 18th century château was the personal home of Napoleon and Josephine, where they spent the happiest years of their married life, and where she spent much of her time between their divorce and her death in 1814. The whole building has been left as it was during their occupation, as a museum devoted to the Emperor and to the wife to whom he was so passionately devoted during the early years of their marriage.

MALMAISON ANIMAL PARK (95)   *45k NW Paris*

Pleasant animal park near Cormeilles-en-Vexin, with deer, geese, swans and horses. There is a little train and picnic area.

MANTES-LA-JOLIE (78)   *60k WNW Paris*

Busy town astride the Seine, with a fine 12th – 14th century church similar in style to Notre-Dame in Paris and which contains the lovely Navarre chapel. There is a 14th century gateway on the riverside, and an interesting 18th century façade to the old hospital; but unfortunately Mantes was badly bombed during the 2nd World War, and much of it has been re-built since.

LE MARAIS CHÂTEAU (91)   *45k SSW Paris, 12k NE Dourdan*

Delightful 18th century château, with park, museum and feudal dungeons.

MEAUX (77)   *55k E Paris*

An ancient town on the River Marne, with a 13th and 14th century cathedral, the contents of which includes the tomb of Bishop Bossuet (1627 – 1704), historian and orator. Part of the Bishop's Palace has been transformed into an interesting museum and the gardens which were laid out by Le Nôtre, are also open.

MELUN (77)   *55k SE Paris*

Busy 'capital' of the Seine et Marne Département, Melun lies on the Seine, just to the north of the great forest country of Fontainebleau. The church of Notre-Dame is an interesting early gothic building, and there is a modest Municipal Museum.

MEUDON (92)   *12k SW Paris*

Here on the edge of pleasant woodlands is a busy town, part of the Paris conurbation, with three interesting museums… the Air Museum, which is believed to house the richest aeronautical collection in the world. The Meudon Museum, situated in the house of Molière's widow, and devoted to the history of the area. The Rodin Museum, in the house where Rodin lived for a long time until his death. This contains many of his sketches and layouts, but should not be confused with the Rodin Museum in Paris.

MILLY-LA-FORÊT (91)   *19k W Fontainebleau*

Attractive little town on the western fringes of the forest of Fontainebleau, with a 15th century wooden market hall and the remains of a medieval castle.

MONTFORT-L'AMAURY (78)   *50k E Paris*

Pleasant medieval town with a ruined castle, held by the De Montforts (Simon de Montfort, the father of the English barons' leader, defeated at the Battle of

continued

Evesham, was born here). See the castle ruins, the interesting 15th – 16th century church with its fine stained glass; and the home of the composer Maurice Ravel, which is a museum in his memory.

MONTMORENCY (95) *20k N Paris*
Large town on the northern outskirts of Paris, with a fine 16th century collegiate church, the ancient burial chapel of the Montmorency family, and a museum relating to Jean-Jacques Rousseau, its most renowned citizen.

MONTREUIL-SOUS-BOIS (93) *8k E Paris*
Very much part of urban Paris, Montreuil has a pleasant park in which is situated a Living History Museum. This illustrates various aspects of French social history.

Moret-sur-Loing

MORET-SUR-LOING (77) *75k SE Paris*
Delightful little town with old houses looking out over the River Loing, with old winding streets, 12th century dungeons, the house 'of François 1st', and the church of Notre-Dame. Sisley painted many of his famous riverside scenes here.

NEMOURS (77) *80k SSE Paris*
Small town astride the River Loing, 15 ks south of Fontainebleau. There is a 16th century church, a local history museum, and pleasant views down the river from the main bridge. Hire bicycles from the station and explore northwards into the forest country of Fontainebleau.

Provins... a distant view

NOGENT-SUR-MARNE (94) *14k E Paris*
Although much built up, there are restaurants by the river, a marina and an aquatic centre. See also the church of St-Saturnin and the 'Maison Nationale des Artistes', an attractive house in a pleasant park.

PONTOISE (95) *35k NW Paris*
The old part of this busy town, now almost within the Paris spread, is attractively sited on slopes above the Oise river. Amongst its steep narrow streets will be found the lovely Gothic churches of St-Maclou and Notre-Dame, and there is an interesting museum in the rue Lemercier. The ancient abbey of Maubuisson lies across the Oise, to the east of the bridge.

PORT-ROYAL DES CHAMPS ABBEY RUINS AND MUSEUMS (78) *30k WSW Paris, 3k S Trappes*
Here are the remains of the ancient abbey of Port Royal, founded in 1204, and a place of retreat for many men of letters in the 17th century, amongst them, Pascal and Racine. There are two interesting museums here.

Medieval walls, Provins *Caesar's Tower, Provins*

PROVINS (77) *85k ESE Paris*
Fascinating medieval town complete with walls, towers, underground passages, three medieval churches, and a fine tithe barn. Explore the narrow, sometimes steep streets, and do not miss the two 13th century houses in the rue des Capucins.

RAMBOUILLET (78) *55k SW Paris*
Pleasant town, with the forest of Rambouillet on almost every side. The great château has had royal connections since medieval times, but the present

continued

The Dining Room, Rambouillet

Île-de-France

Royaumont Abbey *Royaumont Abbey*

In the Bois Préau Museum, Malmaison

St-Denis *Monument in St-Denis*

The Terrace, St-Germain-en-Laye

building, which has been the summer residence of the Presidents of France since 1897, is mostly of 18th century origin. See the richly decorated and furnished interior, the fine gardens, the 'Bergerie Nationale' (The National Sheep Farm, established here by Louis XVI), and the Laiterie de la Reine, built for Marie Antoinette by Louis XVI. Do not miss a visit to the fascinating Rambolitrain Museum in the Place Jeanne d'Arc. This contains over 4,000 different models.

LA ROCHE-GUYON (95)   75k WNW Paris
Small village beautifully situated on the curving banks of the Seine, with a ruined château of the 12th – 16th centuries, and a second more recent château.

ROISSY-EN-FRANCE (95)   25k NE Paris
This is the site of one of the world's most impressive airports, the Charles de Gaulle.

ROSNY CHÂTEAU (78)   68k WNW Paris,
7k W Mantes-la-Jolie
Splendid late 16th and early 17th century mansion, built for the Marshal-Duke Sully, Henry of Navarre's chief minister. The Duchesse de Berry made this her home for 13 years in the early 19th century, and the personality of both of these famous figures is still strongly established here. See the great park laid out by Olivier de Serres, the 17th century agriculturalist, and do not miss the church, in which will be found Corot's 'Flight into Egypt'.

ROYAUMONT (95)   40k N Paris, 10k SW Chantilly
Founded in 1228 by St-Louis, the abbey of Royaumont became one of the great monastic houses of France, and the present remains convey at least something of its former splendour.

RUEIL-MALMAISON (92)   15k W Paris
Busy Paris suburb, but see the church, which contains the tomb of Napoleon's Josephine and a lovely Italian Renaissance organ chest. The châteaux of Malmaison (See Page 124), and Bois Préau, once the respective residences of Napoleon and Josephine, are now both National Museums and well worth visiting.

ST-CLOUD (92)   12k W Paris
Although part of urban Paris, this is noted for its fine park, which was laid out by Le Nôtre. It is possible to explore the park on hired bicycles and there are splendid prospects out over Paris from various viewpoints.

ST-DENIS (93)   10k N Paris
Here is the great medieval church of Saint-Denis... the first important Gothic building in France, and the inspiration of Chartres cathedral. For twelve centuries the kings and queens of France were buried here, and although the graves were desecrated during the Revolution, the tombs themselves were saved, and they now provide a splendid illustration of French history and art. See also the fine Art and History Museum.

ST-GERMAIN-EN-LAYE (78)   20k WNW Paris
Elegant town on the banks of the Seine, with a great château which was the summer residence of the Kings of France from the 12th century. The present château was built in the 16th century in the Renaissance style, and after a chequered career was restored by Napoleon III to house the National Museum of Antiquities, (which should not be missed). See also the formal gardens laid out by the industrious Le Nôtre, and walk in the forest
continued

of St-Germain which lies to the immediate north. The composer Debussy was born here in 1862, and there is a statue of him in the town.

ST-LÉGER-EN-YVELINES (78) *55k WSW Paris*
Minute village in the northern part of the forest of Rambouillet. With two hotels this would make an excellent base from which to explore the forest... either on foot or by car.

ST-MANDÉ (94) *12k E Paris*
Here will be found the City Transport Museum of Paris (60, avenue Ste-Marie), which houses many of the vehicles used in the urban and regional public transport systems.

St-Vrain Zoo Park. A St-Vrain Zoo Photograph

ST-OUEN (93) *7k N Paris*
This busy part of urban Paris is chiefly noted for its Flea Market (Marché aux Puces)... a splendidly mixed second-hand fair which takes place each Saturday, Sunday and Monday; with stalls spreading over a wide area to the immediate north and north west of the Porte de Clignancourt.

ST-VRAIN ZOO PARK (91) *35k S Paris, 9k SE Arpajon*
A splendid wildlife park in the tradition of Longleat and Woburn (It is in fact in association with the Chipperfield Organisation). There are extensive drive-through areas enclosing lions, tigers, elephants, zebras, giraffes, and a wide variety of other wild animals. There are lakes on which boat safaris may be taken, together with picnic areas, restaurants, fishing, etc. Do not miss a visit to this fascinating park.

Sceaux Château

Sceaux Château

SCEAUX (92) *12k SW Paris*
Magnificent park laid out by Le Nôtre for Colbert, containing a Grand Canal, over a kilometre long, an octagonal pond, a waterfall, a château with collections of paintings, tapestries and ceramics, an orangery built by J. H. Mansart, and two exquisite 18th century pavilions. This is all the property of the Hauts-de-Seine Département and is operated as the Museum of the Île de France.

SÈVRES (92) *12k WSW Paris*
Here in this small town, world renowned for its brilliant porcelain, is the great National Ceramics Museum, which is claimed to be the most complete collection in the world. See also the National Porcelain Factory, around which there are guided tours on certain days.

At the Sèvres Porcelain Factory

Dining Room at Vaux-le-Vicomte

THOIRY ANIMAL PARK (78) *50k W Paris, 15k N Monfort-L'Amaury*
Exciting wildlife park in the grounds of Thoiry Château, which itself has fine collections of furniture and porcelain. Drive through the African Wild Game Reserve and Lion Park, and the Bear Park; and visit the Vivarium, the Tiger Park and Monkey Jungle. Restaurant, souvenir shop, etc.

VAUX-LE-VICOMTE (77) *50k SE Paris, 6k E Melun*
Exceptionally beautiful 17th century château, built for Louis XIV's Finance Minister, Fouquet, by three master craftsmen... the architect Le Vau, the decorator Le Brun, and the then young landscape designer Le Nôtre. The resulting masterpiece was too much for the king,

Vaux-le-Vicomte

continued

Île-de-France

Fountains at Versailles

Versailles at night

In the Grand Trianon, Versailles

The Petit Trianon, Versailles

The King's Staircase, Versailles

and having flounced off in the midst of the grand opening, had Fouquet thrown into prison for misappropriation of public money, and soon afterwards embarked on his own grand design for Versailles, having resolved never again to be outshone by a subject.

VERSAILLES (78) *20k W Paris*
Busy modern town of almost 100,000 inhabitants, known throughout the world for its splendid château. This is almost entirely the work of engineers and architects working under the personal supervision of the Louis XIV who, at the age of 23, set out to re-build the previous château. This was in 1661, and by 1682 the grand design was largely completed, and a population of about 20,000 was then in residence. Devote at least a day to Versailles... to see the magnificent apartments, the Museum, the Orangerie, Le Nôtre's great gardens and park, the Petit Trianon, and the Car Museum. In the town, see the stables, the cathedral, the Labinet Museum and the King's Kitchen Garden.

VETHEUIL (95) *70k WNW Paris*
Minute village above the curving Seine, with a church which has a lovely Renaissance façade. There is an attractive gorge between here and Vienne-en-Arthies, a short distance westwards.

VIGNY CHÂTEAU (95) *45k NW Paris, 10k N Meulan*
Splendid château built during the reign of Louis XII for Cardinal Georges d'Amboise. Tour of park from April – November.

VILLARCEAUX *70k NW Paris*
Compact village with a handsome château rebuilt in the 18th century by Jean Courtonne.

VILLECONIN CHÂTEAU (91) *14k N Étampes*
A largely 14th century castle with later alterations including lovely timbered ceilings, and a splendidly vaulted room... the Salle de Montagu.

VILLETTE CHÂTEAU (95) *50k NW Paris*
Nr Condecourt, 4k NNE Meulan
The water gardens here are particularly attractive, and are well worth a visit.

The Seine at Vetheuil

Languedoc-Roussillon

Comprises the following Départements
Aude (11)   Lozère (48)
Gard (30)   Pyrénées Orientales (66)
Hérault (34)

The Languedoc was so named after the language of those who lived in southern France, where 'oc' meant 'yes', rather than 'oïl' or 'oui', as it was spoken in the north. To this has been added Roussillon, the land stretching south and west to the eastern Pyrénées and the border with Spain; and in the north has been added the country of the Cévennes mountains and part of the great plateau country of the Causses.

So here is a region of great contrasts... old sunbaked harbour towns like Sète and Collioure, great new holiday resorts springing up along the previously mosquito-ridden coast, splendid Roman remains at Nîmes and the nearby Pont-du-Gard, lovely medieval fortified towns like Carcassonne and Aigues-Mortes, the old university town of Montpellier, Narbonne with its Archbishop's Palaces, and the 'royal' city of Perpignan, once capital of the long vanished Kingdom of Majorca. But away from the large towns and the sparkling coast, is a hinterland of equally bewildering variety... from the Pyrénées with its sunlit valleys enriched by Romanesque abbeys and churches, to the mountains of the Haut-Languedoc and the Cévennes, with their great forests and fast flowing trout streams, and beyond to the Causses, with their deep gorges, underground rivers and colourful caves.

AGDE (34)   *22k E Béziers, 57k SW Montpellier*
A holiday resort and fishing port on the river Hérault a short distance above its entry to the sea. There is a museum of local folklore and a fine 12th century cathedral with an impressive keep giving it the appearance almost of a fortress. Considering how often the town was sacked over the centuries, it is no wonder that the citizens built their church in such a way.

AIGUES-MORTES (34)   *40k SSW Nîmes*
Small town on the edge of the haunting Camargue (See Page 230), Aigues-Mortes was founded in the 13th century by St-Louis as an embarkation port for the 7th Crusade. However the port and its canal soon silted up, and with the sea now being four miles away, the town's prosperity rapidly declined. We are now left with one of Europe's finest examples of a complete 13th century town fortification. The walk around the walls from the lovely Tower of Constance takes about three quarters of an hour and is well worthwhile.

AIGOUAL, MONT (30)   *39k N Le Vigan,*
102k NNW Montpellier
This is the second highest point in the Cévennes (See Page 133), and it is possible to come quite close to the summit by car (use D48 from Le Vigan). There is a weather observatory on the top, from which there are splendid views on a clear day.

Agde

ALÈS (30)   *45k NNW Nîmes*
A busy mining and industrial town, the old part of which was built by the great fortifier Vauban, on the site of a medieval château. See the handsome 18th century town hall, the former cathedral of St-Jean, and the attractive Bosquet Gardens.

ANDUZE (30)   *13k SW Alès*
Small town in a valley, known as the Gateway to the Cévennes, with some narrow medieval streets, a 13th century clock-tower, and several potters at work. There are interesting caves at Trabuc about 9ks NNW, and a park containing many exotic trees, the Parc Prafrance, about 3ks N of Anduze.

Aigues-Mortes

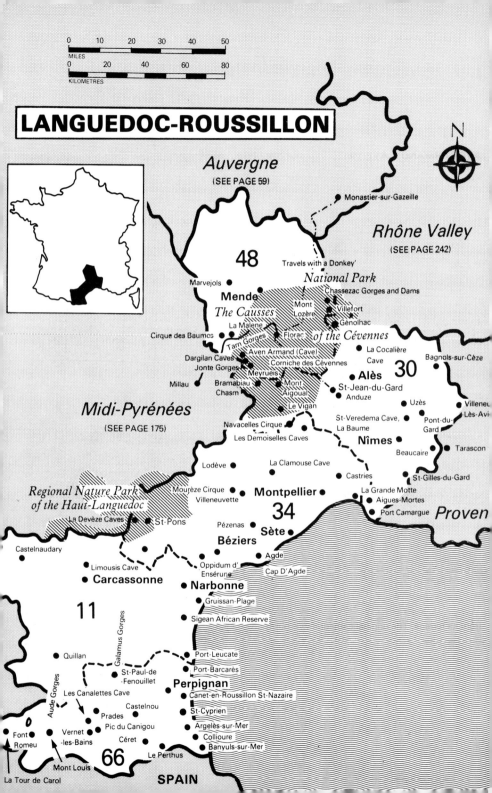

ARGELÈS-SUR-MER (66) *21k SE Perpignan*
Modest coastal town with fine beaches and several small hotels. No special features.

AUDE GORGES (11 & 66) *50k S Carcassonne*
The road southwards up the gorges of the Aude from Quillan (which is 50k S of Carcassonne) to Mont-Louis is just under seventy kilometres in length. It passes through spectacular country and must be one of the most impressive scenic drives in France.

AVEN ARMAND (CAVE) (48) *35k SW Florac*
This is situated in remote country on the southern side of the Causse Méjean. A long tunnel leads to a great chamber 165 to 330 feet wide and 130 feet high, with a great quantity of impressive stalagmites.

In the Aude Gorges   *St-Nazaire Church, Béziers*

BAGNOLS-SUR-CÈZE (30) *33k NW Avignon*
Small town in the Rhône valley with a museum containing a modest collection of Impressionist and Post-Impressionist paintings by Renoir, Monet, Bonnard, etc. Many visitors will wish to drive about eight kilometres eastwards from here to look at the Marcoule Atomic Energy Centre. One cannot enter this, but there is a well illustrated viewing area.

BANYULS-SUR-MER (66) *37k SE Perpignan*
Small fishing port and holiday resort only ten kilo-metres short of the Spanish border. The Pyrénées come down to the sea here, and Banyuls' cove is surrounded by hills. There is an excellent aquarium, attached to the marine biology laboratories. The famous sculptor Aristide Maillol, was born and died here, and there is a monument by him in the town.

Vineyards above Banyuls

BEAUCAIRE (30) *24k E Nîmes*
An old town attractively situated on the banks of the Rhône opposite Tarascon (See Page 239), of which there are fine views from the top of the castle tower. See also the Hôtel-de-Ville, built to the designs of Jules Hardouin Mansart in the late 17th century, the Romanesque chapel of St-Louis, and the museum illustrating life in old Beaucaire which will explain the great fairs held here for so many centuries.

BÉZIERS (34) *823k S Paris, 93k N Perpignan*
Busy market town and centre of the local wine industry (Hérault Département produces about 15% of all France's wine). The old town looks out over the River Orb, which is here crossed by the Canal du Midi (See the bridge and lock by Paul Riquet, who was born at Béziers in 1604, and who built the whole Canal du Midi and the port of Sète). There are fine stained glass windows in the cathedral and splendid views westwards from its terrace. The original cathedral was burnt down and the whole population slaughtered, by Simon de Montfort in 1209, during the crusade against the Albigensian heretics. See also the interesting museums and the three Romanesque churches.

Boules at Banyuls

THE BRAMABIAU CHASM (30) *19k SE Meyrueis*
Here, a river plunges underground and only re-emerges after about seven hundred metres, having dropped some ninety metres in the process. This is situated in the heart of the Cévennes National Park (See Page 133).

The River Orb at Béziers

Languedoc-Roussillon

The Pic du Canigou in springtime

St-Martin du Canigou Photograph by Peter Titchmarsh

At Le Canet

At Cap d'Agde

The Cité, Carcassonne

LES CANALETTES CAVE (66)
3k S Villefranche-de-Conflent, 9k SW Prades, 52k WSW Perpignan
Interesting cave fifty metres below the water level of the nearby river.

CANET-EN-ROUSSILLON ST-NAZAIRE (66)
13k E Perpignan
Brilliant holiday complex with nine kilometres of beach, a large yachting harbour, and a wide range of hotels and other holiday accommodation.

CANIGOU, PIC DU (48)   *About 15k S Prades*
This 2784 metre high mountain has been made famous by many poets and is almost a sacred peak to the inhabitants of Roussillon. There are excursions by jeep from Prades and Vernet-les-Bains. The abbey of St-Martin-du-Canigou which was largely re-built in the early 20th century, is dramatically sited on a rocky plateau to the south of Vernet-les-Bains.

CAP D'AGDE (34)   *28k E Béziers, 6k SE Agde*
Built on a rocky headland and overlooking an enclosed 'bay', this is probably the most architecturally interesting of the seven new holiday resorts in Languedoc-Roussillon (See La Grande Motte, Page 134). There is a good sandy beach, and no fewer than nine independent harbours. Do not miss a visit to Aqualand, an outstanding water 'fun park', with slides, waterfalls and swimming pools.

CARCASSONNE (11) *905k S Paris, 305k W Marseille*
Busy capital town of the Aude Département, with its streets still in the grid-iron pattern of the bastide-type, lower town established here in the 13th century. However it is to the walls and towers of the upper town or Cité that all visitors' eyes are drawn. Although on much earlier foundations, these walls and towers are in the main the faithful reproductions of those built by Louis IX between 1260 and 1270, a few years before he allowed the expelled local Viscount, Raymond II to build his bastide lower town. Carcassonne's walls and towers make this one of Europe's finest fortified towns, but these are mainly the work of Viollet-le-Duc, the celebrated 19th century architect and restorer, who also re-built the walls of Avignon and restored the abbey of Vézelay. However do not let this detract from your enjoyment of this unique spectacle, for le-Duc's work was brilliant, and he no doubt came very near to a true reproduction of Louis IX's great fortification works. See especially the museum in the castle and the nearby church of St-Nazaire, in which is buried Simon de Montfort, grandfather of the Simon who defied King John; walk on the walls and along the space between the two walls. In the lower town, do not overlook the excellent Museum of Art, which has a room devoted to the Surrealists.

CASTELNAUDARY (11)   *36k WNW Carcassonne*
Pleasant little town on the lovely Canal du Midi, with an attractive 14th century church and a tower with a street beneath it.

CASTELNOU (66)   *15k SW Perpignan*
Château and village on a hilltop site on the very edge of the Pyrenean foothills, which is well worth visiting. The château acted as the hub of a network of signal towers operated by the Vicomtes de Castlenou, who held the greater part of Roussillon from the 11th century.

CASTRIES (34)   *13k NE Montpellier*
A small town astride the N110, much quieter now
that the Autoroute A9 is completed. It has a ruined
Romanesque church and a handsome Renaissance
château.

CAUSSES, THE (48)   *Approx. 125k NW of Montpellier*
A series of immense limestone plateaux intersected
by deep gorges, the most famous of which are the
Gorges of the Tarn (See Page 138). The physical
characteristics of the Causses are rather similar to those
of England's Peak District, but all is on a much larger
scale, and much of the area is still remote and unspoilt.
It is of course noted for its caves and underground
rivers... typical features of limestone country.

Aqueduct at Castries

CÉRET (66)   *30k SSW Perpignan*
Small town in the Pyrénées, with plane trees lining its
boulevards and a lovely 15th century fountain in the
Place de la Victoire. This was one of the birthplaces of
Cubism, and was a favourite of Picasso, Braque, Gris,
Manolo and several others. There is a Museum of
Modern Art which has an important collection of these
artists' works. Céret's cherry orchards are renowned for
producing the earliest cherries in France.

NATIONAL PARK OF THE CÉVENNES (30 – 48 – 07)
About 75k NW Nîmes, About 90k NNW Montpellier
Created in 1970, this National Park covers no fewer
than 215,000 acres, and includes the massif of
l'Aigoual, Mont Lozère, and part of the Causse Méjean.
There are various nature walks, and the rare fauna and
flora are specially protected. There are Information
Centres at Florac and Génolhac.

In the Causse Noire, south of the Jonte Gorges
Photograph by Peter Titchmarsh

CHASSEZAC GORGES AND DAMS (48)
100k NNW Nîmes
The large hydro-electric scheme to the north of
Villefort has created delightful lake scenery, and there
are especially fine views from a point near the N106
eight kilometres north of Villefort. See the medieval
village of la Garde-Guérin, close to this point.

LA CLAMOUSE CAVE (34)   *9k N Gignac*
39k WNW Montpellier
A fine cave in the Hérault Gorges, with spectacular
stalagmites and stalactites.

LA COCALIÈRE CAVE (30)   *25k NE Ales, to E of D904*
A complex cave with passages totalling over twenty-
five kilometres in length.

COLLIOURE (66)   *25k SE Perpignan*
This is one of the most attractive little fishing ports in
the whole of southern France, and was a favourite of
Matisse, Picasso and many other painters. There are
three good beaches, a church with a very Spanish-style
interior including some fine Baroque altar-pieces; and
the remains of a castle of the Kings of Majorca (See
Perpignan, Page 137), known as the Château des
Templiers.

CORNICHE DES CÉVENNES (48)
90k NNW Montpellier
This highly scenic mountain road was built by Louis
XIV for the use of his troops, in their campaigns against
the Camisards. It runs from Florac, through
L'Hospitalet, le Pompidou and St-Roman-de-Tousque,
to St-Jean-du-Gard... a total distance of 53 kilometres.

The Harbour at Collioure
Photograph by Peter Titchmarsh

In Les Demoiselles Caves

In the Herault Valley, near Les Demoiselles Caves

The Oppidum d'Ensérune

At the Oppidum d'Ensérune

'The Little Yellow Train' – at Font-Romeu – Odeillo Station
Photograph by Peter Titchmarsh

The Old Village, Gruissan

In the Jonte Gorges
Photograph by Peter Titchmarsh

Languedoc-Roussillon

DARGILAN CAVES (48)　　　　9k WNW Meyrueis
Fascinating caves, with an entrance 850 metres up in the Causse Noir cliffs, overlooking the Jonte Gorge. Passages branch out into a variety of chambers, with stalactites and stalagmites.

LES DEMOISELLES CAVES (34)　　7k SE Ganges, 40k N Montpellier
Vast caves at the foot of cliffs overlooking the lovely Hérault valley, with an imposing central chamber called 'The Cathedral' (50 metres high), at the far end of which is a stalagmite known as 'The Virgin and Child', with all the appearance of a real statue.

LA DEVÈZE CAVES (34)　　　　5k W St-Pons, 55k WNW Béziers
Interesting caves with three chambers discovered in 1929 by the Abbé Giry. There are, as a local guide book states... 'very striking concretions' (carbonate deposits forming stalactites and stalagmites).

ENSÉRUNE, OPPIDUM D' (34)　　12k WSW Béziers
This was a great Celtic hill town dating from the 6th century BC and is believed to have contained about 10,000 inhabitants in its heyday. There is a museum on the site, and there are fine views out over the surrounding plain to the Cévennes and the Pyrénées.

FLORAC (48)　　　　　　115k NW Nîmes
Attractive small town, and administrative centre of the Cévennes National Park, Florac makes an ideal base for the exploration of the Cévennes, and the Causses. A fascinating road runs west and south from here along the fabulous Tarn gorges (83 ks to Millau). Visit the Pécher waterfall, above the town to the SW.

FONT-ROMEU (66)　　　　88k WSW Perpignan
Busy winter sports and summer mountain resort in the heart of the Pyrénées, not far from the border with Spain. There is a casino, cableways and ski-lifts, and a wide variety of hotels. The nearby Chapel of the Hermitage-de-Notre-Dame has a rich Baroque interior.

At Odeillo just to the south the great, mirrored solar furnace may be visited, and not far beyond it is one of the stations on the light railway on which runs the 'Little Yellow Train'. This narrow gauge railway runs from Vernet-les-Bains in the east, to La Tour de Carol beyond Bourg-Madam, and provides a delightful scenic experience.

GALAMUS GORGES (11)　　　40k WNW Perpignan
Dramatic gorges which can be reached by driving north from St-Paul-de-Fenouillet (Use Michelin Map No. 86).

LA GRANDE MOTTE (34)　　　45k SW Nîmes
The largest and best known of the seven new holiday resorts that have been developed along the Languedoc-Roussillon coast since the 1960s. This contains several spectacular white 'pyramids' of apartment buildings... all part of a 'new world' along this coast, with new roads, airports, and a wealth of other holiday facilities.

GRUISSAN-PLAGE (11)　　　14k SE Narbonne
Gruissan is an old fishing harbour linked to the sea by a small canal, and the Plage is one of the seven great developments of the Languedoc-Roussillon coast (See La Grande Motte, above), only being commenced in 1973. It has an attractive frontage of vaulted houses and a splendid beach.

JONTE GORGES (48)   *35k SW Florac*

These run westwards from Meyrueis to Le Rozier, a distance of twenty kilometres, where the Jonte flows into the larger and better-known River Tarn. 3kms to the east of Le Rozier are the Terrasses du Truel, where rare griffon vultures can sometimes be seen hovering in the warm air rising up the cliff faces. These splendid 6ft wingspan birds were extinct here until a few years ago, but have now been re-introduced into the area, and are breeding successfully.

REGIONAL NATURE PARK OF THE HAUT-LANGUEDOC (34, 81)   *(Partly in Midi-Pyrénées)*
About 90k W Montpellier, About 50k N Carcassonne

Created in 1971, this Park covers an area of 105,000 acres, consisting of lovely hill country covered largely with beech forests. There are many foxes and weasels, and wild sheep are increasing in numbers. Ther are park information centres (Maisons du Parc) at Ferrières, Brassac, La Salvetat, Fraisse, Douch, Mons, Roquebrun, Sorèze and Saint-Pons (which is also the Park H.Q.).

The Pont Notre Dame, Mende

LIMOUSIS CAVE (11)   *17k N Carcassonne*
A long cave with many stalagmites and stalactites.

LODÈVE (34)   *55k WNW Montpellier*
Pleasant old town in wooded mountain country at the confluence of the Lergue and Soulondres, the second of which is crossed by a pleasant old bridge. See the fortified cathedral of St-Fulcran, and the many old houses.

In the Pyrénées near Mont Louis
Photograph by Peter Titchmarsh

MARVEJOLS (48)   *29k W Mende*
Minute market town in the Colagne valley with three of its medieval gateways surviving (See especially the Porte de Soubeyran).

MENDE (48)   *155k NW Nîmes, 92k SSW Le Puy*
This town in a pleasant setting on a terrace above the River Lot, is the capital of the Lozère Département. The Penitents' Tower is the only remains of the 12th century fortifications, which have been replaced by a circle of boulevards; but these enclose an old town with narrow streets and many old houses clustered around the cathedral. This building was partially destroyed by the Huguenots, but was re-built in the early years of the 17th century, and contains a splendid set of Aubusson tapestries, and some lovely choir stalls. From the cathedral, old streets descend to a beautiful 14th century bridge over the Lot.

MEYRUEIS (48)   *35k SW Florac*
Small town prettily sited at the head of the Jonte Gorges, and an excellent centre for exploring the gorges of the Causses and the Cévennes National Park.

Meyrueis   *Photograph by Peter Titchmarsh*

MONT LOUIS (66)   *80k WSW Perpignan*
Small town in the Pyrénées, near the head of the Têt valley, and not far from the border with Spain at Bourg-Madame (20 ks). Vauban's citadel is one of the few built by him to have survived almost intact. Five kilometres to the south is the Romanesque church of Planès, sited high above the main valley. Fourteen kilometres to the north-west is the Bouillousses lake, at the end of an attractive road up the Têt valley.

MONTPELLIER (34)   *760k S Paris, 50k SW Nîmes*
This large town is the capital of Hérault Département, and is also the natural capital of Mediterranean Languedoc. It escaped the Albigensian strife of the 13th century, as it became part of the Kingdom of Aragon in
continued

Planès Church, near   *The Promenade de*
Mont Louis   *Peyrou, Montpellier*

At Montpellier Zoo

Narbonne Cathedral

1204, becoming part of the Majorcan Kingdom in 1262, and being ceded to France in 1349. However it suffered badly during the religious wars of the 17th century, and most of its fine buildings are of late 17th or 18th century origin. See especially the Promenade de Peyrou, the Château d'Eau, the public fountains, the Botanical Gardens, and the old town houses (most of which present plain façades, but contain handsome courtyards within). Montpellier has been called the 'Oxford of France', and there has been a University here since the 13th century, which includes one of Europe's oldest and most respected Medical Schools. There are claimed to be about 32,000 students in its University and High Schools, and Montpellier is very much a town of the young. Its art galleries, libraries and museums are outstanding... see especially the Fabre Museum and the Atger Museum, both of which contain outstanding collections of paintings. There is an excellent zoo, the Parc Lunaret, just to the north of the town, off the D17, Quissac road, with a wide collection of mammals, reptiles and birds.

MOURÈZE CIRQUE (34) 50k W Montpellier, 9k W Clermont

Here almost surrounding a minute village is a great mass of dolmen like rocks, giving the impression of some other planet's surface. Be prepared for a rather agile scramble here.

NARBONNE (11) 27k SW Béziers, 56k E Carcassonne

Busy town which is the capital of the Aude Département, and which was one of the largest and most important towns of Roman Gaul. The only surviving item from the Roman period is the bridge over the Canal de la Robine, but there are many medieval buildings to be seen, notably the cathedral, only the choir of which was built, but this is magnificent; and the Archbishop's Palaces. See also the basilica of St-Paul, and the Museums of Art and Ceramics*, and of Archaeology.

*Which is in the 'New' Archbishop's Palace.

NAVACELLES CIRQUE (30 and 34) 98k W Nîmes 34k WSW Ganges

This is a vast hole in the ground, formed by the meandering of the river Vis, which flows through a deep gorge beyond the Cirque. There is a small village on a bend in the river at the very bottom, which is reached by a steeply descending road.

NÎMES (66) 710k SSE Paris, 43k WSW Avignon

This busy city was one of the oldest and most important towns of Roman Gaul, and it has an outstanding collection of historical monuments, including a great amphitheatre, known as Les Arènes, which could once hold 20,000 spectators, and which is now used for bull-fights; The Maison Carrée, a remarkably well preserved Roman temple, built by Agrippa, the son-in-law of the Emperor Augustus, and now used as a museum; the remains of the Thermae... fountain, nymph's shrine and Temple of Diana... which were all incorporated into the Jardin de la Fontaine in the 18th century. See also the Tower Magne, where the water supply for the city terminated (having crossed the famous Pont du Gard, twenty three kilometres to the north-west), and the remains of the Roman walls. There is much to see in Nîmes, with its wide boulevards and charming old streets, and it also makes an ideal centre for the exploration of Roman Provence (Arles, Orange, St-Rémy, Pont du Gard).

The Jardin de la Fontaine, Nîmes

The Maison Carrée, Nîmes. Photograph by Peter Titchmarsh

Les Arènes, Nimes

Languedoc-Roussillon

PERPIGNAN (66) *910k S Paris, 310k SW Marseille*

Capital of the Pyrénées Orientales Département, and also of the Roussillon Region, Perpignan is a busy city of over 100,000 inhabitants. In the 13th and 14th centuries it was the capital of a kingdom including the Balearic Islands, Montpellier, Roussillon and the Cerdagne, and it is largely for this reason that it is so rich in art treasures. See especially the lovely Palace of the Kings of Majorca, the red brick fortress of Le Castillet which incorporates a museum of Catalan Arts, La Loge de Mer, various buildings with commercial origins, and the cathedral of St-Jean. There are four other museums to be visited, and many quiet little streets with old houses.

The Place de la Loge, Perpignan

LE PERTHUS (66) *30k S Perpignan*

Small village on the frontier with Spain, and now happily by-passed by the Autoroute B9. The village shelters beneath a fortress built by the great Vauban, and there is a small winding road westwards to the Col de l'Ouillat and beyond to the Pic Neoulous, from which there are splendid views back over the Roussillon plain, and southwards to Spain.

PÉZENAS (34) *23k NE Béziers*

Attractive small town set amongst vineyards and only about twenty kilometres from the coast. The Governors of Languedoc, the Montmorencys and the Contis, made Pézenas their headquarters, and for this reason it has a wealth of 16th and 17th century buildings. Wander at will amongst the narrow streets, with their old houses, courtyards and staircases, and see especially the Hôtels de Lacoste, d'Alfonce, and de Malibran. The shop of Barber Gély, in which the playwright Molière* is supposed to have spent many hours listening to the customers' chatter, is incorporated in the local Syndicat d'Initiative, and is open to the public. See also the Commandery of St-John of Jerusalem and the church of Ste-Ursule.

*One room of the local museum is devoted to Molière, who spent much time in Pézenas.

Old street in Pézenas

The Pont-du-Gard
Photograph by
Peter Titchmarsh

PONT-DU-GARD (30) *23k NW Nîmes*

Built during the reign of the Emperor Augustus, about 20 BC, this is one of the great wonders of the Roman world, with three tiers of arches, one above the other. It was built to bring water to the city of Nîmes, and is a truly splendid combination of architectural grace and engineering skill. We camped beneath it once, many years ago, but this is no longer possible.

The Pont-du-Gard
Photograph by
Peter Titchmarsh

PORT CAMARGUE (30) *50k SSW Nîmes*

Rapidly developing yachting harbour and beach resort, at the western end of the Camargue.

PORT-LEUCATE (11) *47k S Narbonne*

This together with its neighbour, Port-Barcarès, is part of the great development plan for Languedoc-Roussillon (See La Grande Motte, Page 134), and they were both established in the 1960s. Both are situated on magnificent sandy beaches between the sea and the great lagoon of Salses, and Port-Leucate has one of the largest yacht harbours in Europe. Port-Barcarès, has an ocean liner, the Lydia, on its beach, with various entertainment facilities.

The Lydia... on the sands at Port Barcarès

Doorway, St-Gilles   *Sculptural detail, St-Gilles*

The Port, Sète

In the Tarn Gorges   Photograph by Peter Titchmarsh

Boat trip in the Tarn Gorges near la Malène
Photograph by Peter Titchmarsh

PRADES (66)   *43k WSW Perpignan*

Pleasant town in the Têt valley, beneath the great Canigou peak, with many orchards in the surrounding countryside. The restored abbey of St-Michel-de-Cuxa, three kilometres to the south, was once the religious and intellectual centre of Roussillon. Prades is world famous as the home of the Spanish cellist Pablo Casals, and the music festival that he founded continues each year, a fitting memorial to a very great man.

ST-CYPRIEN (66)   *15k SE Perpignan*

A modern holiday centre with three miles of splendid sandy beaches, and the most southerly of the seven new resorts which have been established in Languedoc-Roussillon since the 1960s (See La Grande Motte, Page 134).

ST-GILLES-DU-GARD (30)   *19k SSE Nîmes*

Pleasant old town on the slopes of a gentle hill. The abbey here was once an important place of pilgrimage as well as being a stopping place on one of the routes to Santiago-de-Compostela. All that remains of interest is the crypt and the splendid west façade, with its three richly carved doorways, all of which dates from the 12th century.

ST-VEREDEMA CAVE, LA BAUME (30)

35k NE Nîmes

An ancient hermitage in a cave in the Gardon Gorge, which also houses an interesting Romanesque chapel. There are several other caves in the area, and the famous Pont du Gard (See Page 137) is only a few kilometres to the east.

SÈTE (34)   *35k SSE Montpellier*

This is the largest French Mediterranean port after Marseille, and it is situated on the north eastern end of a long isthmus between the Bassin de Thau and the sea. This is where the Canal du Midi (See Page 131) meets the sea*, and the 'Canal-du-Rhône-a-Sète' heads north-eastwards from here to join the Rhône at Beaucaire, opposite Tarascon. This is a great fishing and wine shipping port, and ships seem almost to be moored in the streets. The poet Paul Valéry was born here in 1871, and there is a museum dedicated to him.

The port and the Canal du Midi are the work of the same man, Paul Riquet, who built them in the 17th century. He was born at Béziers.

SIGEAN AFRICAN RESERVE (11)

15k S Narbonne, to E of N 9

A large wildlife park on the shores of the Étang-de-Sigean, with lions, antelopes, bears, alligators, rhinoceros, and a wide variety of other animals and birds.

TARN GORGES (12 & 48)

Florac is 90k NNW Montpellier

This great canyon cut by the river Tarn between the Causses de Sauveterre and de Méjean, can be followed by road for eighty kilometres from Florac to Millau (which is in Aveyron Département... part of Midi-Pyrénées Region). From La Malène to the Cirque des Baumes it is possible to take a trip in a small flat bottomed boat. Do not miss a visit to this, one of Europe's great natural wonders.

'TRAVELS WITH A DONKEY' (48)

This classic work describes a journey made by Robert Louis Stevenson in the company of 'a small ass, not much bigger than a dog, and the colour of a mouse', by name 'Modestine'. In twelve days they travelled between the village of le Monastier-sur-Gazeille (22k SE of le Puy in the Haute Loire.) and the small town of St-Jean-du-Gard (just in Gard Département, 60k NW of Nîmes), thus traversing some of the loveliest of the Cévennes country... a distance of about 190 kilometres. The Cévennes is still splendid walking country, and possible the best centre for exploration is Florac (See Page 134), which Stevenson passed through on his famous journey.

Track over Mont Lozère... 'R.L.S.' and Modestine came this way.

UZÈS (30)   *25k N Nîmes*

Delightful old town on a small hill with a castle, still occupied by the premier Duke of France, and which is open daily. See also the cathedral which was largely destroyed both by the Albigensians and the Protestants, but of which the lovely Fenestrelle Tower survives. There are old houses, narrow arcaded streets, and a 'Museum of the Wheel', the contents of which include many vintage cars. The writer Racine spent two years in Uzès, studying theology.

VERNET-LES-BAINS (66)   *55k WSW Perpignan*

Situated in the foothills of the Pyrénées, this is a 19th and early 20th century spa town much favoured by notable English visitors at one time. Above it is an old village complete with medieval castle and a 12th century church. The 'Little Yellow Train' (see Font Romeu, page 134) runs from here, up the Têt Valley and on to the frontier with Spain.

The Fenestrelle Tower, Uzès   *The Duke's Castle, Uzès*

VILLENEUVE-LÈS-AVIGNON (30)   *3k NW Avignon, 44k ENE Nîmes*

This has for centuries been the smart suburb of Avignon, and many cardinals had their summer palaces here. See especially the great tower of Philip the Fair, from the top of which there are fine views out across the Rhône to Avignon itself. See also the church of Notre-Dame, built in the 14th century by a cardinal who was a nephew of Pope John XXII; the Chartreuse, the largest house of the Carthusian order; and the museum which is housed in an elegant 17th century mansion, and which contains an interesting art collection including one of the greatest of French paintings, 'The Coronation of the Virgin Mary' by Enguerrand Charonton.

In the Old Village, Vernet-les-Bains   *The Tower of Philip the Fair, Villeneuve-les-Avignon*

VILLENEUVETTE (34)   *45k W Montpellier, 4k SW Clermont*

A 17th century 'new Town' created by Colbert, Louis XIV's famous First Minister, complete with entrance gate inscribed 'Honneur au Travail', a tree shaded square with fountain, workmen's cottages and a reservoir for washing the cloth once produced here. A number of craftsmen have set up here in recent years.

GREAT WINE AREAS OF FRANCE — LANGUEDOC-ROUSSILLON

Vast quantities of wine are produced in this region. Little of it is superlative in quality, but much of the vin-ordinaire and the mass bottled branded wines originate in whole or in part from this prolific area. With the increasing cost of wines from the classic areas, wines bottled in the Languedoc-Roussillon are becoming much more widely accepted.

The Rhône at Villeneuve-lès-Avignon

Limousin

Comprises the following Départements
Corrèze (19)
Creuse (23)
Haute-Vienne (87)

Centred upon the fine city of Limoges, this region lies in the heart of France, at the cross-roads between the North and the South. It is an area of gently sloping hills, secret valleys, wide forests and tree bordered lakes. The rivers Creuse, Cher, Corrèze and Vienne all rise in the region, and it is also crossed by the lovely Dordogne. Many of these rivers have been dammed to provide electricity, and the resulting lakes add great beauty to the landscape. There are medieval castles and Romanesque churches to be visited, and old towns to be explored. Inevitably you will wish to see the porcelain and enamel work for which Limoges is world famed, and the recently revitalised tapestry works of Aubusson and nearby Felletin. There are also opportunities for water sports on the great lakes, walking and riding in forest country, together with fishing, cycling, arts and crafts courses, and even horse-drawn carriage tours. The lovely countryside of the Limousin will seldom provide high drama, but for those who are prepared to explore quietly, there is a tranquillity to be found here so often lacking in the more popular holiday areas.

AMBAZAC (87)   *19k NE Limoges*
 Modest little town in the hills with a splendid 12th century reliquary chest that used to belong to the abbey of Grandmont, about 8ks N, and now in ruins. This is one of the outstanding examples of Limousin enamelling and should not be missed.

ARGENTAT (19)   *118k SSE Limoges*
 Delightful little town in the Dordogne valley, with the wooden balconies of old houses, jutting out over the river. This is an excellent centre for exploring the granite plateau of Xaintrie over to Merle Towers (See Page 144), and it also lies at the lower end of the great series of dams across the Dordogne, which can be followed by taking the roads north and east to Bort-les-Orgues.

Arnac Pompadour Château

ARNAC-POMPADOUR (19)   *60k S Limoges*
 Small town which owes its importance to Louis XV, who gave the château and the title of Marchioness to his mistress, the great Madame de Pompadour, in 1745. The château is now part of the equally famous National Stud, which was established here by Louis XV in 1761, and which is still fully functional here. It is open most of the year except 1st March to 10th July. Horse shows and race meetings are held here during the summer.

AUBAZINES (19)   *14k E Brive, 106k SSE Limoges*
 Small village attractively set amongst wooded hills, and grouped around the former abbey church, a 12th century Cistercian building, with an interesting interior which includes the splendid 13th century tomb of St-Stephen. The former abbey is now occupied by nuns, but visitors may see the chapterhouse, the kitchen, and the old fish pool, fed by a long canal. There are splendid views from Puy de Pauliac to the NE of the village (road to within short distance of summit).

AUBUSSON (23)   *90k ENE Limoges, 365k S Paris*
 Modest town in quiet hill country, where Flemish weavers settled in the 14th century, bringing with them the art of tapestry weaving, that was to make the name Aubusson synonymous with fine tapestry and carpets. By the time of Louis XIII there were over 1,600 tapestry weavers in Aubusson and neighbouring Felletin (11ks S). Although this art went into decline in the 19th century, it was revived, largely due to Jean Lurcat, in 1939, and continues to flourish. Aubusson claims to be the 'tapestry capital' while the smaller town of Felletin takes the title, 'the birthplace of tapestry'. Both have exhibitions of contemporary tapestry, which are well worth visiting.

Maître Tapissier, Monsieur Tabard, with a modern Aubusson tapestry

Beaulieu-sur-Dordogne

Le Chastang Dam (See Bortes-les-Orgues)

Chambon-sur-Voueize

BEAULIEU-SUR-DORDOGNE (19)

128k SSE Limoges

Small town in the lovely Dordogne valley, with a Romanesque abbey church possessing an outstandingly beautiful tympanum over its south door, illustrating the Last Judgement in dramatic detail.

BORT-LES-ORGUES (19)   *70k ENE Tulle*

This great reservoir was created by the flooding of the first of the five major hydro-electric dams on the Dordogne in 1951, and it is over fifteen kilometres long. There are boat trips from the dam to Val-Château (See also Lanobre Page 62), and there are facilities for bathing, sailing, water skiing and fishing.

It is possible to drive south-west from here, to Argentat, a distance of 135 ks, down the valley of the lovely Dordogne, passing the dams and lakes of Marèges, L'Aigle and Le Chastang.

BOURGANEUF (23)   *50k ENE Limoges*

Small town above the wooded Taurion valley, with a medieval tower, which once housed a Mohammedan prince in semi-captivity, and known since as Zizim's Tower. See also the splendid Aubusson tapestry in the Town Hall.

BOUSSAC (23)   *130k NE Limoges, 40k NE Guéret*

Small town on the Petite Creuse river, overshadowed by a late medieval castle which is well worth visiting. See especially... the kitchens, George Sand's room (the castle was the setting for her novel Jeanne) and Prince Zizim's room (he must have been allowed to come over from Bourganeuf at some time or other) (See Above).

BRIVE-LA-GAILLARDE (19)   *92k SSE Limoges*

This busy town on the river Corrèze is the centre of a prosperous fruit and vegetable area, and is known as La Gaillarde... 'the bold', due to the fortitude of its citizens during several sieges. The remaining buildings of the medieval town are in the vicinity of St-Martin's church, a partially Romanesque building at the very centre of the town, and around which there is a lively market each Saturday. See also the Ernest Rupin Museum, the courtyard of the fine Renaissance, Hotel-de-Lâbenche (not open), and the 16th century Aldermen's Tower, to the immediate south of the church.

LE CHALARD (87)   *40k SSW Limoges*

A striking Romanesque church dominates this small village, but it consists only of a chancel and one transept, as the nave was never built. Do not miss the fine series of capitals.

CHÂLUS (87)   *35k SW Limoges*

Small town set in the wooded Limousin countryside, and dominated by the remains of Château Chabrol, the medieval castle from whose keep a crossbow was discharged at Richard the Lionheart, while he was directing an attack upon it. Although only struck on the shoulder, Richard died some days later of gangrene, and Chalus thus passed into history.

CHAMBON-SUR-VOUEIZE (23)   *47k E Guéret*

Charming little town in the lovely valley of the Voueize with a fine 11th – 12th century abbey church. This has a long, tall and very austere interior, where medieval times still seem very close. If you wish to see the beautiful silver reliquary-bust of the local saint, Ste-Valérie, apply to the presbytery.

LE CHATENET-EN-DULONG (87)

8k N St-Léonard-de Noblat, 25k ENE Limoges

It is possible to hire horse-drawn caravans and carriages by the week or the week-end from le Tourisme Attelé, domaine de St-Agnan, 87400 le Chatenet-en-Dognon. This would be an ideal way to explore the Limousin countryside. (See also Millevaches Plateau, Page 144, for details of another hirer of horse-drawn vehicles).

COLLONGES-LA-ROUGE (19)

113k SSE Limoges
21k SE Brive

Situated in quiet countryside between the Corrèze and Dordogne valleys, Collonges is a delightful red sandstone village where time seems to have stood still. No cars are allowed in the town between 1st June and 15th September, and one can wander at will in the warm sunshine, past such treasures as The Siren's House (thus named after the siren playing a lute, which adorns one of its corners), the Maussac and Vassignat manor houses, and the Romanesque church with its splendid early 12th century tympanum, and its 16th century fortifications (added during the Wars of Religion). A visit here will not be complete without a meal at the Relais de St-Jacques de Compostelle, an ideal restaurant.

COUSSAC-BONNEVAL (87)

44k S Limoges

Minute village in quiet countryside, overlooked by the towers of Bonneval Castle, which was built in the 14th century and much altered in the 18th and 19th centuries. Its interior is enriched by fine tapestries, furniture and paintings, and there is a display relating to one of the lords of Bonneval, who was a soldier of fortune, and became a Pasha in the service of the Sultan of Constantinople.

CROZANT (23)

85k NNE Limoges

Small village in the Creuze valley a few kilometres south of Lake Chambon, with a great ruined fortress above it, dating from the 10th and 13th centuries. Lake Chambon is formed by the massive Éguzon Dam, which was built across the Creuze in 1926. There is a fine viewpoint overlooking the dam, twelve kilometres north of Crozant, on D30 (in Loire-Valley-Centre Region).

LE DORAT (87)

52k NNW Limoges

Small town which has one of the Limousin's outstanding buildings… the Collegiate church of St-Pierre. This is a remarkably complete 12th century church, with its Romanesque flavour tempered by Arabic influences, no doubt brought northwards by pilgrims returning from Santiago-de-Compostella.

FELLETIN (23)

(See Aubusson, Page 141).

FRESSELINES (23)

8k ESE Crozant, 93k NNE Limoges

Attractive 'artist's village' in the lovely Creuse valley, with the studios of the painters, Thiery and Chazaud, both open to view (By appointment only out of season).

MONT GARGAN (87)

40k SE Limoges

There is a road almost to the very summit of this 731 metre high hill top, which is crowned by the ruins of a small chapel. There are outstanding views in every direction, especially westwards to the mountains of the Limousin.

Collonges-la-Rouge

Bonneval Château

143

Bishop's Palace, Limoges... now the Municipal Museum

Porcelain at the Dubouché Museum, Limoges

Merle Towers

On the Millevaches Plateau

GIMEL-LES-CASCADES (19)   *12k NE Tulle*

Situated on the Montane, a tributary of the Corrèze, this minute village is the starting place for a one hour walk past a series of dramatic waterfalls and deep narrow ravines. The church contains splendid medieval treasure which may be seen, on application to the presbytery (See especially the 12th century St-Stephen's shrine, ornamented with Limoges enamels, gold and precious stones). The Étang de Ruffaud, is an attractive small lake two kilometres to the north-east.

GUÉRET (23)   *90k NE Limoges*

This busy little town is 'capital' of the Creuse Département, and is situated in pleasantly wooded countryside not far from the river Creuse. See especially the handsome Hôtel des Moneyroux, which is two buildings joined by a corner turret, and which houses an annual exhibition of contemporary tapestry design from Aubusson; and the Municipal Museum, which has outstanding items combining gold, silver and enamel work, and a fine collection of dolls, amongst its varied exhibits.

LIMOGES (87)   *379k S Paris*

Capital of the Haute-Vienne Département and principal city of the Limousin Region, Limoges is a bright busy place, lying in hilly country on the lovely Vienne river. It has been renowned for its brilliant decorative enamels since the 5th century, and the tradition is kept alive by contemporary artists, some of whose studios may be visited. See especially the cathedral, with its splendid Flamboyant style portal and carved wooden doors, its rood screen and its tombs. See also the churches of St-Pierre and St-Michel, the Bishop's Palace, which is now the Municipal Museum, and the National Museum, Adrien Dubouché, with its outstanding collection of ceramics. This naturally gives pride of place to the porcelain for which Limoges is equally famous.

MERLE TOWERS (19)   *18k ESE Argentat,*
136k SSE Limoges

Dramatically sited ruins of a medieval castle, on a rocky promontory almost surrounded by a loop of the river Maronne. This proved completely impregnable until the coming of artillery. Do not miss the outstanding Son et Lumière... English version 11.30 p.m. Tuesdays & Saturdays July – mid-September.

MILLEVACHES PLATEAU (19, 23)
About 100k E Limoges

This is a great granite plateau stretching from Felletin in the north, almost to Ussel. Much of it is bleak country, with heathland alternating with great conifer forests, and the occasional granite outcrop. The name does not come from vaches (cows), but from the Celtic word batz, which means spring... of which there are multitudes. It is possible to explore this area in an open carriage, which can be hired from Calèches en Limousin, 19250 MEYMAC, with overnight accommodation available in country cottages.

MONTBRUN CASTLE (87)
45k SW Limoges (via Chalus)

An interesting medieval castle on an island in the river Dronne. The towers and curtain wall were built in the 15th century and enclose a massive 12th century keep. The interior was burnt out in 1917, but this castle is still well worth visiting.

MOUTIER-D'AHUN (23)
20k SE Guéret, 80k ENE Limoges

Small village in the upper Creuse valley, with a magnificent abbey church. This has outstanding woodwork, by Simon Baüer between 1673 and 1681, to replace that burnt during the Wars of Religion. Do not miss the splendid 15th century chapel, nor the treasures from the old monastery which are in the Sacristy.

On the Millevaches Plateau

NEUVIC BARRAGE (19)
60k ENE Tulle

This is across the river Triouzoune, a tributary of the Dordogne, and is part of a large hydro-electric scheme in the upper Dordogne valley. There is a beach between the dam and the village of Neuvic, with sailing, water skiing and swimming.

ORADOUR-SUR-GLANE (87)
22k WNW Limoges

It was here in June 1944, four days after the Allies had landed in Normandy that the German occupying forces committed the most savage reprisal of the whole war in France... killing no fewer than 650 men women and children, those who were not burnt in the church or other buildings being killed by guns, grenades or dynamite. The old village has been left as it was following the massacre, as a lesson to us all on the futile brutality of total war.

ROCHECHOUART (87)
42k W Limoges

Small town dominated by a medieval castle situated above a rocky cliff. Much of the castle is occupied by Municipal offices, but one can see the courtyard, the Salle des Chasses, with its series of frecoes and the interesting Municipal Museum. There is a delightful avenue of limes on a terrace, from which there are fine views out over the valley.

ST-JUNIEN (87)
30k W Limoges

Busy town on the lovely Vienne river, here crossed by an attractive 13th century bridge, with a 15th century chapel at its northern end. The collegiate church of St-Junien should be visited for the 12th century tomb of the saint of the same name... a splendid example of Limousin style sculpture and probably the work of an itinerant master mason. St-Junien has been noted as a glove making town since the Middle Ages, and this craft still flourishes today, with about thirty workshops producing some one and a half million pairs a year.

The tragic ruins of Oradour-sur-Glane

ST-LÉONARD-DE-NOBLAT (87)
22k E Limoges

Small market town with a collegiate church which has a fine Romanesque belfry and an interesting interior. There are several medieval houses in the vicinity of the church. Take the D39 south westwards from here to explore the lovely valley of the Maulde, which has been harnessed to provide hydro-electric power by a succession of dams... the Artige, the Fleix, the Martineix, and the Mont-Larron where there is a power station and control centre.

St-Léonard-de-Noblat *St-Léonard-de-Noblat*

Limousin

Solignac Abbey   *Solignac Abbey*

Treignac

West doorway, La
Souterraine
Limousin

Cloisters at Tulle

ST-MAIXANT CASTLE (23)   *6k NE Aubusson,*
96k ENE Limoges

A late 14th century moated building flanked by three round towers, with chestnut shingled roofs above the parapet walks. There are fine paintings and tapestries, and a zoo in the grounds.

ST-YRIEIX-LA-PERCHE (87)   *40k S Limoges*

Busy little market town with a collegiate church, whose simple interior is relieved by a fine series of carved corbel figures. To the east of the town are kaolin quarries, reminding us that St-Yrieix, was the source of the Limoges porcelain industry, here in the 1760s.

SEDIÈRE CHÂTEAU (19)   *3k NW Clergoux, which is*
24k E Tulle

A handsome Renaissance château, standing beside a small lake in lovely forest country. There is a small ethnographic museum and summer exhibitions.

SÉGUR-LE-CHÂTEAU (19)
22k SSE St-Yrieux-la-Perche, 63k S Limoges

Charming little village in a bend of the river Auvézère, and dominated by the creeper-clad ruins of a 12th century castle on a rocky promontory above it.

SOLIGNAC (87)   *11k S Limoges*

Small village with a fine 12th century abbey church (The famous abbey was founded as early as 632, but was plundered in turn by the Vikings, the English and the Huguenots). The château of Chalusset (5ks SE) is an impressive ruin standing on a rocky promontory above the confluence of two streams.

LA SOUTERRAINE (23)   *55k NNE Limoges*

Pleasant little medieval town, built on the site of a Gallo-Roman settlement, with considerable remains of its medieval walls and one gateway... the Porte St-Jean. The 11th – 13th century church reveals, like Le Dorat (Page 143), the extent of Arabic .influence brought northwards by pilgrims returning from Santiago-de-Compostella. But here also will be found traces of the original Gallo-Roman church, and much evidence of Gothic additions and improvements to this largely Romanesque building.

TREIGNAC (19)   *67k SE Limoges*

Attractive little town below the northern end of the lovely Monédières Massif, and bounded by the waters of the turbulent Vézère river, here crossed by a medieval bridge. The Mad Women's Rocks (Les Rochers des Folles) are a short walk away, to the west of the town, from which there are pleasant views of the Vézère gorge.

TULLE (19)   *468k S Paris, 88k SSE Limoges*

Large town extending along the steep sided valley of the Corrèze, this is a place with a very sad history. It was captured twice by the English in the 14th century, sacked by the Protestants in the Wars of Religion, and in 1944, it was liberated by the maquis, only to be re-taken by the Germans the next day, when 99 people were hanged in the streets, and many deported, over a hundred of whom were never heard of again. This is the capital of the Corrèze Département, and has a cathedral with fine bell tower and pleasant cloisters. See also the Maison de Loyac, a 15th century house to the immediate north of the cathedral, which is on the edge of the 'Old Quarter', a fascinating collection of narrow streets with oversailing houses almost meeting each other.

TURENNE (19)   *16k S Brive, 108k SSE Limoges*

Here are the ruins of a great castle, the original stronghold of the Viscounts of Turenne, whose Vicomté was almost entirely independent of France until the 18th century. The two most famous Viscounts were both Henri's... the great leader of the Limousin Huguenots, and Louis XIV's outstanding general. The ruins dominate the little medieval town, and there are splendid views on all sides from 'Caesar's Tower'. 7ks to the NE is the La Fage Chasm, with underground galleries complete with stalagmites and stalactites. It is claimed in a local guide book that in the 'Organ Hall', these are 'played like a xylophone'.

USSEL (19)   *114k ESE Limoges, 60k NE Tulle*

Pleasant old town in the southern foothills of the Millevaches Plateau, with many handsome houses including the Hôtel de Ventadour (not open), an elegant Renaissance building of the late 16th century. There are fine views south and west from the Chapel of Notre-Dame de la Chabanne, on the southern edge of the town.

UZERCHE (19)   *57k SSE Limoges*

A small medieval town, delightfully situated within a deep bend of the Vézère river. Due to this natural protection and its enhancement by fortifications, Uzerche is still able to display its motto with confidence... 'Never Defiled'. A few of the medieval houses are almost castles in themselves, and there is a popular old saying that goes, 'He who has a house in Uzerche, has a castle in Limousin'. See especially the fortified gateway (Porte Bécharie), the fine Romanesque church of St-Pierre, and the charming little Place des Vignerons (The Wine Growers Square).

VASSIVIÈRE, LAKE (87, 23)   *60k E Limoges*

This great artificial lake is bordered by pleasantly wooded hills, and there is a bathing beach and facilities for a wide variety of water sports, on the western side, above 7ks east of Peyrat-le-Château. It is possible to drive completely around the shores of the lake... about sixteen kilometres , and there are holiday villages at Pierrefitte and Masgrangeas, sailing and canoeing facilities at Auphelle and Vauxveix, and numerous camping sites. There are also motor-boats at Auchaize and Broussas. (Use Michelin Map No. 72).

Turenne

Uzerche

Lake Vassivière

Limousin

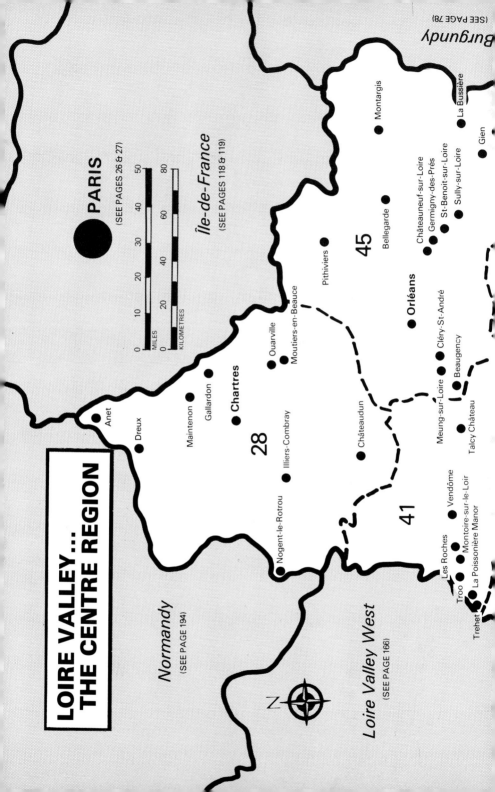

LOIRE VALLEY...
THE CENTRE REGION

PARIS

(SEE PAGES 26 & 27)

```
MILES      0   10   20      30    40      50
KILOMETRES 0   20      40      60        80
```

Normandy
(SEE PAGE 194)

Île-de-France
(SEE PAGES 118 & 119)

Loire Valley West
(SEE PAGE 166)

Burgundy
(SEE PAGE 78)

Anet

Dreux

Maintenon

Gallardon

Chartres

Ouarville

Moutiers-en-Beauce

Pithiviers

Montargis

Bellegarde

Châteauneuf-sur-Loire

Germigny-des-Prés

St-Benoît-sur-Loire

Sully-sur-Loire

La Bussière

Gien

Illiers-Combray

Châteaudun

28

45

Orléans

Meung-sur-Loire

Cléry-St-André

Beaugency

Talcy Château

Nogent-le-Rotrou

Vendôme

Montoire-sur-le-Loir

La Poissonière Manor

Les Roches

Troo

Trehet

41

N

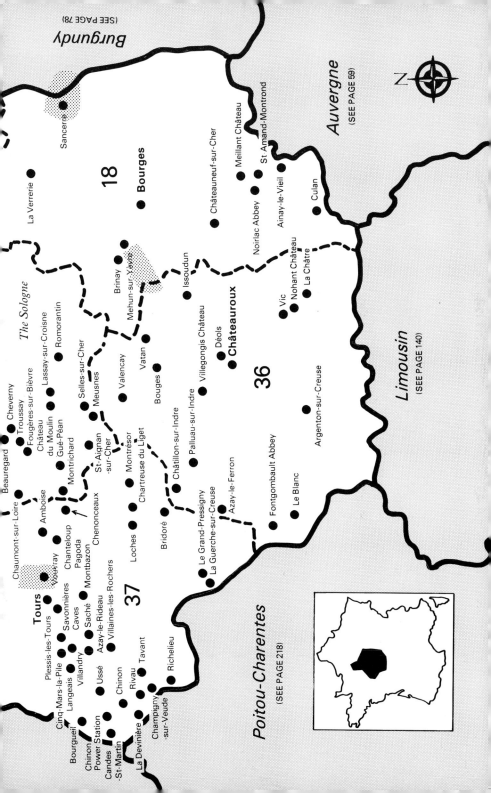

Loire Valley...
The Centre Region

Comprises the following Départements
Cher (18)   Indre-et-Loire (37)
Eure-et-Loir (28)   Loir-et-Cher (41)
Indre (36)   Loiret (45)

Here astride the middle reaches of France's longest river, the capricious Loire, with its lazy, sandy meanderings in summertime, and its great swirling winter floods, is the country's touring area par-excellence. On the banks of the Loire itself, and on or near its tributaries, the Vienne, the Indre and the Cher, will be found a bewilderingly beautiful series of châteaux, with grim medieval strongholds often replaced by splendid Renaissance pleasure palaces.

To the south is the mysterious marshy lake country of the Sologne, and beyond it the Haut Berry around Bourges and the Bas Berry centred upon Chateauroux. North of the Loire is the Loir valley, above which are the rich cornlands of the Beauce, with the splendid cathedral of Chartres rising above its distant horizons.

But everywhere one goes in the Region there is so much to see... not only the châteaux, with their wonderful Son-et-Lumière shows, but its series of old towns and cities, with their cathedrals, churches and museums, and its small villages, with their old houses lazing in the sun, in a gently rolling countryside which seems to go on for ever.

Ainay-le-Vieil   *Ainay-le-Vieil*

The Château terrace, Amboise

Leonardo da Vinci Museum, Clos-Lucé.
Photograph by Studio Henry, Amboise

AINAY-LE-VIEIL (18)   *55k SSE Bourges,*
10k SE St-Amand-Montrond
A moated medieval fortress complete with conical topped, round towers, and moat... or so it would appear from outside... but once within one encounters an elegant Renaissance manor house. Well worth visiting.

AMBOISE (37)   *24k E Tours, 221k SW Paris*
Delightful old town on the south bank of the Loire. There has been a castle here for many centuries, but it was Charles VIII, who was born here in 1470, that built the great château, the remains of which we see today. He started this in 1492, but it was only during the occupation of François I, that this 'tour-de-force' was completed... thus marking the beginnings of the Italian influence upon French art and architecture. It was under François I that life at Ambois was at its richest, and the king brought Leonardo da Vinci to spend his last years at the nearby Clos Lucé. In 1560 the Huguenots plotted to seize the young François II, but their plans were discovered, and the slaughter at Amboise that followed was typical of the excesses of so many religious disputes. From that time onwards Amboise was never again used as a royal residence. Visit the château itself, with its St-Hubert's Chapel, its terrace, the royal apartments and the great towers; the manor of Clos-Lucé, with its splendid collection of models and drawings relating to Leonardo, the apartments where he spent his last years; and the interesting Postal Museum in the town. (Son et Lumière at the Château.)

ANET (28)   *51k N Chartres, 79k W Paris*
Pleasant little town lying between the river Eure and the forest of Dreux. Its magnificent Renaissance château was built for Diane de Poitiers, and there is an exquisite chantry chapel over her tomb.

ARGENTON-SUR-CREUSE (36)   *125k SE Tours*

Delightful little town with old houses on the banks of the river Creuse. There are attractive views from the 'Old Bridge', and from here one can walk up to the Chapel of Notre-Dame-des-Bancs, with its great statue of the Virgin Mary, and its fine views out over the town and the river. Drive south from here to Crozant (See Page 143) to explore the lovely Creuse valley (about 40 kilometres to Crozant).

AZAY-LE-FERRON (36)   *80k SSE Tours, 17k SSW Châtillon*

Impressive 16th, 17th and 18th century château, which despite its belonging to the city of Tours, retains a remarkably 'lived-in' feeling. Its rooms are furnished in a variety of styles from many periods, and there is a 'Voltaire Room', reminding us that Voltaire often came to Azay, as a friend of the Breteuils, the family who lived here. Do not miss the portraits of two of France's most famous royal mistresses... Agnès Sorel, and Diane de Poitiers.

Argenton-sur-Creuse

AZAY-LE-RIDEAU (37)   *28k SW Tours*

Magnificent Renaissance château on the river Indre, which was built between 1518 and 1529, for the great financier, Gilles Berthelot, largely under the personal direction of his wife. The château is in an 'L' shape with one wing over the river, and the interior is now arranged as a museum of the Renaissance with splendid furniture and tapestries. The turrets and machiolations are more fairy-like than medieval, and were intended as an indication of the owner's importance, rather than defensive features. (Son et Lumière.)

Night and Day, at Azay-le-Rideau

BEAUGENCY (45)   *25k SW Orléans*

Pleasant town on the banks of the Loire, with considerable medieval flavour. See especially, the old stone bridge, the remains of the town walls, the 12th century church, the 16th century Town Hall, the Regional Museum in the Château Dunois, and several other interesting buildings, including the Tour de César, an 11th century keep.

BEAUREGARD (41)   *7k SE Blois*

Delightful Renaissance château, much altered in the 17th century, when the splendid gallery was added. This contains no fewer than 363 portraits of famous men of France, and should on no account be missed.

BELLEGARDE (45)   *23k W Montargis*

Small village to the north of the Forest of Orléans with a fine Romanesque facade to its church, and paintings by Carrache, Cortone and Berun within. The château has a 13th century keep complete with moat, and various brick buildings, including some elegant stables, erected by a son of Louis XIV's mistress, Madame de Montespan.

The Tour de César, Beaugency

LE BLANC (36)   *60k WSW Châteauroux*

Interesting old market town on the river Creuse, with three churches of interest and many pleasant riverside views.

BLOIS (41)   *181k SSW Paris, 60k SW Orléans*

Situated on the Loire, and capital of the Loir-et-Cher Département, Blois is a busy light industrial and agricultural centre. Much of the old town was destroyed in 1940, but there are still several old streets to be *continued*

The Loire at Beaugency   *The Château staircase, Blois*

Loire Valley Centre

Blois Château

'Lady at the Window', at Jacques Coeur's Palace, Bourges

Old houses at Bourges

Bourges Cathedral

Bourges Cathedral

The Loire, near Bourgueill

explored. With its wide selection of hotels it is an excellent centre for visiting many of the Loire châteaux, and it also has a château of its own that is quite exceptional. This is a vast building around a central courtyard, in a mixture of styles revealing its present origins to be of the 13th, 15th, 16th and 17th centuries. However it was during its occupation by Louis XII and Francois I during the first half of the 16th century that this became a royal residence without compare... the 'Versailles of the Renaissance'. The story of the building of Blois and those that lived and died in it is too complex to relate here... but a visit should on no account be missed. (Son et Lumière). See also the hump-backed Pont Gabriel over the Loire, the old streets near the cathedral, and the church of St-Nicholas.

BOUGES CHÂTEAU (36)   *30k N Châteauroux*
Handsome 18th century mansion with some fine furniture, and a beautiful garden. There is an exhibition of carriages and a saddle room in the outbuildings.

BOURGES (18)   *227k S Paris*
This fine medieval city was the capital of the ancient Dukedom of Berry, and is today the chief town of the Cher Département. From 1340 to 1416, Duke Jean de Berry, with lavish patronage, made Bourges a great centre of art and culture, and will always be remembered for his commissioning of such splendidly illuminated manuscripts, as the 'Très Riches Heures' which is now in the museum at Chantilly. The university of Bourges was founded by Louis XI in 1463, and Calvin developed many of his ideas here. The great cathedral was completed in 1324, and much of it may have been the work of the same group of craftsmen responsible for Notre Dame in Paris, which it resembles in some respects. See especially the splendid line of five east doorways, which introduce us to the great width of this building, with its double aisles, and no transepts; the glorious series of stained glass windows... possibly second only to Chartres in their richness and variety; the high north tower which can be ascended; and the crypt which contains the marble figure of Duke Jean, the only surviving piece of a magnificent tomb, which was destroyed in the 18th century. While in Bourges you should also see the Berry Museum in the Hôtel Cujas; the Hôtel des Échevins; the Hôtel Lallemant; and Jacques Coeur's Palace, a handsome 15th century building erected by a local merchant who became Master of the Mint to Charles VII, and whose business interests extended southwards as far as the Mediterranean. These are just a few outstanding buildings in a city which has a multitude of old houses, streets and gardens to explore.

BOURGUEIL (37)   *45k SW Tours*
Small town in the centre of a rich wine growing area. Here will be found the delightfully titled 'Cellar of the Divine Bottle'... a pleasant little museum, where the local wine may be tasted free.

BRIARE (45)   *74k ESE Orléans*
Small town on the Loire with an interesting Automobile Museum, and a handsome aqueduct, built by the great civil engineer, Gustave Eiffel, carrying the Canal de Briare over the wide river.

BRIDORÉ (37)   *14k SE Loches*
The 15th century château here is reputed to be that in which the dreaded 'Bluebeard' (see Tiffauges page 174) locked up his wives. It has a fine rectangular keep surrounded by a now dry moat.

BRINAY (18)   *8k SE Vierzon*
Minute village just to the west of the river Cher, with a Romanesque church which has some very fine 12th century wall paintings depicting scenes from the life of Christ.

LA BUSSIÈRE (45)   *12k NE Gien, 76k ESE Orléans*
Handsome 17th and 18th century château, complete with moat and adjoining pool. There is an interesting display relating to angling here.

Candes-St-Martin   *The Loire near Candes-St-Martin*

CANDES-ST-MARTIN (37)   *16k WNW Chinon*
Small village beside the union of the Loire and the Vienne with a lovely 13th century church, which had fortifications added two centuries later. This is built on the site of the house in which St-Martin of Tours is believed to have died. It was in November when his body was carried to Tours and it is said that the countryside burst into flower as it passed... this being the origin of the term 'St-Martin's Summer'.

CHAMBORD (41)   *18k E Blois*
One-hundred and fifty metres in length, one-hundred and fifteen metres in width, Chambord with its 440 rooms, is the largest of the Loire châteaux and arguably the most magnificent. It stands in a vast park of 13,600 acres in which deer and wild boar roam (apart from the 1,500 acres to which the public are admitted, and where these animals may be spotted from observation posts). Chambord was built by François I between 1520 and 1535, and consists of a central 'keep', with four towers enclosed by outer 'walls', also with towers at their corners... a feudal plan, but it was built as a royal pleasure palace, with a fascinating double spiral staircase, and a myriad of luxurious features. The rooms are now only sparsely furnished but the overall effect of Chambord is still breath-taking. (Son et Lumière).

Chambord   *Photograph by Peter Titchmarsh*

CHAMPIGNY-SUR-VEUDE (37)   *65k SW Tours*
Small village noted for its Sainte Chapelle, once the chapel of a long demolished castle, and only saved from destruction by the intervention of Pope Urban VIII. Here is a splendid specimen of the high Renaissance style, with richly sculptured ornament and an outstanding series of stained glass windows.

CHANTELOUP PAGODA (37)   *3k S Amboise*
A charming 18th century 'folly' on the banks of the Loire... all that survives of a fine château built by the Duc de Choiseul. Fine views may be obtained from its topmost tier.

Chanteloup Pagoda   *Sculptured figures, Chartres Cathedral*

CHARTRES (28)   *88k SW Paris*
How can one possibly describe Chartres in a few lines? Rising out of the rich, flat cornlands of the Beauce, the great cathedral with its two spires, with a medieval town on the slopes below, stands above a bustling city, the capital of Eure-et-Loire Département. Medieval and Renaissance houses and churches, old streets, hump-backed bridges over the Eure, the old wash houses beside the river: All should be savoured to

continued   *Chartres*

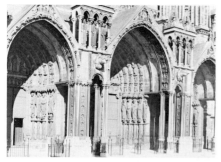

The Western Portal, Chartres

Sculptural detail, the west portal, Chartres. Photograph by Peter Titchmarsh

In Châteaudun Château

Châteaudun Château

Chateauneuf-sur-Cher

Chaumont-sur-Loire

the full... but it is to the cathedral that one is inevitably drawn. The stained glass windows, and the sculptured figures ornamenting the western portal, provide an experience that escapes description. If you never visit anywhere else in France, please spare time to come here, and to experience the hopes, the fears, and the deep faith, of the medieval craftsmen that created this most moving of monuments.

CHÂTEAUDUN (28)
44k SSW Chartres, 48k WNW Orléans

Delightful little town on the banks of the river Loir with several old houses and three interesting medieval churches. However the dominating feature is the great château, part of which rises sheer from the river bank. This has a massive 12th century circular donjon, a 15th century north wing and chapel, built by Jean Dunois, companion of Joan of Arc; and a 16th century Renaissance wing.

CHÂTEAUNEUF-SUR-CHER (18)
29k S Bourges

Small village with a fine castle overlooking its bridge across the Cher. The exterior is very medieval in appearance, but it conceals a courtyard overlooked by a series of Renaissance rooms.

CHÂTEAUNEUF-SUR-LOIRE (45)
25k E Orléans

The château has gone, but there is a fine park surviving, and a most interesting Maritime Museum devoted to 'Navigation on the Loire'. Five kilometres to the south-east is the outstandingly interesting church of Germigny-des-Prés, perhaps the oldest Romanesque church in France. (See Page 156).

CHÂTEAUROUX (36)
96k S Blois

Busy industrial town and capital of the Indre Département, with two churches worth visiting and an interesting museum displaying relics of the Napoleonic period. There are the remains of a 12th century abbey at Déols, two kilometres to the north-east.

CHÂTILLON-SUR-INDRE (36)
22k SE Loches

Charming little town with the remains of a medieval castle including a round 13th century keep, and also a Romanesque church with attractive 16th century choir stalls.

LA CHÂTRE (36)
36k SE Châteauroux

Pleasant little town on the banks of the upper Indre with many old houses and a tall keep housing a George Sand Museum, with various documents relating to the famous 19th century novelist who lived for many years at nearby Nohant (See Page 159).

CHAUMONT-SUR-LOIRE (41)
17k SW Blois

Beautifully sited in a wooded park above the Loire, Chaumont was built between 1465 and 1510, and in 1560 it was acquired by Catherine de Medici, the widow of Henri II. However she then forced her late husband's mistress, Diane de Poitiers to exchange Chaumont for Diane's favourite residence, Chenonceaux. Although feudal in plan and general appearance, it is softened by many Renaissance features, and the apartments contain pleasing furniture, tapestries and medallions (the latter having been made in the stables by the Italian artist, Nini, in the 18th century for his patron, the then owner, Governor Le Ray of 'Les Invalides'.

CHENONCEAUX (37)   *35k E Tours*

Magnificent Renaissance château built between 1513 and 1521, with a two hundred foot long gallery built out across the river Cher in 1560. Henri II gave Chenonceaux to his mistress, Diane de Poitiers, but on his death, his widow Catherine de Medici took it from her in exchange for her château at Chaumont. The interior is splendidly decorated and furnished. There is a Wax Museum depicting fifteen scenes telling the story of Chenonceaux. An electric train connects the entrance gate to the courtyard, and if the water level permits there are boat trips in the summer. (Son et Lumière.)

Chenonceaux   *Photograph by Peter Titchmarsh*

CHEVERNY (41)   *13k SE Blois*

This château is a 17th century mansion, without additions... an untouched period piece whose magnificent decorations and furnishings are almost all contemporary with the building. It is situated in a splendidly wooded park, and the kennels of the Cheverny Hunt can also be visited. The present owner, the Marquis de Vibraye is a descendant of Hurault de Cheverny, who completed the house in 1634.

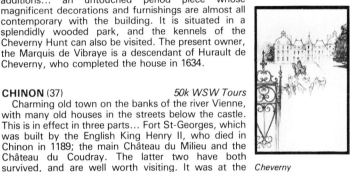

Cheverny   *Old street in Chinon*

CHINON (37)   *50k WSW Tours*

Charming old town on the banks of the river Vienne, with many old houses in the streets below the castle. This is in effect in three parts... Fort St-Georges, which was built by the English King Henry II, who died in Chinon in 1189; the main Château du Milieu and the Château du Coudray. The latter two have both survived, and are well worth visiting. It was at the Château du Milieu that Joan of Arc had her famous encounter with the Dauphin in 1429, some two months before she was able to involve herself in relieving the siege of Orléans by the English. There is a tourist steam train linking Chinon with Richelieu, about twenty kilometres to the south.

CHINON NUCLEAR POWER STATION (37)
          10k NW Chinon

This installation with its great metal globe, was the first station to generate nuclear power in France, and there is a special viewpoint, which is furnished with plans and models explaining the workings of the plant.

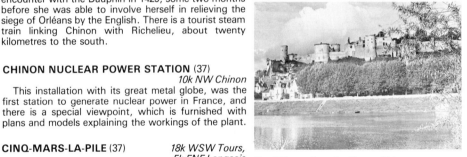

The Château above the Vienne, Chinon

CINQ-MARS-LA-PILE (37)   *18k WSW Tours,*
                    5k ENE Langeais

Small village on the Loire with a curious tower topped by four small pyramids... La Pile... nearby. The only remains of its château are two towers, in one of which there is an interesting display of armour.

CLÉRY-ST-ANDRÉ (45)   *15k SW Orléans*

Modest village with a Flamboyant Gothic basilica containing the tomb of Louis XI and a Renaissance chapel where Jean Dunois, companion of Joan of Arc, is buried.

CULAN (18)   *69k S Bourges*

Dramatically sited medieval fortress which has retained its wooden fighting platforms (a very unusual survival). There are fine views of the Arnon valley, 15th century chimney pieces, interesting tapestries and furniture.

Cinq-Mars-la-Pile   *The Tomb of Louis XI, Cléry*

155   *Loire Valley Centre*

Royal Chapel, Dreux

La Devinière, birthplace of Rabelais

Fougères Château

Germigny-des-Près Church

Hunting Museum in Gien Château

The River Claise, near Le Grand-Pressigny

La Guerche-sur-Creuse Château

LA DEVINIÈRE (37) *5k SW Chinon*
This small manor house was the birthplace of Rabelais in about 1494. It is now a museum devoted to Rabelais, and is a good example of a small country house of the 15th and 16th centuries.

DREUX (28) *83k W Paris, 35k N Chartres*
Busy modern town, which still contains many old timbered buildings, a fine Renaissance style belfry, and the Royal Chapel of the Orléans family... an interesting 19th century building with some fine stained glass windows.

FONTGOMBAULT ABBEY (36) *8k NW Le Blanc, 96k SSE Tours*
A great Benedictine abbey on the banks of the Creuse. Although it was dissolved at the Revolution, it has now been restored and re-occupied by the Benedictines. The church is normally open to visitors.

FOUGÈRES-SUR-BIÈVRE (41) *17k S Blois*
Small village with a 15th century 'medieval castle' built at a time when most of the builder's neighbours were putting up elegant Renaissance châteaux.

GALLARDON (28) *16k ENE Chartres*
Minute town with the remains of a feudal keep, an interesting 11th, 13th and 16th century church with a painted wooden ceiling, and a fine 16th century house situated in the rue Port-Mouton.

GERMIGNY-DES-PRÉS (45) *23k ESE Orléans, 5k SE Châteauneuf-sur-Loire*
Here is one of the oldest religious buildings in France, with its 9th century, Carolingian origins evident in a ground plan in the shape of a Greek cross and in its quite exceptional mosaic of the Ravenna school.

GIEN (45) *64k ESE Orléans*
Situated astride the Loire, this busy town was much bombed in the 1939–45 War, but it has been attractively re-built. See the splendid modern church, and the interesting Museum of Hunting in the château.

LE GRAND-PRESSIGNY (37) *30k SSW Loches*
Small village on the little river Claise, at the foot of a hill on which stands a partly ruined castle. This has a fine 12th century keep, and a 16th century wing containing an interesting prehistoric collection.

GUÉ-PÉAN (41) *13k E Montrichard*
Elegant 16th century Renaissance château, deliciously sited at the head of a tranquil valley. The interior is full of interest, and there are fine tapestries and pictures within.

LA GUERCHE-SUR-CREUSE (37) *37k SSW Loches, 12k NE Chatelleraut*
This little village has a 12th century church and a rather forbidding 15th century château, which was built by Charles VII for his mistress, Antoinette de Maignelais.

ILLIERS-COMBRAY (28) *25k SW Chartres*
Marcel Proust, the well known early 20th century novelist, spent many of his early years in the home of his aunt, Madame Amiot, and her house in the rue Docteur Proust is now a Proust Museum.

ISSOUDUN (36)

27k NE Châteauroux, 38k WSW Bourges

Busy town not far to the north of lovely forest country with a fine 12th century keep which may have been built by Richard The Lionheart, and a 16th century hospice complete with fascinating pharmacy and a splendidly carved 'Tree of Jesse' in its chapel. Balzac wrote one of his novels while staying here.

LANGEAIS (37)

25k WSW Tours

15th century château, built by Jean Bourré for Louis XI, and scene of the marriage of Charles VIII and Anne of Brittany in 1491. The gatehouse complete with drawbridge, looks down threateningly upon the charming little town, but once within there is a contrasting domestic scene, with windows looking out over courtyard and gardens, the most important feature of which is the ruined keep built by a Count of Anjou in the 10th century. The apartments within were splendidly restored and furnished in the 19th century, and give a good impression of life in a château in late medieval times. See especially the Saloon in which the royal marriage took place, and the fine chimney pieces both here and in the guardroom.

Langeais Château

LASSAY-SUR-CROISNE (41)

34k SE Blois

Minute village with 15th century church, situated in the 'secret country' of the Sologne (See Page 161), with the beautiful brick and stone Château du Moulin, a short distance to the west. This is surrounded by a moat, and is delightfully furnished.

Langeais by night

The Château du Moulin, Lassay

LIGET, CHARTREUSE DU (37)

10k E Loches

The ruins of a Carthusian monastery founded by Henry II to obtain forgiveness for the murder of Thomas Becket. The nearby chapel of St-Jean is an interesting little 12th century Romanesque building with wall paintings of the same period.

LOCHES (37)

41k SE Tours

This enchanting little town still has a flavour of medieval and Renaissance times, with its 'Cité Médiévale' on a ridge overlooking the river Indre. This old part of the town is encircled by ramparts over a mile and a half in length, which are pierced by three fine gateways. At the southern end is the great medieval keep or donjon, with its towers and notorious dungeons, while at the northern end there is the partly Renaissance Logis Royal, which amongst other things houses the tomb of the lovely Agnès Sorel, mistress of Charles VII. See also the beautiful Hôtel de Ville, and the church of St-Ours.

Tomb of Agnès Sorel, Loches

Medieval keep, Loches

MAINTENON (28)

19k NNE Chartres, 76k SW Paris

Attractive little town on the river Eure, with the large brick and stone château, that Louis XIV gave to the governess of his children, who was henceforth known as Madame de Maintenon, and who became his wife on the death of the Queen in 1687. Madame de Maintenon's bedroom is on view, and the fine park, laid out by Le Nôtre, contains the remains of the famous aqueduct intended to provide water for the fountains and canals of Versailles. This was started by the great Vauban, but abandoned after four years.

View towards Vauban's aqueduct, Maintenon

The River Yèvre, near Mehun

In Meillant Château

Menars

Castle ruins at Montoire

Wall paintings in the chapel at Montoire

MEHUN-SUR-YÈVRE (18)　　　*16k NW Bourges*
Small town on the attractive Canal de Berry, with the two surviving towers of the great château of the Duc de Berry, the patron of the arts, who will be forever remembered for the Limbourg brothers' illuminated manuscript, 'Les Très Riches Heures du Duc de Berry', which he commissioned, and which shows in such delightful detail the life and work in and around the château here (See Condé Museum, Chantilly, Page 210).

MEILLANT CHÂTEAU (18)　　　*38k SSE Bourges*
Splendidly furnished late 15th century château standing in a lovely park on the north side of a small village, with a stream close by. See especially the handsome east front and the most unusual Tour-de-Lion, an octagonal tower isolated from the main building. There is a collection of carriages and motor cars in the outbuildings.

MÉNARS (41)　　　*8k NE Blois*
Handsome 17th century mansion, enlarged by Madame de Pompadour during the last years of her life. Parts of the château are open to the public and it is also possible to visit its great park. Its delightful gardens stretch right down to the banks of the Loire.

MEUNG-SUR-LOIRE (45)　　　*18k SW Orléans*
Pleasant little town on the Loire with an 18th century château, and beside its Romanesque church, a ruined 12th century keep where the famous vagabond poet François Villon, spent some time in prison (on one of the many occasions when he was in trouble).

MEUSNES (41)　　　*10k E St-Aignan-sur-Cher*
There is an interesting museum in the village, illustrating the history of gun-flints, and flint-knapping.... a local industry for many hundreds of years.

MONTARGIS (45)　　　*71k ESE Orléans, 114k SSE Paris*
Busy town on the edge of the Forest of Montargis, complete with river, canal and lake, and in consequence, many bridges. The fine, lofty 16th century choir of its church is well worth visiting.

MONTBAZON (37)　　　*9k S Tours*
Prosperous village on the left bank of the lovely river Indre, with a bewildering choice of splendid hotels and restaurants nearby (The Red Michelin will reveal all!).

MONTEVRAN ZOOLOGICAL PARK (41)
4k N Chaumont-sur-Tharonne,
which is 36k S of Orléans
A large zoo park containing over two hundred animals from six continents, including a very complete collection of bears and hyenas, wolves and wild boars. Also lions, camels, dromedaries, bison, yak... and many others. Restaurant, souvenir shop, buvette, picnic areas.

MONTOIRE-SUR-LE-LOIR (41)　*19k WSW Vendôme*
Delightful little town on the Loir with many pleasant old buildings including a medieval castle, several Renaissance houses, and a Romanesque chapel with a fine series of wall paintings of the 12th and 13th century.

MONTRÉSOR (37) *52k SE Tours*
Handsome little château with two round towers linked by a Renaissance range, and containing a collection of French and Polish pictures. The nearby church is a largely Renaissance building with a fine tomb and beautiful stained glass windows.

MONTRICHARD (41) *43k E Tours*
Small town on the river Cher, which is overlooked by the great keep of Foulques Nerra's castle. See especially the church of Nanteuil, with its fine series of corbel figures representing kings and bishops, the Archaeological Museum in the Château de Pont-Cher, and the interesting collection of vintage cars.

Montrésor

MOUTIERS-EN-BEAUCE (28) *29k SE Chartres*
There is an interesting windmill to the south-west of this minute village in typical Beauce countryside, which is noted for its great rolling cornlands.

NOGENT-LE-ROTROU (28) *54k WSW Chartres*
Small town with many old houses dominated by the great keep of its castle. See especially the tomb of the Duc de Sully (the famous minister of Henri IV) and his wife, by the sculptor Boudin, in the Hôtel-Dieu; and the delightful 17th century Nativity in terra-cotta in the church of Notre-Dame.

NOHANT CHÂTEAU (36) *30k SE Châteauroux*
The well known female novelist George Sand spent much of her life here, and the handsome 18th century château in which she lived is now a museum devoted to her memory. (See also La Châtre, Page 154, and Vic, Page 163).

At Montrichard

NOIRLAC ABBEY (18) *5k NW St-Amand-Mont-Rond*
38k S Bourges
A fine Cistercian abbey founded in 1150 by a cousin of St-Bernard not far from the banks of the Cher, and which has been lived in ever since. Do not miss a visit here.

ORLÉANS (45) *120k SSW Paris*
Much bombed in the 2nd World War, Orléans is a fine modern city astride the Loire, and is the capital of the Département of Loiret. Its medieval cathedral was largely destroyed by Huguenots in 1586, Orléans being their headquarters during the Wars of Religion, and today it represents a pleasant blend of architectural styles. In the Place du Martroi there is a 19th century statue of Joan of Arc, reminding us that it was Joan that finally succeeded in raising the long siege of Orléans by the English, in May 1429. See also the Fine Arts Museum, Joan of Arc's House, the Hôtel de Ville, the Historical and Archaeological Museum, and several other interesting old churches and houses.

Nogent-le-Rotrou   *Joan of Arc at Orléans*

OUARVILLE (28) *27k ESE Chartres*
There is an attractive windmill a short distance to the west of this village in the heart of the Beauce.

PALLUAU-SUR-INDRE (36) *36k WNW Châteauroux*
This little town above the banks of the Indre has an interesting château from which there are fine views out across the river. See also the choir stalls in the collegiate church, and the wall paintings in the church of St-Laurent.

Orléans

Steam train at Pithiviers.
Photograph by Musée des Transports de Pithiviers

Louis XI's Room at Plessis-les-Tours

Mellow brick at Plessis-les-Tours

St-Aignan Château

St-Benoit Abbey

St-Benoit Abbey

Effigy of Philip 1st at St-Benoit

PITHIVIERS (45)   *42k NE Orléans, 82k S Paris*

Small town with tree lined walks on the site of its old ramparts. There is an interesting, largely 16th and 17th century church, the remains of a medieval collegiate church, and the Château d'Ardoise has some fine timberwork. Children will enjoy the eight kilometre steam train ride from the Pithiviers Transport Museum to Bellebat and back.

PLESSIS-LES-TOURS (37)

To SW of the centre of Tours

A fine brick mansion of the 15th century which contains a small museum devoted to the local silk industry, and other historical mementoes.

LA POISSONIÈRE MANOR (41)   *12k W Montoire*

This handsome Renaissance building was the birthplace in 1524, of the poet Pierre de Ronsard.

RICHELIEU (37)   *60k SSW Tours*

This small town was almost entirely re-built by Cardinal de Richelieu, who commissioned Jacques Le Mercier, the architect of the Palais Royal in Paris; and it is a well nigh perfect example of 17th century town planning. The great château, also built by Richelieu, was demolished in the 19th century, but the town hall contains interesting documents relating both to the town and the family. There is a tourist steam train linking Richelieu with Chinon, about twenty kilometres to the north.

RIVAU (37)   *15k SE Chinon*

A largely 15th century castle mentioned by Rabelais in his 'Gargantua', with its large keep surrounded by towers and a moat… all remarkably unspoilt. It is owned by the painter Pierre-Laurent Brenot, and his works are naturally on display here.

ROMORANTIN (41)   *41k SE Blois*

This is the largest town of the Sologne (See Page 161), on whose southern fringes it lies, attractively sited on the banks of the river Sauldre. It has many picturesque old houses of brick and stone, some with timber framing. See especially the remains of an old royal château, the interesting Museum of the Sologne in the Town Hall, and the Racing Car Museum in the Faubourg d'Orléans.

ST-AIGNAN-SUR-CHER (41)   *39k S Blois*

Charming village on the banks of the Cher, with a fine collegiate church which has a beautiful series of carved capitals, and wall paintings in its Romanesque crypt. There are good views from the terrace of the château, which is itself not open to the public. The extensive caves in the area are used for the storage and fermentation of the local sparkling wines.

ST-AMAND-MONTROND (18)   *44k S Bourges*

Modest town situated just to the west of the river Cher, with a pleasant park occupying the hilly site of a now vanished castle. The largely Romanesque church contains several items of interest.

ST-BENOIT-SUR-LOIRE (45)   *35k ESE Orléans*

The great abbey here was originally known as the Abbaye de Fleury, but in the 7th century one of the monks returned from Monte Cassino (which had been
continued

sacked by the Lombards) with the body of Saint Benedict, the much revered founder of the Benedictine Order. Thereafter it became a great centre of pilgrimage and learning, although it was largely destroyed centuries later, at the time of the Revolution (1792). It has now been rebuilt by the Benedictines, although the abbey church itself had survived, and this remains as an outstanding example of Romanesque architecture. See especially the ambulatory, the porch belfry, the 11th century crypt housing the tomb of St-Benedict, and finally the effigy of Philip Ist. See also the old port on the Loire.

Eleventh century crypt at St-Benoit

SACHÉ (37)   *26k SW Tours*
Pleasant 16th and 17th century château in a park on the banks of the Indre. The author Balzac stayed here regularly for many years, and his bedroom and several other rooms are furnished as a museum, with first editions, portraits, etc. Several of Balzac's novels are based on his knowledge of the surrounding area.

SANCERRE (18)   *45k NE Bourges*
This small town is delightfully situated on a hill to the west of the Loire and there are fine views over the surrounding countryside, which is vine clad in parts and otherwise well wooded. There are many narrow little streets and alleyways, below the Tour des Fiefs, the 15th century castle keep, which is the best viewpoint. The dry, white wine of Sancerre is one of our favourites.

Saché Château

Balzac's Bedroom, at Saché

SAVONNIÈRES CAVES (37)   *2k NE Villandry*
                                      16k WSW Tours
Extensive caves with stalactites and stalagmites, which make a contrast with all those châteaux you have probably been visiting.

SELLES-SUR-CHER (41)   *41k SSE Blois*
Delightfully situated on a bend of the river Cher, this village has an abbey church with a fine Romanesque façade and a château which combines a stark 13th century fortress with an elegant Renaissance building close by. Both buildings are well worth visiting.

THE SOLOGNE (41)   *Approx. 30k S Orléans*
This is quiet, secret countryside, of moorland covered with heather and broom, and interspersed with ponds and plantations of birch, pine and Spanish chestnut. See the interesting Museum of the Sologne at Romorantin (See Page 160).

Off hunting in the Sologne

Sully Château

SULLY-SUR-LOIRE (45)   *42k ESE Orléans*
                                        153k S Paris
Pleasant little town on the banks of the Loire, with a 16th century collegiate church containing several items of interest including two fine stained glass windows. However it is the great château within its broad moat that brings most people to Sully. This consists of a 14th century fortress with great towers and a magnificent chestnut timbered roof, and a Renaissance pavillion, built by the great Duke de Sully, soldier and minister under Henri IV (of Navarre). It was in the old château that Joan of Arc persuaded the Dauphin to be crowned (at Reims, in 1429); and in the 18th century the young Voltaire spent much time here, a theatre being built, in which his plays could be performed.

Sully Château

Loire Valley Centre

Sunlit courtyard at Talcy Château

Tours

Ussé Château

Valençay Château

TALCY CHÂTEAU (41)   *20k NNE Blois*
Small 16th century building standing in a vast expanse of cornland, with a medieval exterior concealing two gentle courtyards complete with wine press and dovecote. The rooms within are delightfully furnished in a combination of 16th, 17th and 18th century styles, and are in fine contrast to the rather plain exterior.

TAVANT (37)   *12k ESE Chinon, 40k SW Tours*
Minute village with a wonderful Romanesque church. This has a crypt decorated with splendidly preserved wall paintings as old as the church itself (about 1150), and rivalled in France only by those found at St-Savin, in Vienne (See Page 224).

TOURS (37)   *233k SW Paris*
The lovely city of Tours stands on a narrow spit of land between the rivers Loire and Cher, not far above their final union. It is built on the site of a Roman town, and in the 4th century it became a great centre of Christianity under St-Martin, Bishop of Tours. The New Basilica of St-Martin is an interesting 19th century Romano-Byzantine style building over the rediscovered tomb of the Saint. This is situated in the old part of the city to the south-west of the fine 18th century bridge, the Pont Wilson. The Cathedral and the Museum of Fine Arts lie some distance eastwards, the former being a delightful mixture of styles, with a splendid 'Flamboyant Gothic' west front, incorporating a rose window which was copied from Bourges. The excellent Museum of Fine Arts is situated in the adjoining old Archbishop's Palace. Space does not allow us to describe this fine city adequately, but spare time to wander in its old streets, along the broad quays beside the Loire, and in its lovely parks and gardens.

TROO (41)   *25k W Vendôme, 50k NW Blois*
Small village on the Loir with considerable remains of its medieval fortifications, and a number of houses carved out of the rock... true troglodyte dwellings. There are also rock dwellings to be found at the villages of Genille, Les Roches, and Trehet... all in the Loir-et-Cher Département.

TROUSSAY (41)   *15k SE Blois, 3k W Cheverny*
Charming little Renaissance style château, the interior of which gives a good impression of life in an old manor house in this part of the world. There is an exhibition of items relating to the Sologne in the stables.

USSÉ (37)   *35k WSW Tours*
Delightful 15th century château above the Indre, with white stonework, turrets and towers, standing out fairy-like against the dark woodlands arising behind it (It is said that Perrault was inspired by it when writing the Sleeping Beauty). See the fine 18th century interiors, the exquisite Renaissance chapel in the park, and the colourful formal gardens between the château and the river.

VALENÇAY (36)   *55k SSE Blois*
A 16th century château in the grand manner, with additions in the 17th and 18th centuries. Valençay is perhaps best known as the château of the great opportunist stateman, Talleyrand, who acquired it with Napoleon's help and encouragement in 1803. See
continued

especially the various mementoes of Talleyrand, and the great park with its flocks of llamas, cranes and flamingoes, and its herd of fallow deer.

VATAN (36) *78k SE Blois*
Small village which has an Automobile Museum which is worth visiting.

VENDÔME (41) *32k NW Blois*
Delightful little town on the Loir with many pleasant old buildings, including an abbey church with a splendid 12th century bell tower, over 260 feet high, and a fine Romanesque interior. There is also a 14th century gateway, which was charmingly embellished two centuries later.

LA VERRERIE (18) *10k SE Aubigny-sur-Nère, 29k WNW Sancerre*
Fine 15th and 16th century château, begun by John Stuart, whose father had been given the lordship of Aubigny by Charles VII, in recognition of his services at the Battle of Baugé in 1421. This is a largely Renaissance building, and it looks magnificent when reflected in the waters of the nearby lake. There is much attractive forest country to the south and east of here.

VIC (36) *2k NW Nohant*
The fine series of wall paintings in the little Romanesque church of St-Martin, were discovered by George Sand and her fellow novelist Prosper Mérimée (See Nohant, Page 159).

Vendôme Abbey

VILLAINES-LES-ROCHERS (37) *25k SW Tours, 7k SSE Azay-le-Rideau*
Small village noted for its basket-making, using green rushes and black and yellow osiers, all found in the flat countryside south of the Indre.

VILLANDRY (37) *20k WSW Tours*
A largely 16th century château, incorporating the keep of an earlier fortress, Villandry is especially noted for its elaborate formal gardens in the 16th century Italo-French style. These were created in this century by Dr. Carvallo, as a result of detailed study of the subject, largely derived from the engravings of the great Du Cerceau, the forerunner of all those other European illustrators of castles, mansions and parks, over the subsequent two hundred years.

Villandry Château

VILLEGONGIS CHÂTEAU (36) *12k NW Châteauroux*
Charming moated château built about 1530 by one of the masons who had been employed at Chambord (See Page 153). It is normally only possible to look at the exterior.

VILLESAVIN CHÂTEAU (41) *16k ESE Blois*
Delightful Renaissance château built by Jean le Breton who had supervised the works at Chambord (See Page 153). Dormer windows look out over an old courtyard in which stands a large marble vase, and there is a 16th century dovecote with a fine spiral ladder giving access to the multitude of nesting places. There is also a collection of horse-drawn vehicles.

Formal gardens at Villandry

Villesavin Château

VOUVRAY (37) *9k E Tours*

Small town on the Loire just above Tours, and a well known wine producing centre. It is possible to visit some of the 'caves' of the wine shippers, many of which are excavated out of the limestone cliffs. The countryside hereabouts was well loved by Balzac who was born at Tours, and in 1934 a statue of Gaudissart, the hero of one of his novels, was erected at Vouvray.

Chimney-piece at Ainay- le-Vieil (See Page 150)

Sculptural detail, Chartres Cathedral (See Page 153)

GREAT WINE AREAS OF THE LOIRE VALLEY

There are vineyards along much of the length of this great river, but we shall try here to summarise the outstanding areas.

THE 'UPPER' LOIRE. The area around Sancerre is noted for its dry white wines, and the two names that stand out are Sancerre itself and Pouilly-Fumé. Several excellent dry white wines are also produced in the Cher valley to the west of Bourges.

THE MIDDLE LOIRE. This is the area extending from Blois to the west of Angers, and is partly in the 'Loire Valley West' Region. It takes in Touraine and Anjou, which includes not only the vineyards of the Loire valley itself, but those in the valleys of its tributaries the Indre, the Cher, the Vienne and the Loir. Here are produced a wide variety of wines, reds, whites and well known rosés. Although these wines do not have the international fame of many of the great wines of Burgundy or Bordeaux, many of them are deservedly popular and eminently drinkable. The white wines of Vouvray and the sparkling wines of Saumur deserve a special mention.

THE LOWER LOIRE. See Loire Valley West, Page 174.

The Loire at Gien (See Page 156)

Loire Valley West

Comprises the following Départements:
Loire-Atlantique (44)   Sarthe (72)
Maine-et-Loire (49)   Vendée (85)
Mayenne (53)

On the western fringes of this great Region are the long Atlantic shores, with miles of golden sands punctuated by a series of sparkling resorts and quiet harbour towns, and backed in places by hauntingly beautiful marshlands. The estuary of the Loire, crossed near its mouth at St-Nazaire by a magnificent bridge, leads us back towards the classic château country, with towns like Nantes, Angers and Saumur adding splendour on the way. There are great forests to the sourth and east of Le Mans, while the northern border with Normandy is characterised by deliciously wooded hill country. Much of the remainder of the region may possibly lack the more obvious appeal of some other holiday areas, but it conceals many charming individual features and will amply repay those who are prepared to seek these out.

ANCENIS (44)   *51k W Angers*
Quiet little town on the north bank of the Loire, with the remains of a 15th and 16th century castle now incorporated into a school.

ANGERS (49)   *284k SW Paris*
This was once the capital of the Anjou, and is now the capital of the Maine-et-Loire Département. It is a busy modern city, but it retains many items of great interest to visitors. The great medieval castle stands on a rock above the river Maine, and has no fewer than 17 massive round towers built into its curtain walls. Within the castle will be found one of the world's great collections of tapestries, housed in a splendid modern building. See also the 12th and 13th century cathedral, the vaulting of whose nave was the first to carried out in what has become known as the Angevin style; the 12th century hospital of St-Jean, also with Angevin vaulting, with its collection of modern tapestries by Jean Lurcat; the Fine Arts Museum in the lovely 15th century Logis Barrault; the 12th century belfry tower of St-Aubin; and the Hôtel Pincé, a fine Renaissance building housing a collection of enamels.

Angers

ASNIÈRES ABBEY (49)   *14k SW Saumur*
This ruined abbey, situated to the north of the Brossay Forest, was founded in the 12th century, and its 13th century chancel is one of the loveliest examples of the Angevin Gothic style. Do not overlook the delightful little oratory, which contains a 14th century crucifix.

ASNIÈRES-SUR-VÈGRE (72) *10k NE Sablé-sur-Sarthe*
Charming little town with views of a 17th century château and an old mill, from its delightful old bridge over the Vègre. There are interesting wall paintings in the church, near which is an unusual Gothic building called the Cour d'Asnières, where the priests of Le Mans used to receive their tithes from the peasants.

MONT DES AVALOIRS (53)   *42k ENE Mayenne,*
                                                5k ESE Pré-en-Pail
This is the highest point in Western France (417 metres, 1,368 feet) and there are splendid views from the summit, which is 'equipped' with a topograph, or orientation table. This is situated in pleasant forest country, and is within the Regional Nature Park of Normandy and Maine (See Page 204).

BATZ-SUR-MER (44)   *7k W La Baule, 80k W Nantes*
Small seaside town with several fine sandy beaches close by. There are fine views from the top of the tall church belfry. Do not miss the interesting little Folklore Museum.

Sculptural detail, Angers Cathedral

BAUGÉ (49)   *38k ENE Angers*
Small town with a château (now the Mairie) on the foundations of an earlier fortress built by that great fortifier, Foulques Nerra. Do not miss a visit to the pharmacy of the Hospice St-Joseph, with its wonderful collection of 16th and 17th century 'chemist's jars'; nor to Vieil-Baugé, which has a church with a twisted spire.

LA BAULE (44)   *73k WNW Nantes*
This is one of the great European holiday resorts, with its great five mile sweep of firm, golden sands, its fashionable shops and its wide variety of accommodation and attractions.

BAZOUGES-SUR-LE-LOIR (72)   *40k NE Angers*
Minute town with a delightul little 16th and 17th century château on the banks of the Loir, and a church with an interesting 15th century painted ceiling.

The Beach at La Baule

BERCÉ FOREST (72)   *Approx. 30k SE Le Mans*
A delightful crescent-shaped piece of forest country including a fine wood of oak trees over three hundred years old... the Futaie des Clos, and several little springs and streams (See Michelin Map 64). There are many forest tracks and paths.

BOURGONNIÈRE CHÂTEAU (49)   *9k ESE Ancenis,*
                                   32k WSW Angers
Here is an early 19th century château with the ruins of a 15th century keep nearby, and a Renaissance chapel with a fine reredos incorporating a Christ in Majesty.

BOUMOIS CHÂTEAU (49)   *9k NW Saumur*
Handsome 16th century château with medieval Gothic giving way to a more relaxed Renaissance style, with windows and other domesticities added in the 17th and 18th centuries. There is a dovecote close to the main entrance, and an attractive little chapel. The contents of the beautiful interior include mementoes of Aristide du Petit-Thouars, an 18th century sea-captain and adventurer, who died at the Battle of Aboukir in 1798, having urged his men to fight on rather than surrender.

Cottage in the Brière

BRIÈRE REGIONAL NATURE PARK (44)
                          Approx 60k WNW Nantes
The marshes of the Grand Brière, and the partially drained flat lands surrounding them, have now all been incorporated into a Regional Nature Park. There are facilities for punting on its quiet waterways (once the inhabitants' only means of transport), for sailing, bird watching, horse riding and camping. But above all this is an area of mystery which can be explored by those who seek tranquillity under broad open skies, where fishing, peat cutting and cattle grazing are the most active local pursuits. (There is an excellent 1:50,000 map of the Park published by the IGN.)

Fishing apparatus in the Brière.
A Brière Regional Nature Park Photograph

BRISSAC CHÂTEAU (49)   *16k SSE Angers*
Charming 17th century building between two 15th century towers, standing in a pleasant park. The interior is magnificently furnished and well worth visiting. There is a well restored windmill on the N 178, Angers road, north of Brissac.

CHÂTEAUBRIANT (44)   *71k WNW Angers*
Busy town on the main route between Paris and La

continued

Peat cutting in the Brière   *Windmill at Brissac*

Courtanvaux Château

Craon Château

Le Croisic

Le Croisic Harbour

Cunault Church

Baule, with a largely 16th century château overlooking the little river Chère. All that remains of the original medieval castle are a great square keep and a few walls and towers, but these and the Renaissance 'new château' into which they are incorporated are well worth visiting.

CHÂTEAU-GONTIER (53) *29k S Laval*
Pleasant little town astride the lovely river Mayenne, bordered here by delightful tree lined quays and pleasant parks. There are two interesting churches here, one Romanesque, and one from the 17th century.

CHOLET (49) *61k SSW Angers*
This is a lively modern town, and five kilometres to the south-east is the lake of Ribou, where there are extensive leisure facilities.

CLERMONT ABBEY (53) *12k W Laval*
The ruins of a Cistercian abbey, with a great abbey church containing some fine monuments to the Sires de Laval.

COURTANVAUX CHÂTEAU (72) *8k S St-Calais, which is 45k E Le Mans*
An imposing 15th and 16th century château, with two domed towers framing its handsome Renaissance gateway.

CRAON (53) *56k NW Angers*
Small town in quiet countryside with a handsome 18th century château in pale stone on its northern edge. Only the delightful park and gardens are open regularly to the public.

LE CROISIC (44) *10k W La Baule*
Lively seaside resort with a colourful fishing port, and plenty of character in its streets. There is a good beach near the town, although this is small enough to become rather crowded at peak times.

CUNAULT (49) *13k NW Saumur*
An 11th – 12th century priory church built by the Benedictines, a largely Romanesque building with Angevin Gothic vaulting in places. It is an outstanding example of the Romanesque style, and its interest is enhanced by wall paintings and many sculptural details within.

DOUÉ-LA-FONTAINE (49) *17k WSW Saumur*
Small town built over a series of springs that mark the beginnings of the little river Doué. These rise up through stone cut 'reservoirs' that are probably the remains of quarrying which dates back here to Roman times. There are the ruins of a castle upon a hill above the town, an interesting 15th century church, and the ruins of a collegiate church some three centuries older. There is a fine Zoological Park a little way out of the town on the Cholet road (SW).

DURTAL (49) *34k NE Angers, 13k W La Flèche*
The late 16th century château retains two of its medieval towers, and dominates this little village, which stands on the river Loir.

DE L'ÉPAU ABBEY (72) *4k E Le Mans*
Here on the eastern outskirts of Le Mans are the ruins

continued

of an abbey and a fine abbey church, all of which was built for the Cistercians by Berengaria, the wife of Richard the Lionheart. She was originally buried here, but her tomb was moved to Le Mans cathedral in the early 19th century.

ÉVRON (53)   *24k SE Mayenne*
Small town with a fine abbey church which is a blend of Romanesque and Gothic styles, and which contains rich relics and ornaments in its Chapel of Our Lady of the Thorn.

LA FERTÉ-BERNARD (72)   *44k NE Le Mans*
Pleasant small town, with a 15th century fortified gateway, an interesting 15th and 16th century church, and many delightful old houses.

La Ferté-Bernard Church

LA FLÈCHE (72)   *42k SW Le Mans*
Small town astride the river Loir, with an interesting church and an outstanding series of buildings housing the Pyrtanée Militaire (a military academy), some of which may be visited. This was once a great Jesuit college, and the great philosopher Descartes was one of its pupils. There is an interesting Zoo Park at Tertre Rouge, five kilometres to the south-east.

FONTENAY-LE-COMTE (85)   *137k SSW Angers,*
                               56k ESE La Roche-sur-Yon
Quiet little town astride the river Vendée, with an interesting late Gothic church, some old streets with 16th and 17th century houses, and a 15th century mansion, the Château de Terre-Neuve, with fine ceilings and chimney-pieces. The writer Rabelais was educated at a Franciscan convent here. There is an interesting museum devoted to the Vendée area.

Fontenay-le-Comte   *The Cloisters at
                              Fontevrault*

FONTEVRAULT-L'ABBAYE (49)   *16k SE Saumur*
Here are the remains of a great abbey founded in 1099 by a wandering preacher, and divided into five separate buildings... for monks, nuns, lepers, the sick and noble ladies who wished to retire from the world... all ruled over by an abbess. This abbey rapidly became a most aristocratic institution, and between 1115 and 1789 it was a well used refuge for ladies of royal or noble birth who were either forced, or who decided of their own free will, to retire here. Early in its history it received the wealth and protection of the Plantagenets, and in the great Romanesque abbey church will be found the tombs of Henry II, his wife Eleanor of Aquitaine, who spent her last years here, their son Richard the Lionheart, and the third wife of their other son, King John, Isabelle of Angoulême.

Effigy of Eleanor of Aquitaine, at Fontevrault...

See the abbey church itself, the cloisters, the fine octagonal kitchen, and outside the bounds of the abbey, the church of St-Michel, which contains many treasures which once belonged to the abbey.

GOULAINE (44)   *18k E Nantes*
Situated on the edge of marsh country, this charming moated château is a blend of late Gothic and Renaissance styles. The interior is largely in the style of the 17th and 18th centuries, and is richly decorated and furnished.

GUÉRANDE (44) *19k WNW St-Nazaire, 77k W Nantes*
Delightful little town between the sea and the south-western fringes of the Grand Brière (See Page 167). It continued

*... and of her son,
Richard the Lionheart*

Gateway at Guérande

Loire Valley West

The 'Mont des Alouettes' (See Les Herbiers)

has a remarkably complete 15th century town wall, pierced with five gateways, and with a watery moat on the northern side. Within the walls, there are old narrow streets which are full of character, and there is a collegiate church with a 12th century interior. About two kilometres to the north there is a stone windmill, the 'Moulin du Diable'.

LES HERBIERS (85)   25k SSW Cholet
Small town with no special features, apart from the dramatic 'Mont des Alouettes' (hill of the larks), with its tower windmills and its shrine... all situated about two kilometres to the north. This is well worth visiting.

ÎLE BÉHUARD (49)   15k SW Angers
Small island in the Loire, on which is a village with 15th and 16th century houses, and a 15th century church built by Louis XI, after he had been saved from drowning. This church has a remarkably unspoilt interior, and is well worth visiting.

L'ISLE-BRIAND NATIONAL STUD FARM (49)
22k NNW Angers, 1k S Le Lion D'Angers
Here on an 'island' immediately above the confluence of the rivers Mayenne and Oudon, is an excellent racecourse, and *the* 'National Stud' of France, with splendid modern buildings in the grounds of an elegant 18th century château.

Château at Lassay

LASSAY (53)   34k NNE Mayenne
Small village dominated by the pepperpot roofs and towers of its 15th century castle, which is an outstanding example of military architecture of the Charles VII period. One kilometre to the north of the town are the romantic ruins of the Renaissance château of Bois-Thibault (apply to the S.I. at Lassay for permission to visit).

LAVAL (53)   75k W Le Mans, 278k WSW Paris
Busy modern town astride the Mayenne, and capital of the Département which takes it name from this river. The old town lies mainly to the immediate west of the river, and the remains of its medieval walls encompass an area of old streets and buildings including a Cathedral with Romanesque origins, two other interesting Romanesque churches, and a château with its keep retaining medieval wooden hoardings. Henri 'Douanier' Rousseau, the 'naïve' painter, was born at Laval in 1844.

Le Lude Château

LUÇON (85)   145k SSW Angers, 51k N La Rochelle
Elegantly spacious town, with a Cathedral displaying styles from the 12th, 17th and 19th centuries (its 19th century spire is 85 metres high). See also the handsome 16th century cloisters in the adjoining Bishop's Palace, and the lovely Dumaine gardens behind the Town Hall.

LE LUDE (72)   44k S Le Mans
A largely 15th century château on the foundations of a medieval stronghold commanding a strategic crossing of the river Loir. The interior of Le Lude is still very much 'lived-in', and has a warmth of feeling so often lacking in great houses open to the public. The son-et-lumière on the river bank is outstanding.

MAILLEZAIS (85)   13k SSE Fontenay-le-Comte
Small village on the northern fringes of the Marais

Son-et-Lumière at Le Lude

continued

Poitevin (See Below), with a fine Romanesque porch to its church, and the ruins of an ancient abbey nearby.

LE MANS (72)   *200k WSW Paris*
Thriving city astride the river Sarthe, and capital of Sarthe Département, Le Mans is perhaps best known for its 24 hour car race. However its history goes back to Roman times, and Henry II, the first Plantagenet king of England, was born here in 1133. See especially the cathedral of St-Julian, with its Romanesque nave and splendid Gothic choir and the tomb of Queen Berengaria, the widow of Richard the Lion-Heart; the lovely 13th century church of Notre Dame de la Couture; the Tesse Museum with its fine art collection and the remains of the Gallo-Roman town walls.

Le Mans Cathedral   *In the Old Quarter, Le Mans*

LE MANS CAR MUSEUM (72)   *5k S Le Mans*
Interesting motor museum attached to the famous racing circuit, with no fewer than 160 cars and 60 cycles and motorcycles on display. Do not miss a visit here.

LE MARAIS BRETON, or VENDEAN MARSHLAND (85)   *Approx. 60k SW Nantes*
Extensive marshy area, from which the Département of Vendée takes it name. Here will be found many attractive, low built farms, situated amongst a bewildering number of small rivers and drainage canals.

LE MARAIS POITEVIN REGIONAL NATURE PARK (17, 79, 85)   *Approx. 45k SE La Roche-sur-Yon*
This is a fascinating area of marshland intersected by a myriad of canals, and sometimes described as 'the Green Venice'. It is shared between this region, and that of Poitou-Charentes. (For details see page 220.)

Mayenne

MAYENNE (53)   *74k NW Le Mans*
Pleasant town astride the Mayenne, with an old castle overlooking the river, with its bridges and granite quays. Mayenne suffered badly in the 1944 Normandy battles, and the saving of one of its bridges by the heroism of an American sergeant is commemorated by a plaque. Visit the castle, and six kilometres to the south-west, the ancient abbey of Fontaine Daniel, beside a lovely pool, and the Forest of Mayenne with its oaks and elms, about twelve kilometres beyond.

MERVENT FOREST (85)   *8k N Fontenay-le-Comte*
Lovely wooded country surrounding a long lake with many branches. There is a zoo at the south end of the lake, and sailing dinghies are to be seen on the sparkling tree bordered waters.

Montgeoffroy Château

MONTGEOFFROY (49)   *23k E Angers, 2k N Mazé*
Elegantly proportioned 18th century château, sited on a slight rise in quiet countryside, with splendid wrought iron gates at the entrance to its park. The rooms within are equally elegant, and their 18th century flavour is well preserved. There are carriages and a litter in the stables, and family tombs in the adjoining 16th century chapel. Do not miss this.

MONTREUIL-BELLAY (49)   *16k SSW Saumur*
Charming little town above the banks of the river Thouet. There is a medieval castle (built by Foulques Nerra in about 1025), with elegant 'new castle' added in the 15th century, when the present town walls were also built. See also the collegiate church, the priory of the Nobis, the hospice of St-Jean and the wonderful selection of old houses within its walls.

In Montgeoffroy Château   *Montreuil-Bellay Château*

Loire Valley West

At the Museum of Popular Art, in the Ducal Palace, Nantes

Sandy beach on the Ile de Noirmoutier

The Port, on the Île de Noirmoutier

Plessis-Bourré

MONTSOREAU (49)　　　　　　　*11k ESE Saumur*

Fine 15th century château situated on the banks of the Loire beside a small village. There is a splendid 16th century staircase and a museum devoted to the French campaigns in Morocco. The Vienne joins the Loire just upstream from here.

MORTIERCROLLES CHÂTEAU (53) *47k NW Angers,*
10k SSE Craon

Imposing 15th century château with fine corner towers overlooking a moat. The entrance building is particularly impressive.

NANTES (44)　　　　　　　　　*370k SW Paris*

Large modern city and seaport, on the lower reaches of the Loire, Nantes is also capital of the Loire Atlantique Département. It suffered greatly in the 1939 – 45 War, both at the hands of the Allied Air Forces, and the retreating Germans, but evidence of this is no longer apparent. See especially the great Ducal Castle, a largely 15th century building which houses two art museums; the fine Cathedral in which will be found the lovely Renaissance tomb of Francis II, Duke of Brittany; the Museum of Fine Arts, which has one of the finest collections in France; and the excellent views ⸍ ut over the port from the pilgrimage church of Ste-Ḁ ɩne (above the north bank of the Loire, on west side of the city).

ÎLE DE NOIRMOUTIER (85)　　　*82k SW Nantes*

This is seventeen kilometres long and six kilometres wide, and can be reached from the mainland at low tide, by a long toll bridge. It is a low island with woods near its northern shore. The rocky coastline is punctuated by many sandy beaches, and there are at least three camping sites.

NORMANDIE-MAINE REGIONAL NATURE PARK
(50, 53, 61, 72)

This lies partly in the Loire Valley West Region, and partly in the Normandy Region, (See Page 204).

OUDON (44)　　　　　　　　　*27k NE Nantes*

Charming little town to the immediate north of the Loire, with the ruins of an 11th and 12th century château and a pleasant yacht harbour on the banks of the tidal river.

PLESSIS-BOURRÉ (49)　　　　　*20k N Angers*

Large square moated château built between 1466 and 1472, by Jean Bourré, who was Finance Minister to Louis XI, Charles VIII and Louis XII. It is unusual in being all of this one period, apart from some of the outbuildings. See the painted ceiling in the guardroom.

PLESSIS-MACÉ (49)　　　　　*11k NW Angers*

A largely 15th century château, with curtain walls and towers three centuries older. The rooms are, at the time of writing, empty; but the chapel with its flamboyant Gothic decoration makes a visit here worthwhile.

PONCÉ-SUR-LOIR (72)　　　　*25k SSW St-Calais*

Small village just to the north of the Loir, with a 12th century church which has some interesting wall paintings, and a fine château, which although partly burnt down at the Revolution, retains a fine 16th century staircase, and some splendidly coffered ceilings.

PORNIC (44)   *51k WSW Nantes*
Charming little market town and seaside resort, complete with many attractive little streets and a medieval castle. There are several sandy beaches close by and a little port which is full of character. There is a regular service to the Isle of Noirmoutier.

POUZAUGES (85)   *81k SE Nantes*
Small town with a medieval castle complete with ivy-clad keep. This was one of several castles owned by Gilles de Rais (Bluebeard) (See Tiffauges, Page 174). There are fine wall paintings in the church at Pouzauges-le-Vieux (2k SE) and excellent views out over the Vendée from the Puy-Crapaud (4k E). The Bois de la Folie, just to the north of the town, is an attractive wooded area with fine views from the top of the hill on which it is situated.

Pleasure craft at Pornic

RAGUIN MANOR (49) *33k NW Angers, 15k ENE Candé*
Lovely 17th manor situated in quiet country just to the north of the village of Chaze-sur-Argos. Its charming interior includes two outstandingly splendid rooms, which have decoration incorporating gold leaf, on their panelled walls. Do not miss this.

LA ROCHE-SUR-YON (85)   *65k S Nantes*
This busy town is the capital of the Vendée Département, and was laid out in its present form on the instructions of Napoleon, following the destruction of the medieval town in 1794 by Republican troops. It was in fact called Napoléon, but reverted to its original name in 1871. With its wide choice of hotels it makes an ideal centre for exploring the Vendée.

Fishing craft at Les Sables-d'Olonne

ST-CALAIS (72)   *45k ESE Le Mans*
Small town with a handsome Renaissance façade to its church, and a modest museum and art gallery. The builder of Durham cathedral was a Benedictine father at the monastery here.

ST-GILLES-CROIX-DE-VIE (85)   *78 SSW Nantes*
Twin resorts, making up a small town, with old ports on either side of the little river Vie, and a fine beach stretching southwards from St-Gilles. There are interesting views of ships going up to the ports from the beach to the west of Croix, and both have a pleasant area of old narrow streets, with busy shops, cafes and restaurants.

ST-NAZAIRE (44)   *428k WSW Paris*
Large shipbuilding and industrial town which is not of great interest to visitors, apart perhaps from a visit to its port.

Horse riding near Les Sables-d'Olonne

STE-SUZANNE (53)   *34k E Laval*
Charmingly sited little town on a rocky promontory, with much of its medieval fortifications still intact. There are fine views from its North Tower, and one can walk around the ramparts. William the Conqueror failed to take this town, despite a siege lasting three years.

LES SABLES-D'OLONNE (85)   *91k S Nantes*
A large, lively holiday resort with splendid bathing beaches of fine sand, a wide selection of hotels and camping sites, an active fishing and pleasure port, many elegant shops and all the usual holiday facilities, including an interesting zoo.

The sunlit beaches of Les Sables-d'Olonne

173

Loire Valley West

The Loire at Saumur

At the Cavalry School, Saumur

Serrant Château

On the shores of the Étang du Defais, in Sillé Forest

SAUMUR (49)   *52k SW Angers*

Charming wine town largely on the south bank of the Loire, with two Romanesque churches and a 14th and 15th century château in which are two museums... A 'Museum of Decorative Arts' and a 'Museum of the Horse'. There is a cavalry and armoured corps school here, the origins of which go back to 1763, and there is an interesting Museum of Armoured Cavalry, with no fewer than sixty armoured vehicles on display.

SERRANT (49)   *16k WSW Angers,*
2k NE St-Georges-sur-Loire

Handsome 16th and 17th century château in the Renaissance style, built around a central courtyard and surrounded by a moat. The beautifully proportioned interior is delightfully furnished, and there are interesting connections with the Jacobites. Do not miss the splendid monument by the fashionable sculptor, Antoine Coysevox in the chapel.

SILLÉ FOREST (72)   *Approx 35k NW Le Mans*

Splendid forest country in the centre of which is the Étang du Defais, where there is a 'plage' from which there is sailing and water-skiing.

SOLESMES (72)   *48k WSW Le Mans,*
3k NE Sablé-sur-Sarthe

Small village on the river Sarthe with the abbey church of a great Benedictine foundation. Here are two fine groups of late 15th and early 16th century sculpture representing the 'Entombment of Christ' and the 'Entombment of the Virgin'.

TIFFAUGES (85)   *45k SE Nantes*

Here are the ruins of the great castle belonging to the dreaded 'Bluebeard', Gilles de Rais, one time companion of Joan of Arc, but in later life notorious as having made a compact with the devil (so goes the tale) which involved him in the daily sacrifice of small boys. He was finally hanged and burnt at Nantes in 1440, at the early age of 36, after what can only be described as an eventful life.

VOUVANT (85)   *15k N Fontenay-le-Comte*

An attractive little fortified town above the river Mère with a great 13th century tower (the only remains of its château) and its town walls and postern gate. The Romanesque church is worth visiting.

ÎLE DE YEU (85)

This small island is reached by ferry* from Fromentine, which is 82k SW of Nantes. Yeu has excellent sandy beaches between its rocky headlands, and is in general a most attractive island.

This takes about 1hr 10mins, but owing to tides, the return journey is not always possible on the same day.

GREAT WINE AREAS OF THE LOIRE VALLEY

(continued from page 164)

THE LOWER LOIRE. This area extends westwards from Angers to the Loire estuary beyond Nantes, and is in fact centred upon this fine city. Going downstream we first encounter Muscadet-Sèvres-et-Maine, and then, close to Nantes, Muscadet-des-Côteaux-de-la-Loire. These light, reasonably dry white wines are admirable companions for sea-food and fish in general and tend to be more modestly priced than those from Chablis, the other splendid choice for all fruits-de-mer.

Midi-Pyrénées

Comprises the following Départements:
Ariège (09) Lot (46)
Aveyron (12) Hautes-Pyrénées (65)
Haute-Garonne (31) Tarn (81)
Gers (32) Tarn-et-Garonne (82)

Bounded on the north by the Dordogne, this region contains a series of equally lovely rivers, which with the exception of the Cère (which joins the Dordogne), all flow into the mighty Garonne, and thus into the Atlantic. The great limestone plateaux of the Causses have been deeply incised by these rivers... the Lot, the Aveyron, the Tarn and many others, and the gorges, caves, cirques and chasms thus created provide more than enough drama to relieve this otherwise gentle landscape. Further south lies the quiet countryside of Gers, noted for the production of Armagnac, and beyond, the Garonne and the Ariége lead us up through the foothills, and then to the mountains, of the central Pyrénées... heroic country with peaks to be climbed and valleys to be explored.

Nature has thus provided a rich bounty for visitors to this diverse region, but it has been further enhanced by the works of man, with medieval towns and villages, busy modern cities, old castles and abbeys... all in rich and bewildering profusion. Select a few from our list, travel slowly, stop often, eat well, drink well (always possible in this most 'gastronomic' area)... and you will have adopted a holiday mode without compare.

ALBI (81) *684k S Paris, 76k NE Toulouse*

This large town on the river Tarn is capital of the Tarn Département, and is an excellent centre for exploration of the southern flanks of the Massif Central. The old town is dominated by the great fortified cathedral and the adjoining Bishop's Palace, the Palais de la Berbie, which houses the Toulouse-Lautrec Museum, the most important collection of his work (Henri de Toulouse-Lautrec was born in Albi in 1864). The lovely mellow brick cathedral is one of the great Gothic buildings of southern France, with its long nave divided by a superb screen built about 1500, and sheltered by a wonderfully decorated Gothic ceiling. See also the Renaissance Town Hall, the old houses in the Rue Timbal, and, at Lescure, five kilometres to the NE, the 11th century priory church with its fine Romanesque doorway. It was in the 12th and 13th centuries that Albi became the centre for a breakaway sect that took its name from the town, the Albigensians; and it was their persecution as heretics and their eventual extermination, that dominated the history of this area for so many years.

Albi

ANDORRA *60k SW Ax-les-Thermes*

Small principality in the Pyrénées, with frontiers facing both France and Spain. It has about 30,000 inhabitants and there are numerous hotels for the visitors that flock here from every corner of Europe. During the holiday season its roads are over-crowded, and those in search of tranquillity will probably fare better in other less popular areas.

A 'Toulouse-Lautrec' at Albi

ARGELÈS-GAZOST (65) *13k SSW Lourdes*

Busy touring centre and 'watering place' in a Pyrenean valley to the south of Lourdes, with magnificent views on every side.

AUCH (32) *77k W Toulouse*

This attractive town was the capital of Gascony, and is now the capital of the Gers Département. The old part of the towns stands well above the banks of the river Gers, and is dominated by its splendid late Gothic cathedral. Do not miss a visit here to look at the fascinating choir stalls, the style of which is a blending of Gothic and Renaissance art forms. The stained glass windows of the choir are by a Gascon craftsman, Arnaud de Moles, and they, like the choir stalls, are a delightful blend of Gothic and Renaissance ideals. Just to the south of the cathedral is the Place Salmis, and there are fine views to the Pyrénées from here.

Albi Cathedral

Choir stall,
Auch Cathedral

AUTOIRE (46)
8k W St-Céré

Delightful little village with half timbered houses and a fountain. Beyond lies the Cirque D'Autoire, a rocky amphitheatre, reached by a path one and a half kilometres to the south-west.

AX-LES-THERMES (09)
42k SSE Foix,
103k SW Carcassonne

Small town in the upper Ariège valley, with many hot sulphur springs, and several Pyrenean peaks nearby. Explore up the attractive valley of the Orlu, to the south-east of the town.

BAGNÈRES-DE-BIGORRE (65)
21k S. Tarbes

A busy and prosperous spa town in a wide valley setting in the Pyrénées complete with a good selection of modest hotels and restaurants, a casino, a museum, a 15th century tower, a 16th century church, and several wooden houses with marble frameworks on their façades.

Medieval tower at Autoire

The Baths at Ax-les-Thermes

BOSC CAVE (82)
3k NE St-Antonin-Noble-Val,
40k ENE Montauban

This long cave was once the course of an underground river, now long dried up. There are the usual stalagmites and stalactites.

BRUNIQUEL (82)
28k E Montauban

Old market town poised dramatically above the river Aveyron, at the western end of the lovely Aveyron Gorges. Its steep little streets and alleys are lined with old houses, and its castle well worth visiting (see especially the Knight's Hall, and the lovely Renaissance fireplace in the guardroom). Explore all the way up the gorges of the Aveyron to Villefranche-de-Rouergue and beyond (use Michelin Map 79).

Château at Cabrerets

CABRERETS (46)
33k ENE Cahors

There are two castles close to this attractive little village in the Célé valley, the ruined Château du Diable or Château des Anglais, and the Château Gontaut-Biron, a Renaissance building, not open to visitors. Combines with a visit to the Pech-Merle Caves (See Page 183).

CAHORS (46)
573k S Paris, 111k N Toulouse

This ancient town is the capital of Lot Département, and stands in a tight horseshoe bend of this lovely river, with only a short wall upon the northern, landward side having been necessary in medieval times. Cahors is famous for its medieval Pont Valentré with its tall towers, but there is much else to see besides... the fine Cathedral with its outstandingly lovely north doorway, the long tree lined Boulevard Gambetta (reminding us that Léon Gambetta was born here in 1838), the many narrow medieval streets, and the Barbecane, a 15th century guardhouse near the tower of St-Jean, which looks out over the river at the north-east of the town.

CARENNAC (46)
63k NNW Figeac

Small village on the banks of the Dordogne with a fortified gateway, attractive little streets and a most interesting 12th century church, the most important features of which are the splendid west doorway with a Christ in Majesty on the tympanum, and a 16th century 'entombment' in the south transept.

The Pont Valentré, Cahors

Mountain stream near Cauterets

Massive press in Condom Museum

The Choir, Condom

Ste-Foye Church, Conques

Conques

Cordès

CASTELNAU-DE-MONTMIRAL (81) *35k WNW Albi*

Pleasant little fortified town with many 14th and 15th century houses.

CASTELNAU CASTLE (46) *86k NE Cahors, 10k NW St-Céré*

A great medieval fortress poised above a valley, with splendid views from its ramparts. The outer defences are more than three miles round, and in its heyday 1,500 men and 100 horses were garrisoned here. The interior is also of considerable interest.

CASTRES (81) *42k S Albi, 65k N Carcassonne*

This is a large industrial town, but visitors should on no account miss the Musée Goya, which contains many splendid paintings and about eighty engravings by this outstanding artist. See also the attractive old houses lining the banks of the river Agout.

CAUTERETS (65) *30k SSW Lourdes*

Yet another spa and winter-sports centre, with the unusually wide selection of hotels making it an excellent base from which to explore the Pyrénées National Park (See Page 183). There are many sulphurous springs in the surrounding hills, and Cauterets has been a spa town since Roman times. Use Michelin Map 85 to explore up the valleys south from here, but do not take to the mountains without more information, equipment *and* experience.

CONDOM (32) *110k WNW Toulouse, 40k SW Agen*

Situated on the river Baise, this little town is prosperous largely from the production of Armagnac. Its Cathedral has outstanding cloisters and a splendid collection of coloured roof bosses. The Gothic vaulted 'Table des Cordeliers' restaurant provides memorable meals in a pleasant setting.

CONQUES (12) *37k NW Rodez*

In this attractively sited small village there is one of the best known Romanesque churches in the south of France, the Église Ste-Foye, with its splendid west doorway, and its 9th – 15th century treasure. The nearby bridge dates from the 14th century.

CORDÈS (81) *25k NW Albi*

An especially interesting village with the remains of four protective walls, with churches and chapels dating from the 14th and 16th century. There are covered markets, and old streets and houses, many of which are now occupied by craftsmen who may be seen at work.

COUESQUE BARRAGE (12) *8k N Entraygues*

See Truyère Gorges, Page 67 for details of access to this great dam across the Truyère.

COUGNAC CAVES (46) *3k NW Gourdon, 49k N Cahors*

Two caves beneath a limestone plateau, with the second one containing two chambers... the Salle des Colonnes, with remarkable columns, and the Salle des Peintures Préhistoriques, with several interesting wall paintings.

LA COUVERTOIRADE (12) *40k SE Millau*

Fascinating village in the remote countryside of the Causse du Larzac, hardly unchanged in the last four hundred years, with a simple church, the ruins of a château, and many 15th and 16th century houses.

DOURBIE GORGES (12) *From 8k E Millau*

There is a fascinating road leading east and then south-east from Millau (See Page 181), a total distance of thirty-two kilometres, which follows the Dourbie Gorges to the village of Nant. Roads east and then north-east from Nant, take one into the heart of the Cévennes National Park (See Page 133). All will be revealed by consulting Michelin Map 80, an invaluable companion in this area.

ENTRAYGUES-SUR-TRUYÈRE (12) *47k N Rodez*

Minute town at the confluence of the Truyère and the Lot, with two medieval bridges and several attractive old houses in its rue Basse. Drive west, or south-east from here to explore the Lot Gorges (See Page 180) and north-east for the Truyère gorges (See page 67).

Espalion   *Estaing*

ESPALION (12) *34k NE Rodez*

Small town with a bridge over the river Lot, many old houses, a Renaissance château, and a covered market. At Perse, a kilometre to the south-east there is an interesting Romanesque church, with a strange 'Last Judgement' over its doorway.

ESTAING (12) *41k NNE Rodez*

Delightful little town in the Lot Gorges, built around a rock on which stands a 15th and 16th century château.

FIGEAC (46) *65k NW Rodez*

Pleasant old town on the river Célé, with an 11th century church, and more unusually, a 13th century mint... the 'Hôtel de la Monnaie'. J. F. Champollion, the founder of Egyptology was born here in 1791. Explore down the Céré valley, on the road to Cahors (70 ks).

Foix Château   *Gaillac*

FOIX (09) *82k S Toulouse*

Small town in the Ariège valley, which despite its size, is the capital of the Ariège Département. It is dominated by a triple towered castle, which stands on a rocky site almost sixty metres above.

GAILLAC (81) *54k NE Toulouse*

Small town on the river Tarn, with a 12th and 13th century abbey church, and another medieval church, both with fortified towers. There is an 18th century château housing an interesting museum, which amongst other things, tells the story of Gaillac wine (for which the area is noted). Do not overlook the 'arcaded house' or the attractive Griffoul Fountain.

GARGAS CAVES (65) *5k SW Montréjeau, 108k SW Toulouse*

Prehistoric caves noted for their stencilled hands on the rock face, and their fine rock formations.

GAVARNIE CIRQUE (65) *51k S Lourdes*

Splendidly vast limestone amphitheatre above which tower several peaks along the Franco-Spanish border. The best viewpoint is about an hour's walk south from Garvarnie village. The famous Cascade de Gavarnie is one of the highest waterfalls in Europe.

GOURDON (46) *46k N Cahors*

Small town on a hill with a fortified gateway and two old churches. The caves of Cougnac are situated three kilometres to the north-west (See Page 178).

Gavarnie Cirque

Midi-Pyrénées

The Church of St-Pierre, Gourdon

In Lacave Caves

In the Lot Valley

Loubressac Château

Quiet faith at Lourdes

In the Subterranean Church, Lourdes

REGIONAL NATURE PARK OF THE HAUT-LANGUEDOC (34, 81)

This is shared with the Languedoc-Rousillon Region, and details are on page 135.

LABASTIDE ST-PIERRE, RIDING HOLIDAYS AT (82)
12k S Montauban

Write for details to 'Le Ranch des 4 As', Route de Fonlongues, 82370 Labastide St-Pierre.

Five day treks take in Bruniquel (See Page 177).

LABOUICHE UNDERGROUND RIVER (09)
7k NNW Foix, 80k S. Toulouse

Here one can take a boat trip along a stretch of this underground river, through illuminated caves with splendid limestone features.

LACAVE CAVES (46) *9k SE Souillac, 63k NNE Cahors*

Over a mile of caves through which a little electric train runs. There is an especially effective section illuminated by ultra-violet light.

LAVAUR (81)
37k ENE Toulouse

A small town on the meandering river Agout which suffered terribly at the hands of Simon de Montfort during his savage crusade against the Albigensian heretics (See Albi, Page 175). The defenders of the besieged town were finally beaten, and were either hanged or burnt, their lady châtelaine being thrown down a well. The 13th and 14th century church which replaced that destroyed by de Montfort contains a fine 15th century altar piece, and it has a four hundred year old clock with a wooden figure striking each half hour.

LECTOURE (32)
36k S Agen

Small town above the river Gers with splendid views southwards to the Pyrénées from the promenade replacing its medieval ramparts. There is an interesting museum and portrait gallery in the former Bishop's Palace, which also houses the Hôtel-de-Ville and the Law Courts.

LOT GORGES (48, 12, 46, 47)

These are perhaps at their most dramatic between Espalion and Entraygues (See Page 179), but the Lot valley is a delight from end to end. Use Michelin Maps 76, 79 and 80.

LOUBRESSAC (46) *57k NNW Figeac, 11k W St-Céré*

Minute fortified village above the Bave valley with narrow streets below its 15th and 17th century château. There are fine views across to the castle of Castelnau (See Page 178).

LOURDES (65)
174k WSW Toulouse, 146k ESE Bayonne

Apart from Rome itself, this is the most famous place of pilgrimage in the Catholic world. Pilgrims come from all over the world to visit the place where in 1858 the young shepherdess Bernadette Soubirous said the Virgin had appeared to her several times. There is a grotto where she had her vision, and a complex of nearby buildings in the 'Cité Religieuse', the most remarkable of which is the great subterranean church, completed in 1958 to celebrate the centenary of Bernadette's visions. The old town lies on the opposite *continued* bank of the Gave de Pau, and its chief point of interest is the great castle rising above it, from which there are fine Pyrenean views, and in which there is an interesting Pyrenean Museum.

LUCHON (31)   *90k SW Tarbes*
The full name of this busy spa town and winter-sports resort is Bagnères-de-Luchon. There is a casino, a small local museum and a wide selection of hotels and restaurants. Luchon makes an excellent base for exploring the central Pyrénées. The road up to Superbagnères (1804 metres) provides adventure in plenty, and superb views are to be had from the top where there is an orientation table. But for details see Michelin Map 85.

Late spring in the Pyrénées near the Col d'Aspin, north-west of Luchon
Photograph by Peter Titchmarsh

LUZECH (46)   *19k W Cahors*
Little medieval town within a neck on the meandering river Lot, which was at one time penetrated by a canal. There are fine views down the valley from its 13th century keep.

MARSOULAS CAVE (31)   *Nr Salies du Salat, 75k SW Toulouse*
This cave is noted for its prehistoric paintings of bison, horses, ibex and reindeer, but we are not certain if it is open at present.

MARTEL (46)   *60k NW Figeac*
Minute fortified town on a plateau a few kilometres north of the Dordogne, with its old streets centred upon a covered market-place. There are several ancient buildings of interest including a 14th century building that now serves as the town hall and a 12th and 14th century church that is heavily fortified and which contains a lovely tympanum depicting the Last Judgement within its porch. There are magnificent views out over the Dordogne valley from the 'Belvedere de Copeyre', four kilometres to the south-east.

MAS-D'AZIL CAVE (09)   *37k NW Foix*
There are two fine engravings of bison in this electrically lit cave, but other prehistoric finds have been removed for display in the Mas-d'Azil Town Hall.

MEDOUS CAVE (65)   *3k S Bagnères de Bigorre, 24k SSE Tarbes*
Interesting cave with imprints left by early man. This can be explored by boat and there are illuminated galleries with stalactites and stalagmites. Combine a visit here with an exploration of the lovely Lesponne valley and walk up beyond it to the Blue Lake (Use Michelin Map 85).

The entrance to Maz d'Azil

MILLAU (12)   *71k SE Rodez, 113k ENE Albi*
Busy, largely modern town on the river Tarn, with the wide selection of hotels making it an excellent base for exploring the gorges of the Tarn and the Causses that lie on every side. It is also possible to explore up the Gorges of the Dourbie, right into the heart of the lovely Cévennes (See Page 133).

MIREPOIX (09)   *34k NE Foix*
Thirteenth century bastide (fortified town) with 14th century half timbered houses on wooden arcading in the Porte d'Aval. The Cathedral has the largest nave in France, and there is a ruined château and a Bishop's Palace nearby.

Millau   *The Cloisters at Moissac*

Romanesque sculptural detail, Moissac Church

In Montal Château

The Chaos de Montpellier-le-Vieux
Photograph by Peter Titchmarsh

Najac
Photograph by
Peter Titchmarsh

Gouffre de Padirac

Midi-Pyrénées

MOISSAC (82)   *29k WNW Montauban*
Pleasant old town on the river Tarn, a short distance above its confluence with the Garonne. Here will be found some outstanding examples of Romanesque sculpture… on the south doorway of the abbey church of St-Pierre, and in the nearby cloisters. Do not miss either of these magnificent series of carvings.

MONTAL (46)   *3k W St-Céré, 70k NE Cahors*
A beautiful medieval and Renaissance château on a wooded hillside above the river Bave. It was demolished in the 19th century, but was later re-built with loving care, using almost all the original stonework which had once been sold and dispersed. The Renaissance façade is particularly impressive, and the interior is of great charm and interest.

MONTAUBAN (82)   *50k N Toulouse*
Capital town of the Tarn-et-Garonne Département, Montauban is a large market town situated on the river Tarn. It was built as a planned city in the 12th century, and has several notable buildings, all in the lovely pinkish brick, used with such distinction at Albi. See especially the medieval Pont Vieux, the fortified church of St-Jacques, the beautifully arcaded Place Nationale, where markets are still held, and the Ingres Museum housing works by Montauban's two artist sons… Ingres and Bourdelle.

CHAOS DE MONTPELLIER-LE-VIEUX (12)
16k ENE Millau
This is a very impressive formation of eroded rocks in a small valley running northwards from the attractive Gorges de la Dourbie. This makes a good introduction to the Cévennes for those travelling eastwards. (For the Cévennes, See Page 133.)

MONTSÉGUR CHÂTEAU (09)   *29k SE Foix,*
12k S Lavelanet
Here are the sad ruins of the Château de Montségur, which witnessed the last stand of the Albigensians (See Albi, Page 175), who were all burnt at the stake in 1244 after a siege lasting six months.

NAJAC (12)   *68k ENE Montauban,*
24k S Villefranche-de-Rouergue
Quiet village in the lovely Gorges de l'Aveyron, with Gothic houses, a 13th century church, and the ruins of a castle, built by Alphonse de Poitiers. This is dramatically situated on a great cliff bounded on three sides by the river Aveyron.

NIAUX CAVE (09)   *4k SSW Tarascon-sur-Ariège,*
20k S Foix
This cave is of outstanding archaeological importance and contains a series of prehistoric wall paintings.

GOUFFRE DE PADIRAC (46)   *13k N Gramat,*
70k NNE Cahors
This is a great crater caused by the collapse of a cave, and is ninety metres across and over ninety metres deep. Through this flows an underground river, and a lift takes visitors down to the landing stage from where an underground journey lasting two hours begins. This is often crowded in summer, but it is a fantastic experience, and not to be missed.

PAMIERS (09)   *63k S Toulouse*

Prosperous town on the river Ariège, with boulevards replacing the ramparts of its old town. Its medieval churches suffered greatly at the hands of the Huguenots in the Wars of Religion and the great abbey remains a ruin to this day. The composer Gabriel Fauré was born here in 1845.

PARELOUP LAKE (12)   *35k SE Rodez*

A great lake formed by a dam in the hills, with a bathing beach on its western side (at Fouletiés). Boats may be hired here.

PECH-MERLE CAVE (46)   *Near Cabrerets,*
33k ENE Cahors

A tour of the cave takes about an hour as the galleries are over three kilometres in length. This cave is renowned for its outstanding prehistoric paintings and should not be missed.

Prehistoric painting, Pech-Merle Cave

PENNE-DU-TARN (81)   *34k ENE Montauban,*
6k E Bruniquel

Minute village and ruined 14th century castle on a rocky spur high up above the Aveyron Gorge. All very fine unless you are worried by heights.

PIC-DU-MIDI-DE-BIGORRE (65)
34k S Bagnères-de-Bigorre

This massive mountain peak stands at 2,865 metres above sea level, and has a television transmitter and an observatory on its summit. It can be reached by cableway from la Mongie during the months of July, August and September. Do not miss this... the mountain views are quite breath-taking.

The Pic-du-Midi-de Bigorre

PLAISANCE DU TOUCH ZOO PARK (31)
15k WSW Toulouse, just to N of D 632 road.

Pleasant zoo in a shady setting, with about two-hundred animals on view, including elephants, hippos, lions, jaguars and black panthers. Buvette, souvenir shop, picnic place.

PRESQUE CAVE (46)   *6k WSW St-Céré, 73k NE Cahors*

Cave with a series of chambers which contain many weirdly shaped stalagmites and stalactites.

PUYLAURENS (81)   *50k E Toulouse*

Small village with medieval ramparts, an interesting church, and old covered markets. There are fine views southwards to the Pyrénées.

Summertime in the Pyrénées

PYRÉNÉES NATIONAL PARK (64 & 65)

Created in 1967, this National Park covers an area of almost 125,000 acres, and is situated in the Départements of Pyrénées-Atlantique (in the Aquitaine Region), and in Hautes-Pyrénées in this Region. It follows the Franco-Spanish frontier for about a hundred kilometres to a depth of between three and fifteen kilometres. Within this area there are many great peaks, but for those who do not wish to climb there are marked footpaths in the wooded valleys. Shooting is naturally forbidden, but opportunities for fishing in lakes and mountain streams are boundless. Wildlife include bear, ibex, genet, and marten, and there is a wealth of fauna and flora for the observant visitor's delight.

The Col-du-Tourmalet, near the Pic-du-Midi

Midi-Pyrénées

QUERCY TOUR HORSE DRAWN HOLIDAYS (46)
These are based near Assier, which is about eighteen kilometres north-west of Figeac (See Page 179). Horse drawn caravans are hired out to those who wish to explore the Gausse de Gramat, the valley of the Célé, or the Limargue (north of Rocamadour). Write for details to Quercy Tour, Domaine de Mons, 46320 Assier.

ROCAMADOUR (46)   *59k N Cahors*
Outstandingly interesting village consisting of a single street, at the foot of a high limestone cliff, and lined with many old houses. There are no fewer than five fortified gateways, a great flight of stairs, and a Bishop's Palace; and above it all, a 14th century castle. Rocamadour takes its name from the almost legendary St-Amadour, whose tomb was one of the great European places of pilgrimage in the Middle Ages. Rocamadour is now once again a place of pilgrimage, and also a great tourist attraction... so please do not expect tranquillity here.

RODEZ (12)   *154k NE Toulouse, 608k S Paris*
This cathedral town is the capital of the Avéyron Département and is situated on a hill within a great bend of the river Aveyron. The cathedral was built between 1277 and 1562, and its great tower is one of the finest in France. See also the 17th century Bishop's Palace, the two interesting museums, the various medieval and Renaissance houses and the 15th century Courbières Tower.

ROQUEFORT-SUR-SOULZON (12)   *25k SSW Millau*
Roquefort cheese is still made here, as it has been for centuries, making use of the milk from the ewes that graze the great limestone plateaux of the Causses (See Page 133). The little town is built beneath the slopes of the Combalou mountain in which there are caves ideally suited for the maturing of the cheese, and which can be visited throughout the year.

ST-BERTRAND-DE-COMMINGES (31)
61k ESE Tarbes, 107k SE Toulouse
Fascinating medieval village above the infant Garonne, with its 'upper town' having old walls, and its Cathedral, a partly Romanesque, partly Gothic building containing a fine 16th century rood screen, and choir stalls of the same period. There is also a gallery of 'Trophies' in the Romanesque cloisters. In the lower town are the steps of a Gallo-Roman theatre, and extensive archaeological excavations of the Gallo-Roman town it once served.

ST-CÉRÉ (46)   *75k NE Cahors*
Small town in the Bave valley overlooked by the towers of St-Laurent, with many old houses, and an interesting exhibition of the works of the great modern tapestry designer Jean-Lurcat, who lived and worked in the castle of St-Laurent prior to his death.

ST-CIRQUE-LAPOPIE (46)   *33k E Cahors*
Picturesque village poised above the Lot valley, with steep little winding streets lined by interesting old houses, many of which have been restored by artists who have settled here. There are the fragmentary ruins of a once important castle, from which there are delicious views out over the Lot. There are also fine views to be had from Le Bancourel car park out on the D 40, Bouziès road, just to the west of the village.

Rocamadour

Roquefort

Cheese cave at Roquefort

Cloisters at St-Bertrand-de-Comminges   *St-Cirque-Lapopie*

Midi-Pyrénées

ST-COME-D'OLT (12) *4k ESE Espalion, 34k NE Rodez*
Small village in the Lot valley, built in a circular shape, and surrounded by the remains of ramparts, with a 15th and 17th century church.

ST-GAUDENS (31) *89k SW Toulouse*
Pleasant town in the upper Garonne valley, with fine views southwards to the Pyrénées from its Boulevard Jean Bepmale. There is an interesting collegiate church of the 11th and 12th centuries and a small cloister rebuilt from the remains of Bonnefont Abbey.

ST-GÉRY CHÂTEAU (81) *40k NE Toulouse*
Elegant, Italian inspired château incorporating parts of an earlier medieval castle, built on the very edge of a cliff overlooking the river Tarn. The interior contains work from most centuries, from the room that used to be a kitchen in the 15th century, to the handsome 18th century bedrooms, and the unique dining room which was refurnished in the 'revolutionary mode' in compensation for the illegal confiscation of the family's property at the time when the seigneur was guillotined (also illegally, but retrospective action was regrettably not possible in this case!)

Horse-drawn Holiday in the Lot Département

ST-LIZIER (09) *3k NW St-Girons, 88k SSW Toulouse*
This small village on a hill above the Salat valley was the site of a Gallo-Roman town, and is especially noted for its Romanesque cloisters. But see also the interior of the Cathedral with its 12th century frescoes, the medieval ramparts, and the many old houses.

St-Lizier

SARRANS BARRAGE (12) *100k NNE Rodez*
Fine dam across the River Truyère forming the long and most attractive Sarrans Lake. See Truyère Gorges (Page 67).

SIDOBRE, LE (81) *10k E Castres*
A high plateau area where weathered granite rocks are to be found in many curious formations, and from whence there are delightful views across the deep valley of the river Agout.

SOUILLAC (46) *66k N Cahors*
This is a busy little market town and holiday centre, on the Dordogne, with the number of small hotels and restaurants making it an ideal centre from which to explore the fascinating countryside through which the Dordogne flows. The lovely 12th century Benedictine abbey church should be visited at all costs, both for its wonderfully spacious interior and for its splendid Romanesque doorway which was moved to the interior of the church in the 17th century. Study this in detail, for it is a triumph of the Romanesque sculptor's art, and many of the figures depicted are deeply moving in their simplicity and in their flowing lines.

Lot Valley near St-Cirque-Lapopie   *Sarrans Barrage*

TARBES (65) *155k WSW Toulouse, 210k SSE Bordeaux*
Capital of the Haute-Pyrénées Département, Tarbes is a busy market town situated in the plain, not far to the north of the Pyrenean foothills. Its Romanesque Cathedral is not of outstanding interest, but it has some very lovely gardens (Le Jardin Massey), in which there is an interesting museum. Its wide choice of hotels makes Tarbes a pleasant base for exploring the central Pyrénées.

In the Sidobre

185   *Midi-Pyrénées*

In the Tarn Gorges   *Photograph by Peter Titchmarsh*

TARN GORGES (12 & 48)   *Millau is 113k ENE Albi*

This great series of gorges are shared with the Languedoc-Roussillon Region, and are described on page 138.

TARN TOURIST RAILWAY (81)   *37k NE Toulouse*

This four kilometre long railway follows the bed of a former local line, and trains run each Sunday from Easter to end October, and every afternoon in July and August. It is situated at St-Lieux-les-Lavaur, eight kilometres east of St-Sulpice (off N88).

TOULOUSE (31)   *684k S Paris, 400k W Marseille, 249k SE Bordeaux*

France's fourth largest city, and 'capital' of the Midi-Pyrénées Region, Toulouse was the centre of a southern kingdom for several hundred years. Almost all its old buildings are of lovely pale pink brick, including the handsome 18th century Capitole, Toulouse's Town Hall. The basilica of St-Sernin is the largest Roman-esque building in France, and surely the most beautiful, with its lovely octagonal tower and its semi-circle of apsidal chapels beneath. See also the delightful 'Église des Jacobins', the large Gothic Cathedral, several fine museums (especially the St-Raymond and the Augustins), and the handsome Renaissance town houses (or hôtels). With its splendid choice of hotels and restaurants, Toulouse makes an excellent base from which to explore this region, and it has much to offer the visitor, with elegant shops, no fewer than six theatres, two orchestras, and a wide selection of tours and visits offered at its lively S.I. in the 16th century Donjon tower next to the Capitole.

TROUMOUSE CIRQUE (65)   *50k SSE Lourdes*

Impressive amphitheatre of cliffs to the immediate north of the Franco-Spanish border. Not as impressive as its immediate western neighbour Gavarnie. There is a toll road to a fine mountain viewpoint fifteen kilometres south-east of Gèdre village.

VILLEFRANCHE-DE-ROUERGUE (12)   *58k W Rodez*

A bastide town on the Aveyron, founded in 1252 by the redoubtable Alphonse de Poitiers. Within the bounds of its vanished walls there is a delightful medieval town, with mostly straight streets (Bastide towns were the first example of planned towns since Roman times), lined with a wonderful variety of old houses. This is all centred upon the square, the Place Notre-Dame, with its arcaded houses overlooked by the great stone tower of the church of Notre-Dame. The interior of this church should not be missed, for it contains a fine set of choir stalls carved by André Sulpice. See also the 17th century chapel of the Black Penitents, and 15th century Carthusian monastery.

The Capitole, Toulouse

La Salle des Illustres, in the Capitole, Toulouse

Carving in the cloister of St-Étienne, Toulouse

Carving in St-Sernin, Toulouse

ARMAGNAC... a great brandy

This area, which is partly in the Aquitaine Region, is situated in the very heart of Gascony, and extends south and south-west from Agen, taking in the rolling countryside in which lie such towns as Nérac, Condom, Auch and Aire-sur-Adour. Here are grown the grapes that are used for Armagnac, the brandy second only in importance to Cognac, and a drink of considerable character, that deserves a greater international reputation than it has so far secured.

Nord—Pas-de-Calais

Comprises the following Départements:
Nord (59)   Pas-de-Calais (62)

Of the many thousands of British visitors that land each year at Calais and Boulogne, how many spare more than a few glances and a hurried overnight stop, in this, the far north-eastern region of France? We must confess that we have done this far too often ourselves, and headed south along the high, wide Routes Nationales, and latterly even along the autoroutes. But, as Frederick Tingey points out in his most readable Guide to the North of France, these main routes so often keep to the high ground, and the quiet beauty and flower-filled villages of the valleys are so easily missed. We hope that with the help of our guide (and also Mr. Tingey's), you will be persuaded to wander away from the main routes, to explore some of the smaller towns and villages, to visit wind and watermills, deep forests and tranquil lakes, to explore along quiet canal banks, and to move at a much slower pace than journeys from one country to another seem to induce.

Also do not let the varied and colourful country scene draw you away too quickly from the beautifully sandy shores of the Pas-de-Calais, which are often backed by great white cliffs and in places by pine shaded dunes. Then spare time for looking round the larger towns and cities, for here will be found the great fortifications of Vauban, fine museums and art galleries proclaiming the culture of Flanders and its peoples, and many old streets and buildings with their Flemish flavour still intact despite the depredations of two World Wars.

During your wanderings you will encounter a bewildering number of war cemeteries and monuments, and see well remembered names of battles long ago on many a signpost. We have not dwelt upon this aspect of the region, but this ground has been fought over for centuries. It is a tribute to the peoples of the region that after each successive conflict and disaster, they have re-built anew, and today the cemeteries and monuments are the only reminder of past tragedies. Spare a thought for all the young men who fought here and did not return to their homes, and also for the men and women of the region, over whose fields and streets they fought... it is indeed an area where courage seems to be in the very air... an area that deserves much more than a passing glance from your car window.

AGINCOURT, BATTLE OF (62)   *14k NNE Hesdin*
It was near the little village of Azincourt, on the 24th October 1415, that one of the grimmest battles of English history was fought. Hoping to reach the safety of Calais, Henry V and his 6,000 men found their way blocked, and were forced to fight a French army of at least 30,000. Victory was achieved with the help of Henry's archers, and the slaughter that ensued must indeed have been terrible, with little quarter being given to the French prisoners when the battle was finally won.

AIRE (62)   *14k SE St-Omer*
Pleasant old town on the river Lys, with several interesting 17th and 18th century houses, a handsome 16th century town hall, known as the Hôtel-de-Bailliage. The collegiate church of St-Pierre has a fine tower and some 16th century wall paintings, while on the N43 just to the west of the town, will be found the hospitable Hostellerie des Trois Mousquetaires. This is well placed for an end-of-holiday treat, and its well-cooked and generously proportioned dinners make this one of our favourite last-night stops.

ARMENTIÈRES (59)   *19k NW Lille*
Busy industrial town on the river Lys. It suffered great damage during both World Wars, but has been effectively rebuilt. The mythical young lady of the World War I marching song popularised Armentières for more than one generation of Englishman, and she is remembered still.

ARRAS (62)   *178k N Paris, 114k SE Calais*
This busy city is the capital of the Pas-de-Calais Département, and despite very great damage suffered in the 1914 – 18 War, it retains a 17th century Flemish flavour. This is especially so in the reconstructed Hôtel-de-Ville, with its high belfry, and the two arcaded squares nearby, the Place-des-Héros, and the wide Grande Place. The Abbey and Palace of St-Vaast adjoining the Cathedral houses a large Museum and Art Gallery, and close by there is a large citadel built by Vauban. Maximilien Robespierre, the great revolutionary leader, was born at Arras in 1758.

The Hôtel-de-Ville,
Armentières

St-Vaast Abbey
Museum, Arras

Canadian War Memorial,
Vimy Ridge (10ks N Arras)

Re-constructed trenches,
Vimy Ridge

Nord — Pas-de-Calais

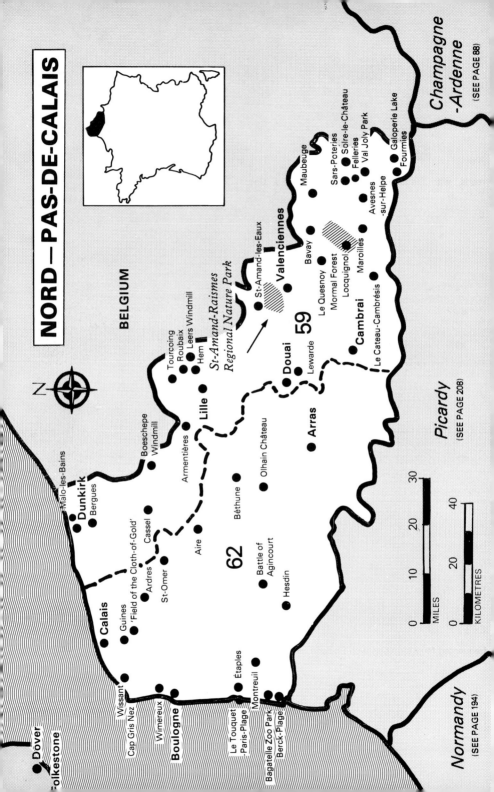

NORD–PAS-DE-CALAIS

BELGIUM

N

Dover
Folkestone

Wissant
Cap Gris Nez
Wimereux
Boulogne
Le Touquet-
Paris-Plage
Bagatelle Zoo Park
Berck-Plage
Montreuil
Étaples

Malo-les-Bains
Dunkirk
Bergues
Cassel
Ardres
St-Omer
Aire
Calais
Guines
'Field of the Cloth-of-Gold'

Boeschepe
Windmill
Armentières
Lille
Tourcoing
Roubaix
Hem
Leers Windmill

62
Béthune
Olhain Château
Battle of
Agincourt
Hesdin

*St-Amand-Raismes
Regional Nature Park*

St-Amand-les-Eaux
Valenciennes

Arras

Douai
Lewarde

59

Bavay
Le Quesnoy
Mormal Forest
Locquignol
Maroilles
Cambrai
Le Cateau-Cambrésis

Maubeuge
Sars-Poteries
Soire-le-Château
Felleries
Val Joly Park
Avesnes
-sur-Helpe
Galoperie Lake
Fourmies

*Champagne
-Ardenne*
(SEE PAGE 88)

Picardy
(SEE PAGE 208)

Normandy
(SEE PAGE 194)

MILES
0   10   20   30
KILOMETRES
0   20   40

AVESNES-SUR-HELPE (59) *49k SE Valenciennes*
Small town which was considerably damaged in the
1939–45 War. Its steep little streets are dominated by
the fine 13th century tower of its collegiate church.

BAGATELLE ZOO PARK (62) *5k N Berck-Plage,*
12k S Le Touquet
This is a pleasure park, with many other attractions in
addition to its animals, including roundabouts, a ghost-
train and a miniature train. Picnic area, cafeteria, gift
shops, etc.

BAVAY (59) *23k ESE Valenciennes*
Small town at the meeting point of several Roman
roads, with the interesting excavations of a Gallo-
Roman town exposed to view.

Berck-Plage

BERCK-PLAGE (62) *44k S. Boulogne*
Holiday resort which is also much used as a centre for
orthopaedic cures. There are miles of fine sands, and a
wide range of amusements for children. Buses run from
here to Bagatelle Park (See above).

BERGUES (59) *9k SE Dunkirk*
Pleasant old town with typical Flemish style houses
and star shaped fortifications so beloved by Vauban.
Bergues suffered badly in the 1939–45 War, but it has
been lovingly restored. The Museum and Art Gallery
contain a fine collection of Flemich paintings which
should on no account be missed.

BÉTHUNE (62) *95k ESE Boulogne*
Prosperous industrial town which suffered great
damage in both World Wars. Despite this, several
interesting old buildings survive, including the partly
ruined 14th century belfry.

The Belfry, Béthune *Fishing boats at*
Boulogne

BOESCHEPE WINDMILL (59) *12k E Cassel*
Restoration of this mill was completed in 1976, and it
is without doubt one of the finest postmills in France.

BOULOGNE (62) *243k NNE Paris*
This is a thriving port and industrial town, and
France's premier fishing port, in addition to being one of
the most popular ferry terminals with England. To the
immediate north of the harbour mouth there is a casino,
and northwards from here a stretch of fine sandy
bathing beaches, with a string of small resorts between
here and Calais, along what is known as the Opal Coast.
The upper town is contained within rectangular walls
built in the 13th century upon Roman foundations. This
is dominated by a stout castle and a medieval Cathedral
which has an 11th century crypt. There is an interesting
Museum with an outstanding collection of Greek vases
in the Hôtel-de-Ville.

Medieval gateway, Boulogne

CALAIS (62) *295k N Paris*
Busy fishing and commercial port, one of the most
frequented ferry terminals with England, and a popular
French holiday resort, Calais is also the largest town of
the Pas-de-Calais Département. It was held by the
English from 1347 until 1558, and the epic statue by
Rodin of the 'Six Burghers of Calais' stands witness
outside the Hôtel-de-Ville. (The burghers were made to
surrender themselves, clad only in their shirts, with
halters around their necks, as the condition of surrender
imposed on the town by Edward III after the eleven

continued *On the beach at Boulogne*

Nord — Pas-de-Calais

Rodin's 'Six Burghers of Calais' outside the Hôtel-de-Ville

Marshal Foch, at Cassel   Cobbled street at Cassel

Henri Matisse Museum, Le Cateau

Canal at Douai

months siege, and their lives were only spared at the request of Edward's queen.) See also the tall lighthouse, from which there are fine views out over the town, and across to the English coast on a clear day. The Museum, with its displays of Flemish lace and linen, is well worth visiting; while to the west of the two lie the bathing beaches of Blériot-Plage (see the monument to Blériot's historic flight across the channel in 1909).

CAMBRAI (59)   *36k ESE Arras*
Bustling cathedral town which suffered great damage in both World Wars. The Cathedral itself is not of outstanding interest, but the church of St-Géry has a fine Renaissance style rood screen, and a painting of the 'Entombment of Christ' by Rubens. Only a little remains of its town walls, but you should not miss the large 14th century 'Porte-de-Paris' gateway. The contents of the Museum include paintings by Vlaminck and sculptures by Rodin.

CAP GRIS NEZ (62) *20k N Boulogne, 30k WSW Calais*
This famous headland, with its lighthouse poised above great cliffs, looks out over the Pas-de-Calais to England, and is well worth a visit. The little resort of Wissant is about ten kilometres to the north-east, and this has miles of sands below its cliffs and dunes. From this beach Thomas à Beckett departed for England, knowing that he risked death. A plaque on the church wall commemorates this fact and his subsequent martyrdom at Canterbury.

CASSEL (59)   *21k WNW St-Omer*
Pleasant little hilltop town which was Marshal Foch's Headquarters in the 1914 – 18 War (he surveys the public gardens from horseback). See the ancient gateways, the old streets, the well restored windmill and the attractive little Folklore Museum. There is a 'Parade of the Giants' here at Easter.

LE CATEAU-CAMBRÉSIS (59)   *24k ESE Cambrai*
Small Flemish town on the river Selle, with a museum devoted to the painter Henri Matisse, who was born here in 1869.

DOUAI (59)   *38k S Lille*
Large industrial town in the centre of a coal mining area, which suffered greatly in both World Wars. However there is a fine belfry to the Hôtel-de-Ville, and the museum has an interesting collection of Flemish paintings. Come here in July and you may be lucky enough to witness the well known 'Parade of the Giants', when great figures are taken through the streets (This custom is a feature in many Flemish towns).

Do not miss a visit to the interesting Mining Museum at Lewarde, just to the east of the town, with its well preserved pit-head complete with picks, miners' lamps and machinery.

DUNKIRK (59)   *292k N Paris, 36k ENE Calais*
This thriving industrial and port town known to the French as Dunkerque, has had a troubled history, and for this reason does not have many buildings of any great age. However its port is well worth visiting as is the fine Museum of Modern Art, and the long sandy beaches of Malo-les-Bains, to the west of the town, are popular with French families. These beaches were of course the scene of the miraculous withdrawal of the defeated British and Allied troops in 1940, when over 300,000 men were taken off the beaches between May 26th and June 3rd.

ÉTAPLES (62)   *29k S Boulogne*
Quiet little fishing port, just up-river from Le Touquet. It was here that Napoleon and Marshal Ney stayed while they were planning the invasion of England, and the house in question, which is in the square, is marked with a plaque.

FELLERIES (59)   *9k ENE Avesnes-sur-Helpe*
Small village with an old water mill and an interesting glassworks, where the blowing of glass still continues.

'FIELD OF THE CLOTH-OF-GOLD' (62)*13k SSE Calais*
Here, just to the south of the Guines – Ardres road (D231), about two kilometres east of Guines, was the scene of the famous meeting between Henry VIII of England and François I of France, with each monarch attempting to outdo the other with the splendour of their pavilions and their entourages. Site marked on Michelin map as 'Camp du Drap d'Or'.

GALOPERIE LAKE (59)*8k E Fourmies, 24k SE Avesnes*
This pleasant lake in woodland country on the Belgian border forms the basis of a leisure area or 'Parc d'Attractions', which is complete with boats and pedalos, and a display of performing dolphins.

HEM (59)   *Just S of Roubaix*
This small 'village' is now almost part of the Lille-Roubaix-Tourcoing complex,but lovers of 20th century architecture should not overlook the lovely modern chapel of La Chapelle de la Face, with its magnificent tapestry and its one wall of impressive stained glass.

Parade of the Giants, Cassel

HESDIN (62)   *59k SE Boulogne*
Attractive old town in the Canche valley, above which is situated the forest of Hesdin, where the wild boar is still hunted. Hesdin was founded by Charles V in 1554, and although its walls have been replaced by boulevards, several pleasant 17th century buildings have survived, including the handsome Hôtel-de-Ville. The Canche flows right through the town below small hump backed bridges, and we have happy memories of strolling over them after a pleasant meal at the little Rôtisserie des Flandres... a fitting end to many of our visits to France. Hesdin was the birthplace of the Abbé Prévost, the author of *Manon Lescaut,* in 1697.

LEERS WINDMILL (59)   *2k E Roubaix*
The restoration of this fine windmill was completed in 1976, and it is well worth visiting.

Quiet fishing in the Pas-de-Calais countryside

LILLE (59)   *219k N Paris, 108k ESE Calais*
Capital of the Nord Département, and one of the great industrial cities of France, Lille has many features of interest for the visitor. Although its city walls have gone, several fine gateways remain, and you should not miss the grandiose Porte-de-Paris, built in 1682 as a triumphal arch in honour of Louis XIV, and second only in size to the Arc-de-Triomphe in Paris. Although the walls restored by Vauban have gone, his great pentagonal citadel is an enduring monument to this great fortifier. It now stands in attractive gardens with a small zoo. See also the Old Bourse, an attractive 17th century Flemish building, the splendid Museum of Fine Arts, the 15th century Ribour Palace, the 13th century Comtesse Almshouse, and the several medieval and Renaissance churches. The great town hall was only completed in 1933, but its high tower is an outstanding feature of the city.

The Porte-de-Paris, Lille   *The Old Bourse, Lille*

Nord — Pas-de-Calais

Vauban's fortifications, Montreuil

Gateway at Montreuil

MAROILLES (59)　　　　*12k W Avesnes-sur-Helpe*
Small village with a lovely 18th century watermill.

MAUBEUGE (59)　　　　*37k E Valenciennes*
This sizeable industrial town suffered terribly in the 1939 – 45 War, and almost ninety per cent of it had to be rebuilt. However there are beautiful gardens below much of Vauban's fortifications, and also close to the walls there is one of France's oldest zoos.

MONTREUIL (62)　　　　*38k SSE Boulogne*
Agreeable little town, which was a port in Roman times. Its river silted up in the early Middle Ages, and it then declined in importance. However it was fortified by Vauban in the 17th century, and there are interesting remains of his citadel and much of the walls too. See also the church of St-Saulve, and the beautifully decorated 15th century chapel of Hôtel Dieu. But above all savour the atmosphere of the sloping, cobbled streets, lined with many old buildings.

MORMAL FOREST (59)　　　*20k SE Valenciennes*
This is a large area of forest intersected by many tracks and pathways, with several picnic areas, an arboretum, and at Locquignol in its very heart, two small hotels. For those with patience there are many roe deer to be spotted in this forest.

OLHAIN CHÂTEAU (62)　　　*21k NW Arras*
Medieval castle/manor house and fortified farm, on two adjoining 'islands' surrounded by an attractive moat. Here is a pleasing blend of stone and mellow brick, with large round towers, and high, pointed roofs. All quite unexpected in this rather bleak country between Arras and Béthune.

LE QUESNOY (59)　　　　*18k SE Valenciennes*
Small town built largely within the star shaped fortifications built by Vauban, who incorporated earlier defence works dating back to Louis XIII and Charles V. The tree-shaded ramparts are surrounded in part by lakes and a moat, and the whole effect is most pleasing.

ROUBAIX (59)
See Lille with which it has been consolidated, along with Tourcoing.

ST-AMAND-LES-EAUX (59)　*14k NNW Valenciennes*
A modest spa town with the only remains of the abbey founded here in the 7th century being a tall 17th century tower housing a splendid carillon of 49 bells... call here at mid-day to hear this being played.

ST-AMAND-RAISMES REGIONAL NATURE PARK
(59)　　　　*To immediate NW of Valenciennes*
This is a large area of forest between Valenciennes and St-Amand-les-Eaux, which was designated in 1968. There are many signed footpaths, and bridleways, and horses can be hired. There is a special reserve north of Raismes where wild boar, wild sheep, and roe and fallow deer may be observed in enclosures, and there is a camping site at St-Amand. But first visit the Information Centre, about two kilometres north-east of Raismes.

ST-OMER (62)　　　　　*40k SE Calais*
Busy town on the river Aa, which at this point
continued

St-Amand-les-Eaux Abbey

In the Museum at St-Amand-les-Eaux

becomes canalised. To the north and east there is flat, fen-like country networked with waterways used both for drainage and transport, and nine kilometres to the east is the lake of Harchelles, an attractive stretch of water in woodlands much loved by local anglers. St-Omer itself is a town of considerable character, despite the damage suffered in both World Wars. See especially the basilica of Notre Dame, a fine 13th – 15th century building containing several items of interest, the Fine Arts Museum with its wide collections of 18th century painting, and the lovely public gardens, parts of which can be explored by boat along the canal.

SARS-POTERIES (59)   *9k NE Avesnes-sur-Helpe*
Village close to the Belgian border, which is noted for its potteries and its Glass Museum. See also Felleries (Page 191).

SOLRE-LE-CHÂTEAU (59)   *14k NE Avesnes-sur-Helpe*
Small village with old houses dating from the 16th century and an interesting 15th century church with fine stained glass windows.

LE TOUQUET-PARIS-PLAGE (62)   *32k S Boulogne*
An elegant resort which was largely created for the aristocratic English and European visitor in the years before and after the 1914 – 18 War, Le Touquet is something of a period-piece. There are splendid sands, two casinos and a racecourse, and a wide variety of hotels and restaurants.

Sand-Yachting at Le Touquet

VALENCIENNES (59)   *69k ENE Arras*
Prosperous industrial town with few buildings of interest to visitors. However the Museum contains many fine paintings and sculptures including works by Watteau and Carpeau, both of whom were born at Valenciennes.

VAL JOLY PARK (59)   *20k E Avesnes-sur-Helpe*
This is centred upon a large lake created by the building of a dam across the river Helpe, and there are opportunities for sailing, and pleasant walking in forest country to the south of the lake.

WIMEREUX (62)   *7k N Boulogne*
Pleasant seaside resort which is ideal for family holidays, although the beach is not as sandy as many of its Pas-de-Calais neighbours.

On Wimereux beach

Go-Karting at Le Touquet

Nord — Pas-de-Calais

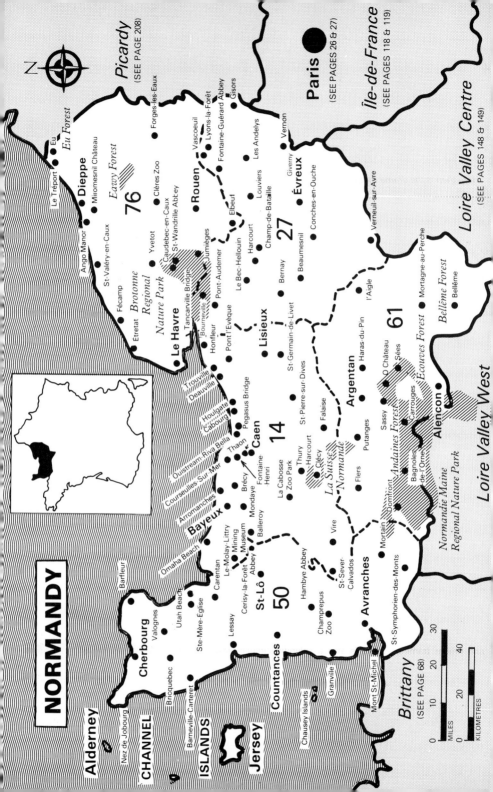

Normandy

Comprises the following Départements:
Calvados (14)   Orne (61)
Eure (27)   Seine-Maritime (76)
Manche (50)

This region is bordered on its north and west by no less than six hundred kilometres of coastline, with a succession of great cliffs, long sandy beaches, and colourful fishing ports and holiday resorts, stretching all the way from Le Tréport to Mont St-Michel. It was from these shores that William, Duke of Normandy, sailed northwards to England, thus earning himself the title, 'William the Conqueror'. His story is told in the great Bayeux Tapestry; and the more recent story of the great Allied invasion force that landed on these shores in June 1944 is told in a succession of fascinating museums in the area.

Here then is the drama that Normandy has to offer its visitors, but once away from its brilliant coastline there is more peaceful fare... in quiet pastoral countryside, with golden plains and gently rolling hills, deep woodlands and sparkling, well stocked rivers.

Here will be found great castles and magnificent abbeys, busy little market towns and colourful villages. Explore areas like 'La Suisse Normande', with its rocky hillsides and tree clad gorges, walk or ride in the great forests of the Normandie-Maine Regional Nature Park, or the forest of Brotonne near Rouen. Drive quietly down country roads, and above all, do not rush through Normandy simply because it is too close to the channel ports; for if you do, you will have missed an amply rewarding experience.

The Hôtel-de Guise, Alençon

The Seine from Château Gaillard

L'AIGLE (61) *55k SSW Évreux*
Busy little town with a 12th and 15th century church and an interesting museum featuring the 1944 Battle of Normandy, complete with maps, waxwork likenesses of the generals involved and various recordings.

ALENÇON (61) *145k SW Rouen, 173k S Le Havre*
Large market town enriched by a fine Flamboyant Gothic church, with splendid porch, and connections with Ste-Theresa who was born in Alençon (See also Lisieux, Page 203). There is an interesting display of the famous Alençon lace in the School of Lace.

LES ANDELYS (27) *39k SE Rouen*
Small town dominated by the splendid ruins of Château Gaillard, the great fortress built by Richard the Lionheart above the banks of the Seine in the closing years of the 12th century. There are splendid views both up and down the Seine valley from its ramparts. See also the interesting church of Notre Dame in Grand Andely, well removed from the Seine.

Château Gaillard, Les Andelys. Photograph by Peter Titchmarsh

ANGO MANOR (76) *9k WSW Dieppe*
Delightful late Gothic buildings grouped around a central courtyard. The farmhouse is built of stone and flints, and the adjoining barns are built of mellow brick and timber framing. There is also a splendid circular dovecote of stone, flint and bricks. This manor was built by Roger Ango, Governor of Dieppe, whose palace there was destroyed in a bombardment in 1694.

ARGENTAN (61) *57k SSE Caen, 137k S Le Havre*
This small town suffered badly during the Normandy Invasion of 1944, and there are only a few old corners remaining. However the church of St-Germanus has been well restored, and is of considerable interest.

Cruisers on the Seine at Les Andelys

ARROMANCHES (14) *10k NW Bayeux*

Small seaside resort famous throughout the world as the site of Mulberry 'B' one of the great artificial harbours created for the landing of British troops in the invasion of France in 1944*. In just 100 days 2,500,000 men, 500,000 vehicles and 4,000,000 tons of equipment were landed here. Do not miss a visit to the fascinating Normandy Landings Museum (which includes a film with an English commentary).

Mulberry 'A' was at Omaha Beach, and this was used for the landing of the American invasion force... See Page 204.

Old Mulberry Harbour caissons, on the beach at Arromanches

In the Museum at Arromanches

AVRANCHES (50) *134k S Cherbourg, 100k SW Caen*

Busy little town on a hill above the Sées estuary, with distant views of Mont St-Michel from its attractive Botanical Gardens. In the small square which marks the site of the former Cathedral there is a paving stone marking the spot where Henry II of England kneeled in penance for the murder of Thomas Becket by his knights in Canterbury cathedral. See also the Avranchin Museum, the church of St-Gervais and St-Protais in which is the shrine of the founder of Mont St-Michel, and the Patton Monument, marking the place where General Patton started his great offensive across France on 1st August 1944.

The Casino, Bagnoles-de-l'Orne

BAGNOLES-DE-L'ORNE (61) *48k WNW Alençon*

This is the largest spa town in western France, and with its wide selection of hotels, it is an excellent centre for exploring the Andaines Forest, and the rest of the area covered by the Normandie-Maine Regional Nature Park (See Page 204). There are numerous attractive walks in the vicinity of the town.

BALLEROY CHÂTEAU (14) *37k W Caen*

This handsome château was built by Mansart between 1626 and 1636, and blends in with the village at the end of which it is situated. The formal gardens were the work of Le Nôtre, and the elaborate interior decoration, furniture and pictures make a visit here well worthwhile. Do not miss the fascinating Museum of Balloons and Ballooning in the main courtyard.

Balleroy Château

BARFLEUR (50) *27k E Cherbourg*

Small fishing port near the far north-east of the Cotentin Peninsula. This is now a holiday resort, with its harbour devoted to sailing dinghies and other pleasure boats. The Gatteville Lighthouse, three kilometres to the north, may be visited. There are fine views from an old German strongpoint at La Pernelle about seven kilometres to the south.

BARNEVILLE-CARTERET (50) *37k SSW Cherbourg*

Pleasant seaside resort on both sides of a small estuary, with a fine rocky headland complete with lighthouse to its immediate north. There is a small harbour at Carteret, and a long sandy beach at Barneville-Plage, with all the usual resort facilities. Do not miss the fascinating Romanesque sculptural details in Barneville church. There are regular sailings to Jersey from here.

Barfleur

Normandy

BAYEUX (14) *92k SE Cherbourg, 27k WNW Caen*

This small but ancient town was the very cradle of the Dukedom of Normandy, for it was the daughter of Bayeux's Governor, that became the wife of Rollo the Viking, and mother of William Longsword... the ancestor of William, Duke of Normandy, the 'Conqueror'. The story of William's conquest of England is wonderfully told in the famous Bayeux Tapestry, which hangs in the one-time Bishop's Palace*, opposite Bayeux Cathedral. The Cathedral is a blend of Romanesque and Gothic styles and is also well worth visiting.

(Do not miss a visit here... there is an English commentary available).

The Bayeux Tapestry displayed

BEAUMESNIL CHÂTEAU (27) *13k SE Bernay, 40k W Évreux*

Handsome 17th century château with a moat beneath its extravagant façade. On the other side of the château there are formal gardens, and these are open to the public except in August.

LE BEC-HELLOUIN (27) *42k SW Rouen, 21k NE Bernay*

A great abbey was founded here in 1034, and it owes its fame as a centre of learning in the years that followed, by providing no fewer that two Archbishops of Canterbury... Lanfranc and Anselm. The abbey church was demolished during the years that followed the Revolution, but the remains are well worth visiting and a new abbey has been established in the former refectory. There is a fine view from the top of St-Nicholas' Tower, and unusually, there is a Car Museum in a building close by.

Bayeux Cathedral

Le Bec-Hellouin Abbey

BELLÊME (61) *40k E Alençon*

This village on hilly ground to the south of Bellême Forest is the 'capital' of the Perche region, and there are fragmentary remains of its medieval walls, and some pleasant 17th and 18th century houses in the Rue Ville-Close. There are fine opportunities for walking in Bellême Forest, especially in the vicinity of the Herse Pool, which is two kilometres to the north on the Mortagne road.

BERNAY (27) *58k SW Rouen*

Busy little town which grew up around an important abbey founded here in the 11th century by the grandmother of William the Conqueror. The Romanesque abbey church is worth visiting and there is a small museum in the former Abbot's Lodge. There are pleasant views out over the town from the Promenade des Monts on a hillside to the north.

Beaumesnil Château

BRÉCY MANOR (14) *8k E Bayeux*

Delightful 17th century manor house, built by the great Mansart as a wedding present for his niece. Although the house itself is not normally open, the lovely Italian gardens are, and from them one can obtain many views of the house, and also take in the charming 'triumphal gateway'.

BRICQUEBEC (50) *22k S Cherbourg*

Small town in the heart of the wooded Cotentin Peninsula with a castle which has an impressive 14th
continued

Brécy Manor

Normandy

Cabourg

Caen by night

William the Conqueror's castle, Caen

Wrought-iron at Carrouges

Carrouges Château

century keep... a high polygonal tower from which there are fine views. There is a Trappist monastery two kilometres to the north which is noted for its Gregorian chants, and which may be visited at times.

BROTONNE REGIONAL NATURE PARK (76)
About 35k W Rouen

This is a 'protected zone' straddling the Seine between Rouen and Tancarville, incorporating almost all of the attractive Brotonne Forest, which lies to the south of Caudebec. There are many opportunities for walking and riding in the forest, and there is a Craft Centre just to the north-west of Bourneville (10k ENE Pont Audemer).

LA CABOSSE ZOO PARK (14) *Near Aunay-sur-Odon, 28k SW Caen*

Interesting zoo with many animals and a large aviary with an outstanding collection of birds.

CABOURG (14)
24k NE Caen

Elegant 19th century seaside resort which was built on a semi-circular plan with its streets all running into a little 'place' just behind the promenade. There are fine sands and a wide variety of holiday entertainments.

CAEN (14) *240k W Paris, 121k ESE Cherbourg*

This busy industrial city, and capital of Lower Normandy, was three quarters destroyed in 1944 following the Normandy Invasion, but it has been imaginatively rebuilt, largely of attractive Caen stone. The two great sights of Caen are the Abbaye aux Hommes, founded by William the Conqueror, who was of course Duke of Normandy, and the Abbaye aux Dames, founded by his Queen, Matilda. Both are outstanding examples of Romanesque (or Norman) architecture, and each houses the remains of their respective founders. See the church of St-Pierre, a Gothic building with a Renaissance east end, and the famous belfry, which fell during the 1944 Battle, but which has since been rebuilt. There are several other medieval churches to be seen, and the courtyard of the Hôtel d'Escoville, a delightful Renaissance style merchant's house, is well worth visiting. See also the remains of William the Conqueror's great citadel, which houses a Fine Arts Museum, and a Normandy Museum.

CARENTAN (50)
50k SE Cherbourg

There is a long tree lined waterway stretching from this little market town to the sea, and the tall spire of its Flamboyant Gothic church must have acted as a shipping mark for sailors coming into the estuary for centuries. The large market place is surrounded with old houses built over arcades and is full of character.

CARROUGES (61)
25k NW Alençon

Large château built in the late 16th and early 17th centuries. The elegant entrance pavilion is flanked by two corner towers, and this sets off the great mass of the main building. The splendid furnishings make a visit here well worthwhile.

CAUDEBEC-EN-CAUX (76)
36k WNW Rouen

This small town on the banks of the Seine was almost entirely destroyed by fire in June 1940, but the fine Flamboyant Gothic church of Notre Dame escaped, and is well worth visiting. See also the Templar's House, an interesting 13th century building.

CERISY-LA-FORÊT ABBEY (50)   *22k SW Bayeux*

Partly ruined 11th century abbey on the north-western edge of the lovely Cerisy Forest, with its beech and oak trees. This abbey is regarded as a fine example of 'Norman Romanesque' and is well worth visiting.

CHAMP-DE-BATAILLE CHÂTEAU (27)
30k NW Évreux, 5k NW Le Neubourg

Splendid late 17th century château consisting of two long brick and stone wings, with a central pavilion complete with a dome. The interior is equally elegant and handsomely furnished, with works by Fragonard, Canova and Carpeaux.

An elegant interior at Champ-de-Bataille

CHAMPREPUS ZOO (50)   *20k NNE Avranches*

A zoo garden with four hundred animals, including panthers, lamas, bears, chimpanzees and many other specimens.

CHAUSEY ISLANDS (50)   *Off Granville*

An attractive group of islands to the west of the Cotentin Peninsula, and best reached from Granville. The Great Island (La Grande Île) is inhabited by about a hundred people, but the rest are uninhabited. There are day trips from Granville, and from Dinard in Britanny.

CHERBOURG (50)   *360k WNW Paris*

Naval base and translantic harbour, Cherbourg is now also an important ferry terminal. Cherbourg is not perhaps a place to stay in, but there is an interesting War and Liberation Museum in the Fort du Roule, which was the main point of resistance by the outflanked Germans in 1944. See also the Emmanuel-Liais Park with its fine collection of tropical plants, and the J. F. Millet Museum, which houses an extensive art collection including more than thirty works by Millet.

In Cherbourg harbour

CLÉCY (14)   *37k SSW Caen*

This village is usually regarded as the 'capital' of the Suisse Normande (See Page 206), although its hotel accommodation is severely limited in size. The 16th century Placy Manor houses an interesting Folklore Museum, and there is cider tasting and a leisure park complete with miniature railway.

CLÈRES ZOOLOGICAL PARK (76)   *20k N Rouen*

An extensive collection of free roaming birds and mammals in the grounds of an elegant château. In the nearby Auberge du Cheval Noir, there is an interesting collection of Vintage cars.

In the Suisse-Normande, near Clécy   *At Clères Zoological Park*

CONCHES-EN-OUCHE (27)   *18k WSW Évreux*

Small market town situated in wooded country between the forests of Conche and Évreux, on a spur around which the river Rouloir sharply bends. The ruined 12th century castle stands in the public gardens, but most visitors come to Conches to see the fine Gothic church of St-Foy, with its splendid series of stained glass windows and its two lovely 15th century alabaster triptychs, thought to be the work of an English craftsman.

COURSEULLES-SUR-MER (14)   *18k NNW Caen*

A small holiday resort with fine beach and well known oyster beds. The small harbour was used by no fewer than three famous visitors to the Allied troops in Normandy in 1944... Sir Winston Churchill, General de Gaulle and King George VI, on 12th, 14th and 16th June respectively.

Stained glass at St-Foy, Conches   *In Courseulles harbour*

Normandy

Sunshine at Deauville

Deauville Casino

Cross-Channel ferry entering Dieppe harbour

COUTANCES (50)   *75k S Cherbourg*
Small town on a little hill crowned by a splendid Cathedral. This is and elegant 13th and 14th century Gothic building, with the light stone of its interior enriched by the warm colours of its fine stained glass. See also the Renaissance church of St-Pierre, and the beautifully terraced public gardens.

DEAUVILLE (14)   *43k ENE Caen, 74k S Le Havre*
Fashionable seaside resort, with fine sandy beach, and a wide variety of holiday facilities, including many hotels and restaurants.

DIEPPE (76)   *200k NW Paris*
Lively seaside resort and harbour town, with three ports... the ferry port, overlooked by old houses, in the heart of the town, with the fishing and commercial ports beyond. See the medieval church of St-Jacques and the castle with its museum, which contains an outstanding collection of ivories (There were no fewer than 350 ivory carvers in Dieppe in the 17th century). But perhaps the best of Dieppe lies in its old streets between the ports and sea front, which are full of character.

DOMFRONT (61) *157k SE Cherbourg, 65k E Avranches*
Small village sited on a rocky spine with the ruins of a medieval fortress incorporated in an attractive public garden from which there are fine views out over the Varenne gorge to the Passais countryside. Those interested in 20th century architecture should not miss St-Julien's church.

EAWY FOREST (76)   *Approx. 30k SE Dieppe*
This large beech forest is one of the loveliest in Normandy, and can best be explored northwards from the village of St-Saens. There are forest roads, picnic spots and ample opportunities for walking. Use Michelin Map 52.

ÉCOUVES FOREST (61)   *Approx. 12k N Alençon*
Delightful area of forest country with oak, beech and coniferous trees. There are fine views northwards from the Rochers du Vignage, and a network of forest tracks gives ample opportunities to walkers. Deer and roebuck may be observed by the patient watcher.

ELBEUF (76)   *18k SSW Rouen*
Busy textile town on the south bank of the Seine. The churches of St-Jean and St-Étienne are both worth visiting and there is an Ornithological Museum in the Hôtel-de-Ville, which is near the river.

ÉTRETAT (76)   *28k N Le Havre*
A dignified little holiday resort town with its pebble and sand beach stretching in front of a promenade which lies between some of the most dramatic cliffs in Europe. There is a rock arch and a solitary needle of rock offshore.

EU (76)   *31k NE Dieppe*
Small town between the sea at Le Tréport and the attractive forest of Eu. It has a fine collegiate church, which is largely 12th and 13th century in origin, and which has not been spoilt by the 19th century restoration of Viollet-le-Duc. See also the two splendid 17th century mausoleums of the Duke and Duchess de

continued

Rock arch at Étretat   Eu Château

Normandy   200

Guise in the College Chapel which was founded by Henri de Guise in 1573. The castle is not of great interest. If possible explore south east from here to the forest of Eu. Here are fine stands of oak and beech, many walks and picnic sites, all of which are easily reached from the forest roads. Use Michelin Map 52.

ÉVREUX (27)   *102k W Paris*
This large town is 'capital' of the Eure Département, and is a busy agricultural centre. The cathedral of Notre Dame illustrates the development of architectural styles and includes Romanesque, Gothic, Flamboyant and Renaissance work. See also the abbey church of St-Taurin, another example of developing styles.

Évreux Cathedral

FALAISE (14)   *34k SSE Caen, 128k S Le Havre*
This small town was the birthplace of William the Conqueror, and despite virtual destruction in the 1944 battles, it is well worth visiting for the sake of the great medieval fortress where William made his plans for the invasion of England. See the memorial to William's companions at the Battle of Hastings in the St-Prix Chapel in the castle, and the fine equestrian statue of William himself in the town square.

FÉCAMP (76)   *64k WSW Dieppe*
Lively fishing town, noted for its deep-sea fishing fleet. It has a great abbey church, with a nave considerably longer than many cathedrals, and the Benedictine Distillery and Museum. It was in the 16th century that one of the monks here set about distilling a liqueur from the aromatic herbs that grew upon the nearby cliffs, and the ensuing story of 'Benedictine' may be followed in the fascinating museum, complete with sound and light. (Commentary in several languages including English). Guy de Maupassant lived here and Fécamp is featured in several of his stories.

Norman fortress, Falaise   *William the Conqueror, at Falaise*

FLERS (61)   *57k SSW Caen*
Prosperous industrial town with a 16th century moated château attractively situated in a park complete with large lake, on its western side. The château contains a museum with items largely of local interest.

FONTAINE-HENRI CHÂTEAU (14)   *15k NNW Caen*
Handsome Renaissance château with a pleasantly furnished interior. See especially the fine staircase and the excellent collection of pictures.

FONTAINE-GUÉRARD ABBEY (27)   *20k SE Rouen*
Extensive ruins of a 12th century abbey on the west bank of the river Andelle, with ruined church and chapter house and a monks dormitory over what was probably their workroom.

Reconstructed square at Falaise

FORGES-LES-EAUX (76)   *54k SE Dieppe*
Fashionable spa town which was 'put on the map' by Louis XIII and Cardinal Richelieu, who both came here to take the waters. There is a 'Thermal Park' complete with a grotto where Louis and his Queen came to drink, and several elegant 17th century features.

GISORS (27)   *58k SE Rouen*
Small town dominated by the ruins of a fine medieval fortress, which was largely the work of the English kings, Henry I and II. See also the interesting 12th – 16th century church of St-Gervase and St-Protase, much damaged in the 39 – 45 war, but since well restored.

Fontaine-Henri Château   *Well-head at Fontaine-Henri Château*

Normandy

Hambye Abbey ruins

A little schooling at Haras-du-Pin

In the Fine Arts Museum, Le Havre

Honfleur harbour

In the Eugène-Boudin Museum, Honfleur

GRANVILLE (50) *104k S Cherbourg*

Busy little seaside resort with an old walled town on a promontory above its harbour, which is an embarkation point for the Chausey Islands (See Page 199). In the Upper Town see Notre Dame church, the Museum in the Main Gate, the Lighthouse, and the Aquarium. In the Lower Town see the Waxworks Museum, the Christian Dior Garden and the pleasant beach.

HAMBYE ABBEY (50) *30k NNE Avranches*

A splendid ruined Romanesque and Gothic abbey in a quiet valley setting. The restored conventual buildings contain much of interest including Norman tapestries in the 'Guest's Dormitory'.

HARAS-DU-PIN (61) *15k E Argentan*

This National Stud is in the heart of the Perche horse breeding area. Fine woodland rides all converge on Colbert's Court (named after the great statesman who founded the stud), and the main château serves as the manager's residence. There are usually about a hundred stallions kept here, and there are race meetings in August and October. The stud is usually open to the public.

HARCOURT (27) *34k NW Évreux*

A fine medieval castle with a double moat and a handsomely furnished interior including a fine 17th century staircase. The surrounding park is regarded as France's second most important arboretum and most of the trees therein are labelled.

LE HAVRE (76) *204k WNW Paris, 86k W Rouen*

This is a great industrial and port town, second only to Marseille in the volume of traffic handled. It suffered terribly during the 39 – 45 war, but since then it has gone from strength to strength. Tours of the harbour may be made by boat, and in addition to the ships and other installations there are views of one of Europe's largest power stations. In the city, see the dramatic modern church of St-Joseph, by architect and town planner, Auguste Perret; and the beautifully designed Fine Arts Museum (Opened 1961). For fine panoramic views over the city, visit Ste-Adresse Fort, and then drive two kilometres north-west to visit the lighthouse of La Hève, from which there are splendid views out over the Seine estuary.

HONFLEUR (76) *63k NE Caen*

Charming old fishing and commercial port on the southern shores of the Seine estuary. The old harbour is surrounded by tall narrow houses, with their slate roofs and some even with slate hung walls, and closed in on the north by the attractive Lieutenance (the Governor's House). Wander in Honfleur's old streets, visit its old churches, and especially the Eugène-Boudin Museum, with its fine collection of paintings reminding us that this town was one of the cradles of the Impressionist school. Do not miss a visit to the unusual all-wooden church of Ste-Catherine... probably built as a 'temporary measure' after the hundred years War, but luckily never replaced.

HOULGATE (14) *15k SW Deauville*

Small holiday resort with beautiful sands beneath its high dark cliffs, known as the Vaches-Noires.

NEZ DE JOBOURG (50)   *26k W Cherbourg*
Explore westwards from Cherbourg to this dramatic headland, which together with Cap de la Hague, make up the far north west of the Cotentin Peninsula.

JUMIÈGES (76)   *28k W Rouen*
A deliciously sited Benedictine abbey, with a great roofless abbey church flanked by the ruins of a smaller church and chapterhouse. All this is situated amongst trees on the south side of the small village.

LESSAY (50)   *54k S Cherbourg*
Small town near the head of a large coastal inlet, with a splendid Romanesque abbey church, and a small zoo.

The Nez de Jobourg   *Jumièges Abbey*

LISIEUX (14)   *49k E Caen*
Busy commercial town, the old parts of which were almost entirely destroyed in 1944. However the Cathedral of St-Pierre is well worth visiting, and Lisieux is also a renowned centre of pilgrimage... to the shrine of Ste Theresa... a young Carmelite nun, who died of consumption a short time after completing the touching story of her life, 'The History of a Soul'.

LOUVIERS (27)   *29k S Rouen*
Small town on the river Eure, with an outstandingly rich example of the Flamboyant style in the shape of its church of Notre Dame. The interior of this building contains several fine sculptures.

Ste-Theresa's Basilica, Lisieux   *Mondaye Abbey*

LYONS-LA-FORÊT (27)   *36k E Rouen*
Delicious little village complete with 18th century market hall and a late medieval church with timber belfry. This is situated in the heart of Lyons Forest, in which are some of the finest beech woods in France. The forest country is interlaced with several roads, and many forest tracks and footpaths, and is well worth exploring.

MIROMESNIL CHÂTEAU (76)   *7k S Dieppe*
This 17th century château was the birthplace of the 19th century writer Guy de Maupassant, and there is a statue of him on its boundary.

LE-MOLAY-LITTRY MINING MUSEUM (14)
                                           14k W Bayeux
This is a most interesting museum and well worth visiting.

Nineteenth Century lifting wheel, Mont-St-Michel   *Defensive tower, Mont-St-Michel*

MONDAYE ABBEY (14)   *11k S Bayeux*
Handsome 17th century classical abbey church and buildings in quiet countryside south of Bayeux.

MONT-ST-MICHEL (50)   *22k SW Avranches*
                                           156k S Cherbourg
This is one of the great spectacles of Europe... a magnificent Romanesque and Gothic abbey built upon a dramatic rocky island rising almost sheer from a wide sandy bay swept by immensely powerful tides. Approach to the island is by a long causeway, and at the foot of the long climb up to the abbey is a little town devoted to the needs of the hundreds of thousands of tourists that come here each year. Space does not allow a detailed description of Mont St-Michel... suffice it to say that a visit here will never be forgotten, despite the crowds and the inevitable commercialization.

Mont-St-Michel by night

Normandy

The Refectory, Mont-St-Michel

In a Normandy forest

O Château

The Pointe du Hoc, just west of Omaha Beach

Ouistream harbour

MORTAGNE-AU-PERCHE (61)   *56k SE Argentan*
Small market town on a hill with fine views out over the wooded Perche country. The Flamboyant Gothic and Renaissance church of Notre-Dame is noted for the interesting carvings on its choir stalls.

MORTAIN (50)   *36k E Avranches*
This small town was almost totally destroyed in 1944, but it has been attractively rebuilt. See the 13th century collegiate church and the Cistercian Blanche Abbey, which is situated just to the north of the town close to the 'Grande Cascade', a fine waterfall in thickly wooded country.

NORMANDIE MAINE REGIONAL NATURE PARK
(50, 53, 61, 72)   *About 160k SE Cherbourg,*
About 170k SSW Le Havre
This great area of richly afforested country extends partly into the Loire Valley West Region. Here in forests of beech, oak and pine will be found roebuck, wild boar, woodpeckers, buzzards and warblers. This is quiet hilly countryside and well worth exploring.

O CHÂTEAU (LE CHÂTEAU D'O) (61)
17k SE Argentan
Early Renaissance château complete with moat. The castle is not (at the time of writing) open, but apart from July to mid September, it is possible to view the exterior from across the moat.

OMAHA BEACH (14)   *About 20k NW Bayeux*
This was the site of one of the two great American landing beaches on June 6th 1944, the other being at Utah Beach, at the foot of the Cotentin Peninsula. The combination of extremely heavy German opposition, strong coastal currents and difficult shingle, made this landing area the bloodiest of them all. Even the artificial Mulberry harbour only lasted until 19th June, when it was swept away by a most unseasonal storm. Along this beach there are three monuments and a fine seafront boulevard running between Vierville and Les Moulins.

OUISTREAM-RIVA BELLA (14)   *14k NNE Caen*
Lively holiday resort with a colourful yacht harbour at the point where the Caen Canal joins the sea, and a fine stretch of sand along its front. There is an interesting Museum of the Normandy Landings, reminding us that Ouistream was one of the first towns to be liberated during the 1944 Landings (by an Anglo-French Commando unit, on the morning of 6th June).

PEGASUS BRIDGE (14) *At Benouville, 12k NNE Caen*
This was renamed to commemorate its capture by British Airborne Forces on the night of 5th/6th June, and there is an interesting Museum devoted to the exploits of the Airborne Forces nearby.

PONT-AUDEMER (27)   *48k ESE Le Havre*
This has a small port on the river Risle and is also noted for its leather tanneries. Although badly damaged in 1944, much of the old town has survived, notably the fine church of St-Ouen, with its Romanesque origins and its alterations and additions in Flamboyant Gothic and Renaissance styles. There is a pleasant Bird Park near here, with birds, monkeys and reptiles.

PONT L'ÉVÊQUE (14)   *48k ENE Caen, 64k S Le Havre*
Charming little town on the banks of the river
Touques. It was badly damaged in the 39 – 45 War, but
there are several pleasant old timbered buildings
including a former convent.

ROUEN (76)   *139k NW Paris, 86k E Le Havre*
Capital of Upper Normandy, this great industrial city
is France's fourth port, after Marseille, Le Havre and
Dunkirk. It suffered greatly in the 2nd World War, but
has been lovingly restored since. The wealth of old
buildings and charming streets has earned it the title of
Museum Town, and the number and diversity of its
buildings make it impossible to describe adequately in
the confines of this guide. See especially, the great
Cathedral, the famous Gros Horloge (The Great Clock),
the Belfry, the Place du Vieux Marché, where the spot
on which Joan of Arc was burnt at the stake is still
marked, the Joan of Arc Tower, where she was
imprisoned and tried, the Fine Arts Museum and several
other museums, St-Maclou church, the lovely Hôtel-de-
Bourgtheroulde, and the Flaubert and History of
Medicine Museum, the 17th century hospital where
Flaubert was born (his father being a surgeon there).
And finally, do not miss a walk along the busy quays
lining the banks of the Seine.

The Old Convent, Pont l'Évêque

A medieval street in   Rouen Cathedral
Rouen

ST-GERMAIN-DE-LIVET (14)   *6k S Lisieux*
Charming 15th and 16th century château surrounded
by a moat. It is a half timbered building with its façade
an attractive pattern of mellow brick and stone, and is
perhaps more a manor than a château in appearance.

ST-LÔ (50)   *78k SSE Cherbourg*
A busy and prosperous town on the banks of the river
Vire with an 'old town' still bordered on three sides by
ancient ramparts. St-Lo suffered disastrously in 1944,
but the town has been re-built to an excellent plan,
revealing the rocky spur upon which the ramparts
stand. Visit the 'old town' within these ramparts, the
restored 14th and 15th century church of Notre-Dame,
the Romanesque church of Ste-Croix, the museum in
the Hôtel-de-Ville, and the fine stud where about 250
Norman, Percheron and English stallions are stabled.

St-Germain-de-Livet Château

ST-PIERRE-SUR-DIVES (14)   *31k SE Caen*
Small town in rich pastoral country, with a fine old
abbey church incorporating Romanesque and Gothic
work. The medieval covered market was unfortunately
burnt down in 1944, but it has been re-built in its original
form.

ST-SEVER-CALVADOS (14)   *36k NW Avranches*
Small market town, with an interesting Wild Animal
Park in the nearby forest.

ST-SYMPHORIEN-DES-MONTS (50)
    *35k SE Avranches, betweeen St-Hilaire and Le
    Teillieul.*
Extensive zoo park with a varied collection of wild
animals in conditions of 'semi-liberty'.

ST-VALÉRY-EN-CAUX (76)   *32k W Dieppe*
Small holiday resort with good sands at low tide, a
harbour for pleasure craft, and a Renaissance house on
the quayside said to have been visited by Henry IV. This
little town was almost entirely destroyed in 1940 when it

continued

Forest country   St-Valery-en-Caux
near St-Sever   harbour

Normandy

Terraced garden at Sassy Château

Sunlit streams in the Suisse-Normande

The Tancarville Bridge   *Thaon church*

Summertime in Trouville

was so gallantly defended by troops the 51st Highland Division, the surrender of which was eventually accepted by General Rommel. There is a monument commemorating their heroism on the cliffs just to the east of the town.

ST-WANDRILLE ABBEY (76)   *34k WNW Rouen*
Here was a great Benedictine abbey, and the ruins of the largely 14th century abbey church and cloisters are well worth visiting. The church of the present monastery is a 15th century tythe barn which was moved here piece by piece in 1969.

STE-MÈRE-ÉGLISE (50)   *37k SE Cherbourg*
Small town with a War Museum reminding us that it was here that the American 82nd Airborne Division landed on 5/6th June 1944. Here is Milestone 0 on Liberty Road... the start of the Americans' long haul across France to Metz and Bastogne.

SASSY CHÂTEAU (61)   *11k S Argentan*
An 18th and early 19th century château, with attractive terraced gardens. Combine with a visit to the lovely forest of Écouves which lies about ten kilometres to the south (See Page 200).

SÉES (61)   *21k NNE Alençon*
Charming little cathedral town not far to the north east of the great Forest of Écouves. See the Cathedral itself, a handsome 13th and 14th century Gothic building, the church of Notre-Dame-de-la-Place, and the 18th century Bishop's Palace.

SUISSE NORMANDE, LA (14)   *30k S Caen,*
20k W Falaise
A highly attractive area mostly in the Orne valley, between Thury-Harcourt and Putanges, with deep gorges, wooded valleys, and rocky peaks, from which there are fine views out over the surrounding countryside. This is well worth exploring in detail with the help of the Michelin Maps 55 and 60, and the Michelin Green Guide to Normandy. The area resembles parts of the Peak District rather more closely than Switzerland.

TANCARVILLE BRIDGE (76)   *30k E Le Havre*
This fine suspension bridge across the Seine estuary is one of the largest in Europe. There is a telescope and recorded commentary (in English) on the bridge's construction, on the south bank.

THAON (14)   *12k NW Caen*
Here in fields to the north of the village is a pure Romanesque church... one of the most unspoilt little buildings in Normandy. Enquire locally for permission to visit.

LE TRÉPORT (76)   *30k NE Dieppe*
Small fishing port and busy holiday resort, with its neighbour Mers-les-Bains just across the river Bresle. There is fine sand at Le Tréport at low tide. Climb on foot or by tele-cabin to the Terrace Calvary, from which there are fine views.

TROUVILLE (14)   *43k ENE Caen, 74k S Le Havre*
Charmingly elegant seaside resort with splendid golden sands and a wide selection of hotels, restaurants and shops. Pleasant walks along the inevitable promenade, but also along the busy quays lining the Touques, with views across to neighbouring Deauville.

UTAH BEACH (50)   *45k SE Cherbourg*
This was one of the two great American landing beaches in the Normandy Invasion of June (the other being Omaha (See Page 204), and there is a commemorative monument here and a War Museum near Ste-Marie-du-Mont.

VALOGNES (50)   *20k SE Cherbourg*
Former capital of the Cotentin peninsula area, much of this attractive old town was destroyed in 1944. However many lovely old buildings have survived, notably the Hôtel de Beaumont and two churches. There is a fascinating Regional Cider Museum here.

Trouville harbour   *In the Suisse-Normande*

VASCOEUIL (27)   *23k E Rouen*
Delightful 14th – 16th century fortified manor house, in a garden on the edge of the Lyons Forest, with several reconstructed half-timbered cottages, and a fine dovecote in mellow brick. The interior of the house is excellently furnished, and its contents includes a well known private art collection.

VERNEUIL-SUR-AVRE (27)   *43k SSW Évreux*
This attractive old town in the wooded Avre valley was built by Henry I of England (at least one French guide book refers to him merely as Henry, Duke of Normandy... but he was of course both) as part of an east west defensive line against the incursions of the French into Normandy. See especially the church of La Madeleine with its splendid tower so like the Butter Tower at Rouen, the church of Notre-Dame with its exceptional number of 16th century statues and carvings, and the remains of Henry Ist's fortifications, from the watchtower of which there are fine views out over the town and the surrounding countryside.

VERNON (27)   *31k ENE Évreux*
Handsome town on the Seine with many wide avenues and fine views of several wooded islands in the river from its bridge. There is a Romanesque collegiate church and an attractive timber-framed house nearby. See also the 'Archives Tower', and at Giverny, 5k SE, the lovely gardens created by the painter Claude Monet, together with his studio, both of which are now open.

VIRE (14)   *60k SW Caen*
Bright, largely new town on the river Vire, built to replace the destruction wrought during 1944. The well restored church of Notre Dame, with its undamaged 15th century clock tower, is worth visiting.

Tranquil Normandy

YVETOT (76)   *35k NW Rouen*
Prosperous market town on the Caux plateau which had to be almost entirely rebuilt following the disastrous air raids of 1940. We include it here in view of the splendid modern church, built of concrete and glass by Yves Marchand, with stained glass by Max Ingrand... this is a tour-de-force which should not be passed by.

'CALVADOS COUNTRY'

Normandy is renowned throughout France for the splendid cider produced from its orchards, but in the Département of Calvados this is distilled into the fiery, apple-flavoured brandy liqueur known as Calvados. This is an excellent drink with which to round off a generously proportioned meal, but it is also popular as a bar drink, as the readers of Simenon's Inspector Maigret will no doubt recall.

Bell-tower at Valognes   *Blossom time in Calvados country*

Normandy

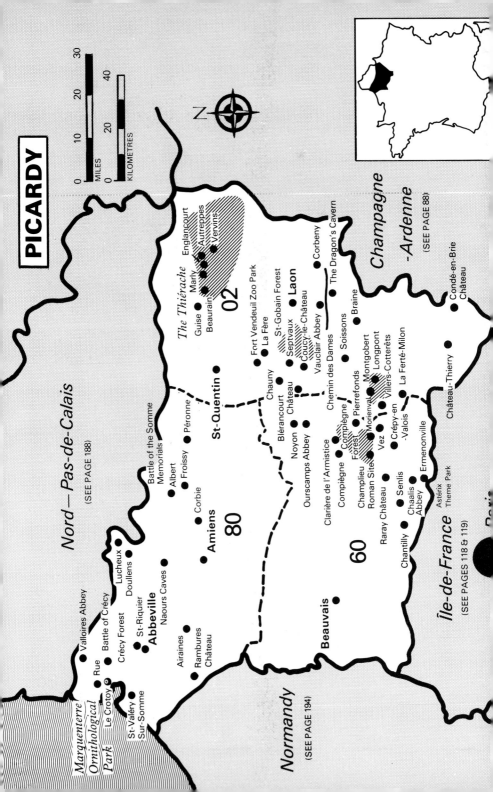

PICARDY

Nord – Pas-de-Calais
(SEE PAGE 188)

Normandy
(SEE PAGE 194)

Champagne
-Ardenne
(SEE PAGE 88)

Île-de-France
(SEE PAGES 118 & 119)

Marguenterre
Ornithological
Park

Le Crotoy
Rue
St-Valéry
Sur-Somme

Valloires Abbey
Battle of Crécy
Crécy Forest
St-Riquier
Lucheux
Doullens

Abbeville
Naours Caves

Airaines
Rambures
Château

Amiens
Albert
Corbie
Froissy
Péronne

Battle of the Somme
Memorials

80

St-Quentin

Ourscamps Abbey

Beauvais

Clairière de l'Armistice
Compiègne
Champlieu
Roman Site
Raray Château
Chantilly

60

Pierrefonds
Compiègne
Forest
Morienval
Vez
Senlis
Chaalis
Abbey
Crépy-en
-Valois
Ermenonville

Astérix
Theme Park

Château-Thierry

Condé-en-Brie
Château

Paris

Noyon
Château
Blérancourt
Chauny

La Fère
Fort Vendeuil Zoo Park

St-Gobain Forest
Septvaux
Coucy-le-Château
Vauclair Abbey

Laon
Chemin des Dames
Soissons
Braine

02

The Thiérache
Guise
Beaurain
Marly
Autreppes
Vervins
Englancourt

Corbeny
The Dragon's Cavern

Montgobert
Longpont
Villers-Cotterêts
La Ferté-Milon

MILES
KILOMETRES
0 10 20 30
0 20 40

N

Picardy

This region is a vast series of plains, with rich cultivations generously interspersed with forests, ponds and gentle wooded valleys, the most notable of which shelter the Somme, the Oise and the Aisne. There are many memories here of battles long ago, and many memorials and cemeteries reminding us of the unimaginable slaughter that took place in the 14 – 18 War, but despite this, the lasting memory of Picardy for most visitors today will be of quiet, sparsely populated countryside punctuated by a few busy industrial towns and a multitude of peaceful country towns and villages, many of whose cathedrals and churches provide glorious evidence that it was here that French Gothic architecture achieved some of its outstanding triumphs.

See especially the cathedrals of Amiens, Beauvais, Laon, Noyons, Soissons and Senlis. Also visit the Asterix Theme Park and the Sea of Sand, two fun parks near Ermenonville. It is only too easy to hurry on through Picardy, down the space-devouring autoroute, to Paris and the South; but please stop awhile to explore its forests, to visit its cathedrals and churches, to amble along its tranquil valley roads, and walk in the narrow streets of its old towns.

ABBEVILLE (80)
81k S Boulogne, 45k NW Amiens

Busy town on the river Somme, only a few miles from its entry to the sea at St-Valéry. It was well nigh destroyed in the 39 – 45 War, but has been rebuilt with style. Do not miss the well restored church of St-Vulfran with its Flamboyant style façade and fine Renaissance doors, nor the handsome 18th century miniature château of Bagatelle, situated on the Paris (N1) road. The re-built Boucher de Perthes Museum contains important collections of art and archaeology and is well worth visiting.

La Bagatelle, Abbeville

AIRAINES (80)
20k SE Abbeville

Small town astride the N1, with the ruins of a 13th century castle, where the English king Edward is believed to have slept while on his way to Crécy (See Page 212). There is also an interesting Romanesque church which has a roof reaching almost to the ground.

ALBERT AND THE BATTLE OF THE SOMME (80)
28k ENE Amiens

This town was almost entirely destroyed in the first World War and even suffered again in the second. However it is the usual starting point for a tour of the various War Memorials which is signposted by the Picardy Rose. This tour takes you to Beaumont-Hamel, the Memorial Park to the Newfoundlanders, with its great bronze reindeer; to the Belfast Tower to the memory of the Irish troops; to Thiepval, Pozières, Longueval, and finally to Doullens where visitors may hear a recorded account of the battle in several languages.

Monument at Beaumont-Hamel

The Belfast Tower, Thiepval

AMIENS (80)
150k N Paris, 125k SSW Boulogne

This large city astride the Somme is the capital of the Somme Département, and ancient capital of Picardy. It suffered terribly in both World Wars, but luckily its great Cathedral escaped serious damage. This magnificent Gothic building is the largest cathedral in France, and is particularly noted for the splendid sculptures adorning its three west portals, and its wonderfully carved 16th century oak choir stalls. There are fine views of the city to be obtained from the concrete Perret Tower near the station and both the Picardy Museum and the Local History Museum in the Hôtel de Berry should be visited. *continued*

The New Zealanders' Memorial, Longueval

In Amiens Cathedral

West doorway, Beauvais Cathedral *Braine Abbey*

Chantilly *Photograph by Peter Titchmarsh.*

The magnificent interior of Chantilly

In the Museum of the Horse, Chantilly
Photograph by Peter Titchmarsh

Amiens is also noted for its market gardens (Les Hortillonnages), which are situated in marshlands on the eastern side of the city, and which can be visited by boats, which leave the Café de l'Île aux Fagots. Most of these gardens can only be reached by boat, and their produce is still brought into the Marché sur l'Eau (by the Place Parmentier) by curious punt-like boats with prows and sterns like gondolas. Do not miss a visit to the excellent Zoo Park on the west side of the city.

THE ASTERIX THEME PARK (60)
(Special Exit from Autoroute, 38k N Paris)
A large fun park with features for all the family, including a Gallic Village, 'Shooting the Rapids', 'Asterix's Travels through Antiquity', a Dolphinarium and 'How the Roman Village of Lutetia became Paris'. There are shows, shops and a number of restaurants and other eating places.

BEAUVAIS (60) *76k N Paris, 166k S Boulogne*
This is the capital of the Oise Département, and having suffered great damage from bombing in 1940, it is largely a modern town. The Cathedral has the highest Gothic choir in the world... the result of no fewer than three attempts to achieve a superlative, when the principles of Gothic architecture were stretched to their very limit. It once had the highest central tower, but this only survived for five years, and was never rebuilt. However the choir is a splendid achievement, with its wonderfully soaring vertical lines, and sense of lightness. Do not miss the Treasury, the tapestries (the famous Beauvais factory was destroyed in the 1940 bombing and never replaced), the cloisters, the famous astronomical clock, nor the pre-Romanesque church of the 'Basse Oeuvre'. Close by is the Romanesque and Gothic church of St-Étienne, which is particularly rich in 16th century stained glass.

BLÉRANCOURT CHÂTEAU (02) *14k SE Noyon*
Not a great deal survives of the château built by Italian born architect, Salomon de Brosse (1565 – 1626), but there are splendid 17th and 18th century gardens with gazebos and triumphal arches, and a Franco-American Historical Museum, which was established here in 1927.

BRAINE (02) *18k E Soissons*
Large village astride the N31, with a handsome early Gothic abbey church (Viollet le Duc reckoned it to be 'one of the most beautiful churches in the north of France').

CHAMPLIEU ROMAN SITE (60) *14k S Compiègne*
The site of a probable wintering place for the Roman legions, with the remains of a large arena, baths, theatre and a temple. All this is pleasantly situated just to the south of the Compiègne Forest (See Page 211).

CHANTILLY (60) *50k N Paris, 10k W Senlis*
Elegant little town in lovely forest country with splendid 18th century stables, which now contain a delightful 'Museum of the Horse', with a series of interesting exhibits and fine displays of dressage and horsemanship in general. These stables adjoin one of the best known and most delightful race-courses in France. To the immediate west of these is the great château of Chantilly, stunningly sited amongst lakes and gardens, much of which were laid out by the great

Le Nôtre. The château houses the Condé Museum with its outstanding collections of tapestries, paintings, sculpture, jewellery and manuscripts, including the world famous 14th century illuminated manuscript, 'Les Très Riches Heures du Duc de Berry.' 5k to the south are the Commelles Lakes, in a lovely forest clearing near to an old hunting lodge known as the Château de la Reine Blanche.

CHÂTEAU-THIERRY (02)
97k ESE Paris, 41k S Soissons

Delightful town on the banks of the Marne, on the western edge of the Champagne country. There is a public park within the walls of the old castle, and nearby is the birthplace of the 17th century French Aesop, La Fontaine. There is an impressive American War Memorial on 'Hill 204', to the immediate west of the town, reminding us of the bitter fighting that took place here in 1918 (The nearby Bois Belleau Cemetery contains the graves of over 2500 American troops).

Craonne, near the eastern end of the Chemin-des-Dames

CHEMIN-DES-DAMES (02)
Starts 15k NE Soissons

This is a famous hill crest road which runs eastwards from the N2 about mid way between Soissons and Laon, and it was first used by the daughters of Louis XV for carriage drives. There are many war cemeteries and memorials along the way, reminding us that this was the scene of intense fighting in 1917. (See also the Dragon's Cavern, Page 212).

Compiègne Palace

Old houses at Compiègne

COMPIÈGNE (60)
82k NE Paris, 77k SE Amiens

Attractive town on the river Oise, and on the very edge of the great Compiègne Forest. It was at Compiègne that Joan of Arc was finally captured by the Burgundians, who handed her over to the English. The present royal palace of Compiègne was built by Louis XV and XVI, but it was Napoleon and Napoleon III who made the fullest use of it. It is now a museum and the richly furnished royal and imperial apartments may be visited. There is also a most interesting Museum of Vehicles and Tourism here. In the town there is a collection of Greek vases (second in France only to the Louvre) in the Vivenel Museum, and a splendid collection of model soldiers in the Town Hall.

COMPIÈGNE FOREST (60)
80k NE Paris.
To the immediate south and east of Compiègne

This is a large state-owned forest, deservedly popular with week-ending Parisians. See especially the 'Clairière de l'Armistice', a forest clearing where you may visit the famous railway carriage where the 1918 Armistice was signed. See also the forest 'villages' of Vieux-Moulin and St-Jean-aux-Bois, and the ponds of St-Pierre; and walk along some of the pathways through this lovely forest country.

In the Vehicle Museum, Compiègne

CONDÉ-EN-BRIE CHÂTEAU (02)
13k ESE Château-Thierry

A 16th century château, much altered in the following centuries. The interior is largely 18th century and is elegantly furnished. It has been in the hands of the de Sade family since 1814 and some of the letters written by the notorious Marquis de Sade during his 28 years in prison may be seen here.

CORBENY (02)
17k SE Laon

Astride the busy N44, this small village is noted for its fascinating Museum of Bees and Honey, which is well worth visiting. There is a Mead Brewery attached.

In the Vehicle Museum, Compiègne

Picardy

King of Bohemia's
Monument, Crécy

Fishing boats at Le
Crotoy

On the evening tide, off Le Crotoy

Poplar Island, Ermenonville

The 'Sea of Sand', Ermenonville

CORBIE (80)   *16k E Amiens*
Small village on the Somme, with two churches and the remains of an abbey which became known as the 'Second Rome of the Middle Ages', due to its great wealth and power. Three kilometres to the south is the great Australian War Memorial near the village of Villers-Bretonneux, commemorating the death of no fewer than 10,000 Australian soldiers who died here in the spring of 1918.

COUCY-LE-CHÂTEAU (02)   *17k N Soissons*
Small village built largely within the walls of a vast ruined castle. The great central keep was blown up by the Germans in 1917, but the long outer walls and towers are well worth visiting. To the north and east lies the great Forest of St-Gobain, in which is situated the village of Septvaux with its fine Romanesque church (9k NE Coucy).

BATTLE OF CRÉCY (80)   *18k N Abbeville*
This took place on Saturday 26th August 1346, a little way to the north of the village of Crécy-en-Ponthieu, when Edward III and the Black Prince (then only a boy of 16) won a resounding victory over the French, at the start of the Hundred Years War. There is a cross marking the spot where the brother in law of the French king, Jean de Luxembourg, the old and blind King of Bohemia, fell... but no other signs remain. To the south and west of the village, there is the extensive Forest of Crécy.

CRÉPY-EN-VALOIS (60)   *70k NE Paris,*
                                                38k S Compiègne
Small town attractively sited above two valleys on the western fringes of forest country. Some of its ramparts remain, and the 12th century keep of the ducal castle houses an interesting museum, much of which is devoted to archery. One of its two medieval churches is dedicated to Thomas à Becket.

LE CROTOY (80)   *21k NW Abbeville*
Lively little seaside resort looking across the Somme estuary to St-Valéry. It is connected with St-Valéry, and with Cayeux-sur-Mer beyond, by a light steam railway which is a great attraction for children.

DOULLENS (80)   *35k SW Arras*
This small town in the lovely Authie valley is overshadowed by one of Vauban's great fortresses, but it has a pleasant 18th and early 19th century flavour. The Lombart Museum is devoted to items of local interest. (See also Albert and the Battle of the Somme, Page 209.)

THE DRAGON'S CAVERN (02)
                                        on the Chemin des Dames,
                                35k ENE Soissons, 20k SE Laon
This a fascinating museum devoted to the battles in the area during the 14–18 War, and it is situated in a vast underground quarry. There is an audio-visual display (with commentary in English) and a tour of the underground galleries. See also the Chemin des Dames (Page 211).

ERMENONVILLE (60)   *47k NE Paris, 14k SE Senlis*
Small village on the edge of the Ermenonville Forest, with a deliciously beautiful park (The Parc Jean-Jacques Rousseau*) situated around a large pond. A little to the north is an excellent zoo (The Jean-Richard Zoo), with a wide variety of animals and also performing dolphins. A short distance further to the north, up the road towards Senlis, is the entrance to the 'Sea of
continued

212

Sand', with the Jean Richard Amusement Park, including 'Redskin Valley'. Away beyond the other side of the Senlis road are the ruins of the Cistercian abbey of Chaalis, complete with lake, woods, rose gardens and the Jacquemart-André Museum.

(Rousseau was originally buried on a poplar-shaded island in the park, but his body was later moved to the Parthenon in Paris).

LA FÈRE (02) — 42k N Soissons
Pleasant little town on the Oise with a 13th century church and a museum containing an excellent collection of pictures.

LA FERTÉ-MILON (02) — 10k S Villers-Cotterêts
Small town on the pretty river Ourcq, above which are the ruins of a great medieval castle. The 17th century playright Jean Racine was born here, and there is a statue of him in the town. Do not miss the lovely stained glass windows in the largely 16th century church of St-Nicholas. Explore southwards down the Ourcq valley to Meaux (See Page 124), along quiet roads to the east of the river.

FORT VENDEUIL ZOO PARK (02)
15k SSE St-Quentin
Attractive Zoo Park and Leisure Park established around the remains of a large 19th century fortress. Picnic areas, refreshments, narrow gauge railway.

FROISSY (80) — 10k SW Albert
Minute village on the Somme, with a delightful little touristic train running 14k between here and the equally small village of Cappy.

GUISE (02) — 27k ENE St-Quentin
Small town on the western fringes of the Thiérache (See Page 216), with a ruined castle which was largely destroyed in the 14 – 18 War, but which is now being excavated and partially restored. This was a medieval castle extensively fortified in the 16th century using brick rather than stone.

LAON (02) — 135k NE Paris, 230k SE Boulogne
This attractive old town is the capital of the Aisne Département, and is situated on a narrow ridge rising some three hundred feet above the plain in which it stands. The early Gothic Cathedral has a fine west front with richly decorated portals and a handsome rose window. There is a 12th century chapel of the Knights Templar in the garden of the nearby museum, and there are pleasant walks around the town walls, considerable lengths of which have survived. There are a number of interesting Romanesque and Gothic churches to be found in the villages situated in attractive countryside to the south and south west of Laon... ask for details at the Aisne Tourist Office in the Hôtel du Petit St-Vincent.

LONGPONT (02)
11k E Villers-Cotterêts, 16k SW Soissons
Here is a 12th century abbey converted into a manor house, in a pleasant setting just to the east of the Retz Forest.

LUCHEUX (80) — 7k NE Doullens, 37k NNE Amiens
Pleasantly situated village with a interesting Romanesque church, the capitals of which include the Seven Deadly Sins amongst their sculptured decoration. The ruined castle above the village housed Joan of Arc for a brief time after her capture at Compiègne.

The Jacquemart-André Museum, Chaalis

Ruins of Chaalis Abbey

Laon Cathedral

Laon Cathedral

Ruins of Longpont Abbey

Picardy

Morienval Abbey

Noyon Cathedral cloisters

MARQUENTERRE ORNITHOLOGICAL PARK (80)

28k NW Abbeville

Opened in 1973, this Bird Sanctuary borders a natural reserve in the Bay of the Somme, and its privileged position between the mouth of the river Maye and the Cape of St-Quentin has always made it a favourite with migrating birds. The Sanctuary comprises three separate areas: a walking areas amongst moors and wooded dunes, an area of ponds and aviaries, and a watching area which is recommended to ornithologists and photographers. Those less interested in birds will head for the nearby Marquenterre Aqualand, a well-equipped and largely indoor aquatic fun-place.

MORIENVAL (60)

10k NNE Crépy-en-Valois

Small village in a valley just to the south of the Compiègne Forest, with a Romanesque abbey church which has three belfries, and which also has within it one of the earliest examples of crossed Gothic arches forming a roof vault… a style of architecture that soon spread across western Europe bringing a new lightness of form made possible by this concept.

The Old Library, Noyon

NAOURS CAVES (80)

17k N Amiens

Here in 1888, beneath this small village the local priest discovered an extensive system of underground tunnels, with over half a mile of 'streets' with many chambers leading off them. Some of the dates carved upon the walls date back to the Hundred Years War. The caves were used by the British in the 14 – 18 War and by the Germans in the 39 – 45 War. There are guided visits.

NOYON (60)

24k NE Compiègne

Pleasant town in the Oise valley with a Romanesque and early Gothic Cathedral. This has a spacious interior with choir and nave both of the same height, while beyond the remains of the cloisters, is a 16th century chapter house with its projecting upper storey supported on wooden pillars. This contains a well known library of over 4000 volumes. There is a small museum in the former Bishop's Palace, and in the street named after Noyon's most famous son, is the birthplace of Jean Calvin, the great founder of Protestantism (1509 – 1564).

Ruins of Ourscamps Abbey

OURSCAMPS ABBEY (60)

5k S Noyon

Here are the ruins of a great Cistercian abbey, which have now been re-occupied by a religious order. As the Picardy Tourist Guide states… 'vaulting technique may be studied 'with the lid off' in the ruins of the abbey church'.

PÉRONNE (80)

51k E Amiens

Small town on the river Somme, which here flows through flat marshy country amongst a series of ponds. There is boating and fishing and much market gardening, and it has a 12th century sandstone castle which formed one of the bastions of the ancient city walls.

PIERREFONDS (60)

14k SE Compiègne

Small village on the eastern fringes of the Compiègne Forest with a great castle, once ruined, and then 'restored' by that inveterate re-builder of ruins, Viollet-le-Duc. There is a small lake close to the castle, where rowing boats and pedalos may be hired.

Pierrefonds Château

RAMBURES CHÂTEAU (80) *23k SW Abbeville*
This is a fine 15th century castle with a mellow red brick keep, and four great towers, all within a moat. This has been lived in by the same family (the Rambures) since it was built, and its interior is rich with period furniture, portraits and other objects collected by them over the years.

RARAY CHÂTEAU (60) *10k NE Senlis*
Fine 17th century château in a quiet situation on the edge of woodlands, with lovely arcades facing on to its courtyard. Visitors may only look round the outside, but this is well worthwhile.

RETZ FOREST (02) *N, S and E of Villers-Cotterêts*
An extensive forest with many opportunities for walking, with the Manor House of Longpont (See Page 213) ten kilometres east of Villers, and the Château of Montgobert with its Wood Museum, seven kilometres north-east of Villers.

Hunting in Retz Forest   *The Town Hall, St-Quentin*

RUE (80) *23k NNW Abbeville*
This minute town was once a busy seaport, but it now lies some distance inland. It has several pleasant old houses and a splendid Flamboyant Gothic chapel with elaborate vaulting. There is a recorded commentary with automatic lighting in this fascinating building.

ST-GOBAIN FOREST (02) *Approx 5k W Laon*
Extensive forest covering much of the high limestone plateau between Laon and Chauny. Use Michelin Map 56 to explore this pleasant area in detail.

ST-QUENTIN (02) *73k E Amiens*
Busy industrial town on the upper reaches of the Somme. It has an imposing 12 – 15th century basilica with a great belfry above it and an interesting 9th century crypt beneath. The town hall has a deliciously Flamboyant façade, and the Lécuyer Museum contains a splendid collection of portraits by the 18th century pastel painter, Maurice Quentin de la Tour, which should not be missed. See also the outstanding collection of butterflies and other insects in the Entomological Museum, and the Children's Museum in the rue Gorodon.

ST-RIQUIER (80) *9k ENE Abbeville*
Small town with a great abbey church mostly in the Flamboyant Gothic style. The adjoining abbey buildings house exhibitions relating to rural life in Picardy, and there is also a town belfry which served as a lookout in medieval times.

In the dunes at La Mollière, west of St-Valéry-sur-Somme

ST-VALÉRY-SUR-SOMME (80) *19k NW Abbeville*
Small holiday resort on the inner shore of the Somme estuary, complete with a fishing port and yacht harbour. The ramparts, from which there are fine views out over the long promenade, still retain two of their old gateways. Do not miss the little seamen's chapel of St-Peter, in which hangs a variety of ship models... offerings in thanks for a safe return from the sea.

SENLIS (60) *51k NNE Paris, 51k SE Beauvais*
An ancient town bordered by forest country on almost every side. The old cathedral, with its fine spire, was built in the 12th and 13th centuries and its west
continued

Romanesque figures, Senlis Cathedral   *Cathedral spire, Senlis*

Picardy

'Diana the Huntress', in the Hunting Museum, Senlis

portals are enriched by splendidly carved tympanums. There are many pleasant old streets close to the Cathedral, and the Royal Castle (where Henry V of England married Catherine of France) now houses a most interesting Hunting Museum. This is built up against the remains of Gallo-Roman town walls, and a considerable length of the medieval town walls have also survived. On the western outskirts of the town are the remains of a large Gallo-Roman amphitheatre.

SOISSONS (02)   *98k NE Paris, 265k SE Boulogne*
This town, lying on the banks of the river Aisne, suffered extensive damage in both World Wars, and even its early Gothic Cathedral did not escape unscathed. See especially the south transept with its splendid arcades and cross vaulting. To the south of the Cathedral lies the ruined abbey of St-Jean-des-Vignes, with its magnificent west front still largely intact, and whose cloisters, refectory and wine cellar may be visited. The ruined 12th century abbey of St-Léger now houses an interesting museum.

THE THIÉRACHE (02)   *NE part of Aisne Département*
This pleasantly pastoral area close to the border with Belgium is noted for its cattle farming and its fifty or so fortified churches, most of which are in brick with coloured designs built into their walls. The church towers, round or square, were built almost entirely without windows and often served as a refuge in this troubled frontier region. Some of the best Thiérache churches are at Beaurain, Marly, Englancourt, St-Algis and Autreppes. Start from Guise 27 kilometres east-north-east of St-Quentin, using Michelin Map No 53. Others lie to the south and south-east of Vervins.

VALLOIRES ABBEY (80)   *15k S Montreuil,*
30k N Abbeville
An interesting 18th century abbey in the valley of the Authie, on the site of an abbey founded here in the 12th century.

VAUCLAIR ABBEY (02)   *17k SE Laon*
The ruins of a Cistercian abbey founded in 1134 by monks from Clairvaux (See Bar-sur-Aube Page 89). These are attractively sited in a wooded valley complete with a small lake and are well worth visiting. They lie to the immediate north of the Chemins des Dames (See Page 211).

Ruined Abbey of St-Jean-des-Vignes, Soissons

VEZ (60)   *8k W Villers-Cotterêts*
Small village on the western fringes of the Retz forest, situated above the attractive oak woods of the Automne valley. Here is the lovely Romanesque church of St-Martin, and the largely 14th century castle of Louis d'Orléans, with a chapel in its courtyard housing an interesting museum devoted to the great Valois family.

VILLERS-COTTERÊTS (02)   *29k SE Compiègne*
Small town almost encircled by the lovely Forest of Retz (See Page 215). It owes its origins to the Dukes of Valois who built a hunting lodge here in the 10th century. This has been replaced by a Renaissance château, built by François I in 1535, and which is now an old peoples home. However it is possible to walk in the lovely park and into the forest beyond. Alexandre Dumas was born here in 1802 and there is a museum bearing his name which is worth visiting.

Soissons Cathedral

Vauclair Abbey ruins

Poitou-Charentes

Comprises the following Départements
Charente (16)   Deux-Sèvres (79)
Charente-Maritime (17) Vienne (86)

Situated between the Loire Valley and the vineyards of the Bordeaux country, Poitou-Charentes consists largely of a great rolling plain of rich pasture-land, through which a few large rivers run, some westwards to the Atlantic and some north to join the Loire. The wooded valleys of these rivers and the dozen or so principal forests add interest to an otherwise rather featureless landscape. However it is the towns and villages, the castles and abbeys, that are the great feature of this region, with its exceptional wealth of Romanesque and Angevin architecture, which was due in part to its lying astride the great pilgrim route to St-James of Compostella in north-western Spain, and its connections with the English, Plantagenet Kings. For a complete contrast, do not miss a visit to the impressive Futuroscope Theme Park near Poitiers.

The other great feature of this region is its sparkling Atlantic seaboard stretching southwards from the mysterious Marais-Poitevin, past La Rochelle, to Royan at the mouth of the lovely Gironde estuary. Its mild and comparatively sunny climate has made this a favourite with the French for many years, and with its delightful offshore islands of Ré, Aix and Oléron, and the architectural treasures of its hinterland, the Charente-Maritime coast provides a wonderful holiday opportunity for those coming from further afield.

AIX, ÎLE D' (17)   *10k NW Fouras by passenger ferry, 17k NW Rochefort*
    Small island which was fortified by the great Vauban in the 17th century. The Maison de l'Empereur is the house where Napoleon spent his last four days before finally surrendering to the English fleet on 15th July 1815, having failed to escape to America. It is now a fascinating small museum with relics of Napoleon. Fortunately no cars are allowed on the island, but a day's visit is well worthwhile, and craftsment working on mother-of pearl may be observed.

ANGLES-SUR-ANGLIN (86)   *49k ENE Poitiers*
    Small village dominated by the romantic ivy-clad ruins of a medieval castle. This takes its name from the tribe of Saxons, the Angles, and the locals rather like to be known as 'les Anglais'.

Angles-sur-Anglin

Abadie's Hôtel-de-Ville, Angoulême

ANGOULÊME (16)   *445k SSW Paris, 110k S Poitiers*
    Prosperous industrial town overlooked by its old upper town which is still called 'le plateau', and which is well sited above the Charente valley, with especially fine views westwards from its medieval ramparts. These can be walked for almost their entire length (about half an hour). The Cathedral is a largely Romanesque building, with splendid carvings on its west front. Its restoration in the 19th century by local architect, Paul Abadie (best known for Sacré Coeur in Paris), was perhaps rather heavy-handed, but it is well worth visiting. See also Abadie's Hôtel-de-Ville, which incorporates a medieval keep; and explore the old streets with their many 17th and 18th century buildings.

Argenton-Château

ARGENTON-CHÂTEAU (79)   *21k W Thouars*
    Delightfully situated on a hill above the valleys of the Argenton and the Ouère, this charming village includes the remains of a castle which was largely destroyed in 1793, and a collegiate church which has a fine Romanesque doorway.

AULNAY (17)   *18k NE St-Jean-d'Angély*
    Small village with a wonderful Romanesque church richly sculptured both outside and within, with a variety of animal and plant motifs. This church of St-Pierre-de-la-Tour was on the famous route southwards from Paris to the shrine of St-James at Compostella in north-west Spain... the greatest of all the medieval pilgrim trails across Europe.

Aulnay church

Romanesque capital, Aulnay church

BARBEZIEUX (16) — *33k SE Angoulême*

Pleasant old town with tree shaded-avenues, and older winding streets near the twin towered castle gateway, which houses a small museum.

BASSAC ABBEY (16) — *35k W Angoulême*
3k ESE Jarnac

Large abbey founded by the Benedictines in about 1000, and now housing a community of nuns. The fine Romanesque façade of the abbey church introduces us to a 13th century 'Angevin' interior which is handsomely furnished with 18th century woodwork.

BOIS DE ST-PIERRE LEISURE PARK (86) — *7k S Poitiers*

An extensive 'leisure area' with woodland and small lakes, with opportunities for walking, fishing, and riding.

Richelieu's defences at Brouage

BRESSUIRE (79) — *82k NW Poitiers*

Small town which was burnt down in the 13th, 16th and 18th centuries, and also suffered greatly in the Vendean uprising of 1791, only three years prior to its third great fire. However the church of Notre Dame with its 12th century nave and Renaissance belfry is well worth visiting,as are the ruins of the great fortress above the town to the west.

BROUAGE (17) — *19k SW Rochefort*

A remarkably atmospheric place situated in a great expanse of salt marshes. This was once one of the great seaports of France and although already in decline due to silting of its channel to the sea, it was massively fortified by Cardinal Richelieu between 1627 and 1640. The sea is now some distance away, the port has gone, and only about two hundred people now live here, but the great fortifications are well worth visiting (twenty minutes to walk all round). Samuel Champlain, the founder of Quebec, was born here in 1567.

Richelieu's defences at Brouage

CHÂTELLERAULT (86) — *35k NNE Poitiers*

A prosperous and charming town on the river Vienne, here crossed by the lovely 16th century Henri IV Bridge with its two stone towers. There are many charming old houses, one of which, the Maison Descartes, was the early home of this great 17th century philosopher, and is now a Descartes Museum. See also the interesting Car Museum, which is situated in an old weapon workshop.

CHAUVIGNY (86) — *23k E Poitiers*

Small town on a hillside above the Vienne, with the ruins of no fewer than four castles, and a Romanesque church with a series of outstandingly interesting sculptured capitals to its nave and choir.

Romanesque capitals, Chauvigny

COGNAC (16) — *42k W Angoulême*

This prosperous and agreeable town astride the Charente is noted the world over for the production of brandy, the export of which only began in the 17th century. Most of the storage buildings where the distillation and maturing takes place, are situated along the quays of the river, and many can be visited. The Scotsman, Otard, established his brandy business in the old château of the Valois family, where François I was born, and this may be visited both for its historical connections and for a view of its brandy storage casks. See also the rambling streets of the old town

Vaulted brandy cellars at Cognac

continued

approached through the 16th century Porte St-Jacques and the interesting Museum and Art Gallery situated in the public gardens.

CONFOLENS (16)   *71k SSE Poitiers*
A pretty little town at the confluence (hence its name) of the rivers Vienne and Goire, with many attractive old houses lining the narrow streets in the angle between the two rivers. The Vienne is spanned by a 14th century bridge and the church of St-Barthélémy has a pleasing Romanesque doorway.

Confolens

DAMPIERRE-SUR-BOUTONNE CHÂTEAU (17)
7k NW Aulnay
A delightful 16th century Renaissance château standing on a lush little island in the river Boutonne. The interior is lightly furnished but the coffered ceiling of the upper of the two galleries is beautifully decorated.

FUTUROSCOPE (86)   *10k N Poitiers*
A large theme park dedicated to advanced technology, with much futuristic architecture, a cinema with a giant screen, a Children's World, 'Galaxies of the Future' and many other attractions. There's something here for those of every age.

FORÊT DE CHIZÉ ZOO (79)   *20k S Niort,*
7k SE Beauvoir-sur-Niort
Twenty five hectares in the heart of the large Chizé Forest with a wide range of mammals, birds and reptiles. There is a bar, and ample space for picnics. Not far away there is an attractive Butterfly Museum. Ask at zoo for directions.

At Forêt-de-Chizé Zoo.
A Forêt-de-Chizé Zoo Photograph

FOURAS (17)   *13k NW Rochefort*
Attractive little seaside resort with sandy beaches and a regular ferry service across to the Île d'Aix (See Page 217), and the Île d'Oléron (See Page 221). The impressive fortress has a 15th century keep and was strengthened by the great Vauban. It was from Fouras that Napoleon left for the Île d'Aix, in July 1815 thus leaving the mainland of France for the last time, and a monument marks the historic place.

LIGUGÉ ABBEY (86)   *10k S Poitiers*
This was the oldest monastery of the Gauls, having been founded by St-Martin in the ruins of a Roman villa. The present abbey chuch dates from the 16th century, but excavations have revealed foundations of several earlier buildings including that of the villa.

LOUDUN (86)   *56k NNW Poitiers*
Small town on a hill, the medieval walls of which have been replaced by attractive tree lined boulevards. There are many narrow winding streets and a wealth of 16th and 17th century houses, some of which are timbered. The 11th century keep, the Tour Carrée, is sited above the town and there are fine views out over the surrounding countryside from its roof. In 1634 a young priest was burned to death in the market place, having been found guilty of bewitching a nun, and it was this event that inspired Aldous Huxley's book,'The Devils of Loudun'.

THE MARAIS POITEVIN REGIONAL NATURE PARK (17, 79, 85)
This is a fascinating area of marshland intersected by a myriad of canals, and sometimes described as the 'Green Venice'. It is shared between this region and that of the Loire Valley West. Over forty kilometres long and *continued*

In the Marais Poitevin

thirty kilometres wide, the former Gulf of Poitou has silted up and has been reclaimed from the sea. In this strange land everything moves by water, including farm animals and harvested crops. A flotilla of 'plattes' (flat bottom boats) still circulates here. Boatmen take visitors along these wonderfully quiet waterways, and some of the better known centres from which to explore are Courçon, St-Hilaire-le-Palud, Sansais, Arcais and Damvix, all of which may be reached by driving approximately westward from Niort (Use Michelin Map No 71).

In the Marais Poitevin, near Niort

MARENNES (17)   *52k S La Rochelle*
Small town on the edge of great oyster beds, with fine views out over the marshes at the mouth of the Seudre river from its 15th century church tower. There is an Oyster Museum at Bourcefranc four kilometres to the north-west, where there are still more oyster beds.

MARTHON (16)   *23k E Angoulême*
Minute village dominated by the ruins of a fine 12th century castle.

MELLE (79)   *56k SW Poitiers*
Small town remarkable only for its three Romanesque churches. St-Savinien has only an exterior doorway, but St-Hilaire is not only pleasantly situated near the riverside, but has a most interesting series of carvings on its capitals. St-Pierre, standing to the north of the town, has a fine south doorway.

Oyster grower at Marennes   *Niort castle*

NIORT (79)   *73k WSW Poitiers*
Busy commercial and industrial town, Niort is the capital of the Deux-Sèvres Département and is situated on the river Sèvres. The great castle was once thought to have been built by Henry II and his son Richard Lionheart, but it was almost certainly a creation of the French. Two keep towers and the buildings between them are all that remain, but these are worth visiting, and there is a Museum of Poitevin costumes within. See also the charming 15th century 'old Town Hall', and the Musée des Beaux Arts next to the present Town Hall.

OIRON (79)   *15k WSW Loudun,*
                        56k NNW Poitiers
Small village with two remarkable Renaissance buildings, both the work of the Gouffiers, the father being Chamberlain to François I, and the son, Claude, being the Master of Horse. The father built the lovely Collegiate church and started the outstandingly fine château, which was completed by his son. See especially the arcaded gallery, with the names of Claude's favourite horses inscribed upon its walls. Claude Gouffier, the Comte de Caravas, inspired by his extravagant life style, the story by Perrault of Le Chat Botté (Puss in Boots), and has achieved immortality as the 'Marquis de Carabas'.

Beach on the Île d'Oléron   *Oyster growers' boats, at the Île d'Oléron*

OLÉRON, ÎLE DE (17)   *40k NW Royan,*
                                164k SW Poitiers
This is the second largest of France's offshore islands after Corsica, and is connected to the mainland by a long toll bridge. There are two small towns... Le Château-d'Oléron, and St-Pierre-d'Oléron, the former being the largest oyster centre in France, the latter being the island's wine-making centre. There is an unusually mild climate, fine beaches, excellent fishing, and several pleasant camping sites and hotels.

Sailing dinghies at the Île d'Oléron

Romanesque church at Parthenay

Notre-Dame-de-la-Grande, Poitiers

St-Hilaire-le-Grand, Poitiers

Pons Castle

LA PALMYRE ZOO PARK (17)   *15k NW Royan*

A fine zoo in eight hectares of pine forest and sand dunes, with over six hundred species in its collection. There is a buvette and a souvenir shop.

PARTHENAY (79)   *51k WSW Poitiers*

Busy little agricultural centre, with a fascinating, partially walled town, which stood on the famous pilgrim route to Compostella. It is best approached over the Pont St-Jacques, through the Porte St-Jacques, and along the lovely old Rue de la Vaux St-Jacques (St-Jacques being the St-James of Compostella). There are the remains of a castle above to our right, with lawns and three surviving towers; and there are three churches surviving intact, and several other ruined ones... all reminding us of Parthenay's importance as a pilgrim's staging post.

PETITES MINAUDIÈRES LEISURE PARK (86)
9k SE Châtellerault

A pleasantly wooded area with two lakes. There are opportunities for fishing, bathing and boating, and a variety of other sports. Also a park with wild boars, and a children's playground (happily well isolated from each other).

POITIERS (86)   *335k SSW Paris,*
178k ESE Nantes

Large industrial city which used to be the capital of the old province of Poitou, and which is now the capital of the Vienne Département. Poitiers still has a largely unspoilt 'old city' bordered on two sides by the river Clain. The victory of the Black Prince and his army of Englishmen over the French King, in 1356, took place at Nouaillé-Maupertuis, about nine kilometres south-east of the city. Poitiers has however been an important town since Roman times, and an early centre of Christianity. See especially the Gothic Cathedral, with its three parallel naves and great apse; the Baptistery of St-Jean, dating from the 4th century and one of the earliest Christian buildings in France, which now houses an interesting museum; the Romanesque churches of Ste-Radegonde, Notre-Dame-de-la-Grande and St-Hilaire-le-Grand; the Musée St-Croix; and the Palais de Justice, with its splendid Gothic Grande Salle and Tour Maubergeon. The Hôtel Fumé was once part of the ancient university, and both Francis Bacon and Descartes studied here, while Rabelais also visited it from time to time.

PONS (17)   *91k SE La Rochelle*

This small town on the river Seugne was astride one of the pilgrim routes to Compostella, and here has survived at least part of a pilgrim hospice, built outside the walls to receive those who arrived after the town gates has closed for the night. This is one of the very few pilgrimage buildings other than churches that has survived. See also the great square keep of Pons castle, and the Château d'Usson to the south-east of the town, which was moved and re-erected here in the 19th century... a most fascinating piece of restoration.

LE QUÉROY CAVES (16)   *15k E Angoulême*

These are in wooded limestone country and are near one end of underground water-courses, the other end of which is to be found at the Sources de la Touvre (8k E Angoulême), a pleasant area with trees and pools, where there is Son-et-Lumière in July and August.

RÉ, ÎLE DE (17)   *480k SW Paris. By Ferry from La Pallice, near La Rochelle.*
A large flat island off La Pallice, with several small villages, many of which have low, white walled houses with green shutters. There are long beaches, salt marshes and oyster beds. There are also vineyards and market gardens that are famous for their asparagus, and at the north-western tip of the island there is a lighthouse from which there are fine views. Visitors to this island will find several hotels and camping sites.

ROCHEBRUNE CHÂTEAU (16)   *18k SE Confolens, 10k W St-Junien*
Fine moated château with four towers dating from the 11th century.

On the Île-de-Ré

ROCHE COURBON CHÂTEAU (17) *19k NW Saintes, 2k N St-Porchaire*
Described by Pierre Loti as the "Castle of the Sleeping Beauty", Roche Courbon is a splendidly romantic 15th century castle, more feudal than Renaissance in feeling. It is wonderfully sited in a narrow valley on the edge of marshes, and there are lovely water gardens and a Renaissance gatehouse. Son et Lumière during the season.

ROCHEFORT (17)   *30k SSE La Rochelle*
This was built by Colbert between 1666 and 1668 in a great bend of the Charente, and its shipyard and arsenal became one of the most important elements of French naval power. Little remains of its great fortifications, but the grid pattern of the old town clearly reveals it as a planned entity. See the interesting Naval Museum and the little Loti Museum in the house where the famous traveller and author, 'Pierre Loti' was born in 1850.

Roche-Courbon Château

Market-place, La Rochelle

LA ROCHEFOUCAULD (16)   *22k NE Angoulême*
Small town on the river Tardoire, with an interesting pharmacy in the old hospital, which is open to visitors, and a splendid château, which is not. This is however well worth looking at from outside, with its great square 12th century keep surrounded by elegant Renaissance château buildings.

LA ROCHELLE (17)   *476k SW Paris, 188k NNW Bordeaux*
Busy commercial and industrial city, and France's fifth largest fishing port, La Rochelle is also a lively holiday resort, with pleasure boating, beaches, good shops, and a frequent ferry service to the Ile de Ré from adjoining La Pallice. The entrance to the old port is still protected by the twin towers of St-Nicolas and de la Chaine (between which there was a chain which could be stretched out to bar the entry of shipping), and overlooked by the older Tour de la Lanterne, the original lighthouse. See also the Porte de la Grosse Horloge, a medieval gateway; the massive Hôtel de Ville, with its fine Renaissance front; and the museums, amongst which is the fascinating New World Museum. Wander along the streets of the old town, but perhaps best of all, sit at one of the many cafés on the quayside watching the comings and goings of boats of all shapes and sizes.

La Rochelle by night

ROYAN (17)   *70k S La Rochelle, 163k SW Poitiers*
A really excellent modern seaside resort, due largely to the fact that it was terribly damaged during the 1939 – 1945 War, and that it was imaginatively re-built
continued

Entrance to the old Port, La Rochelle

Fishing boats at Royan

Poitou-Charentes

St-Savin and the River Gartempe

soon afterwards. There are great stretches of golden sands, every amusement that the seaside holiday-maker could wish for, elegant shops, a wide range of hotels and restaurants, many camp sites and so many car parks that it seldom seems crowded. See the brilliantly designed modern church of Notre-Dame, and take a boat trip across the mouth of the Gironde Estuary to the Pointe de Grave, and beyond to the Cordouan Lighthouse. Drive north-westwards to the Coubre Forest and the Coubre Lighthouse, which may be visited.

ST-GEORGE-DE-DIDONNE (17) *3k SE Royan*
This popular holiday resort is almost part of Royan (See above), but it still has a character of its own, and is a quieter place than its neighbour, and perhaps more suitable for families with young children.

ST-JEAN-D'ANGÉLY (17) *100k SW Poitiers*
Busy market town, with narrow streets, many of which are lined with pleasant old houses. The great Benedictine abbey that gave shelter to pilgrims on their way to Compostella, was largely destroyed during the Wars of Religion and the ambitious plan for its replacement was only partly completed at the Revolution. It therefore stands today, still only half built. However the 14th century gateway with its clock tower, and the handsome 15th century fountain, are well worth seeing.

Painted roof, St-Savin Abbey

St-Trojan Tourist Tramway. Photograph by Philippe Gala

ST-JOUIN-DE-MARNES (79) *18k SE Thouars*
Minute village with a fine fortified abbey church, built by the Benedictines in the 12th century. Its splendidly proportioned interior is well worth visiting, and is convincing evidence of the wealth and power of the Benedictines.

ST-MAIXENT-L'ÉCOLE (79) *50k WSW Poitiers*
Busy little town on the river Sèvre, which grew up around a great abbey, later almost entirely destroyed by the Huguenots. However the 17th century abbey church that largely replaced the medieval one is well worth visiting.

ST-SAVIN (86) *41k E Poitiers*
Pleasant village astride the river Gartempe, with a fine Benedictine abbey church... a Romanesque building with its tower topped by a graceful 14th century spire. Within will be found one of the great art treasures of France, perhaps the finest series of 12th century mural paintings in the whole country. Take a pair of binoculars if you wish to study these in detail.

The Abbaye-aux-Dames, Saintes

Arch of Germanicus, Saintes

ST-TROJAN TOURIST TRAMWAY (17)
At S end of Île d'Oléron
A six kilometres long, narrow gauge line at the southern end of the Île d'Oléron, winding through a pine forest, close to beaches, and ending up beyond the dunes near the shoreline facing the Maumusson Channel which lies between the island and the mainland.

SAINTES (17) *126k SW Poitiers*
This busy town on the river Charente was an important centre in Roman times and its Roman bridge was only replaced in the 19th century. At this time the fine Roman Arch of Germanicus which had stood upon it since the first century was re-erected on the west *continued*

Roman amphitheatre, Saintes

bank of the river. The great Roman Amphitheatre lies to the west of the old town, and is a most impressive monument (it had room for 20,000 spectators). There is also an interesting Archaeological Museum.

However Saintes is not only a Roman town, for it lay astride one of the great medieval pilgrim routes south to Compostella, and within its old town will be found two outstanding Romanesque buildings, the richness of which must have been largely due to their function as pilgrimage churches... the Abbaye aux Dames, and the church of St-Eutrope, with its splendid 12th century crypt. But apart from these fascinating items, the old town of Saintes provides many pleasures amongst its narrow and attractive streets... handsome 18th century houses, several museums, and pleasant quays along the Charente, from whence boat trips may be taken in summer down to Rochefort.

Roman theatre, Sanxay

SANXAY (86)   *31k WSW Poitiers*
Quiet village in the valley of the little river Vonne, with the interesting Gallo-Roman site including the excavated remains of a theatre, baths and temple. This is a pleasantly grassy place surrounded by trees, and well worth visiting.

TALMONT (17)   *16k SE Royan*
Attractive little flower-decked village above white limestone cliffs with the church of Ste-Radegonde on the very edge, above the Gironde Estuary. This only consists of part of the original, as the nave collapsed into the sea several centuries ago.

Ste-Radegonde church, Talmont

THOUARS (79)   *66k NW Poitiers,*
34k SSW Saumur
Attractive little town with its castle perched on a cliff overlooking the river Thouet. The castle is not open to the public, but there is an elegant Italian Renaissance chapel within its walls. See especially the medieval main gateway (the Porte du Prévost), the Romanesque façade of the church of St-Médard, and the 12th century Tour du Prince de Galles.

TOUFFOU CHÂTEAU (86)   *21k ENE Poitiers*
Fine château on the west bank of the river Vienne, with a 16th century Renaissance building linking the St-Georges tower to the keep. This keep was surrounded by dry moats and four angle towers, of which the St-Georges tower was one. The St-Jean tower has attractive wall paintings representing the various agricultural tasks of the four seasons of the year.

Thouars   *Charente countryside*

VILLEBOIS-LA VALETTE (16)   *24k SSE Angoulême*
Medieval hill-top village in delightful wooded countryside, with walls and six towers, and a château which was rebuilt in the 17th century.

COGNAC... the Brandy Country
An extensive area centred upon the town of Cognac, and famous throughout the world for the production of France's finest brandies, distilled here as in Armagnac, from grapes specially grown for the purpose. The word brandy is derived from the Dutch word for burnt wine... brandewijn, and it was the Dutch demand for this drink that first stimulated its production from the often indifferent wines of the area inland from La Rochelle and Rochefort.

Touffou Château

PROVENCE

Savoy and Dauphiny Alps
(SEE PAGE 252)

ITAL

Queyr
Region
Natur
Park

La Grave

Briancon

Ecrins National Park

Vallouise

Château Queyras
St-Véran
Notre-Dar
-de-Clausis

St-Firmin

05

Guillestre

The Route Napoléon

Embrun

Gap

Serrre-Poncon Barrage and La

Rhône Valley
(SEE PAGE 242)

Barcelonette

Praloup

Super-Sauze

Donzère-Mondragon
Barrage

Vaison-la-Romaine

Bollène

Sisteron

04

Mont Ventoux

Brantes

Languedoc
-Roussillon
(SEE PAGE 130)

Orange

84

Digne

Carpentras

Châteauneuf-
du-Pape

Nesque Gorges

Entrevaux

Fontaine-de-Vaucluse

St-Michel
Observatory

Moustiers-
Ste-Marie

Castillon Barrage
and Lake

L'Isle-sur-la-Sorgue

Senanque Abbey

Côte d'Azur

Avignon

Gordes

The Luberon

Riez

Castellane

Apt

Barbentane

Cavaillon

Oppède-le-Vieux

Ménerbes

Manosque

Verdon Gorge

Tarascon

St-Rémy

Lourmarin

Ansouis Château

Ste-Croix Lake

Mons

Beaucaire

Golfe

Fontvieille

Les Baux

Cadanet

Ste-Croix Lake

Bel-Homme Pass

Bargemon

Montmajour Abbey

Les Alpilles

Silvacane Abbey

Villecroze

Fréjus Zoo Par

Arles

Salon-de-
Provence

Barben Zoo Park

Draguignan

Le Tray

Mas du Pont
de Rousty

The

**Aix-en-
-Provence**

Barjols

Les Arcs

St-Raphael

Méjanes

Entrecasteaux

Fréjus

Ginès

13

St-Maximin
la-Ste-Baume

Le Thoronet
Abbey

Ste-Maxime
St-Tropez

Pont de Gau
Bouman Museum

Etang de Berre

Brignoles

Port-Grimaud

Petit
Sauvage
Ferry

Les Saintes
Maries
de-la-Mer

Camargue

Martigues

83

Grimaud

Aubagne

Sanary
Bandol
Zoo

Marseille

Bormes
Le Lavandou

Sormiou
Les Calanques
Port Miou

Cassis

Bandol

Sanary-sur-mer

Toulon

Hyères

Giens

Iles d'Hyères

Ile du Levant

Ile de Port Cros

Ile de Porquerolles

0	10	20	30	40	50

MILES

0	20	40	60	80

KILOMETRES

Provence

Comprises the following Départements
Alpes-de-Haut-Provence (04) Var (83)
Hautes-Alpes (05) Vaucluse (84)
Bouches-du-Rhône (13)

The Romans called this Region PROVINCIA, the 'Province', the most important part of their earliest conquest outside Italy, which itself was regarded as extending westwards to the River Var. Following the gradual decline of the Roman Empire, Provence suffered at the hands of Vandals, Goths and Saracens, but the traditions of Rome and the early Christian church remained much stronger here than in northern France, and the spirit of Roman civilization lingers still in its towns and cities, and in the colourful countryside in which they stand. Provence may have been absorbed into the kingdom of France in 1481, but in many ways the true Provençal still regards himself as someone rather different to those 'northerners' living up beyond Valence. However Provence is itself a region of remarkable contrasts, stretching from the marshes of the Camargue to the snow clad mountain tops and deep valleys of the Alps, from the beautiful and diverse series of coastal resorts between Marseille and the Esterel Massif to sunlit Roman and medieval towns including Arles, Avignon and Aix, and the enchanting Provençal countryside now enriched by massive irrigation schemes, but still retaining the flavour so beloved by Cézanne and Van Gogh, and by so many other artists, writers and musicians who worked here.

Hot, and in places, overcrowded in high summer, Provence is a sheer delight in spring or autumn, and we shall always remember our drives down the Rhône valley out of a northern winter, into the spring sunshine waiting for us somewhere south of Lyons or Vienne. If we have sometimes favoured the autoroute at the expense of quieter and more subtle roads, those who know the strength of Provence's pull in springtime will perhaps overlook our impatience to be re-charged with its magic once again.

AIX-EN-PROVENCE (13)

752k SSE Paris,
31k N Marseille

Established in 122 BC by the Romans, who had destroyed the Celto-Ligurian hill top 'capital' at Entremont, three kilometres to the north, Aix has remained a city of considerable importance ever since. In the 12th century it became the capital of the Counts of Provence, and was perhaps in its heyday during the reign of Good King René in the 15th century. Count Mirabeau, the central figure of the Revolution during its early days, was a member of one of the great families that left their mark on Aix, with many handsome 17th and 18th century houses, and Mirabeau himself is remembered by the name of the finest of Aix's many tree lined avenues, the Cours Mirabeau. There is so much to see in this busy, but delightful city... the Cathedral, with its lovely Romanesque cloisters and its series of tapestries intended originally for Canterbury Cathedral, the elegant streets and charming fountains, the several museums, especially the Musée Granet with its excellent collection of paintings, and the library which includes King René's 'Book of Hours' amongst its treasures. There is much else besides, and a wide selection of hotels and restaurants to tempt the visitor to linger here, and to absorb at least something of the spirit and culture of this sunlit region.

The Cours Mirabeau, Aix   Fountain at Aix

LES ALPILLES (13)

A miniature mountain range with limestone summits bare of vegetation, which consists elsewhere of coarse grass and scrub punctuated by the odd cypress tree, with olives and almonds growing in the valleys. These are one of the best known elements of the Provençal landscape, and are at their best just to the south of St-Rémy.

Cathedral cloisters, Aix

Provence

The Arena at Arles.
Photograph by Peter Titchmarsh

At the Roman theatre, Arles.
Photograph by Peter Titchmarsh

St-Trophime, Arles

Les Alyscamps, Arles

ANSOUIS CHÂTEAU (84)   23k N Aix-en-Provence

Charming château which has been in the hands of the same family since the 9th century. From the outside it appears to be largely a 17th century building, but it incorporates many medieval features within. The hanging gardens are a delight, and there is a Romanesque chapel which is now the parish church.

APT (84)   52k E Avignon

Situated beneath the northern slopes of the Luberon, this small town used to be a Roman colony, and there is Roman stonework in the crypts beneath the former Cathedral of Ste-Anne, which is itself well worth visiting. There are also Roman rooms incorporated in the cellars of many houses nearby, and these are thought to have been looking on to the Forum. See the Archaelogical Museum, and the remains of the Roman 'Julian Bridge' a short distance outside the town.

LES ARCS (83)   10k S Draguignan

Pleasant little medieval village with the remains of a château, and a little church containing a fine 16th century retable with 16 panels.

ARLES (13)   727k SSE Paris, 92k WNW Marseille

Charming southern town astride the main arm of the Rhône a short distance below the point where the 'Little Rhône' branches westwards, to form the western boundary of the Camargue (See Page 230). Arles rose to importance early in the Roman era and soon became the Roman capital of Provence and one of the great capitals of the Roman Empire. Much of the older part of the town is dominated by the great arena, which could once hold 21,000 spectators, and which was turned into a fortified stronghold after the fall of the Empire (hence the remaining square towers). This is now the scene of many bull fights, although happily bull-fighting in France does not involve the killing of bulls. The nearby Roman theatre is, like the arena, remarkably well preserved, and regular performances of drama and opera take place here in summertime. There is so much else to see in Arles, but do not miss the Jesuit church, with its Museum of Christian Art, below which there are three galleries which are actually the foundations of buildings that once stood around the great Roman Forum, the only sign of which, above ground, are two pillars in the Place du Forum. See also the church of St-Trophime, where St-Augustine was consecrated as the first Bishop of Canterbury; the Alyscamps, a wide tree-shaded roadway on either side of which there are a beautiful series of Roman tombs... a favourite subject of the artist Van Gogh; the Museum of Pagan Art; the Réattu Museum; and the Arlaten Museum, which was created by the poet Mistral, using the Nobel Prize money he won in 1904. Our short description cannot do justice to this delightful town, but it is not surprising that it was a favourite not only of Van Gogh and Mistral, but also of Daudet, Bizet and Gounod, amongst a host of other artists and writers.

AUBAGNE (13)   17k E Marseille

Charming old town on a hill from which there are fine views out over the surrounding countryside. Pottery is made here and there is an interesting museum devoted to the Foreign Legion, which moved its headquarters to Aubagne in 1962, this having been based at Sidi-Bel-Abbès in Algeria since its foundation in 1831.

AVIGNON (84)   *686k SSE Paris, 100k NW Marseille*
Situated on the Rhône a short distance above the
point where it is joined by that other great Provençal
river, the Durance, Avignon is one of the most
important cities in the history of France, and remains a
bustling lively place, and full of character. The Pont St-
Bénézet (the Pont d'Avignon) was one of the first stone
bridges to be thrown across the Rhône, and dates from
the 12th or 13th centuries, while the encircling city walls
were built in the 14th century, when the Popes moved
from Rome to Avignon to escape the intimidation of the
great Roman families. The massive Palace of the Popes
was built in the mid 14th century, and is a splendid
example of medieval architecture, with a most
interesting interior. See also the Cathedral, which is
almost next door to the Palace, and then walk a short
distance northwards, to the Rochers des Doms, a
dramatic viewpoint, out over the Rhône to the
mountains including the distant Mont Ventoux (See
Page 240). Near to the Rochers is the Petit Palais which
houses a fine collection of paintings. See also the
handsome 17th century Hôtel des Monnaies, and the
lovely 18th century Calvet Museum, with its
outstanding collection of French paintings, and the
churches of St-Pierre and St-Didier. But above all, take
time to wander at leisure around this lovely old city, for
it is impossible to appreciate its charms in a visit of only
a few hours.

The Pont d'Avignon

BANDOL (83)   *51k ESE Marseille*
Lively seaside resort with many hotels, a long
promenade and a colourful harbour. The little Île-de-
Bendor, just offshore, can be reached by motorboat in
under ten minutes.

The Palace of the Popes, Avignon

BARBEN ZOO PARK (13)   *8k E Salon-de-Provence*
A large zoo with over three hundred animals. Also an
aquarium, a large aviary, and an historic château, once
owned by King René. Buvettes, souvenir shop,
restaurants, picnic areas.

BARBENTANE (13)   *10k SW Avignon*
Small town with two medieval gateways and a 17th
century château, with an elegantly furnished interior
which is well worth visiting.

BARCELONNETTE (04)   *70k ESE Gap*
Delightful summer resort in a splendid mountain
setting, with several skiing centres nearby, notably Pra-
loup and Super-Sauze. There are a variety of hotels in
the three resorts named.

The Palace of the Popes, Avignon   *Sunlit terrace at Bandol*

BARGEMON (83)   *21k NE Draguignan*
Charming little medieval town at the foot of the Pre-
Alps of Grasse, with many old narrow streets within its
ramparts, and several small tree-shaded squares
ornamented with fountains. Both churches are worth
visiting. There are splendid views from the Bel-Homme
Pass, six kilometres to the north.

BARJOLS (83)   *64k E Aix-en-Provence*
Fascinating little medieval market town with a ruined
château overlooking its narrow streets and tree-shaded
squares, with no fewer than thirty three fountains... a
marvellous place on a hot day... and all in a quiet valley
amongst wooded hills. Do not miss a visit to the fine
collegiate church which dates from the 11th century.

The Île-de-Bendor, off Bandol

Provence

High summer at Les Baux
Photograph by Peter Titchmarsh

Spring at Brantes

Riding in the Camargue

Bulls on the Camargue Photograph by Peter Titchmarsh.

Gypsy music and dance, in the Camargue

Flamingoes in the Camargue

LES BAUX-DE-PROVENCE (13) *19k NE Arles*

Now half in ruins, this village, built into the very rock of a hilly spur, was once a thriving town and powerful fortress. There are many curious houses and chapels at least partly hewn out of the solid rock, and there are breath-taking views south and westwards out over Arles, and the Camargue. See especially the delightful little Place St-Vincent, and the ruined château which has a 14th century keep. This is inevitably a popular tourist port of call, and should if possible be visited out of season, or early in the day.

BOLLÈNE (84) *25k NNE Orange*

Small town in the Rhône valley with the great Donzère-Mondragon Barrage only a short distance northwards. This is still regarded as one of the great post-war achievements of France, and is well worth visiting. There is a troglodyte village at Barry, five kilometres to the north.

BRANTES (84) *65k NE Avignon, 30k E Vaison-la-Romaine*

The ruins of an old castle rise above this picturesque village, which is itself situated beneath the northern slopes of Mont Ventoux. The village is well known for its arts and crafts, and several craftsmen can usually be seen at work here.

BRIANCON (05) *680k SE Paris, 116k ESE Grenoble*

Attractive frontier town standing at no less than 1326 metres above sea level, Briançon was fortified by the great Vauban, with walls encircling the old town, to which is attached a separate citadel. Walk up the old town's Grande Rue which has a stream flowing down it, and visit the citadel from which there are splendid views out over the surrounding mountains.

BRIGNOLES (83) *50k NNE Toulon*

This is now a busy little industrial centre, due to the mining of bauxite at several sites nearby, but the old town is being restored, and there is a museum in the château, which was once the Palace of the Counts of Provence.

CAMARGUE, THE (13) *To the South of Arles*

A vast low lying region situated between the Great and Little Rhône... typical 'delta' country, with pools and marshland and great wide meadows inhabited by sheep, horses and herds of bulls intended largely for the bull rings. There is a Nature Reserve* around the Étang de Vaccarès in which live thousands of birds including egrets, flamingoes, Egyptian ibises and Moroccan storks, as well as beavers and a variety of other animals*. The northern part of the Camargue has been drained and turned into rice-fields, while much of the rest is now devoted to 'ranches' where horse riding holidays may be taken.

Drive south-west from Arles, calling first at the Mas du Pont de Rousty, which is now an interesting Museum of the Camargue, and on through Ginès, where there is an Information Centre relating to the Camargue and a fine viewpoint over the adjoining lagoon. Just beyond this, there is a Bird Sanctuary at Pont de Gau, and then the Boumian Museum, with a series of tableaux incorporating wax figures illustrating various aspects of Camargue life. From here it is only a short distance to Stes-Maries-de-la-Mer (See Page *continued*

238). It is possible to take a boat trip on the Petit Rhône from its mouth a short distance to the west of Stes-Maries, up to the Petit Sauvage Ferry, and this provides a fine impression of this mysterious area.
Visits only by special permission from the authorities, although there is a public viewpoint near Méjanes.

CARPENTRAS (84)   23k NE Avignon
Busy agricultural centre, which was noted in Roman times for its manufacture of chariots (its name is derived from the Gallic name for a two-wheeled chariot). See especially the small Gallo-Roman triumphal arch, the 16th century gateway (the Porte d'Orange), the Cathedral of St-Siffrein, the former Bishop's Palace, the 15th century hospital with its fine staircase and pharmacy, and the 18th century Synagogue, the interesting interior of which may be visited.

Little train at Méjanes, in the Camargue

CASSIS (13)   23k S Marseille
Delightful Provençal fishing village in a deep bay. It has several hotels and restaurants and is inevitably crowded at holiday times with day visitors from nearby Marseille. The coast between here and Marseille consists of white limestone cliffs pierced by steep sided fiords (known as Les Calanques). Here, overlooked by deserted scrub country, are a wonderful series of secluded little beaches reached only on foot or by boat.

CASTELLANE (04)   54k SE Digne, 63k NW Grasse
Pleasant old town on the Route Napoléon's crossing of the river Verdon, with a 15th century bridge (the Pont du Roc), a series of little medieval streets, an 11th century Romanesque church, and a small pilgrim chapel, Notre-Dame-du-Roc, on a rocky hill above the old bridge (both to the east of the town).

White horses of the Camargue
Photograph by Peter Titchmarsh

CASTILLON BARRAGE AND LAKE (04)
8k N Castellane
This dam across the Verdon has created a great lake in the hills north of Castellane, and is one of the outstanding features of the upper Verdon valley. Below it there is a smaller lake created by the Chaudanne Barrage, and a visit to this can easily be combined with a visit to the Castillon Barrage.

CAVAILLON (84)   27k SE Avignon
Important market town on the banks of the Durance, at the western end of the Luberon hills. Evidence of its importance as a trading centre as long ago as Roman times may be found in the interesting Archaeological Museum, and in the carvings on the remains of its triumphal arch. See also the church of Notre-Dame, which has delightful Romanesque cloisters.

Beach at Cassis

Port-Miou, in the Calanques, west of Cassis

CHÂTEAUNEUF-DU-PAPE (84)   13k S Orange
Small village dominated by the remains of the keep which was part of the Avignon Popes' summer residence. The vineyards that are now world famous were once the personal property of these Popes, and are now also notable as being the first vineyards to be granted the rights that have since become known as Appellation Contrôlée (in 1923).

DIGNE (04)   744k SE Paris, 134k NW Cannes
This relatively small town is the capital of the Alpes-de-Haute-Provence Département, and is situated on the Route Napoléon, in quiet hill country beside the river Bléone. There are fine views from the little hill village of Courbons about six kilometres to the west.

The Calanque de Sormiou, west of Cassis

Sunlit shore at Dramont, near St-Raphael

Entrevaux

In the Écrins National Park

Le Château Restaurant, Fontaine-de-Vaucluse

Daudet's Windmill, Fontvieille

DRAGUIGNAN (83)   *106k E Aix-en-Provence*
Here is a charming 'old town' centred upon its medieval clock tower, with two old gateways and parts of its town walls. Beyond it is the open planned 19th century town, partly laid out by Baron Haussmann, who is noted for his great re-building of Paris. See the Museum and visit the delightful Botanical Gardens.

ÉCRINS NATIONAL PARK (05, 38)
This was created in 1973 and covers a great mountain mass stretching northwards from Serre-Ponçon Lake almost to the Grenoble — Briançon road. Rare fauna to be seen here include the chamois and the golden eagle, and the area is crossed by the long distance path GR 54, although this is only practical for the experienced, between the end of June and mid September. There is a 'Maison du Parc' at Vallouise, twenty five kilometres south-west of Briançon, and further information may be obtained from the Parc National des Écrins, 7, rue Colonel-Roux, 05000 Gap.

EMBRUN (05)   *49k SSE Briançon*
Small town on a rock overlooking the Durance river a short distance above the point where it flows into Serre-Ponçon Lake. The former Cathedral dates from the 12th to the 14th century and is one of the finest churches in the French alps. See the rose window with its 15th century glass, and its organ of about the same date, making it one of the oldest in France. Its treasury contains a remarkable collection of ornaments, pictures and sacred vessels. There are fine views southwards from the 12th century Tour Brune, which is the only surviving part of the Archbishop's Palace.

ENTRECASTEAUX (83)   *25k NE Brignoles*
Medieval village in a remote valley site, with Roman remains, a fortified medieval church and a 17th century château with gardens laid out by Le Nôtre.

ENTREVAUX (04)   *72k NW Nice*
Charming little town in the middle reaches of the Var. This river once formed the frontier between France and the Dukedom of Savoy, and the great fort here was built by Louis XIV's formidable engineer Vauban in 1695. There is a small Historical Museum, a former Cathedral with a stout bell tower built by the Knights Templar, and many pleasant old houses.

FONTAINE-DE-VAUCLUSE (84)   *29k E Avignon*
Small village at the foot of the Vaucluse plateau, with a spring or 'fountain' where the river Sorgue emerges from a cave at the foot of a cliff. There is son-et-lumière here in summer, and there is a splendid view from the ruins of the 13th century castle. The poet Petrarch lived in this village for sixteen years after his departure from the Papal Court of Avignon, and there is a museum here devoted to his memory.

FONTVIEILLE (13)   *10k NE Arles*
About two kilometres south of this village will be found the interesting remains of the Roman aqueduct that conveyed water from Les Alpilles (See Page 227) to Arles, but Fontvieille is best known for the windmill associated with Alphone Daudet and his 'Letters from my Mill'. This is now a much visited museum containing relics of the novelist.

FRÉJUS (83)　　　　　　　　　　*40k SW Cannes*

This large town, with its plage running into St-Raphael, was founded in 49 BC by Julius Caesar, who gave it the name Forum Julii (hence Fréjus). It became a great naval port during the reign of his successor Augustus, but the sea has long since receded and the only sign of the harbour is a medieval lighthouse misleadingly called the 'Lanterne d'Augustus'. However there are several interesting Roman remains to be visited... especially the arena, the theatre, and the aqueduct, which brought water from the hills, about forty kilometres to the north. See also the fine medieval Cathedral, the cloisters of which lead to an interesting Museum of Local Antiquities; and also the 5th century baptistry attached to the Cathedral which is one of the earliest Christian buildings in France. Those in search of the unusual will find both a mosque and a pagoda in the vicinity of Fréjus. They were both erected for French colonial troops during the first World War.

Typical Provençal countryside

Church porch, at Guillestre

FRÉJUS ZOO PARK (83)　　*8k N Fréjus, at Le Capitou*

Large zoo, much of which is on a 'drive-through' basis, with a wide variety of animals. There are islands on which chimpanzees and gibbons live. Buvette, souvenir shop, restaurant during the summer, picnic areas.

GAP (05)　　*178k NE Avignon, 103k SSE Grenoble*

Capital of the Hautes-Alpes Département, Gap is a busy town with several good hotels and restaurants... a useful resting point on the Route Napoléon. Napoleon himself spent a night here on his dramatic journey northwards, and it was only when he reached here that he received a welcome of any enthusiasm.

GORDES (84)　　　　　　　　*38k E Avignon*

Charming hill village on the southern slopes of the Plateau de Vaucluse, with fine views southwards to the Luberon hills. It has a Renaissance château, a large classical church and steep narrow streets lined with old stone houses.

LA GRAVE (05)　　　　　　*77k ESE Grenoble*

Situated below the Meije, one of the great peaks of the Oisans range, this is a pleasant little winter sports and summer mountain resort, which has long been a favourite with climbers...a depressing number of whom are buried in its churchyard.

Cloisters at Fréjus

GRIMAUD (83)　　　　　　　*11k W St-Tropez*

Delightful little 'perched' village, on a hillside looking down a wide valley to Port Grimaud (See Page 236) and the Gulf of St-Tropez. There are fine views from its ruined castle, a little Romanesque church, and an arcaded building known as the 'Maison des Templiers'.

GUILLESTRE (05)　　　　　　*35k S Briançon*

Small town on the western edge of the Queyras Regional Nature Park (See Page 236) and a good base for exploring this splendid area. Drive north-eastwards up the Combe du Queyras to Château Queyras and then south-eastwards to St-Véran (See Page 238).

Countryside near Gap

Provence

At Le Lavandou

Old gateway at Manosque

Clock-tower at Manosque

The Old Port, Marseille

Marseille from the Château d'If

HYÈRES (83)   *18k E Toulon*

Charming town beneath the ruins of a medieval fortress, with many late 18th and 19th century houses lining its older streets, thus proclaiming its early popularity as a place in which to relax... Napoleon, Tolstoy and Queen Victoria were amongst its illustrious visitors. Its popular plage lies well to the south-east beyond an inevitably busy civil airport. The salt marshes that lie between Hyères and the village of Giens to the south, are still a haven for wild birds... a resting place on the migratory routes between Europe and Africa. There are also flamingoes which come here from the Camargue.

L'ISLE-SUR-LA-SORGUE (84)   *22k E Avignon*

This is a delightfully green and cool place on a hot summer day, with the many arms of the river Sorgue flowing through the town. Do not miss a visit to the church, the interior of which is richly decorated in 18th century Italianate style, with excellent paintings and gilded woodwork.

LE LAVANDOU (83)   *40k E Toulon*

Popular holiday resort based upon the remains of a little fishing port, with splendid sandy beaches especially those stretching southwards to La Favière, where there is a fine marina. Above Le Lavandou is the little medieval hillside town of Bormes-les-Mimosas which is well worth visiting, for the grand views out over the coast from its little 'square'.

LOURMARIN (84)   *37k N Aix-en-Provence*

Attractive little town situated on the southern slopes of the Luberon hills, below a fine medieval and Renaissance château. The author Albert Camus is buried in the cemetery here.

LUBERON, THE (84)   *Approx 50k E Avignon*

Situated to the north of the Durance valley, much of this attractive range of hills is now a Regional Nature Park, and there is a pleasant road winding through them from Cadanet and Lourmarin (See Above). For many hundreds of years the Luberon was the haunt of bandits, and in the 16th century the inhabitants, who for many years had been Protestants, were savagely persecuted for their beliefs. See especially two villages on the northern flanks, Oppède-le-Vieux, and Ménerbes (ten and fifteen kilometres east of Cavaillon respectively).

MANOSQUE (04)   *53k NE Aix-en-Provence*

Busy little market town above the river Durance with two medieval gateways to its old town, which is surrounded by wide boulevards which have replaced the walls. The narrow streets of the old town are full of character and well worth exploring.

MARSEILLE (13)   *777k SSE Paris*

This is the second largest city in France after Paris and it is almost certainly the oldest... having been founded by Greek colonists in the 6th century BC, to control the trade route up the Rhône valley to northern Gaul and Britain with its vital supply of tin. Its prosperity in Roman times was brought to an abrupt halt in 49 BC when it took the wrong side in the struggle between Caesar and Pompey, and it was sacked and replaced by Arles as a provincial capital. The crypt beneath the 11th

continued

century abbey of St-Victor bears witness to the activity of Christians here as early as the 5th century.

After this Marseille seems to have suffered greatly at the hands of the Saracens, who were continually raiding these shores; but from the time of the Crusades it once again became a place of great importance and has remained so ever since.

The enthusiastic singing of its volunteers in the wars that followed the Revolution, led to France's great Revolutionary song being nicknamed The Marseillaise, despite its originating from Strasbourg.

The fine modern city of Marseille is still centred upon its old port, from which the great boulevard... La Canabière... leads inland. Boatmen still vie with each other in their shouts of 'Promenade en Mer', asking tourists to visit the dreaded island fortress of Château d'If, prison of Dumas's Count of Monte-Cristo for so many years; or the Calanques, along the shore towards Cassis (See Page 231). However these boats now pass over a road tunnel beneath the harbour entrance... evidence of the bustling new Marseille, with its great docks, its motorways and towering modern buildings. There is no space to describe all its features here but do not miss a visit to the massive 19th century basilica of Notre-Dame-de-la-Garde, from which there are splendid views out over the city, nor the series of fine museums, which are more than worthy of France's second city.

Outward bound from Marseille

Chapel of Montmajour Abbey

MARTIGUES (13)   *45k SW Aix-en-Provence*
A charming town on the narrow spit of land between the great Étang de Berre and the sea, Martigues still clings to its reputation as the Venice of Provence, due to its numerous canals and little waterways; but it is overshadowed by some of the greatest oil refineries in Europe and it requires some devotion to ignore the effects totally.

MONS (83)   *40k W Grasse*
Picturesque medieval village on a steep hillside, with splendid views from a little terrace on which there is an orientation table. The little 13th century church is also worth visiting.

MONTMAJOUR ABBEY (13)   *6k NE Arles*
The impressive ruins of a Benedictine abbey founded in the 10th century, with a 12th century crypt and a massive keep added two centuries later. Combine with a visit to Alphonse Daudet's windmill and the Roman aqueduct at Barbegal (See Fontvieille, Page 232).

Montmajour Abbey   *Boat trip at Martigues*

MOUSTIERS-STE-MARIE (04)   *48k S Digne*
Small village just to the north of the Verdon Gorge (See Page 240), at a point where a small river pours out of a narrow ravine in the mountains, on its way to the great Ste-Croix lake. Faience pottery was made here from the 15th to the 19th century, and it was recommenced in the 1920's. See the potters at work, the interesting Museum of Faience, the Romanesque and Gothic church, and the chapel of Notre-Dame, dramatically sited above the ravine, and from which there are fine views.

NESQUE GORGES (84)   *Approx 20k E Carpentras*
These deep gorges in the Vaucluse plateau run south and west from the picturesque little town of Sault and provide an adventurous day's motoring if combined with a visit to Mont Ventoux (See Page 240). Use Michelin Map 93.

Moustiers-Ste-Marie

Roman theatre, Orange

ORANGE (84) 660k S Paris, 30k N Avignon

Pleasant town which is famed for its two outstanding Roman remains, the great triumphal arch, the third largest surviving example in the whole Roman empire; and the massive theatre, which can still seat 10,000 spectators.

In the 16th century Orange was inherited by William of Nassau, known as William of Orange, who led the Dutch revolt against the Spaniards, and who was the ancestor of both the present Dutch Royal Family, and of England's William III.

ÎLE DE PORQUEROLLES (83) S of Hyères

This is the largest of the Îles d'Hyères and is best approached by boat from Giens, south of Hyères. There are many attractive walks through woods of pine and cork-oak, and a fine series of sandy beaches on the north side of the island.

Shoreline on the Île-de-Porquerolles

ÎLE DE PORT CROS (83) SE of Hyères

This is the central island of the Îles d'Hyères and may be approached from Le Lavandou or Hyères Plage, boats from which also call at the third island, the Île du Levant*. Port Cros is a National Park and Nature Reserve for Mediterranean flora and fauna, but there are still many pleasant paths that can be followed by the visitor.

*Part occupied by the Navy, and part by nudists.

PORT-GRIMAUD (83) 7k W St-Tropez

This is a fascinating creation of the 1960s and 1970s by the architect François Spoerry, who has provided an idealised Provençal 'fishing village', with almost every one of its luxuriously equipped houses looking out over the sparkling waters of a many branched harbour, but already looking as if they had been built many years ago. No cars are allowed into its little streets, but there is space on the water for as many as two thousand boats.

QUEYRAS REGIONAL NATURE PARK (05)
Approx 50k SE Briançon

A splendid mountain area situated between Guillestre and the border with Italy. The flora and fauna are typically alpine with chamois and marmots inhabiting the higher slopes, although there is a hint of the Mediterranean in the valleys below. There is an interesting small museum at St-Véran (See Page 238), depicting life in the area in times past. Long distance footpath GR 5 passes through the Park on its way northwards from Nice, and there are many splendid opportunities for walking in the valleys and the mountains (But please take care in the latter... don't venture far without proper equipment and expertise). To explore by road use Michelin Map 77.

RHÔNE RIVER TRIPS

Day trips may be made on the Rhône from various points between Lyon, Avignon and Stes-Maries-de-la-Mer on the Mediterranean coast. Full details may be obtained from Agence Francaise de Tourisme, 75 rue de la République, Lyon.

Port Grimaud

Queyras Château

RIEZ (04)
40k SSW Digne

Pleasant little medieval town noted for its lavender and its truffles. To the immediate west of the town, there are the ruins of a 1st century Roman temple, and across the river from it, a 5th century Merovingian baptistery... both providing evidence of Riez's importance as a religious centre for many hundreds of years.

ROUTE NAPOLÉON, THE

This famous montain road follows the route taken by Napoleon on his return from Elba, when he landed at Golfe-Juan on March 1st 1815, and travelled to Grenoble. The Route was opened in full in 1932 and runs from Golfe-Juan, via Cannes, Grasse, Castellane, Digne, Sisteron, Corps and La Mure, to Grenoble. It is marked in places with flying eagles, which were inspired by Napoleon's words, 'The Eagle will fly from steeple to steeple as far as the towers of Notre Dame'. This makes a fine route to the Côte d'Azur, especially now that the autoroutes takes the motorist right to its threshold at Grenoble.

ST-FIRMIN (05)
31k N Gap

Small village at the entrance to the Valgaudemar, a delicious alpine valley extending north-eastwards from the valley of Drac. Here are small villages and little fields bordered by poplar trees, and to the north the great mountain massif de l'Oisans.

ST-MAXIMIN-LA-STE-BAUME (83)
43k E Aix-en-Provence

Modest village which possesses the finest Gothic building in south-east France, the Basilica of St-Maximin in the crypt of which are said to lie the remains not only of St-Maximin himself, but also those of St-Trophime, St-Sidonius and no less a person than Mary Magdalene. There was a dispute in the late 13th century as to which church possessed the true relics, this one or that at Vézelay (See Page 87), the latter of which had already enjoyed two centuries as a prosperous pilgrimage centre. However, the Papacy decreed that St-Maximin's were the true relics, and it was from this time that the great Basilica was commenced. Do not miss a visit to this fine building, with its 18th century furnishings in a starkly simple Gothic interior.

ST-MICHEL OBSERVATORY (04)
21k NNW Manosque

This astrophysical observatory stands on a hill top north of Manosque and it is normally possible to visit it on Thursdays at 3 p.m.

ST-RAPHAËL (83)
43k SW Cannes

Elegant holiday resort with a 19th and early 20th century flavour. However this is countered by its fine modern harbour and its Museum of Marine Archaeology, near which is a Romanesque church built by the Knights Templar complete with a watch tower... an 'early warning system' against the approach of Saracen invaders, who were such a menace along this coast. Napoleon landed here on his return from Egypt, and it was also from here that he departed for what only proved to be his temporary exile on Elba.

Fishing boats at St-Raphael

Shoreline at Le Trayas, east of St-Raphael

St-Raphael beach

237

Mausoleum at 'Les Antiques', St-Rémy

'Les Antiques', St-Rémy

ST-RÉMY-DE-PROVENCE (13)   *21k S Avignon*

Small town below the northern slopes of Les Alpilles, noted for its market gardens and its associations with the 16th century astrologer Nostradamus, who was born here; and with the artist Van Gogh who was a voluntary patient at the local mental home in the Romanesque priory of St-Paul de Mausole, which can be visited.

One kilometre to the south are 'Les Antiques', the ruins of the Roman town of Glanum, the most dramatic elements of which are the lower part of a fine triumphal arch, and a unique 1st century A.D. mausoleum. Recent excavations have revealed that occupation of this site dated back to the Gallo-Greek period... the second century B.C.

ST-TROPEZ (83)   *69k ENE Toulon*

Although desperately crowded during the holiday months, St-Tropez is still a town of very great character, with an old fishing and pleasure port and a newer marina, both protected by the long 'Mole Jean Reveille'. There is a bewildering choice of hotels and restaurants, and many smart and colourful shops. See especially the Annonciade Museum with its outstanding collection of late 19th and early 20th century French paintings and bronzes; the views from the Mole; the citadel and the Maritime Museum, reminding us that the great 18th century seaman, Admiral Suffren was a native of St-Tropez.

Marine luxury at St-Tropez

ST-VÉRAN (05)   *50k SE Briançon*

Standing on a terraced mountainside at 2040 metres this claims to be the highest village in Europe. It is an attractive little place where the peasant way of life is still largely unchanged. There is a small road leading up the valley to the chapel of Notre-Dame-de-Clausis (2390 metres), not far from the Italian border, and the object of pilgrimage from both France and Italy.

LES SAINTES-MARIES-DE-LA-MER (13)
39k SW Arles

Old fishing port and beach resort on the southern fringe of the Camargue (See Page 230). The fine 12th century Romanesque church (fortified in the 14th and 15th centuries) marks the place where the three Mary's and their companions are believed to have landed after their long voyage from the Holy Land. Their negro servant Sarah was long ago 'adopted' by the gypsies as their Patron Saint and on the 23rd of May each year they congregate here in great numbers to do honour to her and to the three Mary's. On 25th May there is a series of ceremonies involving gypsies, cowboys and many others, culminating in the carrying of statues of the saints into the sea, which is blessed by the local bishop.

May 23rd at Les Saintes-Maries-de-la-Mer

STE-MAXIME (83)   *14k N St-Tropez*

Attractive small coastal resort in a sheltered setting on the north side of the Gulf of St-Tropez. Apart from all the usual facilities it has a fascinating Museum of Mechanical Music.

SALON-DE-PROVENCE (13)
36k WNW Aix-en-Provence

Busy market town, where the 16th century astrologer Nostradamus lived, and where he is buried. The 13th and 14th century Château de l'Empéri houses a fascinating Military Museum.

On the beach at Ste-Maxime

SANARY-SUR-MER (83)

54k ESE Marseille,
12k W Toulon

Pleasant holiday resort with a little harbour for fishing and pleasure boats. This is one of the 'sea-side' places that retains a real flavour of times gone by, and we have happy memories of a visit here many years ago.

SANARY-BANDOL ZOO (83)

50k ESE Marseille,
2k NE Bandol

An 'exotic garden' in the hills overlooking Bandol, with an interesting collection of fauna and flora. Its relatively modest size makes it ideal for younger children, but all should enjoy a visit here.

SÉNANQUE ABBEY (84)

4k N Gordes,
17k NE Cavaillon

The waterfront, Sanary   Sénanque Abbey

This was founded by the Cistercians in 1148 in an isolated valley of great beauty (a typical Cistercian choice). It still retains its Romanesque church, and it has returned to the ownership of the Cistercians after an eventful history. It is now a Cultural and Research Centre, which includes an interesting series of drawings of Senanque itself and its two sister abbeys, Silvacane and Le Thoronet. There is also a Sahara Museum.

SERRE-PONÇON BARRAGE AND LAKE (05)

25k E Gap

A great dam across the river Durance has created a vast artificial lake amongst the wooded mountains of northern Provence. There are opportunities for every kind of water-sport here, and many most attractive views.

Distant view of Serre-Ponçon Lake

SILVACANE ABBEY (13) *30k NNW Aix-en-Provence,*
4k SW Cadanet

The splendid ruins of a Cistercian abbey founded in 1147, in the valley of the Durance. It has a chequered history, but is now being restored by the State.

SISTERON (04)

48k S Gap

Small town beside the Durance, which here flows parallel to the Route Napoléon, through wild rocky country. There are fine views out over the 13th – 16th century citadel (guided tour with sound effects). Explore the old vaulted streets to locate the Romanesque Cathedral of Notre-Dame.

TARASCON (13)

23k SW Avignon

Attractive small town on the Rhône with the great castle of Good King René (of Provence) looking across the river to the château of Beaucaire (See Page 131). The reason for the two châteaux being so close was that the Rhône represented the frontier between France and Provence, the second of which was independent until René's death in 1480. See also the church of Ste-Martha which contains the tomb of the saint, and also that of Jean de Cossa, who built René's castle

Vault in Silvacane Abbey   The Durance at Sisteron

LE THORONET ABBEY (83)

17k ENE Brignoles

Founded by the Cistercians in 1146 in a remote valley in thickly wooded country, another typical example of the Cistercians' thirst for tranquillity. It has been excellently restored by the State and is well worth visiting.

THOUZON GROTTO (84)

17k E Avignon,
3k N Le Thor

A long cave beneath a ruined château and monastery, complete with many beautifully coloured stalactites.

Castle of Good King René, Tarascon

Toulon

At Vaison-la-Romaine
Photograph by
Peter Titchmarsh

At Vaison-la-Romaine
Photograph by
Peter Titchmarsh

TOULON (83)   *838k SSE Paris, 64k ESE Marseille*

This has been the great naval base of France since the times of Richelieu and Louis XIV, and it remains so today, with one of the finest roadsteads in the world, landlocked on three sides by colourful mountain-sides. The city of Toulon, with about 200,000 inhabitants, is a fascinating place, with all the vitality and colour of a southern port, many pleasant old streets and quaysides, and the comings and goings of picturesque small craft at all times of the day. See especially the Naval Museum and the adjoining Tour Royale, the Museum of Art and Archaelogy with its fine collections of French and Oriental art, and the museum of the History of Toulon. Take a boat to the Porquerolles (See Page 236), and take the cable car up to the peak of Le Faron, from which there are fabulous views out over the coast, and where there is a museum honouring the two great liberators of Toulon... Napoleon and De Lattre de Tassigny, the Free French general involved in the capture of the city from the Germans in 1944. There is much more to see and do in Toulon, but space does not allow us to do it full justice here.

VAISON-LA-ROMAINE (84)   *46k NE Avignon*

This little town on the river Ouvèze reveals evidence of almost continuous occupation since it was established by a Gallo-Roman tribe in the first century A.D. There are the fascinating remains of the Roman town, with a theatre, baths, and a bridge but here, as opposed to Orange, Arles or Nimes, the emphasis is on private houses and small streets. The former Cathedral of Notre-Dame has evidence of its 6th century origins, and also a Romanesque nave and cloisters. The medieval town was built on the opposite bank of the river, beneath the shelter of a castle built in the 12th century, and it is well worth exploring up through the old streets to its ruins from which there are fine views.

MONT VENTOUX (84)   *62k NE Avignon*

Standing at over 1900 metres above sea level, this offers some of the finest views in the whole of southern France, although the middle of the day should be avoided due to the possibility of haze. Do not expect tranquillity at the summit, as there is an observatory, a radar station and television masts here.

VERDON GORGE (04)   *15k SW Castellane*

This twenty one kilometre long gorge, usually referred to as the Grand Canyon du Verdon, is one of the great natural spectacles of Europe, with cliffs varying in height between two hundred and fifty and seven hundred metres. The turbulent waters of the Verdon sometimes disappear below ground, for this is limestone country, and at the end of the gorge they empty into the great reservoir formed by the Ste-Croix Barrage, beyond which are more gorges, although now not so spectacular. There are roads both to the north and south of the 'Grand Canyon', with frequent viewing points, some of which are very easy to reach. May we suggest that you buy Michelin Map No 81, and head off here without delay.

VILLECROZE (83)   *21k WNW Draguignan*

Small village in remote hill country to the south of the Verdon Gorge, with interesting caves close by. These are illuminated, with several chambers at different levels and a lake. There are traces of usage by Romans, Saracens and Templars.

The Verdon Gorge
Photograph by
Peter Titchmarsh

Provence

Rhône Valley

This Region is perhaps the most 'rushed-through' of all. Using the temptingly simple Autoroute du Soleil, one can drive through it, from Mâcon to Orange, in about two hours, a distance of under two hundred and fifty kilometres. But those who have strength to break away will be rewarded with highly civilized eating and drinking in the restaurants and hotels within a few kilometres of the 'valley', either of the Saône, to the north of Lyon, or of the Rhône to its south. Further beyond, to the west of the valley, will be found quiet towns and villages in richly wooded hill areas like the Monts de la Madeleine, the Monts du Forez, the Pilat Regional Nature Park and the dramatic Ardèche Gorges; while to the east there is the southern end of the lovely Jura mountains, the rugged pre-Alpine Vercors, and the delightful pastoral hill country to the south of the Drôme valley.

Here in the Rhône Valley Region the promise of warmer weather already hinted at in Burgundy, is likely to be fulfilled, and we hope therefore that you will be persuaded to stay awhile and experience the tranquillity and the good life to be found here. It lies such a short distance away from the temptress... the Autoroute du Soleil providing such a smooth, fast route to the Mediterranean. Resist her for a few days at least... you will not regret it.

AIN GORGES (01)   *Approx 20k E Bourg-en-Bresse*
A dramatic series of gorges stretching northwards from the village of Poncin, twenty kilometres south east of Bourg-en-Bresse. Almost all of this may be followed by road, as far as the Vouglans Barrage in the Franche-Comté Region (See Page117), a distance of over fifty kilometres.

AMBIERLE (42)   *18k WNW Roanne*
Small village below the eastern slopes of the Monts-de-la-Madeleine, with a fine 15th century Gothic church, which has splendid stained glass and outstanding woodwork within.

ANNONAY (07)   *72k S Lyon*
Busy town in hill country to the west of the Rhône valley, with the ruins of an ancient castle above its old quarter. The Montgolfier brothers were the sons of an Annonay paper merchant, and it was from here that they made their first balloon ascent in 1783. There is a fascinating minor road south west from Annonay down the valley of the little river Cance to its confluence with the Rhône nineteen kilometres away.

Vallon Pont d'Arc, and the Ardèche

ARDÈCHE GORGES (07)   *40k SW Montélimar*
Splendid series of limestone canyons extending south eastwards from Vallon-Pont-D'Arc to Pont-St-Esprit, where the Ardèche joins the Rhône, a distance of about fifty kilometres. See Canoe Holidays, (Page 8) for details of canoe trips down the Ardèche. There are also locally organised punt trips, and for the most part the gorges may also be followed down by road...the D290, from which there are magnificent views from time to time.

AUBENAS (07)   *44k W Montélimar*
Pleasant old town splendidly sited above the river Ardèche, with its Hôtel-de-Ville in an impressive 13th and 15th century castle. A short distance to the east of this there is an Orientation Table which enables the visitor to identify the main features of the fine views northwards from here.

*Canoeing on the Ardèche.
Photograph by P.G.L. Young Adventure Ltd.*

241

LA BASTIE D'URFÉ (42) 14k N Montbrison

Here, to the east of the wild Monts-du-Forez, is a fine Renaissance château, which owes a great deal to Italian craftsmen who were imported here to do most of the decorative work. Both the château and its surrounding gardens are a sheer delight, and should on no account be missed.

ROUTE DU BEAUJOLAIS (69)

This is a well signed route running down through the villages of the Beaujolais*, approximately parallel with the N6, and starting from Crêches eight kilometres south of Macon, both of which are actually in the Burgundy Region. It finishes at a point to the west of Villefranche-sur-Sâone.
*See Page 250.

At La Bastie d'Urfé   At La Bastie d'Urfé

BELLEY (01) 75k SE Bourg-en-Bresse

Picturesque old town on a plateau which is itself overlooked by high mountains on both sides. See especially the house where the noted writer on good food, Brillat-Savarin, was born in 1775; the cathedral of St-Jean with its fine choir; the college where Lamartine was a student; and the handsome 18th century Bishop's Palace.

LA BÉNISSON-DIEU (42) 15k N Roanne

Small village in rolling wooded country north of Roanne, which has a fine Romanesque and Gothic abbey church, with a 15th century tiled roof.

Brou church, near Bourg-en-Bresse

BOURG-EN-BRESSE (01) 417k SE Paris

This large town is the capital of the Ain Département, and it is noted for its cattle and poultry markets. The church of Notre-Dame is largely 16th century and has some excellent choir stalls. However in Brou, a suburb to the south east of the town, there is one of the most exquisite Flamboyant Gothic buildings ever created... a monastery church built by Marguerite of Austria, daughter of the Emperor Maximilian between the years 1506 and 1525. This is full of lovely features and should on no account be missed. The adjoining monastery, after a very chequered career, now houses an interesting Museum of Local Folklore.

BUIS-LES-BARONNIES (26) 30k SE Nyons

Minute town in the valley of the Ouvèze with an arcaded market place which is the centre of the French herb trade during the famous sales held here on the first two Wednesdays in July. The town is delightfully situated below the Baronnies Massif, amidst groves of cherries, almonds, olives and lavender.

Cloisters at Brou church

CERDON CAVES (01) 17k SW Nantua

Extensive limestone caverns to the immediate west of the small village of Labalme, which is situated in hilly country to the east of the Ain Gorges.

CHAMPDIEU (42) 4k N Montbrison

Minute village at the foot of the Monts-du-Forez with a fortified priory church of the 11th and 12th centuries.

CHARLIEU (42) 19k NNE Roanne

Situated in quiet hill country this pleasant old town is enriched by the remains of a fine Benedictine abbey which include fine 15th century cloisters and a priory chapel. There was a Franciscan monastery nearby, but continued

Marguerite of Austria's tomb, at Brou

Farm near Bourg-en-Bresse

Cloisters at Charlieu

regrettably this has been shipped to America leaving only the handsome cloisters.

CHÂTILLON-EN-DIOIS (26)   *79k SE Valence*
Small village in an alpine valley with a hotel and several camping sites making it an excellent base for exploring the upper Drôme. Eleven kilometres to the north is the Archiane Cirque, with great cliffs forming an amphitheatre at the head of the little Archiane valley.

CONDRIEU (69)   *41k S Lyon*
Small town on a hill above the Rhône wth a ruined castle, and fine views from its calvary. There are pleasant hotels with excellent eating both here and at Roches-de-Condrieu on the opposite bank of the river.

Crest

Golf at Divonne-les-Bains

CREST (26)   *28k SSE Valence*
Pleasant small town on the river Drôme, with a Renaissance house in the rue de l'Hôtel-de-Ville, several ancient arched and stepped alleyways, all overlooked by a tall 12th century keep, one of the finest specimens in France.

LE CROZET (42)   *24k NW Roanne*
Small fortified medieval village on the north-eastern flanks of the Monts-de-la-Madeleine with a wonderful atmosphere of the past.

DIE (26)   *65k ESE Valence*
Small town in the middle reaches of the Drôme valley, at the southern end of the lovely Vercors (See Page 249). There are remains of the Roman town wall, a triumphal arch, and a small local museum with Roman items excavated in the town and its surroundings, including a fine mosaic pavement.

Glass studio at Dieulefit
Photograph by
Peter Titchmarsh

Quiet corner at Dieulefit
Photograph by
Peter Titchmarsh

DIEULEFIT (26)   *27k E Montélimar*
Modest village well served by at least two hotels and two camping sites, and situated in the valley of the Lez, in wooded hill country to the east of the Rhône. Here will be found several craft potteries and the glass studio of two very talented glass-blowers — Claude Morin and his son, Nicolas. Do not miss a visit here.

DIVONNE-LES-BAINS (01)   *19k N Geneva*
Fashionable spa town on the border with Switzerland, and only seven kilometres from the shores of Lake Geneva (Lac Léman). However it also has its own lake, together with a golf course and many other sporting facilities. It is very easy to reach Geneva from here due to the autoroute interchange being only three kilometres from the town.

MONTS DU FOREZ (42)   *10k W Montbrison*
Richly wooded mountain country lying to the west of Montbrison. In winter this is great ski-ing country, while in the summer it offers boundless opportunities for walking.

GRANGENT LAKE (42)   *14k W St-Étienne*
A beautifully wooded, twenty five kilometre long lake formed by a great dam across the upper Loire in the hill country west of St-Étienne. There is a plage and facilities for motor-boating and sailing at St-Victor on the eastern shore.

Grangent Barrage, near St.-Étienne

GRIGNAN (26)   *28k SE Montélimar*

Pleasant little town whose narrow streets are dominated by a fine Renaissance château, much visited by the redoubtable writer of letters, Madame de Sévigné, whose daughter Madame de Grignan lived here. Madme de Sévigné died at Grignan in 1696, and she is buried beneath a slab in front of the fine high altar of the Renaissance church adjoining her daughter's home. There are attractive views from the château terrace which runs partly above the church.

LAMASTRE (07)   *36k W Valence*

Picturesque old town on two hills, with a Romanesque church on one and a ruined 13th century castle on the other. These look across at each other over a steep sided ravine.

Grignan Château

LENTE FOREST (26)   *65k E Valence*

Wonderfully scenic mountain country, thickly wooded with fir and beech, with many opportunities for forest walks. Explore with the help of Michelin Map No 77.

LYON (69)   *462k SSE Paris*

This is France's third largest city, after Paris and Marseille, and stands at the confluence of the two great navigable rivers... the Rhône and Saône. The Romans established a town here called Lugdunum in 42 BC, on a key hilltop site, the only visible remains of which are two theatres. The most interesting part of the city lies to the north of the Place Carnot, which is situated between the two rivers, at a point where motorists coming in on the autoroute from the north have to decide whether to head south for Provence or south-east for Grenoble and the Alps. Why not do neither, but instead drive a short distance northwards to the Place Bellecour, one of France's great squares, with a fine equestrian statue of Louis XIV. Walk northwards from here, having first visited the Syndicat d'Initiative which is in the square, to the Place des Terraux, where many hundreds of Lyon's citizens were guillotined during the Revolution, due to their having tried to take a moderate line during its early stages. Visit the excellent Museum of Fine Arts in the Place, and then walk north again to 'Les Traboules' to explore its numerous old passageways and courtyards. Now head south-westwards across the Saône to visit 'Le Vieux Lyon' with more old streets, passage-ways and courtyards, and the largely Gothic Cathedral, with its Romanesque choir and intriguing astronomical clock. Next take the funicular railway up to the top of Fourvière hill, where there are splendid views out over the city from the tower of the Basilica of Notre-Dame-de-la-Fourvière, and from which it is only a short walk south to the Roman theatres. This short description does little justice to one of France's finest cities, with its broad tree lined quays, its wide streets, its great public gardens, its splendid museums, elegant restaurants and hotels, and busy shops... but you will find the Syndicat in the Place Bellecour most helpful in the supply of further details.

The Hôtel-de-Ville, Lyon   Lyon Cathedral

A corner of old Lyon   Dusk at Lyon

MARSANNE (26)   *16k NE Montélimar*

Small fortified village at the foot of the hilly Marsanne Forest country. Drive north east for seven kilometres to the Col de Tartaiguille, from which there are splendid views.

Lyon by night   Countryside near Lyon

The Bridge at Nyons

In Ornac Caves

Lions at Peaugres Safari Park.
A Peaugres Safari Park Photograph.

MARZAL CAVE (07)   *Approx 55k SW Montélimar*
Interesting limestone cavern in the hills to the north of the Ardèche Gorges.

MONTBRISON (42)   *36k NW St-Étienne*
Busy little town to the east of the Monts-du-Forez, with an interesting 13th century church and behind it a unique hall called 'La Diane' which has a wooden ceiling decorated with heraldic panels, and which contains a Museum of Local History. See also the Doll Museum and the Museum of Mineralogy.

MONTÉLIMAR (26)   *607k SSE Paris   45k S Valence*
Busy town first relieved of the N7's traffic by a by-pass to the west and now made even more pleasant by the autoroute to its east. Famous for its nougat for many years, Montélimar also has a bewildering selection of hotels and restaurants to offer the visitor who is prepared to break away from the autoroute's clutches for a short time at least.

MONTS DE LA MADELEINE (42)   *15k W Roanne*
A wonderfully quiet hill area to the west of Roanne. See especially the lake formed by the Tache Barrage, seventeen kilometres west of Roanne, and the smaller lake up in the hills, Le Gué de la Chaux, from whence there is a little train leading to the ski station of La Loge des Gardes, forty kilometres west-south-west of Roanne.

NANTUA (01)   *54k ESE Bourg-en-Bresse*
Attractive town at the eastern end of a beautiful lake in the southern Jura, with a wide variety of good hotels and restaurants. There is a pleasant walk along the southern shore of the lake.

NYONS (26)   *51k SE Montélimar*
Delightful small town in the deep, wooded valley of the river Eygues, which is crossed here by a pleasant bridge. The old town is known as the Quartier des Grands Forts, and is complete with fortifications and fascinating little medieval streets. Combine a visit here with one to Vaison-la-Romaine in neighbouring Provence, only sixteen kilometres south (See Page 240).

ORGNAC CAVES (07)   *Approx 65k SW Montélimar*
These are a range of large caves in dramatic limestone country south of the Ardèche gorges. They are well illuminated and certainly worth visiting.

LA PACAUDIÈRE (42)   *24k NW Roanne*
This small village was a staging post on the old Route Royale, and there are several old buildings that make a visit here worthwhile.

PEAUGRES SAFARI PARK (07)   *8k NE Annonay*
The full title is 'Safari Parc du Haut Vivarais', and it is situated in wooded hilly country to the west of the Rhône valley. This is a large 'drive-through' safari park with a wide variety of animals to be observed, including bears, bison, lions, zebras, baboons and giraffes. There are also many animals to be visited on foot, and there is a lake overlooked by an attractive bar. Snacks, souvenir shop, picnic areas, and play areas for children.

PÉROUGES (01)   36k NE Lyon

Charming hilltop village complete with a double line of medieval walls and two original gateways. The cobbled streets and the old central square have also survived almost intact from medieval times, and to visit Pérouges is to journey back in time for many hundreds of years. Do not miss this.

Old street in Pérouges   Old street in Pérouges

PILAT REGIONAL NATURE PARK   E St-Étienne

A splendid mountain region stretching eastwards from St-Étienne to the Rhône valley south of Vienne, with its highest peak, the Crêt de la Perdrix standing at 1432 metres above sea level. There is a road almost to the summit on which there is an orientation table (twenty five kilometres east-south-east St-Étienne). This is a largely wooded area and ideally suitable for walking and exploring generally.

POET LAVAL (26)   22k E Montélimar

A small, once abandoned hill village dominated by a ruined chateau of the Knights Hospitallers, beside which is a delectable hotel, Les Hospitaliers, one of our great favourites. The rest of this delightful village is gradually being brought back to life, but with great care and affection. There is also a small museum of Protestantism and a few modest craft studios.

PRIVAS (07)   40k SW Valence

This small town is the capital of the Ardèche Departement, and has several pleasant 17th century houses... anything earlier having been destroyed in 1629 when the town was burnt to the ground by Richelieu due to its Calvinist connections.

Pérouges, on its hilltop

RHÔNE RIVER TRIPS

Day trips may be made on the Rhône from various points between Lyon, Avignon and Stes-Maries-de-la-Mer on the Mediterranean coast. Full details may be obtained from Agence Francaise de Tourisme, 75 rue de la République, 69002 Lyon.

ROANNE (42)   391k SSE Paris,
                      86k WNW Lyon

Busy industrial town and inland navigation centre, Roanne stood on the old Route Royale between Paris and Rome, and still stands astride the N7 mid-way between Paris and Marseille (although the Autoroute du Sud has quietened down the N7 considerably). It also stands on the Loire at a point where it forsakes its mountain gorges for the great central plains of France, and only about five kilometres to the south west there starts a fine walk up the dramatic Loire Gorges between the villages of Villerest and Balbigny, a total distance of about forty five kilometres. In Roanne itself, see the ancient castle remains and the interesting museum.

Poët Laval.................... hill-top gem
Photographs by Peter Titchmarsh

ROCHEMAURE (07)   5k NW Montélimar

This small village on the west bank of the Rhône shelters beneath the dramatic ruins of a medieval castle and the ruins of a walled medieval village. A short distance northwards is the extinct volcano of Chenavari, from which there are splendid views out over the Rhône valley, and beyond to the Alps.

ROCHETAILLÉE CHÂTEAU (69)
              11k N Lyon on RN 433

Here is a splendid collection of vintage and veteran cars displayed in the château itself, and in the adjoining Gordini Hall, a fine series of racing cars. This is known collectively as the Musée Henri Malartre after 'Le Conservateur' himself, who runs a most interesting museum. Do not miss this.

In the Motor Museum, Rochetaillée Château

Road through the Grands Goulets, south-east of St-Nazaire-en-Royans

In the Saou Forest

Photograph by
Peter Titchmarsh

ROMANS-SUR-ISÈRE (26)   *18k NE Valence*

This is a bustling town known throughout France for its shoe manufacture, and the local museum takes the shoe throughout the ages as its main theme. It is situated on the north bank of the Isère and much of its medieval walls have survived. The 12th century abbey church of St-Bernard is noted for its fine tapestries. The bridge across the Isère used to be a toll bridge, and this gave rise to the name of the town there... Bourg-de-Péage, now more a suburb of Romans, but confusing to those coming south on the autoroute, who will already have come to dread the word 'péage', and will encounter a sign to this town at the Tain-Tournon Interchange.

ST-DONAT (26)   *18k NE Tournon*

This charming village is the scene each year of an international Bach festival, much of which takes place in the fine collegiate church, which is well worth visiting. See also the priory, the Bishop's chapel, the cloisters and the Byzantine sculptures.

ST-ÉTIENNE (42)   *521k SSE Paris,*
59k SW Lyon

This is one of the great industrial cities of France, and although it would make a reasonable base for exploring the wonderful countryside of the Loire Département, of which it is the capital, it is not itself an outstanding 'touristic' city. However there are several interesting museums within the Palais des Arts. Take the D8 south-east from here to visit the Gouffre d'Enfer, a deep gorge about eleven kilometres away, and then onwards to the Pilat Regional Nature Park (See Page 247).

ST-HAÔN-LE-CHATEL (42)   *13k W Roanne*

Fascinating little fortified village perched on a hill at the foot of the Monts-de-la-Madeleine, complete with several towers, gateway, ancient hospital and a 15th century château.

ST-NAZAIRE-EN-ROYANS (26)   *36k ENE Valence*

Attractive little village at the confluence of the Isère and the Bourne, with an old aqueduct above the steep river bank on which the houses stand. It is possible to drive eastwards from here up the Bourne Gorges (See Page 253).

ST-PAUL-TROIS-CHÂTEAUX (26)   *27k S Montélimar*

There are fine views eastwards to the foothills of the Alps from the little 11th and 12th century Cathedral, which is itself a splendid example of Romanesque architecture.

ST-ROMAIN-LE-PUY (42)   *6k SE Montbrison*

Small village with its 11th century priory church sited on the top of a little volcanic hill. Do not miss the crypt with its richly sculptured Romanesque capitals.

SAOU (26)   *33k ENE Montélimar*

Minute village at the western end of the lovely Saou Forest. With its good camping site, this makes a fine base for exploring the attractive mountain area between the Drôme and the Rhône, which is typified by the Col de la Chaudiere, some 15 kilometres to the east, a modest pass, but a very pleasant one.

SURY-LE-COMTAL (42)   *24k NW St-Étienne*

Small village with an interesting collection of old vehicles which have been beautifully restored.

TAIN-TOURNON (07)   *88k S Lyon*
The busy old town of Tournon is sited above the west bank of the Rhône, with fine views across to its twin on the east bank, Tain-l'Hermitage from the terrace of its Palais-de-Justice, the former castle, which also houses an interesting Rhône Museum. There is an attractive riverside promenade, and above Tain are the famous Hemitage vineyards planted on steep slopes above the river.

The Hermitage vineyards, above Tain

VALENCE (26)   *561k SSE Paris, 100k S Lyon*
Capital of Drôme Département, Valence is a large, lively market town situated on the banks of the Rhône, but unfortunately largely isolated from it by the ever busy autoroute. However it has a fine selection of hotels and restaurants, many pleasant old houses, a handsome Romanesque cathedral, with the former Bishop's Palace beside it now housing a museum. See also the Maison-des-Têtes with its sculptures and medallions, and the Champ de Mars gardens, from whose terrace there are fine views across the Rhône to the ruined castle on Mont Crussol. Rabelais was once a student of a university at Valence (long since gone) and the young Napoleon was a cadet at the artillery school here for almost a year.

Two views of Tournon

VERCORS, THE (26 & 38)   *Approx 60k E Valence*
Splendid mountain country between Valence and Grenoble. This is a high limestone plateau deeply scoured by various rivers into deep gorges, and often thickly wooded (See Lente Forest, Page 245). This area was the scene of great tragedy in 1944, when German troops 'invaded' what had been regarded as an almost impregnable Resistance stronghold. Memories of savage reprisals still linger here. Use Michelin Map 77 to explore this dramatic outlier of the Alps.

VILLARS-LES-DOMBES ORNITHOLOGICAL RESERVE (07)   *34k SW Bourg-en-Bresse*
This is a fascinating bird park, over half of which is composed of ponds (a habitat typical of the Dombes area* which stretches southwards from Bourg-en-Bresse). There are over three hundred species, either in open-air cages, large enclosures, or living freely on the ponds. There is also a bird house containing a selection of gorgeously coloured exotic species. Do not miss a visit here.
*Sometimes described as the 'Lake District' of France.

Bridge over the Rhône at Valence

VILLEFRANCHE-SUR-SAÔNE (69)   *31k NNW Lyon*
Busy town, now happily relieved by the autoroute which passes just to its east. There are no outstanding items of interest apart from the Romanesque church of Notre-Dame, the 16th century Hôtel-de-Ville, and several late medieval houses. However Villefranche is the market centre for the wines of the Beaujolais, and with at least one good hotel and several excellent restaurants this makes a good base for exploring the Beaujolais hills (See Page 250).

VIVARAIS STEAM RAILWAY (07)   *88k S Lyon*
This is a thirty three kilometre long railway line between Tournon and Lamastre, running for almost its entire length along the gorge of the River Doux.

Bird Park at Villars-les-Dombes

Terrace of Les Hospitaliers Hotel, Poët Laval
(see page 247)   *Photograph by Peter Titchmarsh*

Vivarais Steam Railway (See page 249)

VIVIERS (07)   *11k SSW Montélimar*

Minute town above the west bank of the Rhône, a short distance above the commencement of the Donzère-Mondragon Canal, part of a massive hydro-electric scheme (See Bollène Page 230). The old parts of the town have been compared to some Italian hill town, and are well worth visiting. The Romanesque and Gothic former Cathedral is sited on a rock overlooking the river.

GREAT WINE AREAS OF THE RHÔNE VALLEY

BEAUJOLAIS. This is delightful rolling hill country to the immediate west of the Saône and extends southwards from just south of Pouilly-Fuissé (which is in the Burgundy Region) to the area to the west of Villefranche-sur-Saône. Almost all the wine produced here is red, and much of the lower quality matures very quickly into a very drinkable wine. Explore this splendid area by taking the well signposted 'Route de Beaujolais' (See Page 243).

CÔTES-DU-RHÔNE. These vineyards extend southwards, largely but not entirely, along the western side of the Rhône valley, from Vienne right down to Avignon, and apart from those actually classified as 'Côtes-du-Rhône', include such famous names as Château-Grillet, Condrieu, Hermitage, Chateauneuf-du-Pape, Tavel and Lirac. The lower part of this area is within the Provence Region. The Côtes-du-Rhône provides some fine red wines, and many of them are considerably less expensive than the great wines of Burgundy or Bordeaux. There are also many pleasant white wines including those from the Hermitage vineyards, and of course rosés from Tavel and Lirac.

En route to the Col de la Chaudière (see Saou, page 248)   *Photograph by Peter Titchmarsh*

Savoy and Dauphiny Alps

This is the great alpine Region of France, extending southwards from the fashionable lake-side resorts of Évian-les-Bains and Thonon to the Vanoise massif and eastwards from the wooded mountains of the Vercors to the Mont Cenis Pass and the Italian frontier. Here are most of the great French alpine peaks, presided over by Mont Blanc itself, the deep valleys of such rivers as the Isère, the Arve and the Romanche, a multitude of fashionable winter sports and summer mountain resorts, delightful lake-side towns like Annecy and Aix-les-Bains, and the splendid modern city of Grenoble.

Facilities for winter sports in this region are world renowned, but for those visitors coming here in summer there are limitless opportunities for walking in valleys or upon the mountains, many delightful old towns and villages to be explored, massive dams and their attendant reservoirs to be visited, and numerous cableway trips to be taken into the high mountain country. For those less active there are lake-shore plages, boat trips across the larger lakes, and breath-taking views of the mountains that tower over every valley floor.

Lac du Bourget, near Aix-les-Bains

ABONDANCE (74)   28k SE Thonon-les-Bains
Small skiing and summer mountain resort in the deep valley of the Dranse, with a ruined medieval abbey and abbey church. This has cloisters containing early wall paintings showing scenes from the life of the Virgin Mary.

AIGUEBELETTE LAKE (73)   21k W Chambéry
Pleasant lake below the Épine mountains, with opportunities for fishing, boating and bathing. There are modest hotels at Lepin-le-Lac, Novelais-Lac and St-Alban-de-Montbel.

AIX-LES-BAINS (73)   566k SE Paris   14k N Chambéry
Elegant and still sophisticated watering place on the eastern shore of lovely Lac du Bourget, with a bewildering choice of hotels, many of which date from the days when the Americans and the British rich first came here in considerable numbers (Queen Victoria stayed here in 1885). There is an Archaeological Museum, reminding us that the Romans were the first to take the waters here (their baths are still to be seen in the Thermal Establishment). See also the Musée Faure, with its fine collection of 19th and early 20 century French paintings, including works by Degas and Cézanne. Also take a trip on the lake, and if possible take a boat trip up the little river Sierroz, which flows through a deep gorge to the immediate north east of the town.

Sunlit square at Aix-les-Bains

ALBERTVILLE AND CONFLANS (73)
                    50k ENE Chambéry
Albertville is a busy town at the meeting of the Arly and Isère rivers, looking across to the lovely village of Conflans. Here will be found the 'Grande Rue' with its medieval market stalls and delightful 18th century fountain, the Maison Rouge, a 14th century monastery which is now a local museum, and the nearby Grande Roche, from which there are fine valley and mountain views.

ALLEVARD (38)   35k SE Chambéry
Small spa town in a valley below wooded mountain-sides at the northern end of the Belledonne range. There are several hotels making this a good base for exploring the surrounding mountains.

Lakeside leisure, Aix-les-Bains

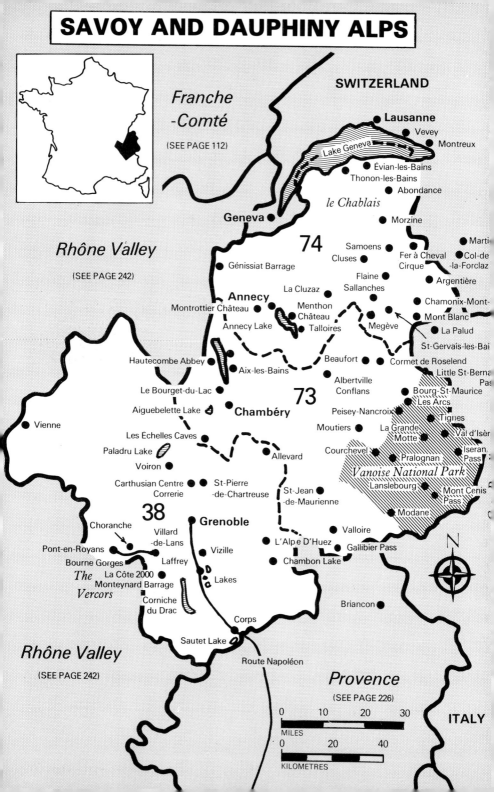

SAVOY AND DAUPHINY ALPS

SWITZERLAND

Franche-Comté
(SEE PAGE 112)

Rhône Valley
(SEE PAGE 242)

Lausanne
Vevey
Montreux

Lake Geneva

Évian-les-Bains
Thonon-les-Bains
Abondance

le Chablais

Morzine

Geneva

74

Samoens
Cluses

Marti
Fer à Cheval
Cirque
Col-de-la-Forclaz

Génissiat Barrage

Flaine
Sallanches

Argentière

Annecy

La Cluzaz

Chamonix-Mont-

Montrottier Château

Menthon
Château
Talloires

Megève

Mont Blanc
La Palud

Annecy Lake

St-Gervais-les-Bai

Hautecombe Abbey

Beaufort

Cormet de Roselend

Aix-les-Bains

Little St-Berna
Pas

Le Bourget-du-Lac

Albertville
Conflans

73

Bourg-St-Maurice
Les Arcs

Aiguebelette Lake

Chambéry

Peisey-Nancroix

Tignes
Val d'Isèr

Vienne

Les Échelles Caves

Moutiers

La Grande
Motte

Iseran
Pass

Paladru Lake

Allevard

Courchevel

Pralognan

Voiron

Vanoise National Park

Carthusian Centre
Correrie

St-Pierre
-de-Chartreuse

Lanslebourg

Mont Cenis
Pass

38

Grenoble

St-Jean
-de-Maurienne

Modane

Choranche

Villard
-de-Lans

Valloire

Pont-en-Royans
Bourne Gorges

Vizille

L'Alpe D'Huez

Gallibier Pass

Laffrey

*The
Vercors*

La Côte 2000
Monteynard Barrage

Lakes

Chambon Lake

Corniche
du Drac

Briancon

Corps

Sautet Lake

Rhône Valley
(SEE PAGE 242)

Route Napoléon

Provence
(SEE PAGE 226)

N

ITALY

0   10   20   30
MILES
0   20   40
KILOMETRES

L'ALPE D'HUEZ (38)   *63k ESE Grenoble*

An outstanding winter-sports and summer mountain resort situated at 1860 metres with many fine hotels and a good network of cableways and ski-lifts. There is a two-stage cableway up to the summit of the Pic-du-Lac-Blanc from which there are awe-inspiring views.

ANNECY (74)   *43k S Geneva*

Lively modern holiday and industrial town at the northern end of lovely Lac d'Annecy, incorporating a delightful 'old town' characterised by narrow streets and little canals bordered by tall flower bedecked houses. There is a small palace on an island formed by two branches of a canal, which is used for exhibitions, and overlooking this is the great château of the Counts of Geneva which houses an interesting local museum. See also the 15th century Dominican church of St-Maurice, with its interesting frescoes, the lakeside gardens with their lovely views down the lake to the mountains beyond, and of course, take a tour of the lake by boat.

ARGENTIÈRE (74)   *8k NE Chamonix*

Charming skiing resort in the Chamonix valley, with several pleasant hotels, and a cableway up beside the great Argentière glacier to the Grands Montets peak (3297 metres), from which there are most dramatic views. In summer drive north from here into Switzerland, and over the Col-de-la-Forclaz, down to Martigny...a really adventurous mountain run.

BEAUFORT (73)   *20k ENE Albertville*

Pleasant village in a deep valley below the Outray massif, with charming old houses and a fine 18th century pulpit in its church. Explore eastwards into the mountains to the Roselend reservoir and the high pastures of the Cormet de Roselend.

LE BOURGET-DU-LAC (73)   *11k NW Chambéry*

Lively holiday town at the southern end of Lac du Bourget, with a plage and boat harbour. Do not miss the 13th century frieze in the church, which is an outstanding example of Savoy sculpture, nor the 'castle' next door to the church, which was given to the monks of Cluny, and which then became a priory. This is complete with an unusual cloister upon which two galleries have been built.

BOURG-ST-MAURICE (73)   *102k E Chambéry*

Small fontier town in the upper Isère valley, on the road north-eastwards to the Little St-Bernard Pass. There is a cableway up from here to the ski resort of Les Arcs and a road running southwards to Val-d'Isère and the Iseran Pass.

BOURNE GORGES (38)   *35k SW Grenoble*

A series of deep gorges formed by the river Bourne in the limestone country of the Vercors (See Page 249) between Pont-en-Royans and Villard-de-Lans. See especially the very impressive caves at Choranche, about twenty kilometres west of Villard-de-Lans. Use Michelin Map 77 to explore this fascinating area in detail.

CHAMBÉRY (73)   *560k SE Paris*

This large but pleasant old town was the capital of the Dukes of Savoy, a state which at one time stretched

continued

L'Alpe d'Huez

Annecy

Lac d'Annecy

High pastures above Beaufort

In the valley of the Bourne

253

Savoy and Dauphiny Alps

Sainte Chapelle, Chambéry

Château gateway, Chambéry

Chambon Lake

In the mountains near Chambéry

On the Route Napoléon, near Corps

Savoy and Dauphiny Alps

from Nice to Berne, and Lyon to Turin, and which only became truly part of France as late as 1860. The narrow streets and winding stairways of the old town are dominated by the great ducal château, the older parts of which may be visited. See also the Cathedral with its 16th century front, and its exquisite 14th century Italian ivory diptych, the fountain with its four massive elephants, commemorating the generosity of General de Boigne, who made a fortune in India in the late 18th century, and the 9th century crypt and baptistry beneath the church of St-Pierre de Lémenc. The number of good hotels and restaurants here make this an ideal base for exploring the western parts of the Savoy Alps.

CHAMBON LAKE (38)   *63k ESE Grenoble*
A large dam across the valley of the upper Romanche has created this beautiful lake in the mountains, below the Grenoble — Briançon road.

CHAMONIX-MONT-BLANC (74)   *615k SE Paris*
                                      83k ESE Geneva
Lively modern holiday centre situated in an outstandingly beautiful alpine valley, no less than 1037 metres above sea level, which for this reason is able to offer 'winter-sports' all the year round. There are a fine variety of hotels, restaurants and sports facilities, and it is one of the best places in France from which the non-mountaineer may 'explore' the world of eternal snows. There is a rack railway up to Montveners, from which there are splendid views across to one of Mont Blanc's great glaciers, the Mer de Glace; and a network of cable-ways taking visitors up to within a thousand metres below the level of Mont Blanc, and on down to the Italian end of the road tunnel at La Palud. This tunnel is eleven and a half kilometres long, and was for some years, subsequent to its opening in 1965, the longest road tunnel in the world. It provides a fine all-weather road link between France and Italy.

CLUSES (74)   *43k ESE Geneva*
Small town in the deep valley of the Arve, noted for the making of small brass parts for clocks and other light industries. There is a national clock making school, the museum and workshops of which may be visited. There is a winding mountain road southwards for ten kilometres, up to the little village of Romme, from which there are fine views out over the Repoisor valley.

LA CLUZAZ (74)   *32k E Annecy*
Pleasant winter-sports and summer mountain holiday resort attractively sited below the Aravis massif. There is a good selection of hotels and restaurants and La Cluzaz is well served by cableways and ski-lifts. Explore south and west from here, over the Col-de-la-Croix-Fry, and down the lovely Manigod valley to Thones. See Michelin Map 74 for several other interesting sorties from here.

CORPS (38)   *63k SEE Grenoble*
Small town astride the Route Napoleon with little cobbled streets, and at least three small hotels. There is a marvellous scenic route around the Sautet lake, crossing a fine single arch bridge over the Drac just below the great dam forming the lake. The isolated mountain church of Notre-Dame-de-la-Salette is at the end of a sixteen kilometre road north from Corps, and is a famous place of pilgrimage in a most attractive setting.

COURCHEVEL (73) *42k SSE Albertville*

Outstanding winter-sports and summer mountain resort with a fine selection of hotels and restaurants. It is the hub of a well planned series of ski-lifts and cableways, which can cope with as many as 30,000 'passengers' per hour. There are splendid views from the summit of 2630 metre high La Saule, which is reached by two cableways.

LES ÉCHELLES CAVES (73) *23k SW Chambéry*

Two caves about five kilometres NE of Les Échelles village and reached from the N6 road, by a tunnel, the construction of which was ordered by Napoleon.

ÉVIAN-LES-BAINS (74) *579k SE Paris, 42k NE Geneva*

Elegant resort on the sothern shore of Lake Geneva, (Lac Léman), with charming views across the water to Lausanne, about twelve kilometres away. There are boat trips across to Lausanne and Vevey, or along the southern shores to Geneva or Montreux, and of course, an excellent choice of hotels and restaurants.

Ski-ing at Courchevel *Génissiat Barrage*

FLAINE (74) *25k SE Cluses*

Fashionable modern ski resort high above the Arve valley with many ski-lifts and two cableways up to the high Désert de Platé.

GÉNISSIAT BARRAGE (74) *42k SW Geneva*

This great dam across the Rhône is well worth visiting. It is built between high cliffs and the waters trapped behind it extend over twenty kilometres northwards to the Swiss border. The hydro-electric generating station at its base is one of the largest in Europe.

Lake steamer at Evian-les-Bains

GRENOBLE (38) *568k SE Paris*

Capital of the Region, and chief city of the French Alps, Grenoble is a dynamic modern city, typified by its splendid plate-glass and marble Hôtel-de-Ville, one of many splendid modern buildings. It lies on a great bend of the Isère, where this river is joined by the equally tumultuous Drac, and Grenoble is noted for its pioneering of hydro-electric power in the 19th century. The old part of the city lies to the immediate south of the Isère, with a much restored Cathedral, a handsome Renaissance Palais de Justice, and a Museum of Fine Arts, which contains one of the great collections of 20th century French art. The old Hôtel-de-Ville contains a Museum illustrating the life of Stendhal, the writer who was born in Grenoble in 1783. However the adventure that most visitors to Grenoble will remember is their trip on the ultra-modern 'téléphérique' (cable car), from the Quai Stephane Jay, over the Isère, and up to the Fort de la Bastille. This is built on a rocky bluff looking out over the city, and at 475 metres, it provides dramatic views which on a clear day even include far off Mont Blanc. There is an orientation table, two restaurants, fortifications by the great Vauban, and a Motor Museum. Grenoble organised the very first 'Syndicat d'Initiative', as early as 1889, and the present Maison du Tourisme in the Rue de la République carries on a fine tradition, with its most helpful supply of tourist information and assistance.

Grenoble *Grenoble*

HAUTECOMBE ABBEY (73) *27k NNW Chambéry*

Benedictine abbey church re-built in the 19th century in elaborate Gothic style, and wonderfuly sited on a

The Tour Perret, Grenoble *Hôtel-de-Ville, Grenoble*

continued,

Laffrey Lake

Swimming pool at Megève

Climbing Mont Blanc

promontory on the western shore of Lac-du-Bourget. Here are the tombs of no fewer than forty one of the Princes and Princesses of Savoy, and many visitors come here across the lake from Aix-les-Bains, both to see the tombs and also to listen to the lovely Gregorian chants of the Benedictine Fathers.

LAFFREY (38)   *24k S Grenoble*
This small village lies just to the north of the 'Prairie de la Rencontre', the spot where Napoleon on his dramatic march north along what has become known as the Route Napoléon (See Page 237), was stopped on March 7th 1815 by a party of soldiers, who were ordered by their young officer to open fire on him. However after a moment's hesitation they broke ranks and shouted 'Vive l'Empereur!', and from this moment his fortunes changed. An equestrian statue of the Emperor marks the spot, and from here there are fine views out over the Grand Lac de Laffrey and the mountains beyond.

LANSLEBOURG (73)   *126k ESE Chambéry*
Small 'frontier village' below the high Mont Cenis Pass (See Below) on the main route between Lyon and Turin. There is an attractive road east and north from here, up over the Iseran Pass, to Val-d'Isère and down to Bourg-St-Maurice. This is the only significant road to penetrate the Vanoise National Park (See Pages 258 – 9).

MEGÈVE (74)   *70k SE Geneva*
Lively alpine holiday resort and winter-sport centre, with a cable-way to the top of Mount Arbois, from which there are fine views to Mont Blanc. There are of course several other cable-ways and ski-lifts, and a wide variety of hotels.

MENTHON CHÂTEAU (74)   *9k SE Annecy*
A 15th and 16th century building replacing an earlier castle in which St-Bernard de Menthon, the founder of the St-Bernard Hospice, was born in the 10th century. Visitors may see an oratory, reproducing the room in which he is said to have been born, and there are exquisite views out over the Lake of Annecy.

MONT BLANC (74)
(See Chamonix, Page 254)

MONT CENIS PASS (73)   *130k ESE Chambéry*
A splendid mountain route leading to the Italian frontier and on down to Susa and eventually Turin. This was built on the orders of Napoleon between 1803 and 1811 and is well worth ascending for its fine views out over the great reservoir lake of Mont Cenis.

MONTEYNARD BARRAGE (38)   *33k S Grenoble*
This massive dam across the river Drac has created a long reservoir in what was a deep valley, and above which there is a fine scenic road, still known as the Corniche du Drac.

MONTROTTIER CHÂTEAU (74)   *11k W Annecy*
13th to 16th century Château with a great round keep and extensive battlements from which there are fine views. The castle contains outstanding collections of armour, oriental porcelain and ivories, and European furniture, and is well worth visiting. If possible combine with a visit to the nearby Fier Gorge (See Michelin Map 74).

Menthon Château

Savoy and Dauphiny Alps

MORZINE (74)   *63k E Geneva*

Lively winter-sports and summer mountain holiday town with cableways giving access to the heights of le Plénay and les Hautforts. Hotels and restaurants abound and this is an ideal base from which to explore the mountain country of le Chablais between here and the shore of Lake Geneva, (Lac Léman).

Two views of Morzine

MOUTIERS (73)   *18k SSE Albertville*

Minute Cathedral and market town in a deep valley at the confluence of the Isère and the Dorons. The 15th century Cathedral contains a richly carved bishop's throne (also 15th century), a Romanesque statue of the Virgin, and a crypt which is believed to date from the 5th century.

PALADRU LAKE (38)

44k NW Grenoble, 14k NW Voiron

Attractive lake in the hills of the Bas-Dauphiné, with several bathing beaches and camping sites, notably at Charavines at the south end. There are two modest hotels at Charavines.

PEISEY-NANCROIX (73)   *15k S Bourg-St-Maurice*

These two villages are attractively situated in a tributary valley high up above the upper Isère, and make up a small but very pleasant mountaineering and skiing resort. Peisey church with its tall thin tower is a picturesque feature of this fine mountain landscape on the northern confines of the Vanoise National Park.

Cableway at Morzine   *Pont-en-Royans*

PONT-EN-ROYANS (38)   *62k WSW Grenoble*

Attractive little village at the mouth of the Bourne gorges (See Page 253), with many old houses poised on the rocky slopes above the river, which has been dammed about two kilometres below. There is an orientation table ('Trois Chateau') well above the village which can only be reached on foot, but is well worth the effort.

ROUTE NAPOLÉON (See Page 237)

ST-GERVAIS-LES-BAINS (74)   *25k W Chamonix*

This is a busy combination of health resort, winter-sports and summer mountain touring centre. It has a number of excellent hotels, and ski-lifts and cableways provide fine access to the mountain slopes above it. The fascinating 'Tramway du Mont Blanc' takes visitors up to the 2386 metre Nid-d'Aigle (The Eagle's Nest) from which there are splendid views over Mont Blanc, only six kilometres away, across the Brionnassay glacier.

Napoleon at Laffrey (See Page 256)

ST-JEAN-DE-MAURIENNE (73)   *72k SE Chambéry*

Old grey stone town sited in a deep valley to the south west of the Vanoise National Park, at the confluence of the rivers Arc and Arvan. See the 11th and 15th century Cathedral, with its detached tower, its handsome 15th century choir stalls and its unique alabaster sculpture, said to contain three fingers of St-John the Baptist.

ST-PIERRE-DE-CHARTREUSE (38)

29k NNE Grenoble

Charming alpine resort in the Massif de la Chartreuse, with at least three small hotels and wonderful views from the terrace of its Mairie. The monastery of La Grande Chartreuse is not open to visitors, but there is

continued

Mont Blanc from St-Gervais   *Tramway du Mont Blanc, St-Gervais*

Savoy and Dauphiny Alps

Carthusian Centre, Correrie, St-Pierre-de-Chartreuse

Talloires

Church at Thonon-les-Bains

Thonon-les-Bains

Ripaille Château near Thonon-les-Bains

an interesting 'Carthusian Centre' at Correrie, four kilometres to the west. The famous green liqueur used to be made at La Grande Chartreuse, but this is now carried out at Voiron (See Page 259).

SALLANCHES (74)　　　*28k W Chamonix*
Busy tourist centre in the Arve valley, now happily by-passed by the autoroute, and noted since the days of early tourism for its splendid views eastwards to Mont Blanc.

SAMOENS (74)　　　*55k ESE Geneva*
This relatively small skiing and summer mountain resort has several modest hotels and a cableway and ski-lifts. It is an excellent base for exploring the upper valley of the Giffre with the dramatic Fer à Cheval Cirque at its head thirteen kilometres to the east, and the Cascade du Rouget (waterfalls) eleven kilometres to the south-east. There are lovely alpine gardens in the village itself, which are well worth visiting.

TALLOIRES (74)　　　*13k SE Annecy*
Charming little resort on the eastern shores of the lovely Annecy Lake, with a larger number of luxury hotels and restaurants per head of the permanent population that anywhere we know. There are fine views out over the lake for those who dare to follow the promptings of the Red Michelin.

THONON-LES-BAINS (74)　　　*33k NE Geneva*
Smaller than nearby Évian, its neighbour along the shore of Lake Geneva (Lac Léman), Thonon is equally elegant as a resort and has several interesting features including two churches and a museum. Two kilometres to the north is the monastery-château of Ripaille, a favourite of the Dukes of Savoy before it was given to the Carthusians, and well worth visiting. There are boat trips across to Lausanne, or along the southern shores to Montreux or Geneva.

TIGNES (73)　　　*30k SE Bourg St-Maurice*
This is a post-war ski-ing resort built below the great Tignes Barrage across the upper Isère, and only thirteen kilometres below Val d'Isère (See Below). There is an attractive little road south-south-west from here up past Tignes Lake, into the heart of the Vanoise National Park, complete with a cable-way at its far end up to the sumiit of La Grande Motte.

VAL D'ISÈRE (73)　　　*31k SE Bourg-St-Maurice*
Fashionable high altitude ski-ing resort, close to the border with Italy. Winter-sport is possible here until May and there is a good network of cable-lifts giving access to the heights of the Vanoise massif. This is an excellent base for exploring the Vanoise National Park in summer, and the Iseran Pass provides adventurous summertime motoring.

VALLOIRE (73)　　　*103k SE Chambéry*
Charming winter-sports village in a valley which leads southwards up to the Gallibier Pass. There is a wide selection of hotels, a cableway and many ski-lifts. The 17th century church is richly decorated within and well worth visiting.

VANOISE NATIONAL PARK (73)
Approx 90k SE Annecy
This encompasses the whole of the Vanoise massif, which extends from the frontier with Italy, south and *continued*

westwards to Modane. It includes 107 peaks above 3000 metres, and the highest of these is La Grande Casse, at 3852 metres. This rugged mountain area can be approached from Pralognan, Tignes, Val d'Isère, Lanslebourg or Modane, but even in high summer, we suggest that you keep to the valleys unless you have experience, or are in experienced company. Long distance paths GR 5 and GR 55 pass right through the Park, but they both represent challenges. This splendid mountain area is noted for its flora and fauna, and ibex and chamois inhabit the remoter slopes. This National Park marches with the equally attractive Gran Paradiso National Park across the border into Italy and together they make up one of Europe's outstanding alpine 'reserves'. For more details write to: Parc de la Vanoise, 15, rue du Docteur-Julliand, B.P. 105, 73003 Chambéry.

Vienne

VIENNE (38)   *492k SSE Paris, 30k S Lyon*

Situated on the east bank of the Rhône this fine town, with its wealth of Roman remains and fine hotels and restaurants belongs more in spirit to the Rhône Valley region, but it does in fact lie in Isère Department, so we have included it here. See especially the great Roman theatre, the Roman temple and the triumphal arch; the splendid Romanesque and Gothic Cathedral, with its fine west portal and its interior rich with stained glass and carved stone, and the church of St-André-le-Bas, which houses a Museum of Christian Art. Lovers of civilized eating and drinking should turn to the Red Michelin Guide, although there will be few who have not heard of 'La Pyramide'.

Cloisters of St-André-le-Bas, Vienne

VILLARD-DE-LANS (38)   *33k SW Grenoble*

Lively winter-sports and summer mountain resort situated at the eastern side of the Vercors (See Page 249). Ski-lifts and cableways connect the town with the great ridge of the Montagne-de-Lans above it to the east, and there is an excellent choice of hotels and restaurants. In summer, take the cablecar to La Côte 2000, a peak from which there are outstanding views. Also drive westwards on N531 to explore the Bourne gorges (See Page 253).

VIZILLE (38)   *17k SSE Grenoble*

Small industrial town in the Romanche valley with only one item of real interest...a fine Renaissance château in which an event of unparallelled importance in French history took place. It was here in 1788 that the nobles, clergy and commoners sat together for the first time, in a united attempt to oppose the suppression of Parliament by Louis XVI, and to proclaim the individual liberty of every Frenchman. It is therefore with some justice that Vizille claims to have been the very cradle of the French Revolution.

Cableway near Villard-de-Lans

In the Vercors, near Villard-de-Lans

VOIRON (38)   *31k NE Grenoble*

Busy light industrial town to the west of the Chartreuse massif. It is here, in the Boulevard Edgar-Coffer, that the Carthusian monks now make the renowned green Chartreuse liqueur*, using a formula over three hundred years old, the secrets of which remain with them still. This process may be watched by visitors on every weekday.

*See St-Pierre-de-Chartreuse, Page 257–8.

Vizille Château, 'Cradle of the Revolution'

Index of Places

A

	Page
Abbadia Château	47
Abbeville	209
L'Aber-Wrac'h	69
Abondance	251
Abreschviller	39
Agde	129
Agen	47
Agincourt, Battle of	187
L'Aigle	195
Aigle Barrage	63, 142
Aigoual, Mont	129
Aiguebelette Lake	251
Aigues-Mortes	129
Ainay-le-Vieil	150
Ain Gorges	241
Airaines	209
Aire	187
Aire-sur-Adour	47
Aitone Forest	97, 98
Aix-en-Provence	227
Aix, Île d'	217
Aix-les-Bains	251
Ajaccio	95
Alagnon Gorges	60
Albert	209
Albertville	251
Albi	175
Alencon	195
Aleria	95
Alès	129
Algajola	95
Alise-Sainte-Reine	79
Alleuze Château	58
Allevard	251
Alma Bridge	28
L'Alpe d'Huez	253
Les Alpilles	227
Alsace and Lorraine-Vosges	39–46
Alsace, Wines of	46
Alsace Wine Road	39
Altkirch	39
Amance	111
Ambazac	141
Ambert	58
Ambierle	241
Amboise	150
Amiens	209–210
Ammerschwihr	39
Ancenis	165
Ancy-le-Franc	79
Ancy-sur-Moselle	42
Andaines Forest	196
Les Andelys	195
Andilly-en-Bassigny	89
Andorra	175
Anduze	129
Anet	150
Angers	165
Angles-sur-Anglin	217
Ango Manor	195
Angoulême	217
Anjony Château	58
Annecy	253
Annecy Lake	256, 258

	Page
Annonay	241
Ansouis Château	228
Antibes	103
Apremont Gorges	120, 122
Apt	228
Aquitaine	47–57
Araggio Castle	99
Arbois	111
Arcachon	47
Arcais	221
Arc de Triomphe	28
Arc-et-Senans	111
Archiane Cirque	244
Les Arcs	228
Arcy-sur-Cure Caves	79
Ardèche Gorges	241
Ardennes Forest	92
Ardres	191
Argelès-Gazost	175
Argelès-sur-Mer	131
Argentan	195
Argentat	141
Argentière	253
Argoat, The	69
Argenton-Château	217
Argenton-sur-Creuse	151
Argonne Forest	39, 89
Arles	228
Armagnac	186
Armentières	187
Armorique Regional Nature Park	69
Arnac-Pompadour	141
Arnay-le-Duc	79
Arras	187
Arromanches	196
Artige Dam	145
Asco	95
Asnières Abbey	165
Asnières-sur-Vègre	165
Assier	184
Asson Zoo Park	47
Asterix Theme Park	210
Aubagne	228
Aubazines	141
Aubenas	241
Auberive	89
Aubusson	141
Auch	175
Aude Gorges	131
Audierne	69
Aulnay	217
Auray	69
Aurillac	58
Auron	103
Austerlitz Column	38
L'Autel Cave	74
Auteuil Racecourse	29
Autoire	177
Autreppes	216
Autun	79
Auvergne	58–67
Auxerre	79
Auxonne	79
Avallon	80
Mont des Avaloirs	165

	Page
Aven Armand (Cave)	131
Avenue de l'Opéra	35
Avesnes-sur-Helpe	189
Avignon	229
Avolsheim	43
Avranches	196
Ax-les-Thermes	177
Azay-le-Ferron	151
Azay-le-Rideau	151
Azé Cave	80
Azincourt	187

B

	Page
Bagatelle (Abbeville)	209
Bagatelle (Bois de Boulogne)	29
Bagatelle Zoo Park	189
Bagnères-de-Bigorre	177
Bagnères-de-Luchon	181
Bagnoles-de-l'Orne	196
Bagnols-sur-Cèze	131
Bairon Lake	89
Balagne, The	99
Balbigny	247
Balleroy Château	196
Bandol	229
La Banne d'Ordanche	60
La Bannie Animal Park	89
Banyuls-sur-Mer	131
Bara-Bahau Cavern	50
Barbegal	235
Barbentane	229
Barben Zoo Park	229
Barbezieux	219
Barbizon	120
Barcelonnette	229
Barfleur	196
Bargemon	229
Barjols	229
Bar-le-Duc	39
Barneville-Carteret	196
Baronnies Massif	243
Barry	230
Barsac	57
Bar-sur-Aube	89
Bar-sur-Seine	89
Bassac Abbey	219
Bastelica	97
Bastia	97
La Bastie d'Urfé	243
Bastille, Place de la	29
Batz, Île de	76
Batz-sur-Mer	165
Baugé	167
La Baule	167
Baume Cirque	111
Baumes Cirque	138
Baume-les-Messieurs	111
Les Baux-de-Provence	230
Bavay	189
Bavella Pass	97
Bayel	89
Bayeux	197
Bayeux Tapestry	197
Bayonne	47
Bazas	49

	Page
Bazeilles	**89**
Bazouges-sur-le-Loir	**167**
Béarn, Kingdom of	**54**
Bellegarde	**151**
Beaubourg Art and Cultural Centre	**29**
Beaucaire	**131**
Beaufort	**253**
Beaugency	**151**
Beaulieu-sur-Dordogne	**142**
Beaulieu-sur-Mer	**103**
Beaumesnil Château	**197**
Beaumont	**49**
Beaumont-Hamel	**209**
Beaumont-sur-Vingeanne Château	**80**
Beaune	**80**
Beauport Abbey	**74**
Beaurain	**216**
Beauregard	**151**
Beauvais	**210**
Le Bec-Hellouin	**197**
Belfast Tower	**209**
Belfort	**111**
Bel-Homme Pass	**229**
Belle-Île	**70, 73, 75**
Bellême	**197**
Belley	**243**
Bel-Val Parc de Vision	**90**
Belvedere de Copeyre	**181**
Béhuard, Île	**170**
Beg-Meil	**69**
Bendor, Île-de-	**229**
Benedictine Liqueur	**201**
La Bénisson-Dieu	**243**
Benodet	**70**
Bercé Forest	**167**
Berck-Plage	**189**
Bergerac	**49**
Bergerie National	**126**
Bergues	**189**
Bernay	**197**
Berzé-le-Château	**80**
Besancon	**113**
Besse-en-Chandesse	**58**
Bétharram Grottoes	**49**
Béthune	**189**
Beuil	**104**
Beynac Château	**49**
Béziers	**131**
Biarritz	**49**
Bibliothèque Nationale	**29**
Bienassis Château	**70**
Bienne Gorges	**116**
Bièvres	**120**
Billaude Falls	**113**
Biot	**103**
Biron Château	**49**
Biron, Hôtel	**36**
Le Blanc	**151**
Blandy-les-Tours	**120**
Blanot Caves	**80**
Blaye	**49**
Blérancourt Château	**210**
Blesle	**60**
Blois	**151 – 2**
Bocognano	**97**

	Page
Boeschepe Windmill	**189**
Bois D'Attilly Zoo Park	**120**
Bois de Boulogne	**29**
Bois de St-Pierre Leisure Park	**219**
Bois Préau	**126**
Bois-Thibault Château	**170**
Bollène	**230**
Bommes	**57**
Bonaguil Château	**50**
Bonhomme, Col du	**41**
Bonifacio	**97**
Bonneval Castle	**143**
Bonzée-en-Woëvre	**42**
Bordeaux	**50**
Bordeaux Wine Areas	**57**
Le Boréon	**108**
Bormes-les-Mimosas	**234**
Bort-les-Orgues	**65, 142**
Bosc Cave	**177**
Bouges Château	**152**
Bougival	**120**
Le Bouilh Château	**50**
Bouillon	**93**
Boulogne	**189**
Boumois Château	**167**
La Bourbansais Zoo Park	**70**
Bourbon-Lancy	**80**
La Bourboule	**60**
Bourcefranc	**221**
Bourdeilles Château	**50**
Bourganeuf	**142**
Bourg-de-Péage	**248**
Bourg-en-Bresse	**243**
Bourges	**152**
Le Bourget-du-Lac	**253**
Bourget, Lac du	**251, 256**
Bourgonnière Château	**167**
Bourg-St-Maurice	**253**
Bourgueil	**152**
Bourne Gorges	**253**
Bourneville	**198**
Boussac	**142**
Le Bouy Zoo Park	**58**
Braine	**210**
The Bramabiau Chasm	**131**
Brancion	**80**
Brando	**98**
Branféré Zoo Park	**70**
Brantes	**230**
Brantôme	**50**
Braux-Ste-Cohière Château	**90**
Brécy Manor	**197**
Bressuire	**219**
Brest	**70**
Breteuil Château	**120 – 121**
Briancon	**230**
Briare	**152**
Bricquebec	**197 – 198**
Bridoré	**153**
Brienne-le-Château	**90**
Brière Regional Nature Park	**167**
Brignoles	**230**
La Brigue	**104**
Brinay	**153**
Brioude	**60**
Brissac Château	**167**
Brittany	**69 – 77**

	Page
Brive-La-Gaillarde	**142**
Brossay Forest	**165**
Brotonne Regional Nature Park	**198**
Brouage	**219**
Brouis, Col de	**109**
Bruniquel	**177**
Bugatti Car Museum	**43**
Bugue, Le	**50**
Buis-les-Baronnies	**243**
Burgundy	**78 – 87**
Burgundy Wine Areas	**87**
La Bussière	**153**
Bussy-Rabutin Château	**81**

C

	Page
La Cabosse Zoo Park	**198**
Cabourg	**198**
Cabrerets	**177**
Cadanet	**234**
Cadouin	**50**
Caen	**198**
Caen Canal	**204**
Cagnes-sur-Mer	**104**
Cahors	**177**
Calacuccia Dam and Reservoir	**97**
Calais	**189 – 190**
Calanques de Piana	**98**
Calanques, Les	**231**
Calenzana	**99**
'Calvados Country'	**207**
Calvaries	**74**
Calvi	**98**
Camaret	**70**
Camargue, The	**230 – 231**
Cambo-les-Bains	**51**
Cambrai	**190**
Canal d'Alsace	**43**
Canal de Briare	**152**
Canal de Bourgogne	**86**
Canal du Centre	**81, 83**
Canal Latéral	**47**
Canal du Midi	**131, 132, 138**
Canal Nantes-Brest	**75, 76**
Canal-du-Rhone-a-Sète	**138**
Les Canalettes Cave	**132**
Cancale	**70**
Candes-St-Martin	**153**
Canet-en-Roussillon St-Nazaire	**132**
Canigou, Pic du	**132**
Canner Valley Touristic Railway	**41**
Cannes	**104**
La Canonica	**98**
Cap D'Agde	**132**
Cap d'Antibes	**103**
Cap Corse	**98**
Cap Ferrat	**108**
Cap Frehel	**70, 71, 77**
Cap Gris Nez	**190**
Cap de la Hague	**203**
Cap Martin	**107**
Caradeuc Château	**70**
Carcassonne	**132**
Carennac	**177**
Cargèse	**98**
Carentan	**198**
Carhaix-Plouguer	**71**
Carlat	**60**

Page

Carnac 71
Carnavalet Hôtel 29
Carozzica Forest 95
Carpentras 231
Carrouges 198
Carteret 196
Carthusian Centre 258
Cascade-du-Rouget 258
Cassel 190
Cassis 231
Castellane 231
Castelnau Castle 178
Castelnau-de-Montmiral 178
Castelnaud Château 51
Castelnaudary 132
Castelnou 132
Castillon Barrage and Lake 231
Castres 178
Castries 133
Catacombs, The 29
Le Cateau-Cambrésis 190
Caudebec-en-Caux 198
Causse de Gramat 184
Causse du Larzac 178
Causse Méjean 131, 133
Causses, The 133
Cauterets 178
Cavaillon 231
Cayeux-sur-Mer 212
Centre Pompidou 29
Cerdon Caves 243
Céret .133
Cerisy-la-Forêt Abbey 199
Cévennes National Park 133
Chaalis Abbey 213
le Chablais 257
Chablis 81
Chaillot Palace . . . . .29 – 30
Chaîne des Volcans 64, 65
La Chaise Dieu 60
Chalain Lake 113
Le Chalard 142
Chalon-sur-Saône 81
Châlons-sur-Marne 90
Chalus 142
Chalusset Château 146
Chambéry . . . . .253 – 254
Chambon Lake (Auvergne) . 60, 64
Chambon Lake (Limousin) 143
Chambon Lake
 (Savoy-Dauphiné) 254
Chambon-sur-Voueize 142
Chambord 153
Chamonix-Mont-Blanc 254
Champagne-Ardenne . . . .88 – 94
'Champagne Country' 94
Champagne Road, The 90
Champagnole 113
Champ-de-Bataille Château . . .199
Champ-de-Mars 30
Champdieu 243
Champigny-sur-Veude 153
Chaplieu Roman Site 210
Champlitte 113
Champrepus Zoo 199
Champs-Élysées 30
Champs-sur-Marne 121

Page

Chanteloup Pagoda 153
Chantilly 210
Chaource 93
Charamande Château 121
Charavines 257
Charenton-le-Pont 121
Charité-sur-Loire 81
Charlannes Plateau 60
Charleville-Mézières 90
Charlieu . . . . .243 – 244
Charolles 81
Charroux 60
Chartres . . . . .153 – 154
Chartreuse Liqueur 259
Chassezac Gorges and Dams . . 133
Chastang Barrage 142
Châteaubriant . . . . .167 – 168
Château-Chalon 113
Château-Chinon 81
Le Château-d'Oléron 221
Châteaudun 154
Château-du-Pin 114
Château Gaillard 195
Château-Gontier 168
Château-Landon 121
Châteaulin 71
Châteauneuf-de-Grasse 107
Châteauneuf-du-Pape 231
Châteauneuf-en Auxois 81
Châteauneuf-sur-Cher 154
Châteauneuf-sur-Loire 154
Château Queyras 233
Châteauroux 154
Château-Thierry 211
Châteldon 60
Châtel-Guyon 61
Châtellerault 219
Châtelot Barrage 117
Le Chatenet-en-Dulong 143
Châtillon-en-Diois 244
Châtillon-sur-Indre 154
Chatillon-sur-Seine 81
La Châtre 154
Chaudanne Barrage 231
Chaumont 90
Chaumont Château 82
Chaumont-sur-Loire 154
Chauny 215
Chausey Islands 199
Chauvigny 219
Chaux Royal Salt Works 111
Chavaniac-Lafayette 61
Chaze-sur-Argos 173
Chemin des Dames 211
Chenavari 247
Chenonceaux 155
Cherbourg 199
Le Chesne 89
Cheverny 155
Chevreuse 121
Chinon 155
Chinon Nuclear Power Station 155
Chizé Forest 220
Cholet .168
Chooz Nuclear Power Station . . 91
Choranche Caves 253
Cians Gorges 104

Page

Ciboure 56
Cimiez 107
Cingle de Trémolat 56
Cinq-Mars-la-Pile 155
Cité, The 30
Cîteaux 82
Clairefontaine Animal Park
 (des Yvelines) 121
Clairvaux Forest 89
Clamecy 82
La Clamouse Cave 133
Clarière de l'Armistice 211
Clécy .199
Clères Zoological Park 199
Clermont Abbey 168
Clermont-Ferrand 61
Cléron .114
Cléry-St-André 155
Clos-Lucé Manor 150
Clos Vougeot 82
Cluny 82
Cluny, Hôtel de 30
Cluny Museum 30
Cluse de Joux 116
Cluses 254
La Cluzaz 254
La Cocalière Cave 133
Cognac 219
Cognac...the Brandy Country 225
Cognacq-Jay Museum 30
Col-de-la-Chaudière 248
Col-de-la-Croix-Fry 254
Col-de-la-Forclaz 253
Col d'Iseran 253, 256
Colettes Forest 67
Collioure 133
Collonges-la-Rouge 143
Colmar .41
Colombey-les-deux-Églises 90
Combarelles Cave 51
Combourg 71
Comédie-Francaise, The 30
Commarin Château 82
Commelles Lake 210
Comper Château 74
Compiègne 211
Compiègne Forest 211
Concarneau 71
Conches-en-Ouche 199
Conciergerie, The 31
Concorde, Place de la 31
Condat .65
Condé-en-Brie Château 211
Condé Museum 210
Condom 178
Condrieu 244
Conflans 251
Conflans-Ste-Honorine 121
Confolens 220
Conques 178
Consolation Cirque 114
Corbeny 211
Corbie .211
Cordès 178
Cordouan Lighthouse 224
Cormatin Château 82
Cormeilles-en-Vexin 124

262

	Page
Cormet-de-Roselend	253
Corniche Bretonne, The	74
Corniche des Cévennes	**133**
Corniche du Drac	256
Cornilloux Waterfall	65
Corps	254
Corsica	**95 – 101**
Corsica Regional Nature Park	**98**
Corte	**98**
Cosne-sur-Loire	**82**
La Côte 2000	259
Côte-d'Azur	**102 – 110**
Cotentin Peninsula	196, 197, 203
Coubre Lighthouse	224
Coucy-le-Château	212
Couesque Barrage	**178**
Cougnac Caves	**178**
Coulommiers	**121**
Courances Château	**121**
Courbevoie	**121 – 122**
Courbons	231
Courchevel	255
Courcon	221
Courmes	105
Courseulles-sur-Mer	**199**
Courtanvaux Château	**168**
Coussac-Bonneval	**143**
Coutances	**200**
La Couvertoirade	**178**
Craon	**168**
Credogne Valley	60
Crêches	243
Battle of Crécy	**212**
Crécy-en-Ponthieu	212
Crécy Forest	212
Crépy-en-Valois	**212**
Crest	**244**
Crêt-de-la-Perdrix	247
Creux-Sailland Waterfalls	60
Le Croisic	**168**
Croix de Valberg	109
Croix-de-Vie	**173**
Le Crotoy	**212**
Crozant	**143**, 151
Le Crozet	**244**
Culan	**155**
Cunault	**168**

D

Daluis	**104**
Daluis Gorges	**104**
Dambach-la-Ville	**41**
Les Dames des Meuse	92
Dampierre	**122**
Dampierre-sur-Boutonne Château	**220**
Damvix	221
Dargilan Caves	**134**
Davayat	**61**
Dax	**51**
Deauville	**200**
Decize	**83**
Decorative Arts, Museum of	**31**
Defais, Étang du	174
La Défense	**122**
Les Demoiselles Caves	**134**
Déols Abbey	154

	Page
Der Lake	**91**
Désert de Platé	255
La Devèze Caves	**134**
La Devinière	**156**
Die	**244**
Dieppe	**200**
Dieulefit	**244**
Digne	107, **231**
Digoin	**83**
Dijon	**83**
Dinan	**71**
Dinard	**71**
Divonne-les-Bains	**244**
Dol-de-Bretagne	**71**
Dole	**114**
Domfront	**200**
Domme	**51**
Domrémy-la-Pucelle	**41**
Donzère-Mondragon Barrage	230
Le Dorat	**143**
Douai	**190**
Douarnenez and Tréboul	**72**
Doué-la-Fontaine	**168**
Doullens	209, **212**
Dourbie Gorges	**179**
Dourdan	**122**
The Dragon's Cavern	**212**
Draguignan	**232**
Dreux	**156**
Dunkirk	**190**
Duras Château	**51**
Durtal	**168**

E

Eawy Forest	**200**
Les Échelles Caves	**255**
École Militaire	30
Ecouen Château	**122**
Écouves Forest	**200**
Écrins National Park	**232**
Eden Roc	103
Effiat Château	**61**
Eguisheim	**41**
Éguzon Dam	**143**
Eiffel Tower, The	**31**
Elbeuf	**200**
Élysée Palace	**31**
Emancé	**122**
Embrun	**232**
Enfer Gorge	**51**
Engelsbourg Castle	45
Englancourt	216
Ensérune, Oppidum d'	**134**
Entraygues-sur-Truyère	67, **179**
Entrecasteaux	**232**
Entrevaux	**232**
De l'Épau Abbey	**168 – 169**
Épernay	**91**
Ephrussi de Rothschild Foundation	108
Épinal	**41**
L'Epine	**91**
Epoisses Château	**83**
Ermenonville	**212 – 213**
Ermenonville Forest	212
Erquy	**72**
Espalion	**179**

	Page
Estaing	**179**
Étampes	**122**
Étang de Berre	235
Étaples	**191**
Etival	45
Étretat	**200**
Eu	**200 – 201**
Évian-les-Bains	**255**
Evisa	**98**
Évreux	**201**
Évron	**169**
Les Eyzies-de-Tayac	**51**
Èze	**105**

F

La Fage Chasm	**147**
Falaise	**201**
Le Faou	**72**
Fargues	**57**
Faubourg St-Germain	31
Faubourg St-Honoré	31
Faucogney	**114**
Faux de Verzy	**92**
La-Favière	**234**
Fayl-Billot	**91**
Fécamp	**201**
Felleries	**191**
Felletin	**141**
Fénelon Château	**51**
Fer-à-Cheval Cirque	**258**
La Fère	**213**
Fermont	42
La Ferté-Bernard	**169**
La Ferté-Milon	**213**
'Field of the Cloth-of-Gold'	**191**
Fier Gorge	256
Figeac	**179**
Filitosa	**99**
Flaine	**255**
Flavigny-sur-Ozerain	**83**
The Flea Market	**32**, 127
La Flèche	**169**
Fleckenstein Castle	46
Fleix Dam	145
Flers	**201**
Fleurigny Château	**83**
Fleury	46
Fléville Château	**41**
Florac	**134**
Flower Markets of Paris	**32**
Foix	**179**
Fontainebleau	**122**
Fontaine Daniel Abbey	171
Fontaine-de-Vaucluse	**232**
Fontaine-Guérard Abbey	**201**
Fontaine-Henri Château	**201**
Font-de-Gaume Cave	51
Fontenay	**83**
Fontenay-le-Comte	**169**
Fontevrault-l'Abbaye	**169**
Fontgombault Abbey	**156**
Fontirou Caves	**52**
Font-Romeu	**134**
Fontvieille	**232**
Foreign Legion, The	228
Forests of the Île-de-France Region	**122 – 123**

Page

Forêst de Chizé Zoo **220**
Forêt d'Orient Regional Nature
   Park **91**
Les Forges 74
Forges-les-Eaux **201**
Fort la Latte 70
Fort Vendeuil Zoo Park **213**
Forum des Halles **32**
Fougères **72**
Fougères-sur-Bièvre **156**
Fouras **220**
Franchard Gorges 122
Franche-Comté . . . . **111 – 117**
Fréjus **233**
Fréjus Zoo Park **233**
Fresselines **143**
Le Fret 70
Froissy **213**
Fromentine 174
Futuroscope **220**

G

Gaillac **179**
Galamus Gorges **134**
Gallardon **156**
Gallibier Pass **258**
Galoperie Lake **191**
Gannat **61**
Gap **233**
Garabit Viaduct **61**
La Garde-Guérin 133
Gargas Caves **179**
Gatteville Lighthouse 196
Gavarnie Cirque **179**
Gavarnie Waterfall **179**
Geneva 255, 258
Geneva, Lake 244, 255, 258
Genille 162
Génissiat Barrage **255**
Génolhac 133
Gérardmer **41**
Géraudot **91**
Germigny-des-Prés **156**
Gergovie Plateau **61**
Ghisoni **99**
Gien **156**
Giens **234**
Gimel-les-Cascades **144**
Ginès 230
Girolata .98
Gironde Estuary 224
Gisors **201**
Givet **91**
Gobelin's Tapestry Factory **32**
Golfe-Juan 109, 237
Gordes **233**
Gouffre d'Enfer 248
Goulaine **169**
Gourdon (Côte-d'Azur) 105
Gourdon (Lot) **179**
Des Gouttes Leisure Park **62**
Grand Ballon, The 41
Grand Brière, The 167, 169
La Grande Chartreuse 258
La Grande Motte **134**
La Grande Motte (near Tignes) 258
Grandmont Abbey 141

Page

Grand Palais, The 35
Le Grand-Pressigny **156**
Grand Roc Cave 51
Grands Montets 253
Grandval Barrage **62**
Grangent Lake **244**
Granville **202**
Grasse **105**
La Grave **233**
Gray **114**
'Green Venice' 171, 220
Grenoble **255**
Grimaud **233**
Grignan **245**
Groix, Île de 73
Gros-Bois Château **123**
Gruissan-Plage **134**
Guebwiller **41**
Guéhenno **72**
Gué-Péan **156**
Guérande . . . . **170 – 171**
La Guerche-sur-Creuse **156**
Guéret **144**
Guermantes Château **123**
Guéthary **52**
Le Gué-de-la-Chaux **246**
Guillaumes 104
Guillestre **233**
Guimiliau **72**
Guines **191**
Guingamp **72**
Guiry-en-Vexin **123**
Guise **213**

H

Haguenau **42**
Haguenau Forest **42**
Halles, Les **32**
Hambye Abbey **202**
Hannonville **42**
Hanvec .69
Haras-du-Pin **202**
Harcourt **202**
Haut Asco 95
Haut-Brion 57
Hautecombe Abbey . . . . . **255 – 256**
Haut-de-Cagnes 104
Hautefort Château **52**
Haut-Koenigsbourg **42**
Regional Park of the
   Haut-Languedoc **135**, 180
Hautvillers **91**
Le Havre **202**
Haye Zoo **42**
L'Hay-les-Roses **123**
Hem **191**
Hendaye **52**
Hennebont **72**
Les Herbiers **170**
Hérisson **62**
Hérisson Waterfalls **114**
Hesdin **191**
'Hill 204' 211
Holography, Museum of **32**
Honfleur **202**
Hossegor **52**
Hôtel de Ville (Paris) **32**

Page

Houlgate **202**
Huelgoat **72**
Hunawihr 42
Hyères **234**
Hyères, Îles d' 236

I

Institute of France, The **32**
Les Invalides **32**
Île-de-France . . . . **118 – 128**
L'Île-Rousse 99
Illiers-Combray **156**
Iseran Pass 253, 256
L'Isle-Adam **123**
L'Isle-Briand National
   Stud Farm **170**
L'Isle-sur-la-Sorgue **234**
Isola 2000 105
Issoire **62**
Issoudun **157**

J

Jardin d'Acclimatation **29**
Jardin des Plantes **33**
Jean-Richard Zoo 212
Jobourg, Nez de **203**
Joigny **83**
Joinville-en-Vallage **91**
Jonas Caves **62**
Jonchery Deer Park **91**
Jonte Gorges **134**
Josselin **72**
Jourarre Abbey Church **123**
Jougne 115
Joux Château **114**
La Joux Forest 117
Juan-les-Pins **103**
Jumièges **203**
Jumilhac-le-Grand **52**

K

Kayserberg **42**
Kerjean Château **73**
Kerylos 103
Kientzheim **42**

L

Labalme 243
Labastide St-Pierre, Riding
   Holidays at **180**
Labouiche Underground River . **180**
Labrède Château **52**
Lacave Caves **180**
Lacq Gasfield **54**
Lafayette Museum **61**
Laffrey **256**
Lagny-sur-Marne **123**
Laiterie de la Reine 126
Lamarque 49
Lamastre **245**
Lamballe **73**
Landernau **73**
Landes, The 52
Landes de Gascogne Regional
   Nature Park **52**
Langeais **157**
Langoiran Zoo **52**

Page

Langonnet **73**
Langres **92**
Languedoc-Roussillon . . . **129 – 139**
Languedoc-Roussillon — Great
　Wine Areas of, ... **139**
Lannion **73**
Lanobre **62**
Lanquais Château **53**
Lanslebourg **256**
Laon **213**
Lapalisse **62**
Lascaux Cave and 'Lascaux 2' . . **53**
Lassay **170**
Lassay-sur-Croisne **157**
Laugerie Deposits **51**
Lausanne **258**
Laval **170**
Le Lavandou **234**
Lavaudieu **62**
Lavaur **180**
Lavoûte-Polignac Château **62**
Lectoure **180**
Leers Windmill **191**
Legion of Honour, Palace of . . **31**
Légué **76**
Léman, Lac **244, 255, 258**
Lente Forest **245**
Lepin-le-Lac **251**
Lérins, Îles de **105**
Lessay **203**
Levant, Île-du- **236**
Levier **117**
Lewarde Mining Museum **190**
Libourne **53**
Liget, Chartreuse du, ... **157**
Ligugé Abbey **220**
Lille **191**
Limargue, The **184**
Limeuil **56**
Limoges **144**
Limousin . . . . **140 – 147**
Limousis Cave **135**
Lisieux **203**
Lison, Source of the River . . . **114**
Little St-Bernard Pass **253**
Little Yellow Train **134, 139**
Loches **157**
Locmariaquer **73**
Locquignol **192**
Locronan **73**
Lodève **135**
La Loge-des-Gardes **246**
Loire Gorges **247**
Loire Valley — The Centre
　Region . . . . **148 – 164**
Loire Valley West . . . . **165 – 174**
Loire Valley, Great Wine
　Areas of **164, 174**
Lombarde, Col de la **105**
Longchamp Racecourse **29**
Longpont **213**
Longueval **209**
Longuyon **42**
Longwy **42**
Lons-le-Saunier **114**
Lorient **73**
Lorraine Regional Nature Park . . **42**

Page

Lot Gorges **180**
Loubressac **180**
Loudun **220**
Loue, Source of the River **115**
Loup Gorges **105**
Lourdes . . . . **180 – 181**
Lourmarin **234**
Louviers **203**
Louvois **92**
Louvre, The **33**
Luberon, The **234**
Lucéram **105**
Lucheux **213**
Luchon **181**
Lucon **170**
Le Lude **170**
Lumio **99**
Lunéville **42**
Lure **115**
Luri **98**
Luxembourg Palace and Gardens **33**
Luxeuil-les-Bains **115**
Luxey **52**
Luzech **181**
Lyon **245**
Lyons Forest **203, 207**
Lyons-la-Forêt **203**

M

Mâcon **84**
Madeleine, The **33**
Maeght Foundation **108**
Maginot Line **42, 45**
Maillezais . . . . **170 – 171**
Maine-Montparnasse Complex . . **33**
Maintenon **157**
Maisons-Lafitte **123**
Malbuisson **115**
La Malène **138**
Malestroit **73**
Malmaison Animal Park **124**
Malmaison Château Museum . . **124**
Malo-les-Bains **190**
Manosque **234**
Le Mans **171**
Le Mans Car Museum **171**
Mantes-la-Jolie **124**
Marais, The **38**
Le Marais Breton **171**
Le Marais Château **124**
Le Marais Poitevin Regional
　Nature Park . . . **171, 220 – 221**
Marché aux Puces **32**
Marcoule Atomic Energy Centre **131**
Maregès Barrage **142**
Marennes **221**
Marineland Zoo Park **106**
Marly **216**
Marmoutier **42**
Marnay **115**
Maroilles **192**
Marquenterre Ornithological
　Park **214**
Marquèze **52**
Marsal **42**
Marsanne **245**
Marseille . . . . **234 – 235**

Page

Marsoulas Cave **181**
Martel **181**
Marthon **221**
Martigues **235**
Martineix Dam 145
Marvejols **135**
Marzal Cave **246**
Mas-d'Azil Cave **181**
Mas du Pont de Rousty 230
Masgrangeas 147
Matignon, Hôtel 31
Maubeuge **192**
Maubuisson Abbey 125
Maulde Valley 145
Mauriac **63**
Maurs **63**
Mauzun **63**
Mayenne **171**
Mayenne Forest **171**
Meaux **124**
Médoc, Route du 57
Medous Cave **181**
Megève **256**
Mehun-sur-Yèvre **158**
Meillant Château **158**
Méjanes 230
Melle **221**
Melun **124**
Ménars **158**
Mende **135**
Menéc, Lines of 71
Ménerbes **234**
Menthon Château **256**
Menton **106**
Mercantour Game Reserve 108
Mer de Glace 254
Merlande Priory **53**
Merle Towers **144**
Mers-les-Bains **206**
Mervent Forest **171**
Mesnil St-Père 91
Messilhac Château 65
Métabief **115**
Metz **43**
Meudon 124
Meung-sur-Loire **158**
Meuse Valley, The 92
Meusnes **158**
Meymac **144**
Meyrueis **135**
Mézières 90
Midi-Pyrénées . . . . **175 – 186**
Les Milandes Château **53**
Millau **181**
Millevaches Plateau **144**
Milly-la-Forêt 124
Mint, The **33**
Mirepoix **181**
Miromesnil Château **203**
Moissac **182**
Le-Molay-Littry Mining Museum 203
Molsheim **43**
Monaco — Monte Carlo **106**
Le Monastier-sur-Gazeille **139**
Monbazillac Château **53**
Monceau Park **33**
Moncley **115**

	Page		Page		Page
Mondaye Abbey	203	Morez-du-Jura	116	Nonette Castle	64
Monédières Massif	146	Morgat	74	Nordheim	39
Monflanquin	53	Morienval	214	Nord — Pas-de-Calais	187 – 193
Monpazier	53	Morlaix	74	Normandie Maine Regional	
Mons	235	Mormal Forest	192	Nature Park	172, 204
Montaigne Château	53 – 54	Morosaglia	99	Normandy	194 – 207
Montal	182	Mortagne-au-Perche	204	Normandy, Battle of	195
Montargis	158	Mortain	204	Normandy Landings	196, 204,
Montauban	182	Mortiercrolles Château	172		206, 207
Montbard	84	Morvan Regional Nature Park	84	Northern Vosges, Regional Nature	
Montbazon	158	Morzine	257	Park of	46
Montbéliard	115	Moulin, Château du,	157	Notre Dame Cathedral	34
Mont Blanc	254	Moulin du Diable	170	Notre-Dame-de-Brusc	107
Montbrison	246	Moulin Richard-le-Bas	58	Notre-Dame-de-Clausis	238
Montbrun Castle	145	Moulins	63	Nouailles Gorges	115
Mont Cenis Pass	256	Les Moulins	204	Novelais-Lac	251
Montculot Château	84	Mountain of the Apes Zoo	42	Novion-Porcien Museum of	
Mont-de-Marsan	54	The Mountain of Reims Regional		Three Wars	92
Mont des Alouettes	170	Nature Park	92	Noyers-sur-Serein	84
Mont Dol	72	Mourèze Cirque	136	Noyon	214
Mont-Dore, Le	63	Moustiers-Ste-Marie	235	Nyons	246
Monte-Carlo	106	La Mouthe Cave	51		
Monte Cinto	99	Mouthier-Haute-Pierre	115	**O**	
Montélimar	246	Moutier-d'Ahun	145	Obernai	43
Montemaggiore	99	Moutiers	257	Observatory, The	35
Montevran Zoological Park	158	Moutiers-en-Beauce	159	O Château	204
Monteynard Barrage	256	Mouton-Rothschild Château	54	Oiron	221
Montfort Château	54	Mozac	63	Oléron, Île de	221
Montfort-l'Amaury	124	Mulberry 'A'	204	Olhain Château	192
Mont Gargan	143	Mulberry 'B'	195	Oloron-Sainte-Marie	54
Montgeoffroy	171	Mulhouse	43	Omaha Beach	204
Montgobert Château	215	Murato	100	Opéra, The	35
Monthermé	92	Murol	64	Oppède-le-Vieux	234
Montier-en-Der	92	Museum of the Horse	210	Oradour-sur-Glane	145
Mont-Larron Dam	145			Orange	236
Mont Louis	131, 135	**N**		Orangerie Museum	35
Mont-Lozère	133	Najac	182	Orcival	64
Montlucon	63	Nancy	43	Orgnac Caves	246
Montmajour Abbey	235	Nans-sous-Sainte-Anne	114	Orléans	159
Montmartre	34	Nantes	172	Orléans Forest	151
Montmédy	43	Nantua	246	Ornans	116
Montmorency	125	Naours Caves	214	Orsay Museum	35
Mont Mouchet	63	La Napoule	106	Orthez	54
Montoire-sur-le-Loir	158	Narbonne	136	Osselle Caves	116
Montparnasse	34	National Archives, The	34	Ouarville	159
Montparnasse Cemetery	34	National Technical Museum, The	34	Oudon	172
Montpellier	135 – 136	Navacelles Cirque	136	Ouessant, Île de	69, 70
Montpellier-le-Vieux, Chaos de	182	Nebbio	100	Ouistréam-Riva Bella	204
Montréal	84	Nemours	125	Ourscamps Abbey	214
Montrésor	159	Nérac	54	Ozoir-la-Ferrière	120
Montreuil	192	Nesque Gorges	235		
Montreuil-Bellay	171	Neuf-Brisach	43	**P**	
Montreuil-sous-Bois	125	Neufchâteau	43	La Pacaudière	246
Montreux	255, 258	Neuvic Barrage	145	Padirac, Gouffre de	182
Montrichard	159	Nevers	84	Pailly Château	92
Montrottier Château	256	Niaux Cave	182	Paimpol	74
Monts de la Madeleine	244, 246	Nice	106	Paimpont	74
Monts Dômes	61, 66	Nice to Digne Railway	107	Paladru Lake	257
Monts Dore	58, 62	Nichet Caves	91	Le Palais	70
Montségur Château	182	Nîmes	136	Palais-Bourbon	31
Monts du Forez	61, 66, 244	Niort	221	Palais de la Découverte	35
Mont St-Michel	203	Nogent-en-Bassingny	92	Palais de Justice	35
Montsoreau	172	Nogent-le-Rotrou	159	Palais-Royale, The	35
Montsouris Park	34	Nogent-sur-Marne	125	La Pallice	223
Mont Ventoux	240	Nohant Château	159	Palluau-sur-Indre	159
Morbihan, Gulf of	69, 74	Noirlac Abbey	159	La Palmyre Zoo Park	222
Moret-sur-Loing	125	Noirmoutier, Île de	172. 173	Pal Zoo Park	64

Page

Pannesière-Chaumard Barrage . . **84**
The Pantheon **36**
Pamiers **183**
La Parata Point **95**
Paray-le-Monial **85**
Parc Jean-Jacques Rousseau . . **212**
Parc Océanique Cousteau **32**
Pardons **74**
Pareloup Lake **183**
Paris . . . . **25 – 38**
Paris by Boat **28**
The Paris Sewers **28**
Paris, Shopping in **28**
Parish Closes and Calvaries **74**
Parthenay **222**
Pau **54**
Pauillac 49, **54**
Pavin, Lake **64**
Peaugres Safari Park **246**
Pécher Waterfall **134**
Pech-Merle Cave **183**
Pegasus Bridge **204**
Peille **107**
Peira-Cava **107**
Peisey-Nancroix **257**
Pen Hir, Pointe de **70**
Penne-du-Tarn **183**
Perche Region 197
Père-Lachaise Cemetery **36**
Périgueux **55**
Péronne **214**
Pérouges **247**
Perpignan **137**
Perros-Guirec **74**
Perse 179
Le Perthus **137**
Pesteils Château **64**
Petites Minaudières Leisure Park **222**
Petit Palais, The **35**
Petit Sauvage Ferry **231**
Peugeot Museum **115**
Pézenas **137**
Piana 98
Picardy . . . . **208 – 216**
Pic-du-Lac-Blanc **253**
Pic-du-Midi-de-Bigorre **183**
Pierrefitte 147
Pierrefonds **214**
Pilat Regional Nature Park **247**
Pino 98
Pithiviers **160**
Plaisance du Touch Zoo Park . **183**
Pleumeur-Bodou Space
    Communication Station **75**
Plessis-Bourré 172
Plessis-les-Tours **160**
Pleissis-Macé 172
Pleyben **75**
Plombières-les-Bains **44**
Plougastel-Daoulas **75**
Plougastel Peninsula **75**
Poët-Laval **247**
Pointe de Grave 224
La Poissonnière Manor **160**
Poissons **93**
Poitiers **222**
Poitou-Charentes . . . . **217 – 225**

Page

Polignac Castle **64**
Poligny **116**
Pomerol 57
'La Pompelle' Fort **93**
Pompidou Centre **29**
Pons **222**
Pontarlier **116**
Pont-Audemer **204**
Pont Aven **75**
Poncé-sur-Loir 172
Poncin **241**
Pont de Gau **230**
Pont-du-Gard **137**
Ponte Leccia 95
Pont-en-Royans **257**
Pontigny Abbey **85**
Pontivy **75**
Pont l'Abbé **75**
Pont l'Évêque **205**
Pontoise **125**
Pornic **173**
Porquerolles, Île de **236**
Port Barcarès **137**
Port Camargue **137**
Port Cros, Île de **236**
Port-Grimaud **236**
Port-Leucate **137**
Porto **99**
Porto Vecchio **99**
Portrieux **77**
Port-Royal des Champs Abbey
    Ruins and Museums **125**
Postal Museum, Riquewihr 44
Pouzauges **173**
Pozières **209**
Prades **138**
Prafrance, Parc **129**
Pralognan **259**
Pra-Loup **229**
Preignac 57
Presque Cave **183**
Prieuré Château 121
Privas **247**
Propriano **100**
Proumeyssac Chasm **50**
Provence . . . . **226 – 240**
Provins **125**
Puget-Théniers **107**
Putanges **206**
Puy-de-Dôme **64**
Puy de Sancy **63**
Le Puy-en-Velay **64**
Puy Ferrand **58**
Puyguilhem Château **55**
Puylaurens **183**
Pyla Dunes **47**
Pyrénées National Park **183**

Q

Quélern **70**
Quercy Tour Horse Drawn
    Holidays **184**
Le Quéroy Caves **222**
Le Quesnoy **192**
Queyras Regional Nature Park . **236**
Quiberon **75**
Quillan **131**

Page

Quimper **75**
Quimperlé **76**

R

Raguin Manor **173**
Railways of Corsica **100**
Raismes **192**
Rambouillet . . . . **125 – 126**
Rambouillet Forest . . 121, 125, 127
Rance Estuary 71
Raray Château **215**
Ratilly Château **85**
Raulhac **65**
Ravel Château **65**
Ravignan Château **55**
Ray-sur-Saône **116**
Raz, Pointe du 69
Ré, Île de **223**
Redon **76**
Reims **93**
Remiremont **44**
Rennes **76**
La Réole **55**
Resistance Monuments **63**
Restonica Gorge 98
Retz Forest **215**
Revin 92
Rhône River Trips **236, 247**
Rhône Valley . . . . **241 – 250**
Rhône Valley, Great Wine
    Areas of **250**
Rhue Gorges **65**
Ribeauvillé **44**
Ribou Lake **168**
Richelieu **160**
Riez **237**
Riom **65**
Riquewihr **44**
Ripaille Monastery **258**
Rivau **160**
Rambures Château **215**
Roanne **247**
Rocamadour **184**
Roc de la Tour 92
Roche aux Sept Villages 92
Rochebrune Château **223**
Rochechouart **145**
Roche Courbon Château **223**
Rochefort **223**
Rochefort-en-Terre **76**
La Rochefoucauld **223**
La Roche-Guyon **126**
La Roche-lès-Aigueperse
    Château **65**
La Rochelle **223**
Rochemaure **247**
La Rochepot Château **85**
Rochers Château **76**
Les Roches (near Troo) 162
Roches-en-Condrieu **244**
La Roche-sur-Yon **173**
Rochetaillée Château **247**
Rocroi **93**
Rodez **184**
Rodin Museum, Meudon 124
Rodin Museum (Paris) **36**
Rogliano 98

	Page
Roissy-en-France	126
Romaneche Zoo Park	85
Romans-sur-Isère	248
Romme	254
Romorantin	160
Roncesvalles Pass	56
Ronchamp	116
Roquebrune-Cap-Martin	107
Roquefort-sur-Soulzon	184
Roque-Gageac, La	55
Roquetaillade Château	55
Les Rosaires	76
Rosanbo Château	76
Roscoff	76
Roselend Reservoir	253
Rosny Château	126
Roubaix	192
Rouen	205
Rouffach	44
de Rouffignac Cave	51
Les Rousses	116
Route du Beaujolais	243
Route des Cretes	41
Route Napoléon, The	237, 256
Route des Sapins	117
Royan	224
Royat	65
Royaumont	126
Rue	215
Rue de Rivoli	36
Rueil-Malmaison	126
Ruffaud, Étang de	144
Rumilly-lès-Vaudes	93

St-

St-Aignan-sur-Cher	160
St-Alban-de-Montbel	251
St-Algis	216
St-Amand-de-Coly	55
St-Amand-les-Eaux	192
St-Amand-Montrond	160
St-Amand-Raismes Regional Nature Park	192
St-Ambroggio	99
St-Antonino	99
St-Augustine Wildlife Park	65
St-Bartholomew's Day Massacre	37
St-Bertrand de Comminges	184
St-Benoit-sur-Loire	160 – 161
St-Briac	76
St-Brieuc	76
St-Calais	173
St-Céré	184
St-Cézaire Caves	108
St-Cirque-Lapopie	184
St-Claude	117
St-Cloud	126
St-Come-d'Olt	185
St-Cyprien	138
St-Denis	126
St-Die	44
St-Dizier	93
St-Donat	248
St-Émilion	56
St-Étienne	248
St-Étienne-du-Mont Church	36
St-Eustache Church	36

	Page
St-Fargeau Château	85
St-Firmin	237
St-Florent	100
St-Florentin	85
St-Flour	66
St-Gaudens	185
St-George-de-Didonne	224
St-Germain-de-Livet	205
St-Germain-des-Prés Church	37
St-Germain-en-Laye	126 – 127
St-Germain-l'Auxerrois Church	37
St-Gervais-les-Bains	257
St-Géry Château	185
St-Gilles-Croix-de-Vie	173
St-Gilles-du-Gard	138
St-Gobain Forest	212, 215
St-Haôn-le-Chatel	248
St-Hilaire-le-Palud	221
St-Hippolyte	117
St-Honorate, Île	105
St-Jean-aux-Bois	211
St-Jean-Cap-Ferrat	108
St-Jean-d'Angély	224
St-Jean-de-Luz and Ciboure	56
St-Jouin-de-Marnes	224
St-Jean-de-Maurienne	257
St-Jean Pied-de-Port	56
St-Jean-du-Gard	139
St-Junien	146
St-Léger-en-Yvelines	127
St-Léonard-de-Noblat	145
St-Lieux-les-Lavaur	186
St-Lizier	185
St-Lô	205
St-Louis	129
St-Louis-Arzviller Inclined Plane	44
St-Louis, The Île	32
St-Maixent-l'École	224
St-Malo	77
St-Mandé	127
St-Maixant Castle	146
St-Martin-du-Canigou	132
St-Martin Vésubie	108
St-Maximin-la-Ste-Baume	237
St-Michel-de-Cuxa Abbey	138
St-Michel-de-Murato	100
St-Michel Observatory	237
St-Mihiel	44
St-Nazaire	173
St-Nazaire-en-Royans	248
St-Nectaire	66
St-Omer	192 – 193
St-Ouen	127
St-Paul-de-Fenouillet	134
St-Paul-de-Vence	108
St-Paul-Trois-Châteaux	248
St-Pierre-de-Chartreuse	258 – 259
St-Pierre-d'Oléron	221
St-Pierre-sur-Dives	205
St-Point Château	85
St-Pol-de-Léon	77
St-Pourcain-sur-Sioule	66
St-Quay-Portrieux	77
St-Quentin	215
St-Raphaël	237
St-Rémy-de-Provence	238
St-Riquier	215

	Page
St-Roch Church	36
St-Romain-le-Puy	248
St-Saens	200
St-Saturnin	66
St-Savin	224
St-Sever-Calvados	205
St-Séverin Church	37
St-Sulpice Church	37
St-Symphorien-des-Monts	205
St-Thégonnec	77
St-Trojan Tourist Tramway	224
St-Tropez	238
St-Valéry-en-Caux	205 – 206
St-Valéry-sur-Somme	215
St-Véran	238
St-Veredema Cave, La Baume	138
St-Victor	244
St-Vrain Zoo Park	127
St-Wandrille Abbey	206
St-Yrieix-la-Perche	146

Ste-

Ste-Croix Lake	235, 240
Ste-Marguerite, Île	105
Ste-Marie-du-Mont	207
Ste-Maxime	238
Ste-Menehould	89
Ste-Mère-Église	206
Ste-Odile	44
Ste-Suzanne	173
Sta-Teresa-Gallura	97
Ste-Theresa	195
Les Stes-Maries-de-la-Mer	238

S

Les Sables d'Olonne	173
Sabres	52
Saché	161
Sacré-Coeur Basilica	37
Sagone	100
Sahara Museum	239
Sainte-Chapelle	37
Saintes	224 – 225
Salers	66
Salins-les-Bains	117
Sallanches	258
Salon-de-Provence	238
Samoens	258
Sanary-Bandol Zoo	239
Sanary-sur-Mer	239
Sancerre	161
Sanguinaires, Îles	95
Sansais	221
Sanxay	225
Saorge	108
Saou	248
Saou Forest	248
Sarlat	56
Sarrans Barrage	185
Sarrazine Cave	114
Sars-Poteries	193
Sartène	100
Sassy Château	206
Saulieu	85
Saumur	174
Saut-du-Doubs	117
Saut-du-Loup	105

	Page
Sauternes	57
Sautet Lake	254
Saverne	45
Savigny-les-Beaune	85
Savonnières Caves	161
Savoy and Dauphiny Alps	251 – 259
Scalella Pass	97
Scandola Peninsula	98
Sceaux	127
Sedan	93
Sedière Château	146
Sées	206
Ségur-le-Château	146
Sein, Île de	69
Seine, Source of the	86
Sélestat	45
Selles-sur-Cher	161
Semoy, Valley of	93
Semur-en-Auxois	86
Semur-en-Brionnais	86
Senanque Abbey	239
Seneca	98
Senlis	215 – 216
Senones	45
Sens	86
Septvaux	212
Serrant	174
Serre-Poncon Barrage and Lake	239
Sète	138
Les Settons	86
Sèvres	127
Sézanne	94
Sidobre, Le	185
Sigean African Reserve	138
Sillé Forest	174
Silvacane Abbey	239
Simserhof Fort	45
Sisco	98
Sisteron	239
Sochaux	115
Soissons	216
Solenzara	100
Solesmes	174
Solignac	146
Sologne, The	161
Solre-le-Château	193
Solutré	86
Somme, Battle of the	209
Sorbonne, The	37
Sospel	109
Souillac	185
Sources de la Touvre	222
La Souterraine	146
Speloncato	100
Spelunca Gorges	100
Strasbourg	45
Suisse Normande, La	206
Sully Château	86
Sully-sur-Loire	161
Super-Besse	58
Super-Sauze	229
Sury-le-Comtal	248

T

	Page
Tache Barrage	246
Tain-l'Hermitage	249
Tain-Tournon	249

	Page
Talcy Château	162
Talloires	258
Talmay Château	86
Talmont	225
Tancarville Bridge	206
Tanlay Château	86
Tarbes	185
Tarn Gorges	138, 186
Tarn Tourist Railway	186
Tarascon	239
Tartaiguille, Col de	245
Tavant	162
Tavignano Gorge	98
Le Teich Ornithological Park	56
Tende	109
Terrasses du Truel	135
Tertre, Place du	37 – 38
Tertre Rouge Zoo	169
Thann	39, 45
Thaon	206
Thiepval	209
Thiérache, La	216
Thiers	66
Thionville	45
Thoiry Animal Park	127
Thonac	56
Thones	254
Thonon-les-Bains	258
Le Thoronet Abbey	239
Thouars	225
Thouzon Grotto	239
Thury-Harcourt	206
Tiffauges	174
Tignes	258
Tignes Lake	258
Tolla Dam and Reservoir	101
Tonnerre	86
Touffou Château	225
Toul	46
Toulon	240
Toulouse	186
Le Touquet-Paris-Plage	193
Tourette-sur-Loup	109
Tournoël Château	66
Tournon	249
Tournus	87
Tours	162
Touvre, Sources de la	222
Tower of Seneca	98
Trabuc Caves	129
Traconne Forest	94
Tramway du Mont Blanc	257
'Travels with a Donkey'	139
Trébeurden	75
Tréboul	72
Trécesson Château	74
Tréguier	77
Trehet	162
Treignac	146
Trémolat	56
Le Tréport	206
Trinité-sur-Mer	77
Troncais Forest	66
Troo	162
Trouée de Belfort	111
Troumouse Cirque	186
Troussay	162

	Page
Trouville	206
Troyes	94
Truyère Gorges	67
Tuileries Gardens	38
Tulle	146
La Turbie	109
Turckheim	46
Turenne	147
Turini Forest	107, 109

U

	Page
Ussé	162
Ussel	147
Usson, Château d'	222
Utah Beach	207
Uzerche	147
Uzès	139

V

	Page
Vaison-la-Romaine	240
Valberg	109
Val Château	62, 142
Val de Sèvres et Vendéc Regional Nature Park	17
Val d'Isère	258
Valdo Niello Forest	97
Valencay	162 – 163
Valence	249
Valenciennes	193
Valgaudemar	237
Valinco, Gulf of	100
Val Joly Park	193
Vallauris	109
Valloire	258
Valloires Abbey	216
Vallouise	232
Valmy Windmil	94
Valognes	207
Vannes	77
Vanoise National Park	258 – 259
Vascoeuil	207
Vassivière, Lake	147
Vatan	163
Vauban Museum	43
Vauclair Abbey	216
Vaucouleurs	46
Vaussaire Barrage	65
Vaux de Cernay	121
Vaux-le-Vicomte	127 – 128
Veauce	67
Vecchio Viaduct	100
Vence	110
Vendean Marshland	171
Vendôme	163
Vendôme, Place	38
Vercors, The	249
Verdon Gorge	240
Verdun	46
Vernet-les-Bains	132, 139
Verneuil-sur-Avre	207
Vernon	207
La Verrerie	163
Versailles	128
Vervins	216
Verzy	92
Vesoul	117
Vesubie Gorges	108

Page		Page		Page
Vetheuil	128	Villefranche-sur-Mer	110	Voelgrun	43
Vez	216	Villefranche-sur-Saône	250	Voiron	259
Vézelay	87	Villegongis Château	163	Volcanoes Regional Nature
Vic	163	La Villette	38	Park	67
Vic-sur-Seille	42	Villeneuvette	139	Vosges, Place des	38
Vichy	67	Villeneuve-lès-Avignon	139	Vouglans Barrage and
Vico	100	Villeneuve-Loubet	110	Lake	241, 117
Vieilles-Forges Lake	94	Villeneuve-sur-Lot	56 – 57	Vouvant	174
Vienne	259	Villeneuve-sur-Yonne	87	Vouvray	164
Vienne-en-Arthies	128	Villéreal	57	Vouziers	90, 94

Vierville	204	Villerest	247	**W**
Vieux-Moulin	211	Villers-Bretonneux	211	Wimereux	193
Le Vigan	129	Villers-Cotterêts	216	Wissant	190
Vigny Château	128	Villers-le-Lac	117	Wissembourg	46
Villaines-les Rochers	163	Villesavin Château	163	
Villandraut	56	Villette Château	128	**X**
Villandry	163	Villiers-en-Lieu	93	Xaintrie Plateau	141
Villarceaux	128	Vincennes, Bois de	38	
Villard-de-Lans	259	Vincennes Château	38	**Y**
Villars-les-Dombes Ornithological		Vire	207	Yeu, Île de	174
Reserve	249	Vitré	77	Yvetot	207
Villebois-la Valette	225	Vivarais Steam Railway	249	
Villeconin Château	128	Viviers	250	**Z**
Villecroze	240	Vix, Treasure of	81	Zicavo	101
Villefort	133	Vizille	259	Zilia	99
Villefranche-de-Rouergue	186	Vizzavona	101	Zonza	101

Index of Persons

A

Page
Abadie, Paul	217
Albigensians, The	175, 180, 182
Ango, Richard	195
Anselm, Archbishop	197

B

Bacon, Francis	222
Balzac, Honoré de	157, 161, 164
Bartholdi, Auguste	41, 113
Becket, Thomas à	85, 196
Berengaria, Queen	169, 171
Bergerac, Savinien Cyrano de	49, 51
Bernadotte, Count Jean (later King Charles XIV, of Sweden)	54
Bernhardt, Sarah	36
Berry, Duchesse de	126
Berry, Duke Jean de	152, 158. 210
Berthier, Marshal Alexandre	122
Bertrand, Claude	115, 116
Bizet, Georges	228
Black Prince	212, 222
Blériot, Louis	190
'Bluebeard'	153, 173, 174
Boëtie, la	56
Boigne, Count Benoit de	254
Boudin, Eugène	159
Bourdelle, Emile	182
Bourré, Jean	172
Brantôme, Pierre de Bourdeilles, Seigneur de	50
Breton, Gilles le	121
Breton, Jean le	163
Brillat-Savarin, Anthelme	243

Page
Brosse, Salomon de	210
Buffon, Georges Comte de	84

C

Calvin, Jean	152, 214
Camus, Albert	234
Caravas, Comte de	221
Carpeaux, Jean	122, 193
Casals, Pablo	138
Cézanne, Paul	227
Chabrier, Emmanuel	58
Champlain, Samuel de	219
Champollion, Jean Francois	179
Charonton, Enguerrand	139
Châteaubriand, Francois René	71, 77
Chopin, Frédéric	36
Churchill, Sir Winston	199
Clement V, Pope	56
Clement VI, Pope	60
Clews, Henry	106
Cocteau, Jean	106, 110
Colbert, Jean Baptiste	127, 139, 202, 223
Corbusier, Le	116
Courbet, Gustave	116
Cousin, Jean	83
Coysevox, Antoine	174

D

Daudet, Alphonse	228, 232
Debussy, Claude	127
Delacroix, Ferdinand	37
Descartes, René	169, 219, 222
Diderot, Denis	92
Duc, Viollet le	55, 132, 200, 214
Dumas, Alexandre	89, 216, 235

Page
Dunois, Jean	154, 155

E

Edward III, King of England	190, 209, 212
Eiffel, Gustave	61, 100, 152
Eleanor of Aquitaine	169
Escoffier, Auguste	110

F

Fauré, Gabriel	183
Fénelon, Francois	51
Flaubert, Gustave	205
Foch, Marshal Ferdinand	190
Fontaine, La	211
Fouquet, Nicholas	127
Fragonard, Jean Honoré	105
Froissart, Jean	54

G

Gambetta, Léon	177
Gauguin, Paul	75
de Gaulle, General Charles	90, 199
George VI, King of England	199
Gouffier, Claude	221
Gounod, Charles Francois	228
Goya	178
Greuze, Jean Baptiste	86
Grimaldi Family	104, 106

H

Haussmann, Baron Georges	34, 35, 36, 232
Henry I, King of England	201, 207
Henry II, King of England	155, 169, 171, 196, 201, 221

Henry V, King of England 187, 216
Henry VIII, King of England . . . 191
Hugo, Victor 36, 89, 113

I

Ingrand, Max 207
Ingres, Jean 182

J

Joan of Arc 41, 46, 155, 159, 161,
174, 205, 211
John, King of England 85
Josephine, The Empress 122,
124, 126

L

Lafayette, Marquis de 61
Lamartine, Alphonse . . 84, 85, 243
Lanfranc, Archbishop 197
Langton, Stephen 85
Le Brun, Charles 128
Léger, Ferdinand 104
Le Nôtre, André 65, 121, 122, 124,
126, 127, 128, 157, 196, 210, 232
Leonardo da Vinci 150
Lisle, Rouget de 115
Lorraine, Dukes of 42
Loti, Pierre 223
Lumière Brothers 113
Lurcat, Jean 165, 184

M

Maillol, Aristide 131
Maintenon, Francoise,
Marquise de 157
Mansart, Francois 121, 123
Mansart, Jules Hardouin 122,
127, 131
Marchand, Yves 207
Marie Antoinette, Queen 126
Matisse, Henri 190
Maupassant, Guy de 201, 203
Medici, Catherine de 154, 155
Mercier, Jacques le 160
Mérimée, Prosper 163
Millet, Jean Francois 120, 199
Mirabeau, Count André . . . 36, 227
Mistral, Frédéric 228
Moles, Arnaud de 175
Molière 137
Monet, Claude 120
Montaigne, Michel de 54, 56
Montesquieu, Charles 52
Montfort, Simon de . 54, 124, 131,
132, 180
Montgolfier Brothers 241
Moulin, Jean 36
Moulins, Maître de 63

N

Napoleon Bonaparte . . 79, 90, 95,
97, 103, 122, 124, 173, 191, 211,
217, 220, 233, 234, 237, 240, 249
Napoleon III 126, 211
Nelson, Admiral Horatio 98
Nerra, Foulques 159, 167, 171
Ney, Marshal Michel 36, 191
Nostradamus 238

O

Orange, William of 236

P

Paoli, Pasquale de 99
Pascal, Blaise 61, 125
Pasteur, Louis 111, 114
Patton, General George 196
Perignon, Dom 91
Perrault, Charles 162, 221
Perret, Auguste 202
Petrarch, Francesco 232
Phoebus, Gaston 54
Piaf, Edith 36
Picasso, Pablo 109
Poitiers, Diane de . . . 150, 154, 155
Pompadour, Madame de 121,
141, 158
Pompon, Francois 85
Prévost, Abbé 191
Proust, Marcel 156
Prudhon, Pierre 114

Q

Quentin de la Tour, Maurice . . 215

R

Rabelais, Francois 43, 156, 160, 169,
222, 249
Racine, Jean 125, 139, 213
Rais, Gilles de 173, 174
Ravel, Maurice 125
Renan, Ernest 77
René, Good King . . . 227, 229, 239
Renoir, Pierre Auguste 120
Richard the Lionheart 87, 142, 157,
169, 195, 221
Richelieu, Cardinal 35, 37, 64, 160,
201, 219, 247
Richier, Ligier 39, 44
Rimbaud, Arthur 90
Riquet, Paul 131, 138
Robespierre, Maximilien 187
Rodin, Auguste 124, 189
Rolland, Romain 87
Rommel, Field-Marshal Erwin . . 205
Ronsard, Pierre de 160
Rostand, Edmond 49, 51
Rousseau, Henri 'Le Douanier' 170

Rousseau, Jean-Jacques 36, 125,
213
Rousseau, Theodore 120

St-

St-Amadour 184
St-Benedict 161
St-Martin of Tours 153, 162

Ste-

Ste-Bernadette 180
Ste-Theresa 203

S

Sade, Marquis de 211
Sand, George . 142, 154, 159, 163
Schweitzer, Dr. Albert 42
Serres, Olivier de 126
Sévigné, Madame de 83, 244
Sisley, Alfred 125
Sorel, Agnès 157
Soubirous, Bernadette 180
Stanislaus, Duke, of Lorraine . . . 43
Stendhal 255
Stevenson, R. L. 120, 139
Suffren, Admiral 238
Sully, Duc de 126, 159, 161
Sylvester, II, Pope 58

T

Talleyrand, Charles 163
Tolstoy, Count 234
Toulouse-Lautrec, Henri 175

V

Valéry, Paul 138
Valois, Dukes of 216
Valois Family 216
Van Gogh, Vincent 227, 228
Vauban, Sébastien 42, 43, 46, 47, 79
103, 113, 129, 135, 137, 157, 187,
192, 212, 217, 220, 232
Vercingétorix 61, 79
Vernier, Pierre 116
Victoria, Queen 234, 251
Villon, Francois 158
Voltaire, Francois 36, 151

W

Watteau, Jean Antoine 193
Wilde, Oscar 36
William the Conqueror . . 173, 195,
197, 198, 201

Z

Zola, Émile 36